AUTHOR'S NOTE

As this book is going off to the printers, Elon Musk has taken the reins of the newly created U.S. DOGE Service and appears to have carte blanche from the Trump administration to remold the federal government as he sees fit. He has identified, as targets, the shrinking of the federal workforce, modernization of outdated federal technology, and $1 trillion in federal spending cuts. His deputies have stormed into multiple federal agencies—some well beyond this mandate—with few guardrails and unclear motives. Some have even refused to identify themselves at times; Musk has suggested that identifying those working for him would be a crime.

He has done little to allay concerns about potential conflicts of interest with his businesses. Meanwhile, much of his early maneuvering has raised legal questions, and some of his actions may or may not knocked down in court one day. But the chilling effects they have on the American population and our country's international standing are immediate and real regardless.

I wish I could say I was surprised by all this. But I've been following Elon Musk's activities for years as a journalist, and what's striking about these developments is not that they are out of character but that they are incredibly consistent with his behavior and business-management approach going back decades. Musk has created a façade of being the hardest-working man in America and the last bastion of the meritocracy—supplemented by fiercely devoted and competent loyalists—that he uses to justify drastic actions, citing his interventions as crucial responses to existential threats. The only thing that has changed is how much power he holds, and the scope of the potential consequences for the American people.

The best way to understand what he's going to do next is to look at how he's wielded his power all along.

HUBRIS MAXIMUS

THE SHATTERING

—— *of* ——

ELON MUSK

FAIZ SIDDIQUI

ST. MARTIN'S PRESS

NEW YORK

First published in the United States by St. Martin's Press, an imprint of St. Martin's Publishing Group

HUBRIS MAXIMUS. Copyright © 2025 by Faiz Siddiqui. All rights reserved. Printed in the United States of America. For information, address St. Martin's Publishing Group, 120 Broadway, New York, NY 10271.

www.stmartins.com

Design by Meryl Sussman Levavi

The Library of Congress Cataloging-in-Publication Data is available upon request.

ISBN 978-1-250-32717-8 (hardcover)
ISBN 978-1-250-32718-5 (ebook)

Our books may be purchased in bulk for promotional, educational, or business use. Please contact your local bookseller or the Macmillan Corporate and Premium Sales Department at 1-800-221-7945, extension 5442, or by email at MacmillanSpecialMarkets@macmillan.com.

First Edition: 2025

10 9 8 7 6 5 4 3 2 1

To the journalists bringing us stories from around the world, with a particular eye to Gaza where so many have been killed, in a singularly deadly time to be a reporter. You are the media.

CONTENTS

HUBRIS
MAXIMUS

INTRODUCTION

There is a large graveyard filled with my enemies.

—Elon Musk[1]

I n retrospect, it was inevitable."[2]

Nothing about what was taking place that Thursday was supposed to be funny. But there sat Elon Musk, huddled among trusted staff at the end of a long row of computer screens inside one of Tesla's Silicon Valley offices, laughing.

Hysterically.

It was a puzzling moment on an unusually eventful weekday for the employees at Tesla's Fremont, California, complex, which hosted overflow from the company's packed Palo Alto headquarters. Musk sat in the open-plan office among his staff—the commander of a white-walled ship, the type of sterile, joyless vessel lined with generic desks and ergonomic chairs where shareholder value is created.

The environment was tense, almost funereal, at least at first. CNBC played frequently in the background of a car company consumed by its reputation, but the coverage on September 27, 2018, was far from the usual stock-pumping, back-seat-driving analysis. This was the day when Musk was meant to face the music, and all eyes were on the TVs.

Musk's latest blunder had gotten the attention of the feds, a sobering moment for anyone—let alone an officer of a public company. But his jovial manner gave the impression that he hardly cared.

Elon and his brain trust sat in rapt attention before a news conference where Securities and Exchange Commission (SEC) enforcement officials laid out the seriousness of Musk's misstep, a false tweet that he had "Funding secured" to take Tesla private.

The SEC was suing Musk for fraud. Its complaint laid out the severity of that charge and its potential consequences. Stephanie Avakian, the SEC's codirector of enforcement, explained that the agency was seeking not only an injunction to prevent future episodes like "Funding secured" but also to impose fines and a return of "ill-gotten gains" and, crucially, "a bar prohibiting Musk from serving as an officer or director of a public company in the future."

Then the stern tone of the news gave way to levity: CNBC showed a split screen of the SEC's press conference and a clip of Musk's recent appearance on the *Joe Rogan Experience* podcast, where he was taking a hit from a joint and blowing out a puff of smoke with a quizzical expression.[3]

Musk, still undaunted, burst out laughing, his unmistakable cackle finally diverting the room's attention from the screen.

The Tesla CEO's erratic behavior had been generating headlines for weeks. In the span of two months, Musk had referred to an internationally recognized good Samaritan as a "pedo guy," posted the tweet that alarmed the SEC, and smoked the offending joint on a podcast stream seen by millions.[4] He had taken the considerable blowback in stride. But as the consequences of Musk's behavior became clear, there was no sugarcoating what this should have meant for him, his board—a body that included his brother Kimbal, a frequent visitor during this tumultuous period—and staffers at every level.

A chastening at least; humiliation at worst.

Musk had floated taking Tesla private for $420 a share, a number that doubled as a weed joke. This particular joke would serve as a running motif of his most colossal screwups. Years later, he'd commit what seemed at the time to be a bigger blunder—arguably the largest of his professional life—by purchasing Twitter for $54.20 per share.

And yet, in that moment as the SEC sought to bring him to heel, all Musk did was laugh. Maybe he knew something his employees didn't?

Though the securities fraud finding would precipitate Musk's removal as Tesla's board chairman and result in fines of $20 million each for him and Tesla, in the long run, Musk himself only became wealthier and more powerful.

I've long been fascinated by power. As a teenager and young adult, I devoured books about people—often shady, contemptible characters—who left their mark on society through sheer force of will, maneuvering at the edges of legal, moral, and ethical responsibility: Chicago mayor Richard Daley, New York's shadow city planner Robert Moses, presidents from LBJ to George W. Bush to Donald Trump, and tech titans like Steve Jobs.

I launched my career at *The Washington Post*, where my work as a beat reporter covering local transit quickly collided with Elon Musk's ambitions to disrupt not only the way we get around but also how decisions shaping society at the highest levels were made.

The conditions that allowed Musk to gain a foothold in the tech industry were clear. By the time I arrived in Silicon Valley in 2019, tech innovation seemed to be languishing. Apple was struggling to find its next revolutionary product even as it "unlocked shareholder value"; social media companies were alienating their customers with their exploitation of user data; and the autonomous car was a mere glimmer in the eyes of many tech founders. Uber's reputation had cratered on the mistakes of its founder and the broader recognition that its model was exploitative and low margin. There was a thirst to anoint the next Steve Jobs, and Musk—armed with the party trick of Tesla's fossil fuel abstention and head-turning acceleration, a product that gave customers the magical experience of the first iPhone—was the prime candidate.

Elon Musk also appeared to fit the model of the powerful figure pushing the limits. He was the latest stress test on our system, on our collective notion that we live in a society governed by rules, regulations, and shared, commonly accepted principles. Were we willing to sacrifice them to get what he promised us? The promise felt big: Tesla's mission is "to accelerate the world's transition to sustainable energy." Wasn't that more important than a few pesky societal norms?

In Tesla, I found a company that was brilliantly innovative and unparalleled in the automotive and technological realms, but also paranoid and hostile to scrutiny, led by a man with little appetite for transparency or

accountability, someone who saw the meddling of the minor sideline players as roadblocks to the society he hoped to unleash. The attitude spread
throughout the organization. Tesla, the thinking went, was smarter than
the people in charge. It had more data. Its mission was righteous. Why
was it being attacked?

Musk was something I had learned about in my studies of power but
had yet to encounter in its physical form: a true-to-life hero from an Ayn
Rand novel—a man with little regard for the consequences of his actions,
for the minor aftereffects one might describe as *fallout*—as long as he
was convinced that he was on the true and correct path. His unconcealed
disdain for the bureaucrats and mediocrities who stood in his way, his
tendency to justify his myopic pursuit of self-interest with supposedly
virtuous ends, and his blame for myriad world problems on the abandonment of meritocracy, all suggested a Randian character brought to life.

"Survival is the organism's ultimate value, the 'final goal or end to
which all [its] lesser goals are the means,' and the standard of all its other
values: 'that which furthers its life is the good, that which threatens it is
the evil,'" reads the *Stanford Encyclopedia of Philosophy*, summing up one
of Ayn Rand's core tenets.[5]

Here's Musk, by comparison: "Making life multiplanetary expands
the scope & scale of consciousness.... Humanity is life's steward, as no
other species can transport life to Mars. We can't let them down." And:
"If civilization collapses before Mars becomes self-sustaining, then nothing else matters."[6]

Musk has even applied the "good versus evil" framing, writing: "Unless it is stopped, the woke mind virus will destroy civilization and humanity will never reached [*sic*] Mars."[7]

Crucially, though, Musk mirrored Randian thought on more practical
matters.

As the *Stanford* publication put it:

Conspicuous by their absence from Rand's list of the cardinal virtues are the 'virtues of benevolence,' such as kindness, charity, generosity, and forgiveness.... Whether, and how much, one should
help others depends on their place in one's rationally defined
hierarchy of values, and on the particular circumstances.... The
greater their value vis-à-vis one's rational self-interest, the greater

the help that one should be willing to give. . . . What is never morally appropriate is to make a sacrifice, that is, to surrender something of value to oneself for the sake of something of less or no value to oneself.[8]

Despite their merit, it is hard to ignore the fact that Musk has gained a huge personal benefit from the vast majority—and each of the major elements—of his business pursuits.

Musk, of course, has justified his accumulation of wealth and power as a means to an end and has appeared to defend his seeming lack of philanthropic motivation as a stand against virtue signaling: "It is extremely difficult to donate money at scale if you care about the reality of goodness, rather than the appearance of it," he has written.[9]

He sees himself providing the ultimate value by helping humanity reach Mars, ushering in an era of green energy, and, more recently, restoring "free speech" to the internet's public square. His plan for a Department of Government Efficiency, an outside group seeking to wield tremendous influence over government regulations and spending, represents yet another extension of this thesis.

During the time I've reported on him, Musk has made it clear that he is no fan of my work, replying to my requests for comment on repeated occasions with some version of the refrain "Give my regards to your puppetmaster," an apparent shot at the *Post*'s owner, rival tech tycoon Jeff Bezos.[10]

Musk, born in Pretoria, South Africa, on June 28, 1971, was a precocious youth who turned to reading to understand the world—a world in which he suffered bullying and what has been described as "psychological torture" as a child—and found his home in computer programming, writing, and selling a video game when he was twelve.[11] He found his answers not in religious texts but in the writings of sci-fi authors like Isaac Asimov and Douglas Adams.[12] He immigrated to Canada as a teenager, enrolling at Queen's University at Kingston before completing his undergraduate studies at the University of Pennsylvania, where he received degrees in physics and economics.

In 1995, he founded Zip2, an online city guide platform that allowed newspapers to offer web-based city directories and supplement them with ads. Zip2 arrived on the scene just in time for the dot-com boom (and before the collapse of online advertising). When Compaq bought Zip2 for more than $300 million, Musk netted more than $20 million, around $10 million of which he'd pour into his next venture, an online payments service that had started as X.com, the domain name that would bookend the chapters of his business career.[13] Musk made his initial fortune on X.com, a payments service that merged with a competitor led by venture capitalist Peter Thiel and became PayPal. Musk used his roughly $180 million in proceeds from PayPal's eventual sale to eBay to fund his two largest ventures—the companies we associate him with today—SpaceX and Tesla.[14] He founded SpaceX in 2002, became a Tesla investor in 2004, and ascended to CEO in 2008, the year Tesla launched its initial model: the Roadster. For years, Musk enjoyed an unimpeachable reputation for reinvigorating the United States' dormant space program and delivering the long-promised car of the future to the masses.

He was a household name, a figure prominent—and safe—enough for mainstream pop culture consumption. Musk appeared on the TV show *The Big Bang Theory* and the sequel to *Iron Man*, a movie series in which a billionaire business mogul invents a technologically sophisticated super suit that enables him to fly and ward off powerful enemies.

And it made perfect sense. He *was* Iron Man or at least our closest approximation to it. Tesla, aided by auto industry peers and government incentives—including a $465 million loan from the Department of Energy—outlasted the challenges of the Great Recession and grew to new heights.[15]

The Model S sedan—and ultimately the Model 3 and Model Y—propelled Tesla into the mass market. Musk's power grew. SpaceX, meanwhile, proved its concept of a reusable rocket and became the first private company to put people in orbit.

Many of Musk's successes stem from his hubris, which is his superpower and, as we'll explore in this book, his greatest weakness. Speaking once about the nearly four-hundred-foot SpaceX rocket he hopes will take humans to Mars, he said: "I can't say for sure that Starship will reach escape velocity, but my hubris certainly has."[16]

Musk propelled Tesla to success by daring to depart from the traditional EV formula. Until Tesla came along with head-twisting acceleration and promises of autonomy, electric vehicles—lumbering econo-boxes that saddled owners with range anxiety and served as little more than rolling political statements—barely even registered on sales charts, as manufacturers used them merely to comply with emissions targets.

Tesla's sudden success made it a hub for engineering whiz kids, a corporate destination that inspired envy in a largely rudderless Silicon Valley, where the era of social media had triggered a wave of disillusion. Many great minds went to work there, but they soon found the company's core approach—rule by one man, eschewing market research and rigorous internal testing before product releases—was hardly scientific. It was inevitable that the limits of this approach would one day be exposed.[17]

Employees who spent enough time around Musk were sometimes left unimpressed with the experience. Even so, the nobility of his goals commanded a type of loyalty rarely seen toward corporate leaders. Those who had left under unceremonious circumstances somehow still occasionally found themselves still rooting for him, crediting him for his vision or drive, still believing in the ultimate mission. Their last memory at Tesla might be of a heated argument with Musk that they won on the technical merits but that rendered them unemployable to the man in charge. It was only when Musk's intellectual laziness became public with his disastrous takeover of Twitter that the public at large began to realize that maybe the man wasn't all he'd been cracked up to be. For me, he was a persistent subject of fascination—not because of his heroism or follies, his awkward mannerisms, or his ability to inspire, but in the way he wielded his power.

Around the time I was conducting research into *Hubris Maximus*, as the Twitter debacle was still fresh in the minds of so many, I stumbled upon a tweet from writer and podcast host Peter Kafka that gave me some clarity of purpose: "I'm increasingly less interested in the future of Twitter, [because] it's been clear for some time. More interested in this q: What happened to Elon Musk? And if the answer is 'this is who he always was' then how did he make Tesla and SpaceX?"[18]

Indeed, how did the man revered as the modern-day Thomas Edison go from real-life action hero and undisputed genius to part-time and perpetually distracted CEO, a divisive and polarizing figure—less charitably, the village idiot of the internet—right-wing ideologue, and, arguably, the biggest bag fumbler in human history? It's true: Musk now owns the Guinness World Record for the largest loss of a personal fortune of all time.[19] Somehow he recovered, bringing Tesla's valuation back over $1 trillion—and boosting his own net worth back to its peaks—in part with a timely election bet.

The story of how all of that happened is quite spectacular. The explanation for Musk's erratic behavior, on an increasingly consequential scale with a bigger and bigger imprint on society, is not that he bought Twitter. It's not that he destroyed his brain with drugs. Nor did he suddenly morph into a tool of the Republican Party, a vector of political interests domestic or foreign, or, perhaps the laziest explanation, just a troll out to provoke people.

Elon Musk put his entire empire at risk—and torched his public reputation before emerging as a political force—simply by unleashing Elon Musk. He had never been a conventional CEO, but at his most powerful, he was completely unbound from the rules of society. By the time he was pulling public stunts like erecting a giant, pulsing X logo in the middle of San Francisco to signify Twitter's rebrand—directing "rave levels of brightness," as one person put it to me, into residential high-rises (including an apartment complex of senior and low-income residents and people with disabilities)—no one expected him to face any real consequences.

San Francisco resident Christina DiEdoardo told me: "It's not a bad bet from Musk that he's going to get away with it, but he shouldn't." DiEdoardo is a lawyer with a propensity for digging into such technical matters as city permitting rules. "It's the latest example of a pattern of scofflawery from a guy that behaves with no consideration for everybody else."

Was it any surprise? That pattern of "scofflawery" had unfolded over several years as Musk realized it resulted in few real consequences.

There was hardly anyone capable of stopping him, as *Hubris Maximus* will demonstrate. And there was no one to save him from himself.

Over a six-year span, Musk made himself indispensable, a man of colossal strategic importance, bringing electric cars into the mainstream, turning Tesla into the world's most valuable automaker, and earning himself the title of world's richest person, all while putting himself at the center of the country's most ambitious undertakings with implications for manufacturing, defense and technology, and politics. Musk cast himself as a potential savior of humanity, an altruist whose fortune was tied to noble pursuits such as halting the world's dependence on fossil fuels and expanding the reach of consciousness into the cosmos. He offered a sense of optimism to many people trapped in the doom loop of a perceived societal and environmental decline. And he had a track record of success, what observers hailed as a Midas touch, along with the rare qualities of possessing a vision—that stretched beyond income statements—and a relentless drive to see it through.[20]

Along the way, he relished his increasing power, firing people who stood in his way; spurning regulators, watchdogs, and whistleblowers; and severing ties with those who dared question him and appointing loyalists in their place.

Musk's rapid ascent and precipitous reputational decline have been a remarkable case study in a few things: the limits of hubris as a leadership style, the pitfalls of corporate mismanagement and unyielding loyalty to one man, the fecklessness of a gridlocked and neutered government (an at-times scientifically challenged gerontocracy), and the drain and outright rejection of expertise in a corporate environment ruled by the short-term dopamine hit of earnings reports. It also demonstrates the power of a platform to shape the public narrative—to write one's own hagiography—compared to quietly demonstrating competence in a world that can't turn away from its screens. Somehow, the rules of meritocracy don't apply to those who can leverage their fame and fortune well enough.

Musk, to be sure, reinvented what it meant to be a CEO in the twenty-first century. He led Tesla using the bully pulpit, eroding guardrails and cutting through red tape whenever possible, dismantling once and for all the image of the CEO as a faceless corporate suit who didn't believe in anything but profits or was otherwise hamstrung by bureaucracy. There was a time when Musk's approach—unfiltered, authentic, raw—was refreshing. I spoke with the CEO of a rival major automaker who said he envied Musk's power—the pure efficiency of his rule and the autocratic nature of his management made it hard to compete.

Musk didn't have to wait for the green light of a board to usher in his most ambitious bets: promising to turn a fleet of a million vehicles into self-driving cars; building a futuristic pickup that looked like nothing else; reopening a crowded and chaotic production line during the height of a pandemic; and making a surprise pivot to social media on the strength of those accomplishments and somehow keeping the lights on after firing 75 percent of the staff.[21] In the process, Musk told powerful government regulators to piss off and influential corporate advertisers to screw themselves.[22]

Who wouldn't dream of having that kind of power?

At the same time, Musk ruled by intimidation, conducting arbitrary firings, setting spontaneous timelines that demanded his subordinates to deliver on massive goals faster than seemingly possible, leading to perpetual burnout and historic turnover.

Soon, so many became all too comfortable with problem-solving approaches that were far from rigorous, blindly following as if Musk's edicts were dogma. The downsides of the approach revealed themselves in quick succession: a trail of disappointed acolytes—philosophical allies who were caught flatfooted by the inconsistency of Musk's positions, investors who grew exhausted by his impulsive behavior, former employees who were lured in by his high-flying promises to change the world and then found themselves on the wrong end of tough business decisions. Past results became an indicator of future success—Wall Street and Silicon Valley investors would follow Musk in walking off a cliff in exchange for a little equity. Case in point: the immense support he rallied to crowd-fund his purchase of X, at the time known as Twitter, a struggling social media company that couldn't justify its $44 billion price tag in any world where Musk wasn't involved. By late 2024, prior to the election that likely impacted X's value, the largest of those shareholders were hundreds of millions of dollars underwater on their investments, and some had publicly turned against Musk.[23] The magnitude of the blunder had become apparent with reports such as one in *The Wall Street Journal* that declared: "Elon Musk's Twitter Takeover Is Now the Worst Buyout for Banks since the Financial Crisis."[24]

This implosion of Musk's public and business reputation had long been in the making. The question now is: Can anyone get through to him before the fallout of his decision-making unleashes even more severe consequences? Is it already too late?

Maybe the signs had been apparent all along—for anyone willing to look. In *Hubris Maximus*, I will make exactly that case—the one that could have served Musk's most ardent backers; Twitter's equity investors; the Morgan Stanley bankers who backed his takeover; now-disillusioned believers in his self-driving tech, customers harmed by his false promises;

and, most of all, the public that was so willing to go along with the aura of Musk, desperately in need of another Steve Jobs, proof of America's place in bringing order to a chaotic and depressing world.

I'll answer troubling questions, ones that might be especially uncomfortable for inhabitants of Musk-world: What if everyone got taken for a ride?

What if Elon Musk wasn't really a genius?

"Everybody loved Napoleon while he cleaned up the mess of the French Revolution but when he got to the top that's when he put his brother in charge and his uncles in charge, and now he picks fights with everybody. And what ended up happening to Napoleon this is exactly what's happening to Elon," investor Ross Gerber, once Musk's biggest defender on television, told me.

"You've got somebody who thinks he's Caesar, or thinks he's Napoleon, who thinks he can do no wrong."

As I write these lines, car buyers have signaled increasing skepticism of Tesla, the crown jewel of Musk's portfolio that recently recorded its first annual sales decline in more than a decade,[25] surely at least in part, because of the damage done by Musk's takeover of Twitter, his relentless and controversial political conjectures—including hard-line anti-immigration rhetoric—and his repeated unforced errors that have revealed a kind of selfishness and led to charges of incompetence or worse—that he's a charlatan.[26] Now Musk has bet the company's future on robots, artificial intelligence, and autonomous cars—to skepticism from some key former colleagues, concern from spurned investors, and the ire of one-time fans—while boosters see it as yet another stroke of brilliance from an unpredictable genius who cannot afford to sit still and reap the rewards of yesterday's formula for success.

On the other hand, it's hard to see how Musk should take away any lessons from the blunders of the recent past, given Tesla's valuation, as of this writing and in large part due to his astute political maneuvering, has been restored to more than $1 trillion. Musk has even gained a position of influence over the agencies that had previously sought to rein him in.

The following chapters will methodically deconstruct the making and mind of that man, the Silicon Valley Caesar, the self-anointed Technoking. This is a book about what should have been predictable from the beginning and details a devastating autopsy of how it was allowed to happen.

1

ELON MUSK'S WAR AGAINST WASHINGTON

The thirty-eight-year-old father dropped his son at preschool and set off for work. He'd recently purchased a Tesla Model X P100D, an SUV with a six-figure price tag that boasted falcon-wing doors, the dream car he'd saved up for and bought himself as a birthday gift.[1]

Walter Huang believed in Tesla. His lawyers would later say that he thought his car, when placed in Tesla's Autopilot mode, was safer than one driven by a human driver.

He was such a dedicated enthusiast that he joined a Facebook Model X ownership group and regularly talked to a friend about the performance of the Autopilot software.[2] His wife said he would watch YouTube videos of Autopilot in his spare time.[3]

This reconstruction of Huang's drive is based substantially on documents from the National Transportation Safety Board's (NTSB) accident docket.

Lately, Huang had been having problems with his Model X. The car, which he regularly used in Autopilot mode, repeatedly veered toward a highway barrier on US 101 that he passed daily on his way to work, prompting him to correct its course.

At around 9:00 a.m. on March 23, 2018, minutes after dropping off his son Tristan at preschool, Huang, an Apple software engineer, flicked on Autopilot and headed south on 101 toward work. At around the same time, he fired up a mobile strategy game he had been playing—Three Kingdoms.[4]

Noting his lack of attention, the car repeatedly prompted him—a visual warning escalating to an annoying beep, the kind meant to provoke a reaction. Tesla detected whether a driver was holding the steering wheel, but Huang didn't nudge it in response to the warnings—a phenomenon familiar to drivers who tend to tune out alerts from the automated systems. Autopilot, programmed to follow lane lines and keep its distance from vehicles ahead, stayed engaged.

At around twenty-seven minutes into his drive, near the interchange between US 101 and State Route 85 north of San Jose, Huang reached the spot where his car had veered off before. Apparently, he did not react quickly enough, and the car lost its lane. From there, it followed a "faded and nearly obliterated" lane line into an empty space between two lanes; ahead, the bustling US 101 and the on-ramp for Route 85 were separated by a concrete highway median.[5]

Once in that no-man's-land and with no traffic ahead of it, Huang's SUV did what it had been programmed to do—it accelerated to the maximum speed the driver had set. It climbed from the 62 mph speed of traffic up to 65 two seconds later, then 68 a second later, then 70 in the final second.[6]

It never reached the speed of 75 mph to which Huang's Autopilot had been preset. Huang's car was an unstoppable force about to meet an immovable object. Huang crashed into the median at around 71 mph, investigators said, spinning "the SUV counterclockwise and [causing] the front body structure to separate from the rear of the vehicle." It also struck two other vehicles, leaving the twenty-five-year-old driver of a Mazda 3 with minor injuries—and the car's front driver's side fender heavily damaged—when the Tesla rotated into the lane of traffic before coming to a rest. The Tesla, its battery compartment ripped open, erupted in flames.[7]

Bystanders found Huang strapped into the driver's seat. They pulled him out of the wreckage, and he was taken by ambulance to Stanford Health Care Hospital.[8]

At 1:02 p.m., Walter Huang was pronounced dead.

Robert Sumwalt's job had sent him to the sites of devastating plane crashes, train derailments, and infrastructure failures over a more than decade-long career at the NTSB.

But seated at a conference table in his sixth-floor Washington, DC, office, one corner in the labyrinth of federal agencies known as L'Enfant Plaza, the nation's top federal safety investigator looked at his iPhone and was stunned as never before.

"He hung up on us."

"Yeah, he did," said Dennis Jones, a nearly forty-year veteran of the agency sitting across the table, also trying to process the ordeal.

Over twenty-seven contentious minutes on April 11, 2018, in Sumwalt's later recollection, Elon Musk had fumed, protested, threatened to sue, and abruptly exited the conversation when safety investigators refused to bend to his will. It was a textbook example of Musk's disregard for a public that had imbued him with godlike power—and his contempt for the safety establishment charged with ensuring he didn't abuse it.

Autopilot, Musk believed, would play a pivotal role in advancing traffic safety, ushering in a future where people no longer had to die on the road. Its very origins were tied to an internal meeting at Tesla where the subject of eradicating road deaths had gripped the engineering staff as one of them wrote out the annual number of yearly road deaths on a whiteboard. Already, major tech companies such as Google and Uber were envisioning populating the roads with self-driving fleets, but Tesla would be unique in pursuing autonomy through privately owned personal vehicles. And the company wanted to make it happen as quickly as possible.

Autopilot is a set of driver-assistance features that enable Teslas to maneuver from highway on-ramps to off-ramps without the driver's physical input, a type of hyperadvanced cruise control that gave consumers a tangible demonstration of Tesla's technological lead over other automakers. It controls the cars' speed and distance from other cars, follows lane lines, and can even make lane changes along a route. Full Self-Driving, meanwhile, sought to bring those capabilities to city and residential streets, adding the ability to make turns, halt for red lights and stop signs, and follow turn-by-turn directions.

Tesla had developed a handy talking point for its discussions of Autopilot: it was safer than normal driving when crash data was compared. (The argument carried a fundamental flaw: Autopilot was intended for highways, and highway driving was inherently less complicated.) But even years later, Musk's position had hardly evolved. He applied the same logic to Full Self-Driving, Tesla's more advanced iteration of Autopilot, designed for use during much more complicated city and residential street driving. Musk's arguments here were at best unproven and at worst reckless: he was encouraging drivers to view systems geared at convenience as lifesaving breakthroughs that could prevent crashes.

Regardless, Musk seemed to believe that even if some lives were lost in the process, those who opposed his vision of the future were roadblocks to progress. He fully articulated this philosophy at an autonomy-focused event years later, in 2022: "At the point of which you believe that adding autonomy reduces injury and death, I think you have a moral obligation to deploy it even though you're going to get sued and blamed by a lot of people. Because the people whose lives you saved don't know that their lives were saved, and the people who do occasionally die or get injured, they definitely know—or their state does."[9]

His position was that the processes established by society to prevent automotive calamities were ineffective or, worse, obstacles to this moral imperative. Musk had legions of admirers and online fanboys who validated this belief; his methods were the right ones, and his way was the only path forward. Who was the government to stand in the way? How could they possibly possess the requisite knowledge, technological know-how, and raw data to undermine him? What had they ever built?

Musk and Tesla already had a fraught history with regulators in Washington. Tesla was staking its future on the artificial intelligence bet of the century: putting a fully autonomous vehicle in the hands of customers, a moon shot that differed from the mostly commercial ambitions of the robotaxi projects from Big Tech competitors like Google and Apple. Regulators and safety officials in the federal government who were building a set of rules to regulate Silicon Valley's lab experiments—small-scale testing in a highly regulated space—were caught largely flatfooted when Tesla started adding features that resembled autonomy to its cars beginning in late 2014.

Musk may have resented Washington's meddling, but he also owed much of Tesla's success to it. In 2009, the company was on the verge of collapse as the Great Recession promised to wipe out demand for its pricey electric cars. Tesla had produced a sleek sports car, the Roadster, which offered the thrill of instant torque combined with an electric power train, in part inspired by the mid-engine Lotus Elise.[10] That thrill came at a price: the vehicle cost around $100,000, or more than double the sticker price of the Elise. Faced with a souring economy that threatened its ability to produce the Model S—the car that would later make the company a household name—Tesla found two saviors. Daimler, the auto group that encompassed Mercedes-Benz, approached Tesla to build power trains for its electric Smart cars. Meanwhile, the US government, aiming to bring electric cars to the masses, made a bet on Tesla. The Department of Energy provided the company with a $465 million loan, critical cash at a time of existential uncertainty.

In a 2011 interview with *The Atlantic*, Musk acknowledged Tesla's reliance on the government.

"Tesla has received a loan from the government," he said. "If Tesla is to compete effectively against GM, Ford, Chrysler and others and those guys are getting massive amounts of money from the government at zero cost of capital and we don't participate in that game it makes a very difficult job even harder. And so it just would be really unwise if we didn't do that."[11]

In the coming years, Tesla would secure another coup. The government was encouraging big automakers to go electric, but they didn't have the capacity or willpower to do so, especially in a declining economy. Tesla, on the other hand, would pump out thousands of electric vehicles per quarter. Why couldn't Detroit simply take credit for their work? Automakers such as Chrysler started buying what were called "regulatory credits" from Tesla so they could surpass state emissions requirements under the federal Clean Air Act. This arrangement propelled Tesla to the profitability that helped make Musk the world's richest person.[12] Not only would his company get a yearslong head start on the competition, it could also cash in on their failure to adapt.

Musk may have outmaneuvered competitors in Silicon Valley and Detroit, but the threat of regulation still hung over him. Though the safety investigators with the NTSB had a different mandate from their counterparts at the National Highway Traffic Safety Administration (NHTSA), Sumwalt felt that Musk lumped all the DC suits together. Musk had been irate when NHTSA regulators called him after another, similar crash in 2016; a Tesla in Autopilot had slammed into a tractor-trailer at 70 mph after failing to distinguish the rig from the sky behind it, in Tesla's explanation, killing the driver. Musk yelled on the phone and threatened a lawsuit when he was told regulators were getting involved, a former safety official, speaking on the condition of anonymity to discuss a sensitive matter, said.[13]

Musk's view was simple: "We're all beating up on him," Dennis Jones recalled.

Musk's relationship with regulators and safety officials fully eroded during the five most critical years in his self-driving push. As he promoted his vision of consumer robotaxis, Musk tested a strategy of harnessing online armies of fanboys—oftentimes, enthusiastic investors whose toxic digital personas were aimed at silencing short sellers or naysayers—against those who threatened to slow the progress of Autopilot and its companion mode, Full Self-Driving, making life a nightmare for those who stood in his way. All in the name, Musk argued, of safety. One official was forced to flee her home in response to what local authorities regarded as a dangerous threat after Tesla fans erupted over her appointment as an NHTSA adviser, and Musk joined in the public attack. In another instance, authorities had to get involved after criticism of a government official escalated into personal threats from online trolls.[14]

On April 6, 2018—the Friday before Musk would angrily hang up on him—Robert Sumwalt knew that he was faced with a potentially unpleasant task: calling the CEO about the latest deadly crash involving a Tesla on Autopilot. Things began quite cordially, but Sumwalt would soon learn the same lesson as so many who have crossed Musk's path over the years: the mercurial billionaire can charm and play nice with those who have power over his empire, but he can turn on them just as quickly if he feels they're threatening to stand in his way.

Federal safety investigators have a duty to the public: ensuring that the errors contributing to fatal crashes are not repeated or, worse, built into safety-critical systems. Many feel this responsibility deeply. Sumwalt—an easygoing but direct communicator who had spent decades as a commercial pilot—certainly did. Even so, he was starstruck as he first dialed Musk's cell phone to discuss the matter.

"In fact, I was amazed . . . I thought 'this was pretty cool, I'm talking to Elon Musk,'" said Sumwalt, now retired from the safety board, recalling the conversation after a recent dinner at Cracker Barrel in Florida.

The two men exchanged pleasantries. Sumwalt, flanked by a coterie of Washington officials huddled around a speakerphone on a sofa outside his office, explained to Musk that he wanted Tesla to be a party to the investigation. This was an especially critical step for a company with vast amounts of internal data, whose technical understanding of its own systems far outmatched that of safety officials. Dennis Jones, the NTSB's longtime managing director, liked to joke that the agency was charged with investigating airplane manufacturers who could pay for its whole budget with a single airliner. In Tesla's case, investigators were helpless in retrieving and decoding the proprietary data from the company's on-board computers without internal assistance. Musk should have been well aware of this knowledge gap.

But the investigative process also benefited Tesla: if the company played a part in the investigation, it would be aware of potentially damaging information and could offer input and clarity about possible damning investigative findings. The ultimate goal was to keep the public safe—and a company that didn't want to mask wrongdoing had little reason not to cooperate.

There were also rules: a party to a federal investigation could not unilaterally release information that might factor into the NTSB probe. I had broken a story earlier in the month about how the NTSB was "unhappy" with Tesla's release of investigative information in the Huang crash, which had implied Huang's inattention was a factor.[15]

Basically, Tesla wasn't allowed to spin its own version of the crash if it wanted to collaborate with safety officials in good faith. Sumwalt had been concerned about Tesla preemptively disclosing data that was subject to the investigation and wanted to make sure Musk understood the rules.

On that spring day, Musk was polite and professional on the phone with Sumwalt—and he expressed openness to cooperating. He wanted Tesla to be part of the probe, he said. Sumwalt took that as an indication that Musk intended to follow the rules. So Elon Musk and the country's top transportation safety investigator agreed to work together.

With the business portion of their conversation concluded, Sumwalt had more questions.

Musk had yet to become the richest person on earth, but he was quickly becoming a household name, a celebrity CEO whom many already regarded as the real-life Tony Stark.

What's a day in the life of Elon Musk? Sumwalt asked.

Musk sounded tired to Sumwalt as he explained that his work schedule was intense. He had been sleeping on the floor of Tesla's factory. The year 2018 had been the most painful of his career, as the company tried to sort out production problems with its mass market Model 3.[16] He told Sumwalt that around 75 to 80 percent of his time was dedicated to Tesla, around 20 percent to SpaceX, and the rest—a figure over the remaining 5 percent or less—was devoted to his other companies. "I think that was intentional," Sumwalt told me of Musk's description exceeding 100 percent.

The conversation lasted thirty minutes.

Sumwalt left feeling good about it.

But over the next few days, as Tesla continued to release information about the crash, even speculating on its cause, the situation deteriorated. Tesla was under pressure as the gruesome details of the crash were revealed. Other crashes had garnered NTSB attention, of course: a later case in Delray Beach, Florida, and an earlier one in Williston, Florida, which was among the most troubling: the Tesla, operating in Autopilot mode, failed to distinguish the side of a tractor-trailer from a bright-colored sky.[17]

In that crash, forty-year-old Joshua David Brown was killed when a truck turned across the path of his 2015 Tesla Model S, which failed to slow down. The top of the Tesla was sheared off in a crash safety officials attributed to distraction after the driver ignored at least seven visual safety warnings, on-screen prompts to pay attention.[18] Investigators cited both Brown's overreliance on the software and a more novel concept, the car's "operational design domain," or the set of conditions and locations in which Autopilot could be activated. Regulators at NHTSA, meanwhile, held Tesla largely free from blame, and Musk called their findings "very positive."[19]

But in the crash involving Huang, Tesla risked losing control. Musk was on the verge of positioning Autopilot as the most important product in Tesla's portfolio, with potential value exceeding that of the company's automotive business. He had seemed to realize the company's image was taking a hit, so Tesla chose a strategy that most big automakers in its position wouldn't think of: it started running interference. Again.

Suddenly, days after the call in which Musk agreed to the ground rules, details of the crash that were under investigation by the NTSB started pouring out of Tesla, directly from its PR department.[20]

"According to the family, Mr. Huang was well aware that Autopilot was not perfect and, specifically, he told them it was not reliable in that exact location, yet he nonetheless engaged Autopilot at that location," the company said in a press statement reported by outlets such as *Fortune* and ABC News.[21] "The crash happened on a clear day with several hundred feet of visibility ahead, which means that the only way for this accident to have occurred is if Mr. Huang was not paying attention to the road, despite the car providing multiple warnings to do so."

When his agency stumbled on the press clippings a day after Tesla's statement went out, Sumwalt couldn't believe it. Tesla was blaming the driver for the crash that had killed him, after Sumwalt had explicitly warned Musk about the rules. It was beyond inappropriate; it was unconscionable.

He picked up the phone and dialed Musk, who wasn't immediately available.

Later that day, Jones had been visiting with Sumwalt in his office when a call popped up on Sumwalt's screen.

Jones remembers the moment vividly.

"Wow, that's Elon Musk," Sumwalt said.

Sumwalt signaled for Jones to stay—they'd finish their conversation once the call had concluded. He knew it would serve him well to have a witness to their exchange.

They put Musk on speakerphone, and Sumwalt quickly got to the point.

"What you did, Elon, was a violation of our party agreement. We spoke about this last week. You agreed that you would abide by our requirements."

There was nothing but silence for almost ten seconds.

Then Musk, growing agitated and shorter with his words, launched into a tirade. Sumwalt recalled him arguing: "You're making a bad mistake. More people [will] die because of this, because of what you're doing."

The investigators were out of line, he indicated, behind the curve with their slow bureaucratic process, as Tesla had already drawn conclusions about the crash using its vast amounts of data, and there was no doubt that the driver had been at fault.

"He goes into a diatribe," Sumwalt said, "about 'well you're decreasing safety by virtue of the fact that our car is safer when it's on Autopilot, we're saving more lives because of Autopilot than people are lost but by your removing us from the investigation you're decreasing safety.'"

Musk then threatened to sue, though it was not clear what standing he would have had.

"That's fine, go ahead," Sumwalt responded.

Musk launched back into his argument about the safety of Autopilot, reminding them of its potential lifesaving capabilities. Sumwalt wondered: How many times do I need to tell you this?

After Musk had finished, Sumwalt signaled for Jones to weigh in. The managing director explained how the parties were expected to work collaboratively, how the agency maintained productive relationships with automakers subject to its investigations, and he noted the harmonious relationship the agency had had with SpaceX in the past. Musk didn't respond right away.

"I don't want us to be removed from the investigation," Musk finally said, as if the prior twenty-seven minutes hadn't happened.

"It's too late for that," Sumwalt said, at no small risk to his agency, which relied on Tesla's expertise to decode its data.

The line went dead.

Sumwalt and Jones looked at each other in shock, trying to process what had happened. It wasn't just being hung up on; Musk's demeanor and attitude and his unconvincing argument—a repetition-filled script— had left Sumwalt thoroughly unimpressed. There simply wasn't enough evidence to demonstrate that Autopilot, a suite of driver-assistance features with a catchy name, was the transformative and revolutionary system with the lifesaving capabilities Musk touted; in this particular instance, it was at the center of a fatal crash, a high-tech calamity that safety investigators could examine to uncover new findings about the intersection of technology, driver distraction, and speed.

It was clear to them both that Musk didn't even recognize the difference between the roles of the safety investigators from the NTSB and the regulators from NHTSA, an important distinction that the head of an automaker should understand.

Tesla would later claim it hadn't been booted from the investigation—it had withdrawn on its own.[22] In a statement reported by outlets including CNBC, Tesla elaborated on its apparent decision to withdraw. "It's been clear in our conversations with the NTSB that they're more concerned with press headlines than actually promoting safety," the company said. "Among other things, they repeatedly released partial bits of incomplete information to the media in violation of their own rules, at the same time that they were trying to prevent us from telling all the facts."[23]

"You can't fire me, I quit," Sumwalt called the maneuver.

The Sumwalt saga was just a preview of how Musk's tumultuous relationship with his overseers in Washington would unfold in the years to come.

In late 2021, Missy Cummings set off from her townhome in North Carolina for the Appalachian trailhead, packing up her teardrop camper for a few days off the grid. She ended up in the middle of the Appalachian Mountains, on the North Carolina–Tennessee border, in her "own *Breaking Bad* world."

Cummings, a single-seat fighter pilot turned college professor, had known her appointment to NHTSA wouldn't be easy. But she hadn't expected it would lead to email messages from strangers threatening to kill her and her family.

Only days earlier, Reuters had reported her appointment to NHTSA as senior adviser for safety in what would have otherwise been a footnote in a set of appointments by President Joe Biden.[24] Cummings, an engineering professor, had served as director of Duke University's Humans and Autonomy Lab and had extensively studied autonomous vehicles. She was able to offer a needed dose of expertise to an agency that was often being outmaneuvered by Silicon Valley. Soon, Tesla's defenders on Twitter, particularly a Musk fanboy named Omar Qazi who'd become a Tesla influencer, started looking into her record. Qazi, a software engineer and California native who shared the liberal politics of people his age and background, started a series of pro-Tesla accounts after purchasing a Tesla Model 3 in 2018, a time when he said he was "just going through a lot of transitions in my life in a sense, coming into adulthood." Qazi studied computer science and economics at Santa Clara University but didn't finish.

Soon, his Tesla advocacy became an all-consuming task; he regularly fought with detractors and short sellers online, incensed by their attacks on a vehicle and a company that he saw as making world-changing progress on the crucial issue of climate change. Above all, Qazi's Tesla made him feel good at a formative time in his life. His willingness to stick his neck out for Tesla—and to *go there* when it came to fighting naysayers online—soon won him the attention of Musk himself.

"I honestly have no clue how I got here," he says. "Really what it was for me was I loved that car. At that time in my life I just got in it, when I went and I drove that car I just felt great. The music, Autopilot—you went places, you have life experiences. It just legitimately made me upset to hear people saying, 'Ah, the company's going to die, the company's going to go away.' To think that car and the company might not be there."

Qazi and the fanboys set their sights on Cummings.

They quickly found that she had criticized Tesla in the past. Some of her comments seemed to stray into advocacy; on Tesla's release of its most advanced driver-assistance software, Full Self-Driving, for example, she'd said: "I'd want my money back."[25] Other comments seemed misguided for someone in her position. One of her tweets said a person would be there to "hold me back" in a spat with Musk, alongside an animated GIF of a punch.[26]

Even worse, in their view, she had served on the board of a company developing LiDAR, a type of sensor technology Tesla and Musk opposed.[27] They believed Teslas could achieve autonomy simply and at a lower cost by using a camera-only approach.

Things escalated from there. Cummings was soon forced to lock down her Twitter account as her mentions were flooded with hateful and misogynistic vitriol. Qazi, drawing attention to the matter with his Twitter handle @wholemarsblog, launched a petition on Change.org that garnered tens of thousands of signatures calling for a review of Cummings's appointment.[28] (Qazi, in an interview, expressed regret about the petition's role in fueling vitriol against Cummings.) Officials at NHTSA were caught flatfooted by what they seemed to regard as more of a public relations storm than a bad-faith smear campaign, in Cummings's view.

(Cummings would ultimately agree to recuse herself from matters related to Tesla.)

But the problem was about to become much worse.

Elon Musk took to his Twitter account.

"Objectively," Musk tweeted, hours after Cummings's appointment was reported, "her track record is extremely biased against Tesla."[29]

Those nine words altered the course of Missy Cummings's life. (Musk has expressed sensitivity to doxxing, which mostly refers to the practice of posting private information of online figures, saying, "Doxxing places people in danger."[30] X's definition of doxxing is expansive, encompassing "contexts suggesting abusive intent, harassment or incitement to harass, as well as the distribution of media that may lead to emotional or physical harm."[31] Musk's actions at the time would not have constituted doxxing but the reactions it incited may have risen to that level.)

Now Cummings wasn't just fielding tweets calling her "evil"; she was facing threats to her safety.

Musk couldn't control how strangers behaved online, but the "Funding secured" stock market furor that prompted intervention by the SEC had surely taught him the power of his Twitter megaphone. The attacks against Cummings had stretched far beyond any concern over a perceived conflict of interest.

Following his 2018 run-in with the SEC that he treated as a slap on the wrist, Musk grew increasingly comfortable using his Twitter following of tens of millions to target people directly. The consequences were starting to become clear. No government official—whether incoming, incumbent, or former—is beyond criticism. But at this point in his journey as a public figure, CEO, and maybe the most prominent personality on Twitter, Musk could not have feigned ignorance about the disproportionate power of his bully pulpit. Women tended to suffer the most severe effects of his Twitter targeting, as the experiences with Washington and California officials showed, and the harassment unleashed by Musk's army of fanboys was far from organic. With Musk's involvement, an argument that could have been confined to a niche, hobbyist—yet still-toxic—corner of the internet would suddenly be projected to the top of many users' Twitter feeds. The pattern would be demonstrated repeatedly over this period as Musk escalated technical matters, even paltry concerns over issues such as insurance rules, into highly public, and messy, online disputes with officials.[32] His actions mirrored the behavior of another public figure with a propensity for petty spats.

In a tweet to Musk, Cummings offered an olive branch: an opportunity to talk through their differences. But it didn't help.

At 12:31 a.m. on October 21, Cummings received an email.

> We know you own LIDAR companies and if you accept NHTSA adviser position we will kill you and your family.

Worried about the safety of her thirteen-year-old daughter, Cummings called the police. The authorities told her that they understood her concern and that she did not have to stay at home. She agreed that it might not be a good idea to stick around. She sent her teenage daughter to her dad's, packed up, and soon was making camp in the wilderness with her RV. She reassured herself that if anything were going to happen, it would be in the next few days. Then things would calm down and she could return to her life.

"I'm not the only person this has happened to," she said in an interview with me in early 2023. "I am the nth person who he has made some kind of negative comment about, and it's completely upended someone's life."

Among Washington officials, Cummings's story is a cautionary tale of what can happen when one dares to mention Tesla or Musk, whose legions of online fans are extremely sensitive to the slightest hint of criticism. Musk's tweets to those groups serve to fan the flames, providing a set of marching orders. Today, so many with strong opinions on Musk refrain from expressing them outright for fear of disturbing the hornet's nest and inviting an online swarm of vitriol turbocharged by Musk's megaphone.

"Being a single-seat fighter pilot, I am such a self-reliant person," Cummings recalled. "My attitude was more like 'come and get me.'"

Still, Cummings soon took action to preserve her mental peace.

She wiped her Twitter account from the internet. She was a professional with a career, and she didn't need to subject herself to the cesspool.

*   *   *

In the time since the Huang crash, Tesla largely resisted making changes the feds recommended, particularly limiting Autopilot to the locations and conditions for which it was designed. Almost a year after Walter Huang's death, another man, Jeremy Banner, was killed when his Tesla in Autopilot crashed into the side of a semitruck trailer at around 70 mph.[33]

Yet Tesla was soon enabling its software to operate in other locations, giving thousands of vehicles the freedom to activate "self-driving" features on city and residential streets.

Jennifer Homendy couldn't believe it.

Years after his spat with the NTSB chair, Elon Musk had a new critic in Washington: Robert Sumwalt's successor, following his retirement after more than a decade at the NTSB.

In October 2020, Tesla released the most advanced iteration of its driver-assistance system, Full Self-Driving. Starting that month, drivers could try the new features, which allowed Teslas to follow a local route, making turns and heeding traffic signals along the way, with the touch of an icon.[34] Homendy, the new chair of the NTSB, had long-standing concerns. Tesla still hadn't followed recommendations made after a 2016 crash in Williston, Florida, when a car in Autopilot mode slammed into a tractor-trailer, let alone those made after the Mountain View, California, crash that killed Walter Huang. The NTSB wanted the company to build in better safeguards that would ensure Autopilot only operated in areas it was supposed to, and drivers couldn't use it while distracted.[35] Teslas in Autopilot shouldn't be slamming into the sides of semitrucks because Autopilot shouldn't be operating at all on roads with cross traffic. Walter Huang's car shouldn't have stayed in Autopilot mode after alerting him repeatedly to pay attention.

Homendy was alarmed that Tesla was putting an even more sophisticated product into the hands of drivers without addressing the safety board's recommendations. Full Self-Driving, she said, was "misleading."[36]

"Tesla has not responded to any of our requests," she told *The Washington Post* in a September 2021 story. "From our standpoint they've ignored us—they haven't responded to us."[37]

"And if those are not addressed and you're making additional upgrades, that's a problem," she added.

Like clockwork, Musk responded with a tweet the same day as the *Post*'s report. This time, he didn't need to say anything to set the mob in motion. He merely posted a link to Homendy's Wikipedia page, in a reply to a report that summarized Homendy's earlier comments to *The Wall Street Journal* about Full Self-Driving.[38]

Homendy remembers where she was when it started. Suddenly, her Twitter was blowing up with vitriol, threats, misogyny. As she watched her feed populate with toxic posts from a rental home in Emerald Isle, North Carolina, that Saturday morning, she remembers feeling oddly at peace. Meanwhile, her Wikipedia page had to be locked down amid attempts to vandalize it

Fellow users were also warning her about the coming onslaught: "I hope you have security; Musk is threatening you," Homendy recalls one of the posts.

Linette Lopez, a journalist who had been attacked by Musk fanboys, also warned Homendy about the fallout. Homendy contacted her local sheriff in Spotsylvania County, Virginia, to alert authorities to specific posts in which people threatened to show up at her home, and one she vaguely recalled mentioning a bomb.

Inside the NTSB, the agency's chief of special operations was briefed on the security situation involving the chair.

The threats soon died down. But Homendy's focus on Tesla continued.

Nearly a month later, Homendy posted a tweet as she drank her morning coffee and took in some music. "An 'anthem of strength' for all the #safety champions out there," she wrote, and pasted a YouTube link: It was to Tom Petty and the Heartbreakers' "I Won't Back Down."[39]

Three days later, Homendy issued a stern letter to Musk.

"The National Transportation Safety Board (NTSB) appreciates the productive and professional cooperation extended by Tesla's technical staff to our investigators over the course of our various crash and incident investigations," she wrote. "I am deeply concerned, however, that Tesla's action—or rather, inaction—to implement critical NTSB safety recommendations has not demonstrated the same productivity or professionalism."[40]

Months after sending the letter, Homendy was in her sixth-floor office at L'Enfant Plaza. The NTSB had agreed to a meeting requested by Rohan Patel, Tesla's DC-based senior global director of public policy.

Musk, for all of the trouble he could cause, had a short memory and a pragmatic streak. He knew there was little benefit to feuding with officials in Washington, especially over the long term. He was an impulsive tweeter, and his acerbic online personality sometimes had the potential to cut into his long-term vision. Patel's invite gave the appearance of a clean-up effort, the type that would sometimes happen after Musk came to his senses.

There was little stated purpose for the meeting, according to Homendy's recollection. Patel briefed her on the latest developments at Tesla, describing the state of the company along with the latest statistics on its cutting-edge safety features and Autopilot system. Homendy applauded Tesla for its passive safety development, which aims to prevent vehicle occupant deaths using devices such as seat belts and airbags, calling it the leader in the field. This was interesting but not particularly germane to the key issue of Tesla's failure to follow NTSB guidance. Patel soon expressed his dismay at the recurring issue of a four-year-old recommendation.

"It doesn't make a lot of sense to me," he told her. In Patel's view, it wasn't only that the order wasn't relevant to Tesla's current technology; NTSB, an investigative body, didn't have the authority to order Tesla around. As far as Patel was concerned, Homendy should be talking to her counterparts at NHTSA.

"[If you] want to develop regulations and . . . think NHTSA should be developing regulations," he said, "that's a good place . . . to have that discussion."

Meanwhile, he was dismayed at seeing Homendy take to the public airwaves to lambaste Tesla for its failure to follow through on an order he saw as irrelevant.

"Look, before you get on TV saying what I think to be really bombastic things about Tesla, why don't you call me ahead of time?" he said.

Patel finished his presentation and then paused.

Oh, there's one other thing.

"[We] want to develop a better relationship with the NTSB."

2

A "DIFFICULT AND PAINFUL YEAR"
AND A HANDSOME REWARD

Ira Ehrenpreis couldn't have known that he was sending one of the most expensive text messages of all time. On April 8, 2017, wary of the fact that Tesla's board had not struck a long-term commitment with its extremely valuable chief executive, the longtime board member tapped out a message to Elon Musk.

The content of the text was tame. Could Musk "pls chat for a few minutes this weekend re a few comp related issues"?[1] Musk, the chief executive of the most exciting car company on the planet, the one gearing up to put self-driving technology directly in the hands of consumers, the one about to roll out a mass market sedan that would propel Tesla into the mainstream, was in a unique position of leverage.

They spoke by phone the following day, starting a process that would soon make Musk the richest person on earth.

Ehrenpreis's goal when he sent that message in 2017 had been to ascertain whether Musk—on the tail end of a 2012 package that had awarded him Tesla stock when the company's valuation reached certain milestones—was ready to re-up his commitment to the company. The 2012 package had been lucrative. "In the end, the value of Musk's [Tesla] holdings increased from approximately $981 million to $13 billion," a later court decision said.[2]

Musk was intrigued by the idea of re-upping his commitment—so much so that he offered specifics over the phone.

The court summarized Musk's ask, a proposal he saw as "really crazy," it said.

"He envisioned a purely performance-based compensation plan, structured like the 2012 Grant but with more challenging market capitalization milestones and proposed 15 milestones of $50 billion in market capitalization—a total possible award of 15% of Tesla's outstanding shares," the filing says.

It was a classic Musk game of *Risk*: he would forgo a salary in favor of a moon shot that could ultimately be worth more than the GDP of some small countries. Musk would receive stock options worth 1 percent of Tesla each time the company's valuation increased by $50 billion.

One could easily discern the inherent flaws with this process—that it was hardly independent and it incentivized Musk to tell Wall Street a story of uninhibited growth in order to build up the Tesla hype as much as possible. Tesla was effectively handcuffing its future to one man, turning a publicly traded company into an automotive fiefdom.

That was before accounting for the fact that Tesla's general counsel, the person responsible for laying out such a proposal, was none other than Musk's one-time divorce attorney Todd Maron, a man described as "totally beholden to Musk."[3]

The context hanging over this "negotiation" was Tesla's unusual level of dependence on Musk. As one Wall Street analyst told me repeatedly, Tesla *was* Musk—the company's valuation was tied to him more than anything. As Musk consolidated his power, that became increasingly true, a maxim by which even large institutional investors would abide.

Tesla has included a version of this disclosure for years in its annual financial report, even before the expansion of Musk's business empire to include X and artificial intelligence bets.

The heading reads: "We are highly dependent on the services of Elon Musk, our Chief Executive Officer," then the document lays out the risk: "Although Mr. Musk spends significant time with Tesla and is highly active in our management, he does not devote his full time and attention to Tesla. Mr. Musk also currently serves as Chief Executive Officer and Chief Technical Officer of Space Exploration Technologies, a developer and manufacturer of space launch vehicles, and is involved in other emerging technology ventures."[4]

Another disclosure is even more telling.

"If we are unable to attract and/or retain key employees and hire qualified personnel, our ability to compete could be harmed," the heading says. The disclosure explains, "In particular, we are highly dependent on the services of Elon Musk."

In that particular report, Tesla's annual filing for 2017, the company hinted at its mindset during the negotiations—laying out the ultimate risk: What if it couldn't keep Musk? He had forgone a salary and opted instead for an unusual arrangement whereby he was compensated with an escalating series of stock awards based on performance targets. With his 2012 agreement nearing its conclusion, it was time to pay Musk again, Tesla said, and "there is no assurance that the CEO Performance Award will receive stockholder approval."[5] Translation: if shareholders did not award Musk handsomely for his efforts to put electric vehicles on the map, he could walk away from Tesla once and for all.

Tesla's board, however, was determined to do its part. As the judge would later put it, "Musk launched a self-driving process, recalibrating the speed and direction along the way as he saw fit."[6]

Over the next several months, Tesla board members met repeatedly to discuss a compensation package that had been shaped largely by its CEO on a timeline that he had the singular power to speed up or slow down, as the filing suggested. Tesla's board did not provide any detailed justification for the astronomical value of the package, just that it risked losing Musk. Another unusual aspect of the negotiation was that by coming to terms with Musk, Tesla was also funding ambitions entirely separate from the company.

According to court documents, Musk told his divorce attorney that "the added comp is just so that I can put as much as possible towards minimizing existential risk by putting the money towards Mars if I am successful in leading Tesla to be one of the world's most valuable companies. This is kinda crazy, but it is true."[7] Musk's other major company, the rocket builder SpaceX, has long aimed to put humans on Mars—a planet Musk sees as essential for the continuation of the human species.[8] This section is based substantially on Judge Kathaleen McCormick's post-trial opinion in the case, *Tornetta v. Musk*.

With little resistance from the company, Musk continued to promote the idea of the pay package. He even modified it to lower his terms and simplify the package—ostensibly to make it less painful, though it was hardly less outrageous. Musk was transparent with Maron, Tesla's general counsel, about his ambitions for the package.

"Given that this will all go to causes that at least aspirationally maximize the probability of a good future for humanity, plus all Tesla shareholders will be super happy, I think this will be received well," Musk wrote. "It should come across as an ultra bullish view of the future, given that this comp package is worth nothing if 'all' I do is almost double Tesla's market cap."[9]

In the end, the board agreed to a deal that would grant Musk 1 percent of Tesla's outstanding stock—in the form of options—for each $50 billion increase in the company's valuation. Court documents stated that the vote was unanimous, aside from a member on leave, Steve Jurvetson, and Musk and his brother, who recused themselves.[10]

Now they just had to secure the approval of the shareholders.

In a financial filing explaining the package to shareholders, Tesla board members undersold the extent of Musk's involvement.

"We created the award after more than six months of careful analysis with a leading independent compensation consultant as well as discussions with Elon, who along with Kimbal otherwise recused themselves from the Board process," they said, adding later, "Early in 2017, with the 2012 Performance Award heading to substantial completion, the independent members of the Board began preliminary discussions about how to continue to incentivize Mr. Musk to lead Tesla through the next phase of its development."[11]

There was no mention of how Musk had laid out the terms, guaranteeing a package of the scope he'd envisioned, accelerated and decelerated the process at his whim, as the court documents say, and had—with "no meaningful negotiation"—won over a board consisting mostly of those "beholden to" him or bearing "compromising conflicts."[12]

The shareholder vote, in March 2018, wasn't close. Musk won the pay package with around 73 percent approval—and that was before accounting for his and his brother's stake.[13]

That same year, an investor named Richard Tornetta filed suit in Delaware's Court of Chancery, alleging breach of fiduciary duty on the part of Musk and the board members. The case wouldn't be decided for years. Few could have predicted that in the meantime, Musk would win every one of the stock awards—twelve tranches in all—and become the richest person on earth, delivering on each target, and well ahead of schedule, leaving shareholders delighted beyond even Musk's original prediction of "super happy."

By mid-2018, the year of the largest pay package in human history, the people around Musk had grown worried. The CEO of Tesla was spending nights in a sleeping bag on the floor of his factory—if he was sleeping at all—and his unpredictable moods had his workers on edge. On any given day, they didn't know which Musk would show up to meetings: the one who had inspired them to solve the conundrum of self-driving cars, or the one who would lash out and fire them if they didn't.

Musk's surly manner could be openly observed by anyone curious to see it: his interactions with reporters, strangers on Twitter, and even company-friendly analysts on Tesla's earnings calls started to take on an increasingly antagonistic tone. Musk erupted on one corporate earnings call—for any other company, a dry, hourlong rundown of quarterly results. In response to analysts' questions, Musk slammed them as "bone-headed" and "dry." Analysts had dared to query Musk on Tesla's capital requirements and Tesla's Model 3 reservations.[14]

Inside Tesla, workers took measures to protect their colleagues against Musk's antics. When he flew into a rage and went for blood—over an unsatisfactory presentation, a project gone awry, an answer to a question he found stupid—they closed ranks, concealing the extent of any given person's responsibility for the failures. When Musk took team leaders aside and asked questions that suggested he was trying to fire someone, they clammed up.

There were two Elon Musks: one deeply thoughtful, effusive in his praise, and relentlessly optimistic about the future to the point that he believed humanity could colonize Mars. The other was angry, paranoid, and essentially solipsistic in his interactions with other human beings. The workers had signed up to join Musk's mission of changing the world, not to deal with an irascible, petty leader who dressed down staffers in far lower positions to the point of tears.

Musk was failing to abide by the golden rule: to treat his fellow humans with the decency and respect that he expected to be afforded. In that instance, after his outburst with the analysts, he recognized it.

To make amends to the analysts, Musk blamed his impoliteness on a lack of sleep, a problem he would cite repeatedly over the years. He was contrite, *Business Insider* reported: "Honestly, I really think there's no excuse for bad manners, and I was kind of violating my own rule in that regard. There are reasons for it in that I had gotten no sleep, had been working 110 hour, 120 hour weeks, but nonetheless, there's still no excuse."[15]

Musk has publicly discussed his use of sleeping medication and how it could alter his behavior ("tweeting on Ambien isn't wise," he once wrote); the question for some was what had driven this sudden spiral and made it so much worse.[16] They wondered: Was there something else?

As it turned out, there may have been. That year, *The Wall Street Journal* reported, Musk had engaged in a series of erratic activities including incidents that left Tesla board members concerned he was using drugs, such as a party he hosted where "he took multiple tabs of acid."[17] (Musk would later tell TV host Don Lemon that he uses ketamine, under a doctor's prescription, in limited doses—"a small amount every other week," Musk said in response to a "negative chemical state in my brain, like depression I guess.")[18]

Musk was transparent about one thing.

"A little red wine, vintage record, some Ambien . . . and magic!" Musk had tweeted in 2017, alarming some of his followers about a potentially dangerous combination.[19]

Even more troubling, Musk rebuffed offers of help and began to retreat into his habits—and circular arguments about a Puritan work ethic, failing to retain the advice of experts and extensive scientific research that suggested his views were outdated. Media and business mogul Arianna Huffington published an open letter to Musk at the time, urging him to prioritize his sleep. "People are not machines," the letter read. "For machines—whether of the First or Fourth Industrial Revolution variety—downtime is a bug; for humans, downtime is a feature. The science is clear. And what it tells us is that there's simply no way you can make good decisions and achieve your world-changing ambitions while running on empty."[20]

Musk replied in a tweet at 2:32 a.m.: "I just got home from the factory," he wrote. "You think this is an option. It is not."[21]

Huffington, who wrote a 2016 book on the importance of sleep, had heard the argument so many times from people convinced the world around them would fall apart without their heroic efforts. But the extent of Musk's theatrics came as a particular surprise.

As Musk's behavior grew more erratic, messages poured in from friends and close confidants who echoed at least one constant refrain: For the love of God, don't tweet. Musk's friend, Tesla board member Antonio Gracias, and his chief of staff, Sam Teller, both urged him to avoid the social media site during times of distress.[22]

"If something really upsets you, go for a walk around the factory," Tesla investor Ron Baron wrote in a private email to Musk in July 2018. "Get an ice cream cone. Just don't use Twitter."[23]

Less than a month later, Musk was racing to the Van Nuys Airport in Los Angeles where his Gulfstream G650ER jet was parked. He pulled up close to his plane and checked his phone.[24]

In the hour it took to reach the tarmac, Musk had missed an important email from Dave Arnold, his chief communications officer at Tesla. The *Financial Times* was about to run a story that included details of the Saudi Public Investment Fund's plans to make a large investment in Tesla, putting a significant stake in the hands of the oil-rich country's sovereign wealth fund.[25] Musk had been in talks days earlier with Yasir al-Rumayyan, the head of the fund, about a potential investment in Tesla, but there was no firm amount or ironclad guarantee.

The news of Saudi interest in Tesla was guaranteed to send shock waves through the public markets. Tesla was one of the most watched—and shorted—stocks in existence.[26] Investors were betting at record levels on the company's failure, believing they could cash in on a looming stock decline.

Musk wanted investors to learn about the Saudi investment directly from him. According to court testimony, he believed that without context, the revelation could raise too many questions. What if the *Financial Times* knew more than it was letting on—that there had been discussions, for example, about taking Tesla private?

Musk took a moment to decide his next steps. He was about to board his plane, and he wanted to respond right then before possibly losing his connection in the sky.

He didn't consult his board. He didn't consult anyone at Tesla. Instead, he opened his Twitter app.

From his car at the airport, Musk decided to clarify things with a sixty-one-character tweet.

"Am considering taking Tesla private at $420," he wrote at 12:48 p.m. "Funding secured."[27]

Musk then boarded his plane.

Days later, in an interview with *The New York Times*, Musk broke down and described how he was in the midst of "the most difficult and painful year of my career."[28] Tesla was in a fight for its survival. The company was struggling to produce its Model 3 sedan, which was supposed to be a $35,000 car aimed at the mass market. Musk had leaned heavily on an automation-centered approach, but it was clear Tesla had gravely underestimated the utility of human hands in car assembly. The company pitched a tent outside its headquarters to expand its production line, a step prompted by its effort to reach a five-thousand-unit-per-week production goal.[29]

"A new building was impossible, so we built a giant tent in 2 weeks," Musk said.[30]

Months earlier, a fire in the paint shop added another troubling wrinkle to Model 3 production.[31] Musk was slowly learning why every new American auto company since Chrysler had failed.

He was obsessive about problem-solving, and no aspect of production was too small, too narrow to command the CEO's personal attention. The flaw inherent in this strategy is obvious: it's a whack-a-mole approach to management, where the sudden all-consuming task, posing the latest insurmountable challenge, could merely scratch the surface of the problems facing the company. Musk's command of the big picture, though, was hardly in question. When an idea or ambition occupied his attention, he would assemble and engage a crack team aimed at delivering. Together, they conducted late-night problem-solving calls, held "hackathon"-style events, and redirected company talent and resources to the moon shot.

But not every problem was a moon shot.

Still, once Musk learned of a compelling engineering challenge, he would make it his personal mission to resolve it—even if it was outside his areas of expertise. Musk was convinced of his genius, and he sometimes seemed to believe he was better equipped to solve big problems than the actual subject-matter experts he was overseeing.

Amid production problems, Musk moved into the paint shop of Tesla's factory. Tesla had struggled to manage issues such as dirt and debris contamination in a facility that needed to be cleaned more often, and it wasn't devoting enough time to painting its cars, instead performing rush jobs to meet ambitious production targets. The quality control issues were becoming a serious problem. So Musk, the CEO of two major companies, spent two weeks sorting out issues with orange-peel—distorted paint on what should be a clean, glossy surface—and clear coats. Soon, he would have much bigger problems.[32]

At 1:00 p.m. on August 7, twelve minutes after Musk had sent his tweet about taking Tesla private, his chief of staff Sam Teller received a text from the company's head of investor relations, its liaison with Wall Street: "Was this text legit?"[33]

A Tesla investor was similarly puzzled, texting Teller at 1:13: "What's Elon's tweet about? Can't make any sense of it. Would be incredibly disappointing for shareholders that have stuck it out for so long."[34] Many of these devoted Tesla investors were in it for the long haul, not for a quick payday from a $420 per share take-private transaction. How did that align with Tesla's mission of "accelerating the world's transition to sustainable energy"?

Even Tesla's chief financial officer was in the dark. Deepak Ahuja texted Musk at 1:23, asking if it might make sense for Tesla to prepare some formal outreach to employees and possible investors in a newly privatized company—an eager group of backers who wouldn't simply be bought out of their positions, something that might have typically happened before the CEO publicly announced a transaction to take the company off the stock market.[35]

"Yeah, that would be great," Musk responded.

"Working on it. Will send you shortly," Ahuja replied.[36]

Tesla's stock was soaring. Musk's announcement had signaled to investors that shares that had been trading around $355 would suddenly be worth $420—even as some were still trying to figure out if it was a weed joke.[37]

At the NASDAQ, officials weren't amused. Its rules require companies releasing material information during the trading day to notify the exchange ten minutes before doing so.[38] It wanted to prevent frenetic trading that could spill into the broader market. Panic sales of Tesla could trigger a ripple effect across tech or other high-value stocks, one that would hardly be rooted in the economic realities of the affected companies. But with Musk announcing a potential $420 per share valuation, some investors would be eager to off-load shares they'd bought at a far lower price.

At 2:08 p.m., NASDAQ halted trading on Tesla.[39]

Musk wasn't done tweeting.

Five minutes after Tesla's shares were halted, when Musk was presumably on his plane, he appended a tweet to his initial post. It gave shareholders hope that if they held out, maybe they would get $420.

"Shareholders could either to sell at 420 or hold shares & go private," he wrote.[40]

If Musk's statement was real, it didn't seem unlikely that shareholders could secure $420 per share for their Tesla stock. Sure, investors might hedge a bit on the possibility that the deal might not go through—keeping the price hovering below that number up until the moment Tesla went private—but as the deal became more likely to close, the shares could become more valuable, climbing toward the $420 Musk's tweet was promising.

For people like Timothy Fries and Glen Littleton, investors who hung on to Musk's every word, his utterances had the potential to shift their fortunes by thousands—in Littleton's case, millions—of dollars.[41]

The only problem was the whole thing might not be true.

To understand why Musk's actions were so cataclysmic, it helps to know the rules of Wall Street. For maturing but still-young companies like Tesla, publicly listing your stock on an exchange such as the New York Stock Exchange or NASDAQ opens up a world of new exposure—and cash—

that smaller-time shareholders, known as retail investors, can bring. But it also subjects them to public reporting requirements. They can no longer conceal how much cash they are burning to drive massive early-stage growth. Companies that trade their stock publicly are accountable to their shareholders, and that means holding quarterly earnings presentations, releasing public financial statements, and making officials such as the CEO and CFO publicly available to answer questions and provide company outlooks—and answer directly for failures to meet expectations. They also have to maintain a board of directors, a governance panel that has the power to appoint and oversee the performance of the CEO and protect the interests of shareholders.

"The parasitic load of being a public company," Musk termed it.[42]

Companies that are publicly traded are subject to federal securities law, a set of rules collectively known as the Securities Exchange Act.

These rules are geared toward ensuring a level playing field for investors so traders can't secure an unfair advantage by buying and selling stock on inside information not known to the rest of the investors, for example. There's also the problem of "selective disclosure" whereby one set of investors learns of material information ahead of another—giving them a jump on everyone else.

Musk's tweet was certainly unorthodox. Wall Street had never known a CEO like Musk, who openly tweeted company information—during the trading day—when investors could readily react and send the stock soaring or plummeting within seconds. The SEC had investigated a case years earlier where Netflix CEO Reed Hastings posted to his Facebook page that the streaming service had surpassed one billion monthly viewing hours. It determined that disclosure of company information on social media was acceptable, provided the company told investors where they could routinely find such information.[43]

By 2018, Tesla investors had gotten used to seeing information about Tesla on Musk's personal Twitter account. But nothing could have prepared them for the thermonuclear bomb that "Funding secured" became.

In the minutes after Musk's tweet, investors, analysts, and reporters scrambled for clarification. But the Tesla CEO sent a second tweet later in the day that only raised more questions: "Investor support is confirmed," he wrote. "Only reason this is not certain is that it's contingent on a shareholder vote."[44]

Much of what was unfolding was news to Tesla's board. While they were aware of Musk's prior discussions with the Saudis—conversations about a potential stake in Tesla, not an unusual line of inquiry for a fund aimed at building out Saudi Arabia's investments beyond oil—board members had not greenlit going private.

The following day, August 8, *The Wall Street Journal* ran an ominous headline, one that hardly inspired confidence for believers in the Musk tweet: "SEC Probes Tesla CEO Musk's Tweets."[45] Regulators were scrambling to determine whether Musk's "Funding secured" claim was true. If it wasn't, and Tesla was the momentary beneficiary of a wild stock swing based on a false statement, Musk and the company could be on the hook for fraud.

Two days later, an investor sued Musk and Tesla in a class-action lawsuit alleging Musk and the company had engaged in "materially false and misleading statements," in addition to behavior that amounted to "market manipulation," and had cost investors hundreds of millions of dollars.[46]

By August 13, Tesla and Musk were playing clean-up. Musk disclosed in a blog post on Tesla's website—usually an extraordinary step for crisis PR situations, such as a negative news story or impending bad news—that he had notified the board days earlier, on August 2, of his desire to take Tesla private at $420 per share. In the same post, Musk said he had updated the board on funding discussions he'd held with the Saudis on July 31. The language was more measured than Musk's tweet, even as he sought to justify his unambiguous declaration of "Funding secured."

"Obviously, the Saudi sovereign fund has more than enough capital needed to execute on such a transaction," he said.[47]

But Musk's blog post made clear that the result of the discussions was far from definitive. The Saudi fund had been interested in taking Tesla private in the past, Musk said. At the July 31 meeting, the fund's director relayed his disappointment that a prior take-private transaction had not materialized. And this time, Musk said, they were eager to see it through.

"I left the July 31st meeting with no question that a deal with the Saudi sovereign fund could be closed, and that it was just a matter of getting the process moving," Musk wrote. "This is why I referred to 'funding secured' in the August 7th announcement."[48]

On August 24, Musk penned another blog post. This time, the head-line was much more definitive: "Staying Public."

Musk relayed that after talking to investors, who urged him against taking Tesla private, he had decided the company would remain publicly traded. The overwhelming sentiment, he wrote, was "please don't do this."

There was, of course, the classic Musk backpedaling and equivocating. Even if they were staying public, he wrote, "my belief that there is more than enough funding to take Tesla private was reinforced during this process."

As it happened, "Funding secured" was only Musk's most damaging tweet since the prior month. As far as streaks of bad behavior and highly public unforced errors go, Musk was on a roll.

The only thing he seemed to crave more than an engineering challenge was public acclaim. The case of a dozen children trapped in a flooded Thai cave earlier that summer offered the opportunity for both.

At the end of June, the world was transfixed by the story of a children's soccer team and their coach who had been exploring a cave deep within a mountain range in Thailand and ended up trapped after torrential rains. The group was initially located in early July, but the rescue proved highly dangerous—and, ultimately, deadly.[49]

Musk, showing signs of a hero complex that would develop further in the years to come, enlisted a team at SpaceX to build what was termed a "kid-size submarine." After initially conceding that the Thai government likely had the situation handled, he offered his help via Twitter, in response to a suggestion from a fan.[50]

The contraption, which Musk described as a rocket tube that was "extremely robust," was developed using SpaceX rocket components.[51] It was completed in early July, and the group, including Musk, ventured to Thailand to deliver it.[52] But it was never used. The lead of the search operation rejected it, *The New York Times* reported, saying it was impractical for the mission.[53] The actual rescue was a treacherous operation, in which around one hundred divers, including Thai Navy SEALs, raced against time to reach the boys and then pull them out one by one using a rope-and-pulley system that guided them through parts of the cave as they laid on stretchers. The cave was extremely difficult for the divers to navigate. As the

BBC reported: "At times they had to navigate sections so ridiculously narrow that they could only just about fit a body through."[54]

Shortly after the rescue, a volunteer who assisted in the cave mission, Vernon Unsworth, gave an interview to CNN where he was asked about Musk's idea for the submarine. Unsworth wasn't impressed.

"He can stick his submarine where it hurts," Unsworth said. "It just had absolutely no chance of working," he added. "The submarine, I believe, was about 5-foot-6 long rigid, so it wouldn't have gone around corners or around any obstacles," he said. "It wouldn't have made the first 50 meters into the cave from the dive start point." He called Musk's effort "just a PR stunt."[55]

Further, Musk had been "asked to leave [the cave] very quickly."[56]

The interview made the rounds on Twitter. By the end of 2018, Musk had become alternately the site's main character and chief instigator, blasting a mix of memes, political opinions, middle school–level jokes, and legitimate news about his companies to his tens of millions of followers. Much of the action took place in the replies to his tweets—where Musk's biggest fans and detractors waged battles over his latest spontaneous utterances, and Musk often expressed his most incendiary takes. Twitter's one-on-one nature flattens the global power structure such that the most famous entrepreneur on earth can boost the views of a no-name anonymous account with fewer than one hundred followers or react instantly to any hint of criticism that comes across his timeline. No one is without their critics, but suddenly, Musk could use his megaphone to make an example of his critics before millions.

As *The Washington Post* noted, it was a Twitter post that prompted Musk to build the submarine in the first place, and the same pattern played out after the Unsworth interview.[57] As Musk's role in the cave rescue—or the lack thereof—was exposed, he vented his frustration by unleashing it on one of the people involved.

He went down a rabbit hole. He googled Unsworth and learned where he lived. And he stumbled on an article claiming it was in a part of Thailand associated with child prostitution and sex trafficking.[58]

That was it. Musk had his angle against Unsworth. He went back to Twitter.

At first, his clapbacks were tame—by Musk's standards. He had never seen Unsworth while he was in Thailand, he claimed, calling that "sus," short for "suspect" or "suspicious."[59] Next, he took issue with Unsworth's description of the caves; the water level, he said, "was actually very low & still (not flowing)," arguing that conditions were favorable enough that his submarine could have made it to the cave in question "no problemo."[60] But it was the last line of that third tweet that held the coup de grace.

"Sorry pedo guy, you really did ask for it."[61]

Far from just throwing a tantrum over his failed effort to help, Musk was baselessly smearing one of the people involved in the rescue of a dozen children as a pedophile.

Musk quickly doubled down. "Bet ya a signed dollar it's true," he tweeted hours later, shortly before taking his posts down.[62] He was soon facing almost universal backlash—not just from skeptics and detractors but also from Tesla fans and investors who were dismayed by his public actions. It was amid that swarm of criticism that Musk had received the email from Baron, the Tesla investor—the one telling him to go get an ice cream cone. "You should not respond to any criticism in the news or on Twitter," he wrote.[63]

Two days after Musk's "pedo guy" insult, he received an email from a private investigator named James Howard, who claimed that Unsworth had "skeletons in his cupboard." Howard offered his services to chase down and substantiate some of Musk's claims. Through Jared Birchall, who manages Musk's family office, Musk hired Howard to conduct an investigation for $50,000.[64]

By now, Musk was facing a heap of criticism for his behavior. Investor Gene Munster, who said he was representing enthusiastic Tesla share-holders, wrote an open letter to Musk saying the Unsworth insult "crossed the line."[65]

"I suspect you would agree given you deleted the string from Twitter, but it will take more than that to regain investor confidence," he wrote. "Your behavior is fueling an unhelpful perception of your leadership—thin-skinned and short-tempered."

The unabating criticism seemed to get through to Musk, and he appeared to realize the potential implications of his accusation. On July 18, three days after slinging his insult, Musk issued an apology. He qualified it by noting that Unsworth had spoken "several untruths & suggested I engage in a sexual act with the mini-sub, which had been built as an act of kindness." Still, Musk conceded, those actions did not "justify my actions against him, and for that I apologize to Mr. Unsworth and to the companies I represent as leader. The fault is mine and mine alone."[66]

The matter could have ended there. But Musk failed to call off Howard, who continued his investigation into Unsworth.

On August 6, an attorney for Unsworth, L. Lin Wood, sent Musk a demand letter. Unsworth's camp was preparing a libel lawsuit, the letter read, inviting Musk to correct the public record and contact Unsworth to discuss the matter.[67] In the weeks that followed, Ryan Mac, then a reporter for *BuzzFeed News*, found out about the letter and emailed Musk to ask for comment. A day later, Mac followed up.

Soon, there was a response from Musk. It was headed by the words "Off the record," an agreement he had not made with Mac beforehand, followed by the opening line: "I suggest that you call people you know in Thailand, find out what's actually going on and stop defending child rapists, you fucking asshole."[68]

The email contained new, explosive—and completely baseless—claims about Unsworth. "He's an old, single white guy from England who's been traveling to or living in Thailand for 30 to 40 years, mostly Pattaya Beach, until moving to Chiang Rai for a child bride who was about 12 years old at the time," Musk wrote to Mac. "He may claim to know how to cave dive, but he wasn't on the cave dive rescue team and most of the actual dive team refused to hang out with him."

The email concluded with, "I fucking hope he sues me."

Days earlier, Howard had begun reporting his findings to Birchall. He claimed to have found a Thai newspaper article that quoted Unsworth's wife, reporting that they had married when she was eighteen or nineteen but met years earlier, before she was an adult. Hours later, Birchall told Musk about his unverified findings.

Unsworth, Birchall told Musk, often traveled to a location known for sex tourism.[69]

Musk's conversations with Birchall, one of his closest confidants, appeared to inform his behavior over the next few days. Before he emailed Mac his unsubstantiated allegations, Musk replied to another journalist on Twitter, writing of Unsworth: "You don't think it's strange he hasn't sued me? He was offered free legal services."[70]

On September 4, *BuzzFeed* published its Musk story with the headline "In a New Email, Elon Musk Accused a Cave Rescuer of Being a 'Child Rapist' and Said He 'Hopes' There's a Lawsuit."[71]

Almost immediately, the fact that this was a shitstorm of his own making seemed to dawn on Musk. The Tesla CEO sent contrite emails to his outside PR representative, Juleanna Glover.

"Yes, this is extremely bad," he wrote. "I didn't expect *BuzzFeed* to publish an off the record email. My intent was to have them investigate and come to their own conclusions, not publish my email directly."[72]

"Still, I'm a fucking idiot."

Musk had been fed a series of potentially damning claims and wanted to make sure they were given due diligence. He was "upset that no one cared to investigate." And *BuzzFeed* had not honored his "off the record" statement as it would have in the past, he claimed.

"It was still one of the dumbest things I've ever done and this distraction couldn't come at a worse time," Musk wrote of this latest misstep coming right on the heels of his "Funding secured" blunder.[73]

Musk's apparent contrition did not seem to make him any more cautious. Two days later, on Joe Rogan's podcast, Musk again made news. For the first two hours and ten minutes of the show, he and Rogan sat across from each other at a desk, covering subjects ranging from a Musk company's creation of a flamethrower-like device billed as "Not-a-Flamethrower" to the intricacies of mechanical wristwatches. At that point, Rogan fired up a joint and turned to his guest with a quizzical expression on his face.

"You probably can't because stockholders, right?"

Musk, who had conceded to maybe smoking marijuana this way once before, conducted a bit of due diligence.

"I mean it's legal, right?" he said.

"Totally legal," replied Rogan.

"How does that work? Do people get upset at you if you do certain things?" Rogan asked.

Musk grabbed the joint and looked at it skeptically, ignoring the question. Having examined it to his satisfaction, he pressed it to his lips, took a puff—and blew out a plume of smoke.

Then he shrugged.

The podcast moved on to other topics: the braking abilities of Teslas, the transition from horses to gasoline cars. "Back when Manhattan had three hundred thousand horses, you figure like if a horse lives fifteen years, [you] got twenty thousand horses dropping dead every year," Musk said, continuing the tenor of a freewheeling podcast, occasionally sipping from a glass of whiskey and briefly playing with a jar on Rogan's desk.

Around seven minutes after the hit, Musk looked at his phone.

"I'm getting text messages from friends saying 'what the hell are you doing smoking weed?'" he said.

It's worth noting that the stigma associated with smoking marijuana—not to mention doing so publicly—has drastically decreased in recent years as more states have legalized its recreational use and many workplaces have removed cannabis from their drug-testing protocols. But back in 2018, Musk was unintentionally breaking a barrier for Fortune 500 CEOs, not to mention federal contractors, by publicly taking a hit on a live-streamed podcast. Regardless of whether it should have been controversial in the first place, it was clear that he wouldn't face the same consequences as a lower-level associate of the federal government or even one of his own companies, were they to engage in the same behavior.

What would have happened if someone had lit up a joint on the Tesla or SpaceX factory floor?

By the start of fall, Musk's streak of controversies and unusual behavior caught up with him, or so it appeared.

A lawsuit over his gargantuan pay package, launched on June 5, 2018, by an investor—a thrash metal drummer, as later described by *Newsweek*, named Richard Tornetta—was not the only chicken that would come home to roost over the next few months.[74]

On September 17, Unsworth, the Thai cave rescuer Musk had baselessly smeared as a pedophile, filed suit alleging defamation, according to a complaint filed in the US District Court.

Ten days later, it was the SEC's turn to hold Musk accountable. The agency issued a press release on September 27 saying it had charged Musk with securities fraud.[75] It took Musk, Tesla, and the SEC two days to announce a settlement.[76]

The penalties facing Musk were steep. He and Tesla were each ordered to pay $20 million in fines. Crucially, Musk would relinquish a key aspect of his power: removing himself from a position that gave him unilateral control over the most important automaker of the twenty-first century. "As a result of the settlement, Elon Musk will no longer be Chairman of Tesla," Steven Peikin, codirector of the SEC's Enforcement Division, said in a statement.[77]

Musk had tweeted his company out of tens of millions of dollars, and himself out of one of his most important jobs.

Now the calls for Musk to step aside as Tesla CEO grew. There were even some Wall Street investors who had been firmly in his corner who felt he was hurting the company and that he wasn't suited for the role of chief executive.

One of these critics was Gene Munster, an investor who would emerge as one of the most vocal backers of Tesla on Wall Street. Munster had followed his earlier criticism of Musk's behavior in the Unsworth affair by saying Tesla could be in a "much healthier place" if Musk took on a role focused on strategy and product development.[78]

"I think if this wasn't happening, the company would be in a better place of hitting its goals," he said, according to *Business Insider*.[79]

A full explanation for Musk's "Funding secured" fiasco remains elusive. An uncharitable read of the situation is that Musk, whose pay was tied to market capitalization goals, had plenty of incentive to drive up Tesla's stock price at any cost, and he quickly learned he could get away with doing so. However, Musk, like certain others in public memory, had a clear tendency to double down when confronted with evidence of his wrongdoing.

It's possible he simply did not want to own up to his mistake.

Whatever the explanation, Musk had rattled investors' confidence with "Funding secured." He had recklessly smeared a good Samaritan in a bout of jealousy.

And it wasn't just Tesla that would be hurt by Musk's rebellious streak.

On November 20, *The Washington Post* reported NASA had ordered a safety review of SpaceX, a move "prompted by the recent behavior of SpaceX's founder, Elon Musk . . . after he took a hit of marijuana and sipped whiskey" on the Rogan podcast.[80]

The agency required adherence to a "drug-free environment."

Elon Musk's speedrun of high-profile corporate controversies—any one of which would have taken down the CEO of most publicly traded companies—confirmed the weakness of the safeguards society had established to prevent someone with practically unlimited financial capacity from running roughshod. They were a stress test on multiple systems: the ability of financial regulators to intervene, the courts' capacity for justice in cases where money was no object, the limits of corporate governance when times are good, and the meager rights of consumers and investors. What would happen when Musk applied his rule-breaking ethos to his own workers and production targets, to a safety-critical system for his cars, or to a social media network that served as a crucial vector for disseminating information on current events and elections worldwide?

Ordinarily, for example, the CEO losing the role of board chair over a misguided tweet—an unforced error and preventable blunder—would have prompted a broader internal reckoning over the governance of a publicly traded company, especially one as important as Tesla.

But in Musk's case, the fact that he no longer commanded the dual roles of CEO and board chairman clarified his duties, allowing him to cement his grip on Tesla even further. Musk would recover from the SEC's reprimand by consolidating his control over the company that would soon become the world's most valuable automaker.

On November 7, 2018, Tesla announced that Robyn Denholm, CFO of Australia's largest telecommunications firm, would leave that role to become Tesla's board chair.[81] So commenced a trademark Musk arrangement: the appointment of well-credentialed but lesser-known loyalists to high-powered positions—those with oversight of his performance or crucial roles in the success of his businesses. (Look no further than the fact that Musk's own brother held a lucrative board seat, alongside friends such as Antonio Gracias and Ira Ehrenpreis.) Denholm was an independent board member who shied away from headlines and was hailed for her potential to bring "stable leadership" to the panel.[82]

But she beat out another potential candidate who'd emerged as the subject of speculation, James Murdoch, of the Murdoch media empire, whose apparent candidacy was described in the tech press as "bad news for Elon Musk."[83] In a later television interview, Musk would acknowledge handpicking Denholm for the role.[84]

Musk may have tweeted himself out of the chairman role, which had given him the reins on Tesla's governance—eliminating one potential check on his moves as chief executive—but he could effectively have free rein as CEO with a subservient board. "Denholm derived the vast majority of her wealth from her compensation as a Tesla director," the same court opinion on Musk's compensation deal had said, including a sum she described as "life-changing."[85]

It's worth remembering that just months before all the behavior that had called his leadership into question in 2018, Musk had been handsomely rewarded—in record-breaking fashion—with the largest pay package in history.

Well before his litany of controversies that ultimately solidified his grip over the company, his control of the Tesla board was perhaps best highlighted by the delivery of that lucrative compensation package. According to the 2024 court opinion, it was worth as much as about $56 billion. It was "250 times larger than the contemporaneous median peer compensation plan and over 33 times larger than the plan's closest comparison, which was Musk's prior compensation plan," it said.[86] The opinion, issued by chancellor Kathaleen St. J. McCormick in the Delaware Court of Chancery, describes in vivid detail how Musk exerted control over the officers who should have been charged with overseeing Tesla—a body that included Denholm, then as a director—in addition to Musk's close friend Antonio Gracias, longtime associate Ehrenpreis, and his own brother, Kimbal. By comparison, the handsomely compensated tech CEOs in Silicon Valley were paid in a combination of salary and stock totaling in the tens of millions of dollars in the most exceptional cases. Uber CEO Dara Khosrowshahi's 2019 employment agreement offered a $1 million base salary and a bonus of at least $2 million, though his total compensation would balloon into the tens of millions in the years to come.[87] *Axios* reported on the shareholder consternation over

Apple CEO Tim Cook's proposed $99 million compensation in 2022, which he ended up receiving.[88]

"How much is too much when it comes to CEO compensation?" the story asked.

Musk's pay package would net him around one hundred times that, on an annual basis.

Musk's actions may have meant he was no longer in charge of the Tesla board, but he was very much in control of the company, which had put an astronomical price tag on his value to the enterprise, leaving little doubt as to who was running the show.

Denholm, the Australian business executive who had stepped in as Tesla board chair, held meetings described in *The Wall Street Journal* as "family-style" affairs, with little scrutiny of the man who would help make her enormously rich.[89] Any question that she would be a check on Musk's power was extinguished practically from the moment she was announced for the role.

"I believe in this company, I believe in its mission and I look forward to helping Elon and the Tesla team achieve sustainable profitability and drive long-term shareholder value," she said in a written statement delivered on the heels of Musk's trifecta of scandals. Musk in turn endorsed his successor and said he looked "forward to working even more closely with Robyn as we continue accelerating the advent of sustainable energy."[90]

That year, Musk gave an interview on *60 Minutes* that shed light on the specifics of their arrangement. Musk couldn't have been more transparent.[91]

"Did you hand-pick her?" asked Lesley Stahl. "Yes," he replied, his eyes seeming to well up as he was pressed about the most difficult year of his life.

Stahl continued, "The impression was that she was put in to kind of watch over you."

Musk's face contorted in what looked like disgust.

"Yeah, I mean that's not realistic," he began to say.

Stahl interjected: "like a babysitter."

"It's not realistic in the sense I am the largest shareholder in the company and I can just call for a shareholder vote and get anything done that I want," Musk declared.

Would he want to return as board chair?

"No. I actually prefer to have no titles at all," Musk told Stahl. This declaration would age especially poorly.

The takeaway was clear: Musk, stripped of his second-most important title, was home free. He'd faced accountability on paper; fines of $20 million each for himself and Tesla; and the appointment of the "Twitter sitter," which would have been a humiliation in any normal circumstance. Outwardly, it might have looked like the SEC had won this battle. In reality, Musk was demonstrating how financial regulators' attempt to assign consequences for one irresponsible act would embolden him for years to come.

In January 2023, I ran into former board member Brad W. Buss outside the San Francisco federal court. He was there to testify in the shareholder trial over Musk's "Funding secured" tweet. I tossed a question in his direction, but he dismissed it with a terse "Say hi to Jeff," virtually the same quip Musk had hurled at me only a few months earlier.[92] The nonanswer aside, the exchange was still revelatory in its own way. It suggested that even after the hijinks of the past several years, the supposed adults in the room were still taking their cues from Musk. That was a sustainable arrangement just as long as Tesla was shattering expectations left and right, becoming the most valuable automaker on earth, and delighting shareholders on its glide path to a more than $1 trillion valuation.

Nobody could have predicted where the biggest threat to Tesla's fortunes would soon come from—least of all a board that had been controlled by Musk, consisting of a significant share of members who, in the findings of the Delaware Chancery Court, "lacked independence" from the company's chief executive.[93]

3

UP IN SMOKE

The man in black appeared before the crowd as the backdrop of fog machines, flames, and ceiling-to-floor lasers came to rest. Elon Musk regarded the audience of fanboys and investors who'd gathered in Los Angeles for the debut of Tesla's latest creation before turning toward a vehicle that had just rolled onto the stage. A few years later, it's hard to truly remember the strangeness of that moment, as everyone took in the alien-looking contraption, its trapezoidal silhouette and stainless steel body gleaming under the klieg lights. Musk then turned back to the crowd and shrugged as if to say: "Well, what do you think?"

After a pause, he acknowledged what everyone was thinking. "It doesn't look like anything else."

The sheer weirdness of Tesla's new pickup truck would have stolen the show if it weren't for the comedy of errors that followed. Around a year after the chaotic events of 2018, Musk was here to show that Tesla still had it. Could it continue its streak of hit products, building on the success of the Model 3 and the recently announced Model Y crossover SUV that promised to continue that momentum?

Musk, clad in his version of a cyberpunk uniform—head-to-toe black—had wanted an environment of hypermachismo for Tesla's newest product unveil: a truck like no other, a shot at the bow of the American auto industry, where a pickup had been the best-selling vehicle for four decades.[1] But his presentation wasn't going to lean into heritage.

It had opened bizarrely, even for a Musk show. The audience was greeted by a mysterious character dubbed "Cyber Girl," a hologram of an ethereal figure with platinum blonde hair and a blue dress. A conspicuous tattoo on her left leg revealed that she was likely portrayed by Elon's girl-friend, Claire Boucher (a Canadian musician known as Grimes).[2] Cyber Girl extolled the virtues of the newest invention of the man she referred to as "my creator."

"The skies are polluted. The world is addicted to oil. But we're here to offer a solution: the Cybertruck. The number one mode of transport for a cyber girl. The greatest evolution in vehicular fashion and function."[3]

Now Musk, looking healthier than he had in years—fit, without bags under his eyes, and beaming under the stage lights—confidently threw his arms in the air and declared, "Welcome to the Cybertruck unveil!"

The Cybertruck continued a long tradition of over-the-top truck unveils, where the vehicles served as a proxy for the values of the person who owned it. It's tempting to think that until Tesla came along with its glitzy, extravagant presentation style that continued in the tradition of tech giants like Apple, major auto presentations were bland affairs, glorified informercials loaded with industry jargon. But oh, were there gimmicks.

Look no further than the 2014 Chevy Silverado debut.

"Silverado customers want a truck that's honest, hardworking and dependable just like they are—one they can pass on to their children," Mark Reuss, General Motors North America president at the time, told an audience in Detroit. "This has been the Silverado mission for generations and we will not waver from it. Our top competitors may think that they have smooth sailing ahead, but let me tell you the *weather* is about to change."[4]

Boom.

The room darkened as a loud crash of thunder was piped in. Heavy clouds and lightning bolts illuminated a set of screens followed by a shower of sparks as a Chevrolet badge and gleaming headlights peeked through a stone wall, shrouded in smoke. The deep, suspenseful bass drum rhythm of a movie chase scene gave way to a triumphant victory score as the ruby-colored Chevy Silverado LTZ revealed itself to the world.

Reuss, acting as if nothing had happened, returned to a scene that evoked the action film *Tomb Raider,* a crimson glow painting the stones in the background as fog continued to pour out.

"Ladies and gentlemen, the 2014 Silverado is stronger, smart and more capable than ever before," he said. "It offers a high-torque standard

V6, the most capable V8 available in a light-duty pickup, smart technology that optimizes power and fuel efficiency based on how you drive and towing and hauling capability to handle even the most tough jobs."[5]

For all the buzz around its announcement in November 2019, Tesla was in no rush to make good on its plans to bring customers the pickup truck of the future. Employees were scrambling at the time to deliver the first units of the Model Y, the vehicle the company hoped would become its bestseller. Tesla couldn't cannibalize its already limited battery supply with a heavy, energy-hogging truck, and Musk seemed to have a limited appetite for starting up a new production line. They had already shown off prototypes of two other vehicles as well, an electric Semi for long-haul trucking, and the revamped Roadster convertible sports car. In fact, this new sheet metal–clad behemoth was merely a repurposed Roadster prototype with the guts transferred to a truck body—Tesla was recycling its old work to generate market hype. These upcoming vehicles were plagued with constantly shifting timelines and wouldn't be delivered for years (at the time of this writing in December 2024, the Roadster still hadn't been delivered).

That said, the company had genuine ambitions to build an electric truck for quite some time. Musk knew that electric cars would never supplant the internal combustion engine if Tesla was merely the brand for liberal California yuppies making their morning Starbucks runs. An electric pickup would be the purest embodiment of the company's mission to wean the world off fossil fuels. It didn't hurt that pickups carried notoriously high profit margins.[6]

This message resonated with executives like company automotive president Jerome Guillen, who saw a genuine need for utility and work vehicles—such as the Semi—in Tesla's catalog. The problem was that Musk himself was starting to waver on his commitment to the long-haul truck, citing the need to put Tesla's finite supply of battery cells toward its existing products.

In the meantime, Tesla went back to the drawing board to design a pickup truck. The initial design that Musk put forward was a bastardized hybrid of a low-slung supercar and a Ute, one that no automaker would have settled for—for good reason.

"It was a monstrosity," said a person familiar with the design, calling it "absolutely horrible and horrid."

The executives around Musk weren't happy with that direction, to say the least, so they got to work on an alternative. The man who took the project on, Franz von Holzhausen, had made his name at Mazda, pioneering a forward-looking design language there before Musk tasked him with establishing one for Tesla, which came in the form of the Model S sedan and the Model X SUV, products that vaulted the company into the mainstream.[7]

Now he was stepping in once again, hopefully to save Musk from letting his worst impulses ruin Tesla's sleek aesthetic. Von Holzhausen and his team quietly got to work on a new truck design, the idea being that they'd present Musk with a far superior alternative. They knew one thing for sure; Musk was wedded to the notion that a Tesla truck shouldn't look like any other pickup.

So they discreetly built a clay model of what would become the Cybertruck. When it came time to sell Musk on the idea, they recruited Guillen, the head of trucking, to deliver the pitch.

There stood the clay model of the Cybertruck, displayed next to three other models of similar proportions for comparison: a Ford F-150, a Chevy Silverado, and a Ram.

Musk appeared to be in a good mood. After surveying the other models, he turned to the Cybertruck.

"Yeah, I think this is better," he said.

And that was that—Tesla employees wheeled out and dismantled the previously designed eyesore. It would never be seen again.

Months after Tesla executives' intervention, the Cybertruck was ready to be debuted to the public. When the new alien contraption rolled onto the stage and a series of leather-clad figures stepped out in shades and black boots, even longtime Tesla observers were in disbelief.

Von Holzhausen and his team had settled on an industrial, sci-fi-inspired design that embraced the cyberpunk aesthetic from the movie *Blade Runner* while making a brutalist showcase of raw materials. Gone was any hint of the early 2000s "Bubble" era design that had swept the automotive industry; Tesla replaced swooping, curvaceous lines with sweeping flat panels of sheet metal, creating a side profile that resembled a pitched roof atop an industrial refrigerator laid flat. The windshield, a massive pane of glass, appeared to sit flush with the hood and met the top of the truck at a single point, without a flat panel to distinguish the roof. Another panel of glass swept from there to the bed area, where a flush-mounted automated tonneau cover sleekly completed the polygonal silhouette.

The headlights were one unbroken light bar, a thin sliver that stretched across the front of the car clear to the side panels. On the rear was a solid red light bar that spanned the truck bed and bled to the truck's edges.

It would have been perfectly at home in the apocalypse.

Musk's idea for an electric truck with no paint—which aimed to save energy both in production and on the road—aligned with Tesla's ethos. While his original design direction for it, which echoed the Chevy El Camino, demanded an intervention, he had a track record for picking quirks that would intrigue potential customers: the falcon-wing doors on the Model X were hardly conventional, but they also alerted people to the brand.

Soon enough, Tesla's designers were joining Musk in thinking outside the box. Mirrors? No. Too conventional. Circular steering wheel? Boring. How about a squircle?

On stage, assistants wheeled in demo equipment to dramatic music, and the presentation took on the aura of TV show *Deal or No Deal*. They were going to conduct a series of tests of the rugged stainless steel truck's apparent toughness. Tesla claimed it was bulletproof—as in literally able to resist 9mm rounds. And it wasn't just the metal body that could resist violent impacts, they said.

In came design mastermind von Holzhausen, wielding a sledgehammer. (Or perhaps it was a "large mallet," as it was referred to in *The Washington Post*.[8] One can't really be sure.)

Biceps bulging from his black T-shirt, a pair of leather gloves hanging out the back of his skinny jeans, he removed his leather jacket. "Want me to do this?" he asked.

He cranked back and took a swing at a large white door, one from a regular pickup.

BANG! It left a large dent.

"Hit it a couple times," Musk urged.

BANG! BANG!

The competitor's door sufficiently mangled, Musk's attention turned to Tesla's version.

"Now hit the Cybertruck. Hit it harder."

Thump. Nothing.

"Really wind up. Nail it," Musk insisted.

THUMP. An anticlimax. The hammer just bounced right off.

Musk was satisfied—but he wasn't done.

"You want a truck that's tough. You want a truck that's really tough? Not fake tough?" he asked the audience. "You want a truck you can take a sledgehammer to, a truck that won't scratch, doesn't dent. What else can we do with this truck?"

Musk, searching for ways to convey the full strength of his 4×4 built from "ULTRA HARD 30X COLD-ROLLED STAINLESS STEEL," floated an idea.

"What if we shot it? Let's shoot it," he declared.

The assembled crowd returned the energy. "SHOOT IT!" one person urged, in the purest expression of the testosterone levels in the room.

"We're in California, unfortunately," Musk replied.

But Tesla was going to demonstrate the toughness of this truck one way or another. In came the assistants, rolling a table onto the stage with regular automotive window glass and a sheet of what the presentation referred to as "TESLA ARMOR GLASS." This time, they dropped steel balls onto the panels from above. The regular glass shattered. Tesla glass, however, merely flexed and snapped back into place.

Normally, that would have been enough to convince an audience. But Tesla's truck, after all, wasn't fake tough like the others.

So back came von Holzhausen—this time toting a large steel ball.

"Franz, could you try to break this glass please?" asked Musk.

"[You] sure?" he asked Musk, who signaled to proceed.

Again, the man in the black T-shirt and tall black boots, toned arms exposed, wound up. He fell back into a full pitcher's pose, kicking back and delivering an overhand strike.

And suddenly, the air was sucked out of the room.

Splat.

The glass on the surface had shattered, leaving a spherical spiderweb imprint right where the driver's head would be. Musk was mortified.

"Oh my fucking god!" he said.

"Well," he concluded, "maybe that was a little too hard."

Grinning, unsure what to do next, von Holzhausen inquired, "Should we try on the door?"

Musk quickly settled on a positive spin.

"It didn't go through, so that was the plus side," he said.

Meanwhile, von Holzhausen was trying to salvage the demo. "Let's try [that one]," he suggested, indicating the rear left passenger window.

"Try that one? Really?" Musk asked, showing a prescient bit of skepticism.

This time, von Holzhausen barely wound up. He tossed the ball gingerly, both feet planted on the floor.

Splat. The window shattered. Farther away from the would-be occupant this time. Same embarrassing sphere-shaped imprint.

"Ohhhh . . . man!" he groaned.

Musk could only laugh.

"It didn't go through," he said. "Ehh . . . not bad. Room for improvement."

Amid the nervous laughter, von Holzhausen hastily exited stage left.

"SHOOT IT!" demanded the audience member once again, breaking the awkward silence.

Musk, flustered and not in the mood for the joke this time, didn't respond directly.

"We—we did actually throw everything," he said. "We threw wrenches, we threw everything, we even literally threw the kitchen sink at the glass and it didn't break. For a little weird reason it broke now, don't know why."

And then he mumbled: "Should have fixed it in post," as the audience laughed.

Then he went back on script—a complete non sequitur.

"In addition, the car has an adaptive air suspension . . ."

"Tesla Unveiled a Bulletproof Pickup. Then the Window Broke," blared the headline in *The Wall Street Journal*.[9] Reuters, hardly a haven for clickbait, framed the debacle: "Tesla's Cybertruck Launch Takes Hit as 'Shatterproof' Windows Crack."[10] The presentation had gone so badly that Musk's own wealth took a hit. "Elon Musk's Net Worth Plunges $768m in a Day after Cybertruck Fiasco," read a headline in the *Guardian*.[11]

It was another area where the Steve Jobs comparisons fell short.

Unlike the meticulously scripted, perfectionistic, and entirely predictable nature of an Apple presentation conducted by Jobs—who once famously made a rare gaffe by asking audience members to turn off their Wi-Fi after connection problems arose during a demo, a notable exception—Musk's live appearances regularly turned into viral punch-lines.[12] The theme would recur over the years as Musk's profile grew: being booed in front of a live crowd at a Dave Chappelle comedy show in San Francisco or Twitter flubbing the presidential campaign announcement of Ron DeSantis when its signature audio feature couldn't handle the load on its servers.[13]

At these times, Musk switched to fight-or-flight mode. You could see his brain working out a million calculations per second to find a way out of the jam. After all, presentations like these—reserved for fawning investors, Tesla-friendly bloggers, and fanboys—are meant to be a safe space for him.

Indeed, Musk rarely puts himself in situations with unpredictable outcomes, as he is wary of the potential for embarrassment. That's why he doesn't often take interviews with adversarial journalists; it seemed he would rather surround himself with sycophants. Years later, as the crowd at the Chappelle comedy show in San Francisco—where he had just laid off thousands of Twitter staff—erupted in a chorus of boos after Chappelle welcomed him onstage, Musk turned to the comedian for help, a rare moment when he wasn't in full control of his audience.

"Dave, what should I say?"[14]

But on his own turf, Musk was in charge of cleaning up the mess. Even after the Cybertruck event, which was supposed to be a triumph, he was left answering for the company's failure.

He was still incredulous the day after the presentation, and key Tesla executives were at a loss.

"We threw same steel ball at same window several times right before event & didn't even scratch the glass!" he tweeted. As proof, Musk posted a slow-motion video of von Holzhausen hurling the steel ball at the truck window before the unveil and the glass panel staying completely intact. "Guess we have some improvements to make before production ha-ha," he wrote.[15]

It wasn't until the following Sunday, three days after the presentation, that Musk came up with a satisfactory explanation. It should have been an entirely predictable outcome: The repeated hammer blows to the door had "cracked base of glass," Musk wrote, "which is why steel ball didn't bounce off. Should have done steel ball on window, *then* sledgehammer the door. Next time . . ."[16]

* * *

Though it would live in meme infamy forever, the matter of the bullet-proof window that wasn't soon blew over. Once it had, the only thing left to process about the presentation was the truck itself. In the days after the demo, Tesla's hyperbolic claims about the truck's utility were called into question by numerous publications, a persistent theme over the course of its development. The automaker even claimed at one point that the truck would be able to "pull near infinite mass."[17]

While the truck was clearly geared toward a certain subset of fans, analysis and auto industry veterans were skeptical about its polarizing looks and potential utility for the vast majority of truck users.

The whole thing left Wall Street puzzled. "[It is] somewhat unclear to us who the core buyer will be," a Credit Suisse analyst wrote, according to *Business Insider*.[18] The truck would likely be a niche offering, said others, describing it as everything from a "stealth bomber" look-alike to, as one Morgan Stanley analyst called it, "more fitting for a work site in a Martian colony."

Not everyone thought the strategy was doomed. Writing for CNN Business Perspectives on "Why Tesla's Weird New Cybertruck Could Be a Hit," Brett Smith of the Center for Automotive Research said, "Musk can use the edgy design as a proof of concept—a first step to show the world that an all-electric pickup really is viable."[19]

Even the praise was tempered with skepticism. But the hype was undeniable. Days after the unveiling, Musk announced that the Cybertruck had garnered around 250,000 reservations in a week.[20] The figure would soon grow into the millions, surely accelerated by Tesla's low and fully refundable reservation fee of $100.[21] A reservation didn't guarantee a sale.

But Tesla had gotten the attention it wanted for a truck it would not deliver for another four years: confirmation that the apocalyptic pickup truck that had become an overnight punchline had the potential to be an instant hit.

There was no word on where auto regulations fit into the picture. If Tesla had wanted to indicate it was serious about building this truck, it could have at least tried to make it look roadworthy.

Where were the amber-colored turn signals? Where was the third brake light? Side-view mirrors were nowhere to be seen. Tesla hadn't checked off some of the most basic automotive regulations.

And even inside the company, some, like Guillen, were concerned about an angular design that posed risks for pedestrians and bicycles. The sharp edges, the nearly impenetrable panels, and the steep viewing angles from the driver's seat all might give the appearance of aggressively protecting the driver, but they flew in the face of years of measures aimed at the safety of pedestrians and other vehicles that might not fare well in a collision with "ULTRA HARD 30X COLD-ROLLED STAINLESS STEEL."

Missy Cummings, who would go on to serve as a senior safety adviser at the country's top federal auto safety regulator, feared the consequences of what Tesla would unleash.

"It is not a good situation: a combination of an even bigger, heavier vehicle—the bad AI. There's nothing good that [can] come out of this scenario."

Tesla pressed on with its plans to build the Cybertruck—but as its initial production date approached in late 2021, the first orders were still nearly two years away from being fulfilled.

Announcing a new model is one thing, but actually building a vehicle requires a highly complex interplay of processes that can stretch over years before the first assembly lines are running. Issues with any one of them—supply contract snags, regulatory hiccups, flaws with the validation builds that precede the production cars—can slow the process down considerably. At its 2019 debut, the Cybertruck was little more than a concept car.

Tesla had set a benchmark for itself with an out-of-this-world prototype and set off on a four-year mission to make a roadworthy version. As Musk himself has put it countless times, "Prototypes are easy, production is hard."[22]

For a glimpse into how hard it is, one need look no further than Tesla's Sparks, Nevada, gigafactory, the primary battery hub for its fleet. Tesla's factories can operate largely independently of one another—production arms serving their individual global regions—but if this facility outside Reno encountered backups, the entire company's production capacity could be brought to its knees.

That was exactly what happened in 2017 and 2018 as Tesla was desperately trying to ramp up production of the Model 3, its mass market–aimed sedan. Here was one example of a production snag that proved Musk's thesis and demonstrated just how far Tesla was from delivering a mass-production pickup truck, using multiple times the battery capacity of its other offerings.

At its bustling Nevada plant, Tesla had installed a sophisticated system of conveyor belts to whisk equipment from the ground floor to a second-floor mezzanine twelve feet up, part of its heavy emphasis on automation. The only problem was that it didn't work.

A two-axis web of conveyor belts and dozens of elevators that lifted parts upstairs had been deemed necessary to complete the battery modules for the Model 3, a final step before they could be shipped to Fremont. But the system was hobbled so often by basic tasks that employees found it was more effective to simply carry parts upstairs by hand.

The conveyor and elevator system was eventually dismantled and scrapped from that part of the factory.

The *Reno Gazette-Journal* in 2018 described sections devoted to battery assembly as "among the most human-intensive areas of the Gigafactory," attributing the need for manual assembly to the less rigid components whose complex forms could confuse the machines, such as wiring, among the parts that had to be walked upstairs.[23]

It wasn't a coincidence. After Guillen arrived and surveyed the system, he got working on a fix: deautomating the process. It was a precursor to his work at Fremont, where he'd take the same series of steps to boost Model 3 production.

"The process of figuring out that people are better than machines at some jobs was part of the reason behind bottlenecks that caused headaches last year as Tesla struggled to meet Model 3 production goals," the *Gazette-Journal* wrote.[24]

Musk likes to tell war stories about his time sleeping at the Tesla factory. In the case of Reno, his decision to do so was hardly a productivity boost. Musk quite literally set up camp on the roof of the factory, using equipment purchased from REI, as one person who remembers the experience vividly recalled.

"They had smores and they drank two-thousand-dollar bottles of whiskey," the person said.

* * *

With the Cybertruck a distant fantasy, Tesla proceeded with a more attainable goal: building the Model Y, which shared 75 percent of its components with the existing Model 3.[25]

In early 2020, Tesla began to deliver the first of its long-promised crossovers that represented the future of the company. After initial hiccups, which included price cuts to stimulate demand amid the COVID-19 pandemic and quality control issues such as a glass roof allegedly blowing off midride, the Model Y delivered on its meteoric sales projections, becoming Tesla's best-selling vehicle and, ultimately, the best-selling car on earth.[26]

The Model Y had been announced in 2019, the same year Tesla unveiled its pickup. Meanwhile, the Cybertruck languished in the background—years after it was promised—with not a single unit delivered.[27]

Musk tried to keep the public intrigue alive. Paparazzi spotted him leaving dinner in a prototype Cybertruck in Los Angeles in December 2019, and Tesla paraded the truck around, filming a segment with famed car collector Jay Leno in 2020.[28] The Cybertruck made a trip to New York City in 2021, where it was spotted maneuvering cobblestone streets. With its futuristic light bars illuminating its narrow path, it looked like it had rolled in from another planet.

Tesla had planned to start production in late 2021, but as that deadline quietly came and went, Musk was pressed to explain the delays. His response? The pandemic's supply chain havoc and chip shortages had shifted Tesla's manufacturing timeline, preventing it from producing any new vehicle model in 2022.[29]

Tesla's main factory had shut down for weeks. Musk had gone to war with California officials over the mandatory closures, prompting him to announce that Tesla's new headquarters would be in Texas. What better place to build the Cybertruck?

The new pickup would be built at Tesla's factory outside Austin, the production hub for the Model Y, in the state Musk had made his new home. Since moving to Texas, Musk had adopted a faux cowboy persona complete with a "Don't Mess with [Tesla]" belt buckle adorned with a lone star and Tesla's "T" logo. The futuristic pickup would fit the image completely, assuming it was ever built.

"We will not be introducing new vehicle models this year," Musk said on a corporate earnings call in early 2022. "It would not make any sense. We will still be parts constrained. We will, however, do a lot of engineering, tooling, whatnot to create those vehicles: Cybertruck, Semi, Roadster."[30]

Meanwhile, his claims about the truck's abilities became increasingly far-fetched—as a constantly shifting set of features and even dimensions inspired little confidence that it was a serious undertaking anywhere close to becoming a reality. Among the more outlandish of these claims: "Cybertruck will be waterproof enough to serve briefly as a boat, so it can cross rivers, lakes & even seas that aren't too choppy," he wrote in late 2022.[31]

Investors like Ross Gerber were becoming agitated.

There was no disputing Tesla's success since 2019; the company's mainstream popularity made it the world's most valuable automaker and Musk the richest person on earth. The Model Y had been a runaway success. But its parts overlap with the Model 3 meant that many of its production kinks had been sorted out years earlier, during the periods Musk termed "production hell" and "delivery logistics hell."[32]

To investors, it appeared the company might have lost a step since then. It had been drained of veteran auto and manufacturing expertise from the likes of Doug Field, the company's former senior vice president of engineering, and Jerome Guillen, who had led the Model 3 production turnaround. In their place were Musk loyalists—the kind of people who scrambled to respond to erratic demands such as building a Cybertruck that could also float but were powerless to tell Musk why they shouldn't.

"People have surrendered," Gerber told me. "He killed off any people that could run Tesla without him . . . and what he's got left now . . . is his group of hardcore enthusiasts."

And then there was the fact that Musk, increasingly consumed with his takeover of Twitter, was distracted. Wall Street had taken notice: Tesla's once unstoppable stock had fallen from more than a $1 trillion valuation in November 2021 to less than $500 billion a year later.[33] The company's value was cut in half. Increasingly, it looked like Tesla's lack of a full-time leader was hurting it.

Production problems with the Model 3 had once prompted Musk to move into the factory, but there would be no such urgency with the Cybertruck. And it was Guillen who had managed to unlock Tesla's full manufacturing capacity for that vehicle. Now Musk was dawdling with Twitter, and Guillen was gone. On top of that, Musk's appetite for mass vehicle production appeared to have waned. The Model 3 and Model Y production crunches had taken everything out of him, and executives found it increasingly difficult to sell Musk on a vehicle with the potential to be a mainstream hit. In their places were Tesla projects that would gain dedicated followings—the Semi, the Roadster, the Cybertruck—but would hardly make the same impact.

Was Tesla still capable of mounting a new assembly line and delivering on another Musk moon shot?

In late November 2023, Tesla was finally ready to deliver the first of its Cybertrucks. Despite being around two years behind schedule, the event drew an enormous level of public interest. Thanks to a smashed window gone viral, anticipation for the futuristic pickups had evolved into a mainstream phenomenon.

Hordes of fanboys, investors, and the otherwise Tesla-obsessed showed up at the Austin, Texas, gigafactory to see what all the hype was about. They were greeted by their first in-person glimpses of the stainless steel–clad behemoth—every bit the alien-looking machine they were promised, for better or worse. The vehicle was mostly faithful to the prototype—the front-facing single horizontal light bar that looked like it was pulled off a space rover, hexagonal cutouts for the massive aerodynamic wheels, the long, uninterrupted blade constituting the windshield wiper, the raised pane of glass extending from hood to roof, the rugged tires, the raw metal body.

Hundreds were in the audience, cheering before Tesla's graffiti-inspired Cybertruck logo and industrial techno beats, echoing the mood of the unveiling. Then a single horizontal bright white beam of light approached, growing larger until the reflection of the metal bumper glinted before the studio lights. The Cybertruck was here.

Out stepped Elon Musk, climbing onto the stage behind his newest creation: "It's very rare that a product comes along that is seemingly impossible," he blared. "That people said was impossible. That experts said was impossible. And this is one of those times."

He turned his attention to the Cybertruck.

"We have a car here that experts said was impossible," he continued, referring to naysayers who, for example, questioned its ability to meet safety regulations. "That experts said would never be made.

"That really is the most . . . I think it's our best product. I think it's the most unique thing on the road.

"And finally," he said, "the future will look like the future."

Musk's speech focused on Tesla's ability to deliver on big promises, and, to the company's credit, it had finally produced the product that had once been the subject of such widespread skepticism, some even from loyal fans and bullish investors—though it had its devotees as well.[34]

However, amid the glitz of the Cybertruck reveal, it was left unsaid that the company had in fact failed to deliver on some of the promised specifics, particularly regarding the truck's performance and price point.

"Tesla Cybertruck is notably the first time that Tesla is straight up not delivering on some of the key specs they promised." This X post came from tech YouTuber Marques Brownlee, who pointed out that the company had promised a truck with a 500-plus mile range for $70,000, and delivered one with a 340-mile range for $100,000.[35]

It was a far cry from when Tesla had inarguably disrupted the automotive industry with its mass market Model 3, which brought the company into the mainstream, and its Model Y crossover, which was soon proclaimed to be the world's best-selling vehicle.[36]

In the days after the Cybertruck launch, Tesla faced several embarrassing incidents. A video purported to show a Cybertruck struggling to navigate up a snowy hill before being rescued by a Ford Super Duty pickup. Ford CEO Jim Farley playfully gloated over the achievement. "Glad a @ Ford owner was there to help," he wrote on X.[37] Even worse, after the Cybertruck reveal and once deliveries of the stainless steel pickup were underway, customers began to report noticeable corrosion on the surface. Photos showed newly delivered Cybertrucks with apparent rust spots. Complaints were picked up by news outlets, which Tesla tried to explain away as "surface contamination," in the words of one company engineer.[38]

Meanwhile, concerns about pedestrian safety, sharp edges, and build quality persisted. The truck was late, overpriced, and unobtainable to many reservation-holders at this phase. A recall added to the problems, demonstrating apparent oversights in the workmanship of a truck that had been billed as extraordinarily tough: an accelerator pedal cover could slide off under force, dislodging and jamming the pedal toward the floor and causing unintended acceleration.[39] Tesla acknowledged that it had received reports from multiple customers about the issue when it recalled the nearly four thousand trucks it had delivered up until that point in April 2024.

Tesla's apparent fix—though seemingly effective—was amusing even to the Tesla community for its standard of finishing: fastening the loose cover with what appeared to be a single rivet, one that wasn't always centered on the trim piece it was holding down.[40]

Meanwhile, demonstration after demonstration showed the Cybertruck straining under the weight of basic towing and hauling—pretty important tasks for pickup trucks—including one YouTuber's experiment that snapped part of the rear frame and the tow hitch clear off the truck.[41]

On the bright side, someone was able to demonstrate that it could briefly serve as a boat after all.[42]

In some ways, the Cybertruck represented Tesla's direction in the new era of Musk. Consider the pushback executives encountered when they tried to pitch Musk on finally building a long-planned economy car, informally dubbed the Model 2, that had the potential to be a worldwide hit, bolstering Tesla's mission "to accelerate the world's transition to sustainable energy." Executives had gathered in Palo Alto to sway Musk on the project, but the Tesla CEO's attention was elsewhere as he ran through the budget numbers. As he reviewed Tesla's capital spending, with the company's heavy focus on artificial intelligence and robotics, Musk decided to sacrifice the project that represented Tesla's future, a development that led Tesla's stock to plummet once the decision to scrap the economy car was reported by Reuters.[43]

It was a trade off, as one former employee put it, that was not aligned with the mission of the company as workers understood it.

Musk, as the former employee put it, had moved on from personal transportation. But there were still flings, as in the case of the Cybertruck and the Roadster. The night Musk killed the Model 2, his Twitter posts highlighted a different project that had managed to capture his attention, the long-promised convertible.

"Tonight, we radically increased the design goals for the new Tesla Roadster," Musk wrote, before implying Tesla's sleek sports car may be able to fly.[44]

4

THE MIND-KILLER

In late March 2020, as the COVID-19 pandemic threatened to bring the world to a halt, Elon Musk was nowhere to be found.

Jerome Guillen had been trying to reach the Tesla CEO for days. He tried calling. He tried texting. His emails—the company president's usual way of corresponding with Musk—went unanswered too.

After three weeks and an appeal to Musk's brother Kimbal, the CEO finally emerged. Musk's absence had been partly strategic: he'd sought to curb Tesla's spending through brute force during a difficult downturn, preventing money from leaving the company by making it nearly impossible to secure his approval. When Musk did surface, it was with an impossible request: reopen the Bay Area factory—now. The plant, built by General Motors in 1962, stretched over more than five million square feet.[1] Now, around the initial peak of the pandemic and the uncertainty over how the disease spread and the severity of its long-term effects—and, critically, long before a vaccine that could minimize its impacts was available—Musk wanted to call ten thousand of his employees back to work.[2]

By 2020, Tesla had finally gotten its manufacturing footing and was ready to produce half a million vehicles that year. Musk wasn't about to let COVID-19 get in the way of what was supposed to be the company's best year on record.

But that wasn't what political officials in California and across the US were signaling. The Bay Area enacted some of the earliest and farthest-reaching pandemic response measures to date. Soon, a surreal stream of news alerts came pouring in, offering a grim preview of what was about to unfold. The NBA suspended play indefinitely after Utah Jazz player Rudy Gobert's positive test, and actor Tom Hanks and actress Rita Wilson, his wife, announced their COVID-19 diagnosis.[3] Alameda County issued its shelter-in-place order by March 16.[4]

By March 19, California governor Gavin Newsom ordered residents statewide to stay at home.[5]

Even while Musk was MIA, his Twitter feed provided sufficient confirmation of life. He had managed to escape the litany of controversies of the prior two years largely unscathed, but the COVID-19 shutdowns left him with a dangerous combination at his fingertips: a keyboard and a lot of spare time.

Much of the world had come to a standstill. Tesla's factory in Fremont, California, had been shuttered during a county-level shelter-in-place order, despite Musk's efforts to resist the restrictions. Musk told his workers he would be reporting to work personally, but they shouldn't feel obligated to do so. His resistance to the shutdowns made Tesla unique among the tech companies and automakers subject to the widespread orders.

A March 14 tweet made Musk's position on the matter clear: "Fear is the mind-killer," he wrote.[6]

In the days that followed, I learned that Tesla's parking lot was filling up with cars just like any normal day. Tesla was defying the county's orders to close the factory. Thousands of employees were reporting to work and putting their health at risk at a time when authorities were struggling to figure out how to best treat the new illness, which would ultimately kill over one hundred thousand people in California alone.[7]

The public was unsure about so many aspects of the novel coronavirus—whether it was airborne, whether masking by the general public could prevent transmission, whether the disease could be transmitted through surfaces or other means. Yet Tesla and Musk believed they had already learned enough about COVID-19 from their work in China, where Tesla operated another gigafactory, to continue operating their facilities safely.[8]

Once Fremont police and the Alameda County sheriff's office stepped in, however, the company had no choice but to shut its doors. Tesla was only allowed to maintain what was called "minimum basic operation," essentially a skeleton staff to make sure payroll went through and facilities didn't fall into disrepair, for example.[9]

That's when Elon Musk practically disappeared, leaving the people in charge of Tesla awaiting marching orders from a CEO who was increasingly letting his company run on Autopilot. Musk was prone to these momentary absences from public view—periods of relative quiet that typically followed his biggest controversies.

At Tesla, executives knew that the longer the closures went on, the more their production goals would be imperiled. But Musk wasn't giving them any direction on long-term planning or any signal of how to proceed. Instead, he was fuming over the fact that his factory was going to be shuttered at all, adopting a war-time policy of stockpiling resources and implementing austerity. Tesla had already been dealing with the shutdown of its sprawling car factory in China, so the company considered itself weeks ahead of others when it came to COVID-19 protocols.

Musk felt he knew something others didn't.[10]

"The coronavirus panic is dumb," he wrote on March 6, the opening shot in what would be weeks of pandemic-related skepticism.[11]

"Kids are essentially immune," he wrote.[12] The danger of panic "far exceeds" that of the virus.[13] Had people considered chloroquine as a treatment?[14]

But Musk also couldn't help suggesting that Tesla could provide assistance. As the world fixated on the virus that was creeping into every facet of daily life, Musk—reprising the rent-a-superhero role he'd enacted during the cave rescue mission—offered Tesla's resources to help build ventilators, the medical devices that were becoming an essential part of the pandemic response.

He hedged his promise, however, noting that by the time Tesla could deliver, the shortage would have been resolved, rendering its efforts unnecessary.[15] In this way, his altruistic offer of help was a win-win: Musk could pledge his resources to a matter of global importance and earn the public's goodwill while never being held to his promises.

Tesla did ultimately scrounge together a ventilator prototype made of car parts; it never appears to have been used. After Musk promised ventilator shipments to officials, including Newsom and New York City mayor Bill de Blasio, Tesla sent over an assortment of devices including BiPAP and CPAP machines—noninvasive devices that were not central to the demands and anticipated shortages associated with the spread of the virus.[16]

All the while, executives at the empty factory that had been bustling with thousands of workers only days earlier found themselves plotting the company's future without its leader. Guillen and chief financial officer Zach Kirkhorn huddled together and settled on a plan: pause the supply chain for now, halting deliveries while the factory was closed in March and April, but hold off on giving long-term directions to Tesla's suppliers.

Major automakers such as Ford and General Motors, vast bureaucracies with layers on layers of management and following a much clearer organizational chart, had a different plan. They were prepared for a disruption that was likely to stretch for months. They ground almost completely to a halt, shifting to a different mission: building ventilators under the Defense Production Act, an undertaking they would be held to by agreements with the federal government.[17]

Meanwhile, with no direction from Musk, Tesla's suppliers were ready to help build cars as soon as the company was ready to resume.

In a sense, Elon Musk was about to stumble into becoming the richest person on earth and running the most valuable automaker on the planet—all because he wasn't answering the phone.

Jerome Guillen, a longtime auto executive who hailed from France and cut his teeth at Daimler, the company that owned Mercedes-Benz, was surprised to wake up one day and discover that he had been appointed president of Tesla.

In 2018, the company was struggling to hit its production targets after making a bet on automation that hadn't panned out. Musk had envisioned a highly efficient and essentially autonomous production line where giant robots assembled cars to precise tolerances more quickly than humans could, besting automakers in Detroit, Europe, and Japan, many of whom had tried this type of automation themselves.

Instead, the mix of human and robot hands had proved too complicated and slowed the whole process down. Guillen's solution was primitive by contrast: set up a giant tent outside the factory to house a third production line where staffers would work through the night assembling cars by hand.[18]

And, just like that, Guillen solved what had been an existential problem for Tesla.

"Jerome Guillen saved Tesla," investor Ross Gerber later put it.

Guillen had stepped in while Musk was engulfed in controversy and managed to shift the narrative around the company's ability to deliver. Suddenly, the question was no longer if Tesla would survive but how high its stock could soar. And he had won the affection of his staff in the process.

"He's a leader," Gerber said, a "hard-charging" executive who "gets people to do stuff."

And he hadn't even wanted the job. As Musk was set to appoint him to head the Fremont factory, he knew that any Tesla leadership position was ephemeral, and he didn't want any major publicity around his inevitable firing. His title, he told leadership, should reflect his technical role and preferably downplay the extent of his power.

Musk agreed, giving Guillen his word.

The next day, Guillen learned of his title in an email—President of Automotive at Tesla.

By April 2020, with no reopening on the horizon, Musk's anger about the shutdown was growing. His ten-thousand-employee factory had not been deemed an essential business, so workers had to remain at home along with much of the country.

It wasn't as if the millions of Americans suddenly sheltering in place needed pricey electric cars. To Musk, however, the shutdown was an affront—a tyrannical government overreach. He would later say it was "fascist."[19]

Behind the scenes, Tesla was angling for an exception that would have made it the only major American automaker to resume production. Musk even appealed directly to President Donald Trump in a phone call with other CEOs in which he praised Trump and expressed his hope to reopen by May 1.[20]

Musk told Trump the reopening could be executed without significant risk, and Trump said he agreed 100 percent, *The Washington Post* reported.[21]

At the time, Musk was also breaking more explicitly with the pandemic orthodoxy. On April 26, he endorsed a YouTube video—since taken down—that advised against continuing lockdowns, contending that social distancing and quarantines could make people less immune.[22]

Back at Tesla, executives had finally managed to reach Musk through his brother Kimbal. Approval or not, Musk was ready for everyone to report back to work.

Guillen was dismayed. Thousands of workers, many with families, would suddenly be placed at risk not only of contracting COVID-19 but also spreading it to others. He'd had to make tough decisions already, contemplating whether to furlough his staff, conduct mass layoffs, or proceed as normal. If they lost their jobs, what would they do about health care, so critical at a time like this?

One thing was for sure: Tesla was not going to suddenly play with the health of thousands of employees and their families because the CEO wanted to hit production targets. The disconnect between the two men, Gerber said, stemmed from their relationship with their workforce; Guillen was a "man of the people," Gerber said.

But Musk had the final word—for the time being at least.

Tesla made plans to return everyone to work on April 29 but was forced to abruptly scuttle them once Alameda County and the surrounding jurisdictions announced their intention to extend their shelter-in-place orders through the end of May.[23]

That sent Musk into a fury.

On April 29, the day Tesla was supposed to reopen, Musk lashed out in a highly unusual corporate earnings call that went off script. Chief financial officer Zachary Kirkhorn—who spoke in a soothing, almost sleepy tone—had been calmly addressing a question about "company liquidity," referring to Tesla's financial flexibility, "given the circumstances" of the pandemic-induced economic shutdown.[24]

Unprompted, Musk chimed in to highlight the "serious risk" of being unable to resume production. He characterized the shelter-in-place orders as "forcibly imprisoning people in their homes against all their constitutional rights in my opinion. And breaking people's freedoms in ways that are horrible and wrong and not why people came to America or built this country," he added, his tone escalating.[25]

In a rage, he tore into the political officials keeping his workers at home. "What the fuck?" he said on the call. "Excuse me."[26]

"To say that they cannot leave their house and they will be arrested if they do, this is fascist," he said at one point. "Give people back their goddamn freedom," Musk demanded.

Musk's line soon cut out, replaced by hold music as a voice on the other end of the line said, "Ladies and gentlemen, please stand by: your conference will resume momentarily. Thank you." It was a brief interruption, around three minutes, but it seemed like someone—a lawyer, a friend, perhaps Kirkhorn himself—was stepping in to calm Musk down.

Later that night, Musk doubled down in a tweet: "FREE AMERICA NOW."[27]

By May, Musk's mood appeared to be greatly improved, if the flurries of erratic tweets on a wide range of topics were any indication. On May 1, he announced he was shedding most of his material possessions, including his Bel Air home. Then he shared that his girlfriend Grimes was mad at him. But perhaps Musk's strangest tweet of the day came when he said Tesla's stock price was "too high" in his opinion, which sent the share price plummeting.[28]

Here he was again, tweeting market-moving information—this time, overtly questioning the share price—smack-dab in the middle of the trading day.

Musk's streak of oversharing was hardly over. On May 4, he announced that he and Grimes had welcomed a new baby whom they'd named X Æ A-12. This invited such questions as: Could a person legally name their baby that? (The answer: Likely, no. Musk and Grimes tweaked the spelling to X Æ A-Xii amid speculation about whether California regulations would permit using numerals.)[29]

My editor at the *Post* asked me to write a story about how to pronounce the baby's name. It was a valid question, and people were likely curious about it. No thanks, I said—we should prioritize more important targets. (This was a clear lapse in news judgment. The baby name story, which a dear colleague enthusiastically took on, was one of the most-read stories in our section that entire year.) As for the pronunciation, Musk told Joe Rogan the middle character was pronounced "ash" (so, ex-ash-A-12), but Musk took to calling the baby "X."[30]

But by May 9, Musk was furious once again.

This time, he was at war with the county health official overseeing the shelter-in-place mandate. As he had grown so used to doing, he turned his Twitter megaphone on a woman in government, a low-level official who had dared to risk halting his momentum: Dr. Erica Pan.

"The unelected & ignorant 'Interim Health Officer' of Alameda is acting contrary to the Governor, the President, our Constitutional freedoms & just plain common sense!" Musk tweeted, announcing that Tesla was suing the county over its inability to reopen.[31] Indeed, the orders in this liberal Bay Area county were more restrictive than those in many other locations—even within California itself—but they were hardly defying the governor.

Newsom hadn't helped matters by text messaging Musk that he could reopen, according to a person in close contact with Musk at the time, convincing the Tesla CEO that he was in the clear. It was only on closer inspection of reopening guidelines—including the federal government's list of critical infrastructure sectors, which did not include auto manufacturing—that company executives realized Tesla was still at the mercy of its factory's home county.[32]

Local jurisdictions had broad discretion to set their own reopening timelines. "Other local orders that are more restrictive than statewide reopening plans would supersede any changes the governor makes, Newsom said," the *Los Angeles Times* reported.[33]

Pan was subjected to the usual stream of reflexive online hate and bullying and left the position weeks later.[34] But Musk's fury wasn't reserved for her alone. He was done, it seemed, with the state of California itself.

"Frankly, this is the final straw," he wrote. "Tesla will now move its HQ and future programs to Texas/Nevada immediately. If we even retain Fremont manufacturing activity at all, it will be dependent on how Tesla is treated in the future. Tesla is the last carmaker left in CA."[35]

It didn't help when state assembly member Lorena Gonzalez chimed in with an angry reaction, the type Musk would use to justify moving on from a state he now saw as wedded to a radical left wing. "F*ck Elon Musk," she wrote. ("Message received," Musk replied the following day.)[36]

Musk had made his decision. The Tesla factory was going to restart production in defiance of the county orders. In a post and playbook on its website, Tesla detailed the measures it had taken to ensure workers' safety, including providing personal protective equipment, requiring social distancing, and adjusting some shifts to reduce the concentration of workers in certain spaces, before taking aim at the county once again.[37]

"Contrary to the Governor's recent guidance and support from the City of Fremont, Alameda County is insisting we should not resume operations. This is not for lack of trying or transparency since we have met with and collaborated on our restart plans with the Alameda County Health Care Services Agency. Unfortunately, the County Public Health Officer who is making these decisions has not returned our calls or emails."[38]

Workers were being ordered back to the factory. In fact, the post said, they were "excited to get back to work." And as the post made clear with its opening lines, officials should think twice before stepping in.

"Tesla is the last major carmaker remaining in California, and the largest manufacturing employer in the State with more than 10,000 employees at our Fremont factory and 20,000 statewide."

Guillen had made his position clear to Musk: he wasn't going to play with workers' lives by ordering everyone back to the factory.

But matters came to a head when Tesla board member Antonio Gracias, a close friend of Musk's, confronted Guillen in a heated back-and-forth that played out in front of Musk deputy Omead Afshar. At one point, as remembered by a person familiar with the exchange, Gracias called Tesla's factory workers people with "stupid jobs" who "could do whatever" Tesla told them to do.

Guillen, appalled at the way his staff had been dehumanized by a corporate officer, couldn't help but laugh at the insensitivity of the view from on high.

But the decision had already been made.

The following Monday, after the email announcing the factory's reopening, Elon Musk made good on his promise. "Tesla is restarting production today against Alameda County rules," Musk wrote. "I will be on the line with everyone else. If anyone is arrested, I ask that it only be me."[39]

Alameda County officials weren't pleased. That day, Tesla received a letter from a county official ordering it to cease production.[40] In an accompanying statement, officials also explained that the county health department had been collaborating "in good faith" with Tesla since April 30 on a reopening plan, contrary to the company's claim that Pan hadn't returned its calls. Indeed, officials expressed hope that Tesla would comply and return to minimum basic operations "without further enforcement measures."[41]

Any doubts that Musk meant business were gone by the following morning, as Tesla's parking lot again began to fill up with cars.

While every other American automaker had ground to a halt, Tesla was back in business. And unlike the others, Tesla had the supplies to keep going. Without Musk's detailed input on how to proceed back in late March, Tesla executives never halted the company's supply chain.

Suddenly, Musk—who had galvanized the auto industry in a race to build electric cars to save the planet from climate change—had fashioned himself into a right-wing hero.

"California should let Tesla & @elonmusk open the plant, NOW," President Trump tweeted. "It can be done Fast & Safely!"[42]

"Thank you!" Musk wrote back.

More importantly, his company was on a path to dominate an auto industry hobbled by a chip shortage and the impacts of an ongoing pandemic that Tesla seemed to regard as a nuisance.

Over the coming days and weeks, as Tesla sought to ramp up production back to normal, there was still the matter of the workers Musk needed to build his cars.

With them, Musk struck a reassuring tone.

Tesla had bullied the county into reopening, effectively consequence-free.[43]

In an early May email to the factory workers, he said that if any of them had reservations about returning, they could stay home and take unpaid leave.

If "you feel uncomfortable coming back to work at this time, please do not feel obligated to do so."[44]

As I soon learned, some concerned workers decided to take him up on this, opting to stay home over their worries about exposing their spouses and kids to COVID-19, as in the case of a worker with a one-year-old son born with respiratory problems, or another with a fiancée who'd recently had heart surgery.

Before long, they were among the group of workers who received termination notices, alleging they had abandoned their jobs. Tesla was accusing employees of "failure to return to work." They could keep their positions—if they agreed to come back.

But the workers' COVID-19 concerns hadn't been unwarranted.

On June 9, I broke a story revealing that Tesla's plant had recorded positive COVID-19 cases just days after Musk reopened the factory in May. In reporting the story, I was struck by the dismissive reaction of a company official whom I reached by phone, a comment amounting to "Who cares?" Tesla seemingly didn't think it was a big deal that its workers were getting sick.

Despite apparent social distancing measures, including keeping workers spread apart on the assembly line, sanitizing machinery, and mandating masks, Tesla's factory became the site of hundreds of COVID-19 cases in the months following Musk's forced reopening.[45]

Tesla's COVID-19 measures appeared to be little more than lip service. Company workers bunched up at the time clock to begin their shifts after having their temperatures taken upon entry and being offered masks.[46]

But once in place, they found little was being done to keep everyone a safe distance apart.

Workers who installed interior components such as steering wheels piled into cars next to each other. Groups of workers huddled close together at job stations alongside factory components. At lunch, the workers gathered together with masks down.[47]

Musk and Guillen had starkly different views on their responsibility to protect workers and their families. Ultimately, that disagreement would mark the end of a duo that had vaulted Tesla to the heights of automotive success.

From the time Musk reopened the plant in May through December, Tesla recorded about 450 COVID-19 cases, including 125 in December alone, according to data obtained by the legal transparency organization PlainSite.[48]

As cases surged inside the plant, something else happened: Tesla's stock value exploded. Supply chain disruptions, chip shortages, and pandemic restrictions combined to wreak havoc on the auto industry. The CEO's refusal to accept the pandemic shutdowns and Tesla's vertical integration and ability to resume because its supply chain had been uninterrupted combined to give the company a unique advantage over its competitors.

By July, Tesla would become the most valuable car company on earth, surpassing Toyota and Volkswagen.[49]

By the end of the year, it was worth eight times as much as it had been that fateful week in March 2020.

Despite his nearly decade-long service to the company, including work widely credited for saving Tesla, Jerome Guillen's undoing was likely in daring to question Musk and his circle of trusted advisers.

Within minutes of objecting to the factory's premature reopening, Musk placed the call that Guillen had been expecting all along. He answered right away and learned he was no longer in charge of Fremont.

Guillen took the news in stride. He was resolute in his belief that the stand he made for his workers had been the right thing to do.

But there was a final indignity. Sidelined and demoted, soon to be moved to Tesla's heavy trucking division, Guillen received another call from Musk: he'd have to give up his unvested stock options.[50] He was no longer going to be company president, and those awards were granted when he'd had more responsibility.

The Wall Street Journal reported on the spat between the two, noting an Equilar analysis that valued Guillen's unvested stock at $600 million.[51]

After the company's valuation had exploded, Musk's actions suggested he thought Guillen and potentially others were making far too much money. Musk, who had been awarded the most lucrative pay package in history just two years earlier, appeared to have been convinced by Tesla board member Ira Ehrenpreis—the chair of the compensation committee that had kicked off the process—that Tesla had been too generous with its equity.

Tesla wanted to claw back some of the equity it had handed out in leaner times, stock suddenly worth tens—in Guillen's case, hundreds—of millions.

At some level, Tesla must have known its request was absurd. The options were contractually guaranteed. Why should they be returned? And what standing did the company have to take them back?

Guillen told them to take a hike.

Tesla announced his departure in a brief SEC filing in June 2021.

"We thank him for his many contributions and wish him well in his future career."[52]

In its reporting on Musk's "unusual request," *The Wall Street Journal* noted what Guillen did next.

"In the weeks that followed, securities filings show, Mr. Guillen sold hundreds of millions of dollars' worth of Tesla stock."[53]

5

ARMS RACE

Elon Musk barely gave Uber a second thought.

In the mid- to late 2010s, before its initial public offering, the ride-hailing giant was the darling of Silicon Valley, and its leader, Travis Kalanick, was *the* genius founder of the moment. The company had coasted to a massive predicted valuation, partly because of its ability to one day unleash a fleet of self-driving cars, which, unlike taxi drivers, could operate around the clock and would not need to be paid.[1]

If that sounds familiar, it's because Tesla's gargantuan valuation a few years later hinged on precisely the same bet.

But back in the Uber boom times of 2017 and 2018, even as Kalanick's repeated public scandals were beginning to tarnish the reputation of the ride-hailing start-up, Tesla was in need of a savior—the company had put all its hopes into a mass market car, the Model 3, that it was struggling to build.[2]

For Musk and Tesla, the success of the Model S and the intriguing prospect of an SUV built on the same platform, the Model X, didn't guarantee future survival. Musk had poured any gains from prior successes into his next moon shot. Rather than rest on its laurels, the company would invest billions in the Model 3. The consequences of that bet were becoming clear. Tesla, hardly too big to fail and banking on a massive investment in a product aimed at the mass market—one whose $35,000 price tag could only be borne out by economies of scale—could either be added to the long lineage of failed American automakers since Chrysler, or it could seek an infusion of cash. Musk famously turned to computing giant Apple at around the same time to see if it would buy the company at a heavy discount. According to Musk, Apple CEO Tim Cook refused to take the meeting.[3]

But another potential suitor emerged. Early Uber investor Jason Calacanis, a friend of Musk's who took delivery of the very first Tesla Model S, said the ride-hailing company and Tesla were on a "collision course" and urged a merger.[4] It seemed like the ideal pairing: the gig economy "unicorn," a glimmering success in a sea of failed start-ups that seemed to hold the keys to the future of transportation, and the world's leading electric vehicle manufacturer, building a propulsion system for the twenty-first century together.

For Uber, acquiring Tesla could serve to change the narrative, over-shadowing the founder's mistakes with a massive investment in the future. It would also remove a potential competitor. Uber executives understood that Musk was making a uniquely ambitious bet on self-driving: enabling a fleet of consumer-owned vehicles to be fully autonomous. What if Tesla emerged as Uber's biggest competitor down the line?

Among top Uber officials, according to a person familiar with the matter, the idea of a merger seemed an attractive possibility—so much so that they solicited Musk's interest in a deal. Through a mutual friend, one executive took Musk's temperature on the idea.

The answer? A swift no. Uber's valuation was far too high, Musk said.

Apparently, he didn't like the fundamentals of the business, which was headed toward a $100 billion initial public offering, one hardly justified by its loss-leading business model. A self-driving Uber test vehicle was also involved in the first fatal crash involving a fully autonomous vehicle, which called into question the viability of its plans for a self-driving future.[5]

Uber's tepid IPO in 2019 further confirmed that investors saw it as a ride-hailing and delivery company that still had to sort out how to make a profit, rather than a safe bet to oversee a massive fleet of autonomous vehicles.

Still, one aspect of Uber's business did stick with Musk, part of the reason for its sky-high valuation. It was the same thing that he'd fixated on when the cofounder of Uber's rival, Lyft, met with him at Tesla's headquarters around 2017.

John Zimmer had been discussing Lyft's own big bet on self-driving cars when he divulged an internal finding: the value of a single robotaxi was $250,000, far more than the equivalent passenger vehicle. A car that could shuttle people around without a driver could be worth five times as much as a regular road car. Zimmer had hardly divulged a state secret, but Musk was fixated on the potential. Sitting in the conference room that day, Musk became fired up as the subject turned to safety: People would be hurt if the government got in the way of autonomous vehicles, he argued, expressing his belief that, at some point, failure to allow the technology would result in numerous preventable deaths.

Musk was still thinking about the $250,000 figure after Zimmer left.

"I can't believe he let that go," he said aloud.

The self-driving car was the moon shot of the 2010s—a pipe dream that would become an albatross for many companies, fueled by widely available venture capital from investors who couldn't resist the prospect of a revenue-generating robotaxi. At the time, it seemed that any company that could cobble together an Engineering 101–level science project—fitting a normal passenger car with sensors that jutted out from every corner, aesthetics be damned—could amass a valuation in the millions. As far as the public was concerned, self-driving cars were always two years away—a timeline that seemed to reset every two years.

Development was incremental, as the companies took baby steps or, more accurately, moved at a geriatric pace. Toward the end of the decade, though, the major players were starting to test out their cars on public roads. For residents living in test labs such as Tempe, Arizona; Pittsburgh; and Palo Alto, California, the autonomous vehicle became a regular sighting—if not a daily nuisance.

Elon Musk took notice of the fleets of futuristic-looking vehicles popping up on area roads, the same way he would zero in on the emergence of AI chatbots years later—and scrambled to react.

"Elon looked at that landscape and was like: 'There's a whole landscape of self-driving cars; we should do something too,'" recalled one former Silicon Valley executive familiar with Musk's thinking.

For all their promise, however, self-driving cars had a fundamental problem—one especially relevant to Tesla. Companies kept touting how they might herald the end of personal car ownership. This was not inevitable, but as they struggled to square the unit economics—a single autonomous car could cost hundreds of thousands of dollars to build—they settled on the obvious solution: build fleets that ultimately pay for themselves by conducting passenger rides, collecting revenue in the process.[6] Practically every consumer-facing autonomous vehicle company chased this model.

Only one company settled on a different vision: selling customers a car that would one day "wake up" and become autonomous.

Elon Musk, standing before a roomful of investors in a pressed white button-up shirt and fitted suit, nudged his clicker and took a deep breath. It was April 2019, and he was ready to make his most definitive pronouncement yet on Tesla's role in the self-driving race.

"By the middle of next year, we'll have over a million Tesla cars on the road with full self-driving hardware, feature-complete, at a reliability level that we would consider that no one needs to pay attention. Meaning you could go to sleep."[7]

Tesla, despite facing intense scrutiny of its Autopilot features at the federal level—the crash that killed Walter Huang, a father of two, had occurred a little over a year earlier—was promising to put even more autonomy at the disposal of millions of drivers.

It was a bold proclamation, but Musk wasn't finished.

"From our standpoint, if you fast-forward a year, maybe a year, maybe a year and three months, but next year for sure, we will have over a million robotaxis on the road. The fleet wakes up with an over-the-air update. That's all it takes."[8]

Musk surveyed the room.

"You say, 'what is the net present value of a robotaxi?' Probably on the order of a couple hundred thousand dollars?"

At the investor event, dubbed "Autonomy Day," Musk had taken the stage and given a highly technical breakdown of Tesla's progress on its various initiatives, including a product road map it billed as its "Master Plan."

But this statement, more than two hours in, was unambiguous: Tesla was throwing its hat into the ring and was highly confident about its chances of prevailing. Musk was known for overpromising, and he liked to quip that while he might sometimes botch the timeline—something fans acknowledged, noting that "two weeks" often meant a few months in Musk-speak—in the end, he'd deliver. But this was a promise on an entirely different scale.

The implications were immediately apparent. Tesla would no longer be just a bit player in the low-margin business of auto manufacturing but a technology firm pursuing artificial intelligence, a company whose valuation should reflect its soaring ambitions.

The race was on.

From the beginning, Musk's vision for a robotaxi differed notably from Silicon Valley's mutually understood principles of a self-driving car. The major players quibbled about ideal locations for cameras and sensors—where best to place a LiDAR sensor, for example—but the basic formula was the same. Use a combination of cameras and radar to detect obstacles, and LiDAR to sense depth and motion in order to stitch together an accurate picture of the operating environment—one that often surpassed what a human driver could see—by using roof sensors to gather data about what lies beyond the summit of a hill, for example. However, while human drivers are far from infallible, they break down the task of driving into a series of subtle judgments, such as how smoothly to follow the lane lines, how hard to tap the brakes, or how far to "creep" out into an intersection and peek at the traffic before making a turn. Self-driving cars, by contrast, were like computers—binary in their thinking, with a tendency to commit. This made them susceptible to dramatic false positives—they might come to a screeching halt to avoid colliding with an imagined obstacle—or worse, false negatives—where they might fail to detect actual ones, putting the occupants at risk.[9]

If there was one thing to know about Musk, though, it was that he wasn't going to follow the competition just because they had all found one specific way to approach a problem. He had a strong preference for design and engineering simplicity, and his characteristic stubbornness—or, more charitably, unyielding set of standards—meant that he would fight hard before compromising his vision.

Indeed, the argument could be made that Musk's preference for simplicity sometimes went too far, to the chagrin of his customers. At one point, Tesla outlined plans to phase out a gear selector, relying instead on the cars' intelligence to determine whether they should be in drive or reverse. "Almost all input is error. Car should do the right thing automatically," he would later tweet in response to concerns over its increasingly closed-off user interface, where basic features such as seat heaters were buried within menus.[10] One cutting-edge Tesla design traded a steering wheel for a racing- and aviation-inspired steering "yoke," prompting complaints over poor control and ergonomics.[11]

Musk's pursuit of automation in Teslas hadn't started with the ride-hailing and Silicon Valley tech giants. But by 2019, the features weren't merely a perk of owning its cars; Tesla was chasing autonomy full bore.

With Autopilot, cars could change lanes, steer through curves, and match the speed of traffic on their own, though the driver was expected to pay attention at all times. "While using Autopilot, it is your responsibility to stay alert, keep your hands on the steering wheel at all times and maintain control of your vehicle," reads one disclaimer on Tesla's website.[12] When it was first developed, Autopilot was merely a catch-all for a suite of driver-assistance features that would grow to encompass others, such as summon, which allowed drivers to remotely move their vehicles in driveways and parking lots and, eventually, through an iteration called Smart Summon, call their cars over to where they were standing.

Autopilot had hatched from a noble place—as a response to the around forty thousand annual road deaths in America, many of which Tesla believed it could help eliminate by removing the chance for human error.[13]

Musk has spoken of this goal. "Reason we hustled so much to get Autopilot V1 out was that someone driving non-Autopilot Tesla fell asleep, crashed & killed cyclist (Tesla driver was uninjured)" he wrote in a tweet years later.[14] (He added that the same driver had unsuccessfully sued Tesla in the matter.)

In the coming years, Tesla put increasing levels of automation in drivers' hands, even as regulators and government officials pushed back against the aspirational naming; this wasn't a system to which a person could trust the task of driving—it could miss lane lines, disengage for no apparent reason, and fail to see obstacles. At one point, the company was even threatened with potential Federal Trade Commission action over the alleged misleading marketing.[15]

Nonetheless, Tesla continued down its path. Nothing—not high-profile crashes, the threat of regulatory action, or fiery and horrific deaths—could slow it down.

But Autopilot, blamed for at least three fatal crashes by mid-2018, wasn't the endgame.

Around that time, Musk and Tesla began promising something else entirely: Teslas would soon be "Full Self-Driving," equipped with capabilities well beyond the driver-assistance features of Autopilot. Drivers could pay $3,000 for a capability that the ride-hailing companies could only dream of one day advertising. "All you will need to do is get in and tell your car where to go," Tesla's website read.[16]

Tesla's claim that its cars are "Full Self-Driving" means that they can function in the three key operating environments of a road car: on the highway, on city and residential streets, and in parking lots and private roads. Tesla's regulatory filings with NHTSA reflect this reality. In those, "Full Self-Driving" is referred to by what one might call its government name: "Autosteer on City Streets."[17]

Essentially, the software brought the capabilities of Autopilot to public roads. Cars could (emphasis: *could*) steer, speed up or slow down, make turns, and follow a point-to-point route without the driver's intervention.

Here's how it would work: Each Tesla with the Full Self-Driving Beta software was equipped with eight cameras that provided a view of its surroundings. The cameras would collect real-time footage of the world around the car, feeding it to powerful internal computer hardware that would interpret the data on its environment—including lane markings, street signs and traffic lights, and potential hazards and obstacles. It's important, for example, for a car to distinguish a deer galloping toward the road from a cow grazing behind a fence adjacent to it.

To understand what the car was seeing, the Tesla would cross-reference footage from its surroundings against a large collection of images labeled by workers so obstacles could be positively identified in real time. Workers would spend hours per day hand-tracing roadway features, such as stop signs, crosswalks, and bike lanes, and feeding them to internal databases.

That way, whenever a Tesla encountered one of these features, it had a point of reference for what it was seeing—and could know how to react.

Cameras have a key weakness: their lenses can be blocked by drops of rain or snowflakes, and their images can be washed out by bright sunlight. This is why autonomous vehicles, the rolling lab experiments deployed by Google and others, have additional sensors building on the camera data. For example, they use LiDAR sensors that shoot light at objects and build complex dot matrixes of their features, providing far higher accuracy than flat camera images.[18] They also use radar sensors—commonly seen in meteorology—which send out radio waves to detect hazards at long ranges, further supplementing cameras.

Perhaps most critically, the competitors' autonomous vehicles rely heavily on a structural framework built on rules and high-definition maps. The rules are simple: a car should never travel down railroad tracks, for example. An autonomous vehicle might be preprogrammed with that knowledge. High-definition maps, meanwhile, might identify every relevant road feature and obstacle—not just stop signs and traffic lights but also painted bus lanes, wheelchair ramps, and even storm drains.

How Tesla's Full Self-Driving cars came to be shipped without these critical components is a story of one man's stubborn insistence on an alternative vision—one that Tesla alone was pursuing.

From its 2020 launch onward, Tesla's pursuit of Full Self-Driving, together with Autopilot, commanded Musk's attention more than anything else. He held late-night meetings with his staff, soliciting updates on its progress. He tested the features on his own cars, usually in their earliest iterations, known as "Alpha" builds, before trying out the customer versions ahead of their wider rollouts.[19]

And he frequently promised new capabilities to his audience of millions on Twitter, sometimes catching his engineers by surprise. One former employee told me that workers sometimes first learned about their deadlines for shipping the latest version of its driver-assistance features through Musk's Twitter feed.

By this time, it was a mainstream practice to hail Musk as the modern iteration of Apple founder Steve Jobs. Fanboys like Omar Qazi—at the time, tweeting under a pro-Tesla handle @tesla_truth, with the display name "Steve Jobs" (later: "Steve Jobs' Ghost")—only added to the myth surrounding Tesla's leader.

But the differences in the two tech leaders' mannerisms, management approach, and communication styles, paired with their attention to detail (or lack thereof, in one's case), could hardly support such comparisons. Still, there are areas where they have proven similar: obsession with the seemingly unachievable, exerting maximum control and ruling with an iron fist, and a preference for hardware and software simplicity. Jobs famously lobbied for the touch-based iPhone to work independent of a stylus—a common device for touch screens at the time—saying, "Yuck! Nobody wants a stylus" and that the iPhone would instead work with the "'best pointing device in the world,' the human finger," as *Time* put it.[20]

These impulses manifested in Musk's approach to making cars he hoped would one day become autonomous. In Musk's view, Tesla should solve the problem of autonomy with the simplest possible approach: using cameras, which mimic human eyesight, and neural nets, a system of computer code that tries to imbue products with brain-like sensibilities.

One might be inclined to attribute Musk's product decisions to some deeper philosophy, but some who have worked for him say certain choices are purely pragmatic. Musk's decision to pursue autonomy without LiDAR sensors—and, later, radar—provides a clear example of this.

"Strictly from a vanity cosmetic perspective he doesn't want to put that on cars because it doesn't look good," said a software engineer who previously worked for Tesla. "And then from a cost perspective [it's] expensive to add these technologies."

If omitting this hardware compromised the systems' performance, Musk had a solution for that too: re-creating it using the technology available. In this case, it would be called Tesla Vision.

Instead of using sensor fusion—the interplay among cameras, radar, and LiDAR—to obtain a sense of scale, Tesla would create a so-called virtual LiDAR using only its suite of cameras. It would use computing power to stitch all the images together to provide a sense of depth.[21] Still, using pictures as a stand-in for the detailed dot matrix built from laser lights that LiDAR could provide was, at best, an unproven shortcut.[22]

Meanwhile, because of their advanced computing systems, Teslas wouldn't need to be preprogrammed with all the rules and map data of their competitors. If Musk's vision were to come true, a Tesla could be dropped in any location—from San Francisco to Cairo, Illinois—and instinctively know how to navigate it.

As far as Musk was concerned, all of that complex hardware and coding was a crutch—and in a sense, he was right. The competitors' autonomous vehicles were largely confined to small service areas that had been programmed with "geofences," or operating areas with well-understood features and obstacles, supplemented by high-definition mapping.

"What's special about FSD [Full Self-Driving] Supervised is that it works anywhere in the US & Canada," Tesla's AI unit said years later, in a 2024 post on X. "No high definition maps, no geofence. This means you can even use it in places that no Tesla has never [sic] traveled to before."[23]

Teslas, in contrast to their competitors, would have all any driver needed: eyes and a brain.

But even within the company, the idea that Autopilot was going to be expanded into a Full Self-Driving system gave engineers pause. As if Musk's one-year timeline for release wasn't enough, Tesla was still having trouble grappling with basic issues such as curbs and painted lines in parking lots, low-speed situations of the lowest possible stakes. Even worse, Autopilot was still failing to detect major obstacles, with devastating consequences. Jeremy Banner, a father of four, was killed in March 2019 when his Tesla in Autopilot plowed beneath a tractor-trailer after the driver crossed into the road; Banner's hands had not been on the steering wheel in the lead-up to the crash, investigators said, and Autopilot did not "consistently detect and track the truck as an object or threat as it crossed the path of the car." Banner died at the moment of impact; his red Tesla Model 3 hurtled another 1,680 feet down the road before coming to a rest, the *Post* reported.[24]

Tesla stuck to its argument that the driver is responsible for maintaining attention, noting Banner had removed his hands from the wheel, according to a statement obtained by ABC News, and saying, "We are deeply saddened by this accident and our thoughts are with everyone affected by this tragedy."[25]

Tesla forged ahead with its Full Self-Driving plans.

By mid-2019, Musk was pushing for expedited delivery on what Tesla called "Smart Summon," the system that would deliver a vehicle from a parking space to a driver, navigating a parking lot all on its own.[26] Taking a trip to the mall and it starts to rain? No problem, your car will meet you at the entrance.

Tesla massively expanded its in-house labeling efforts in part to meet that demand, as it put dozens of new staffers to work on image labeling, suddenly aware that its existing collection of data from Autopilot wasn't enough. If Full Self-Driving was going to operate practically anywhere, including private parking lots and residential streets with unpredictable lane markings, it needed a far larger set of reference images.

Autopilot was a highway-only system with a comparably simple task: guiding a car down the widest type of road with well-understood rules and behavioral constraints, with largely uniform design standards. The car needed to have a set speed limit that it could not exceed—adjusting that speed to keep the appropriate following distance in front of it—it needed to know how to follow painted lane lines, and it needed to understand features such as the shoulder, lane dividers, construction zones, on-ramps and off-ramps.

Cars traveling down an interstate highway were unlikely to encounter a yellow traffic light, a stroller in a crosswalk, a dog on a leash, a cyclist in their blind spot, or another car pulling out of a parallel parking space—let alone all of these at once.

The man in charge of delivering on Musk's vision was Andrej Karpathy, a Stanford PhD who had written a thesis on neural networks and worked for OpenAI before joining Tesla.[27] It was a tall task for someone who seemed most comfortable articulating his vision on paper, but Musk trusted him to lead a team focused on making Teslas autonomous, and, critically, Karpathy, like so many who reported to Musk, was willing to follow his orders.

To get a sense of the challenge Karpathy and his team faced, it's helpful to think of an autonomous vehicle as a beginner driver. It meets all the physical criteria to maneuver the roads—it can see, accelerate, steer, brake—but that doesn't mean it knows what it's doing once it's actually out there.

Now think of image labeling as a sort of brain training that imbues the car's computer with a supply of life experiences, a stash of memories. Drivers in training might experience close calls and remember not to repeat their mistakes, but autonomous vehicles take this to the extreme:

they need to draw on their stash of memories to remember what a stop sign looks like or to interpret the meaning of the lines on the road.

At Tesla, closing this gap took the form of a massive catch-up effort to identify and label anything its vehicles might encounter in the real world, particularly obstacles that might not be found on the highways so familiar to Autopilot.

Karpathy's staff got to work tracing lines around shopping carts, street trees, and bus shelters and dropping pixels with their computer mouses to create a database for Tesla to build off. The goal wasn't perfection—the computer could help with that.

Instead, their priority was speed; Tesla had a lot of catching up to do. Three hundred in-house labelers were charged with delivering fifty labeled images per day—more than six per hour. It was tedious work, and the time crunch made it all the more stressful.

The release of Smart Summon would provide the first test of their abilities.

After hinting at the feature's upcoming release in a May 2019 tweet,[28] by August, Musk had announced a release date of four to eight weeks.[29] Finally, Tesla began rolling out Smart Summon in September, beaming the software to thousands of vehicles at once through an over-the-air update.[30]

Tesla owners marveled at its capabilities, posting videos of their cars traveling clear across parking lots of apartment complexes and shopping centers to find them.[31]

But within days, new videos were posted. In these, the cars looked helplessly confused, dawdling as they tried to plot their next move and even allegedly crashing. One video showed a Tesla pulling back and forth out of a parking spot in a Walmart lot, spending around two minutes waffling on what to do before heading for the owner, meeting him in the middle of traffic.[32] A *Business Insider* report highlighted that and two other incidents—one in which a Tesla allegedly mounted a curb and found itself shrouded in tree leaves.[33] In the other, a Tesla scraped against the side of a garage, leaving a massive dent.

By early October, Musk was touting Smart Summon's widespread use, after it had been activated more than half a million times.[34] When it worked, it was magical, and owners reveled in the ability to show off to their family and friends.

But as the scrutiny piled up, Musk soon had to acknowledge some faults.

"Several finesse improvements coming to Smart Summon in coming weeks. Will be smooth as silk," he tweeted.[35]

Now that the new features were out, he wrote, Tesla was raising the price of its Full Self-Driving package by $1,000.[36] The package would enable users to access the soon-to-arrive software beta of the same name.

Tesla planned to charge $7,000 for a set of features that not only had yet to make cars autonomous—they couldn't even always successfully traverse a parking lot.[37]

In the end, the promised Smart Summon improvements failed to address the highly publicized problems with prediction and perception of obstacles. Tesla abandoned the software as a development priority, and in 2022, Musk announced a rebrand called Actually Smart Summon (ASS), a full revamp that he said was "probably a month or two" away the following year. Owners finally began receiving it in late summer 2024, though it was not long until NHTSA, in January 2025, opened an investigation into reported crashes involving Actually Smart Summon, with investigators noting the similarities to prior crashes involving the earlier Smart Summon iteration.[38]

As Tesla was ramping up its efforts to pursue self-driving, Uber's autonomous vehicle program was imploding—a decline that would culminate in the unit's eventual sale to a self-driving start-up, Aurora, for about $4 billion in December 2020—a once-unthinkable end for the outfit that represented the future of Silicon Valley's hottest unicorn of the mid-2010s. The program's collapse, after a tragedy involving one of its test drivers and a pedestrian in Arizona, would leave a vacuum for another player among the tech giants to audaciously pursue autonomy.

On March 18, 2018, a self-driving Uber struck and killed Elaine Herzberg, a forty-nine-year-old woman who had been pushing a bicycle across a dark street in Tempe, Arizona.[39] Herzberg, a homeless woman who had been well-liked in her community in Tempe, was described by a friend who was also homeless as "like everyone's aunt" in a story by Reuters.[40] Tens of thousands of road users are killed every year in motor vehicle crashes across the United States, but this one carried historical significance: it was the first known fatality at the hands of an autonomous vehicle.

Rafaela Vasquez, the driver of the Volvo XC90 outfitted with Uber's self-driving technology, had been streaming NBC's TV show *The Voice* before the 10 p.m. crash, authorities said. In video footage, Vasquez is seen glancing down before looking up again and then becoming visibly distraught as the vehicle strikes Herzberg. The National Transportation Safety Board (NTSB) cited Vasquez's failure to adequately monitor the road and the car's performance—and her readily observable distraction—as the probable cause. Vasquez was charged with negligent homicide in the crash. She later pleaded guilty to a lesser charge of endangerment.[41]

It would have been easy to pin the crash on the actions of one distracted driver, a backup operator who had shirked her duty to oversee the SUV's performance, but Uber wasn't blameless for what happened. As the *Post* later reported: "Uber's automated driving system failed to classify Herzberg as a pedestrian because she was crossing in an area without a crosswalk, according to the NTSB. Uber's modifications to the Volvo also gutted some of the vehicle's safety features, including an automatic emergency braking feature that might have been able to save Herzberg's life, investigators wrote."[42] The investigators' findings echoed what they would pinpoint as a factor in Tesla crashes; operating in Autopilot mode in cross traffic—areas where Teslas had not been designed to reliably function in that mode—contributed to crashes such as the one that killed Banner when his car slammed into a tractor-trailer. It had been an unexpected obstacle that the vehicle had seemingly not been taught yet to reliably anticipate, like someone crossing the street outside of a marked crosswalk.

For Uber, the additional controversy couldn't have come at a worse time.

A short while earlier, the company had ousted Kalanick, its cofounder and CEO, after a series of embarrassing scandals that called into question not only his maturity and ability to lead the transportation start-up but the culture of the whole company as well.

In late January 2017, hundreds of thousands of customers revolted against the company, deleting their apps in a movement known as #DeleteUber, after the ride-hailing firm continued to give rides during a taxi strike.[43] The strike, organized in opposition to President Trump's travel ban on Muslim-majority countries, attracted thousands of demonstrators to New York City's John F. Kennedy International Airport.

In response, Uber said it was lifting its surge pricing, which would multiply customer fares at busier times, in an effort to avoid excessive rates. That act was interpreted as indifference, and Kalanick and Uber faced fierce backlash, culminating in the viral hashtag.

The following month, former Uber engineer Susan Fowler penned a blog post alleging a widespread culture of harassment at the company.[44] It reignited the outrage against the ride-hailing company and its leader—and Uber agreed to commission a thorough investigation, led by former US attorney general Eric Holder, of its internal culture.[45]

By the end of the month, Kalanick was in hot water again, this time after video footage captured him scolding an Uber driver who had pressed him about declining wages. Kalanick issued an apology, but the writing was on the wall.[46]

"I must fundamentally change as a leader and grow up," he said.[47]

By the end of June, Kalanick was out. He resigned from his position, paving the way for a newer, more mature—more boring—Uber.[48] By December 2020, Uber was off-loading the self-driving project that had been so pivotal to its ambitions only a few years earlier.[49] The company had gone public in 2019 and was suddenly faced with new urgency to control costs and pare down its driver incentives, growth-fueling discounts, and experimentation. The fallout from the scandals and the scrutiny of the company's low-margin business model took much of the momentum out of the one-time "unicorn," which struggled for a long time to reach its initial public offering price after going public.

In many ways, Kalanick's repeated controversies, documented immaturity, and worship of a cutthroat culture with a side of hard partying—one that invited the attention of Arianna Huffington—prepared Silicon Valley for the implosion of Musk, a figure who would loom so much larger in the public imagination.[50]

Even as his star crashed back to earth, Kalanick saw himself as a once-in-a-generation entrepreneur, someone who had changed the world and reinvented the fabric of urban mobility. As Tesla was still grappling with how to break into the mainstream, Uber had already made itself into a verb.

At Uber's peak, countless applicants were clamoring to get the hottest job in Silicon Valley and go to work for a bombastic and decisive leader in Kalanick.

But even Kalanick knew Musk was on a different level years before he became the richest person on earth, according to a one-time executive in their orbit. The former Silicon Valley executive said that even then, Kalanick had looked up to Musk, rather than the other way around.

"Elon is one of the few where he's like 'damn, that guy is an entrepreneur.'"

Now Musk was taking up his mantle in more ways than one.

For Uber, it had taken one fatal crash—and the fallout from its aftermath—to spell the end of the division that had once represented the future of the company. Tesla, however, was held to a different standard regarding its safety lapses, leaning on its argument that drivers were responsible for paying attention at all times. Because Tesla's technology was put in passenger models sold to consumers, much of the scrutiny of it was limited to whether its cars complied with federal motor vehicle regulations— unlike the experimental autonomous vehicles operating under a different set of standards. In the most crucial years of Musk's "self-driving" push, Teslas operating with their advanced driver-assistance features would be involved in hundreds of crashes, dozens of them serious—including at least two dozen fatalities—any one of which could have ground any competing autonomous fleet to a halt, regardless of fault.[51] But Teslas weren't autonomous, the company argued.

They were merely "self-driving."

In court, defending against a Northern California civil lawsuit seeking refunds for owners who alleged they were defrauded by Tesla's technological promises for its self-driving features, the company presented a novel argument. The cars could indeed handle the driving, but they required "active, constant, and attentive driver supervision."[52]

"This makes the vehicles self-driving, but not autonomous," Tesla said.[53]

6

"TO THE F_____ MATTRESSES"

The Tesla executive was beside himself on his call to Steven Cliff, administrator at the National Highway Traffic Safety Administration (NHTSA).

"Why are we being excluded?" he asked, perhaps rightfully incredulous that Tesla would be left out of a White House event promoting electric vehicles in August 2021, according to a person familiar with the matter. Tesla, he noted, was an "American company making all electric vehicles," the poster child for the type of renewable energy success story President Joe Biden was trying to tell months after taking office and making EVs a priority. The White House electric vehicle summit featured General Motors, Ford, and Chrysler parent Stellantis, the big three automakers whose EV sales paled in comparison to Tesla's. It also included a Tesla foe in the form of the United Auto Workers (UAW), who had tried to unionize Tesla's Fremont factory, which became the site of unfair labor practice allegations.[1]

Was the snub intentional, the Tesla official asked, "or is this just a union thing?"

Numerous Biden officials ran interference in the meantime, according to a person familiar with the matter, trying to placate Rohan Patel, Tesla's liaison to Washington, while explaining that the decision was above their pay grade.

"The president made a decision that he wanted to make sure that the UAW knew that he was there for them," one said.

Musk could only sigh.

This retelling of Tesla's exclusion from the Biden electric vehicle sum-mit is based on the recollection of two individuals with direct knowledge of the events.

Two things could be true at once: Biden was trying to generate ex-citement for his plans among those who had not already embraced EVs, and space was limited at the White House South Lawn event at a time when many in attendance were still wearing masks to protect against COVID-19. Regardless, Biden officials seemingly underestimated the fallout and went out of their way to include Musk in future events.

But for Musk, the snub seemed to confirm a growing suspicion—raised years earlier when the NTSB investigated the Huang crash—that power-ful government forces were mobilizing against him. It would cement Musk's metamorphosis from political opportunist to full-fledged sup-porter of the Republican Party, even if he'd go on to weaponize perceived personal slights to justify far more radical behavior in the political arena.

More than a year earlier, Musk had sat in the Oval Office opposite Presi-dent Trump, who was desperate to secure a victory for the domestic man-ufacturing industry he had promised to revive. Far from snubbing a top automaker, Trump was appealing to Musk directly, proclaiming himself a Tesla owner and emphasizing the importance of Musk's company to the crucial domestic manufacturing aspect of his agenda. Still, Trump was far from the EV booster that his successor, who made electric cars a key component of his green energy domestic agenda, would become.

"Look, I don't know about all this electric vehicle stuff," Trump said, according to one source. "I have two Teslas," but there was nowhere to charge them.

Musk turned to a Tesla executive in the room. "Can you take out your phone?" he asked.

The executive showed Trump a sea of red dots on his screen, demon-strating the extent of Tesla's vast network of Superchargers, stations where drivers of the electric vehicles could quickly top up their cars' batteries, before an incredulous president. This retelling is based on the recollection of a person familiar with the matter.

For all his skepticism, Trump needed Musk and Tesla. The electric vehicle manufacturer was deciding on a location for its next gigafactory where it would build such vehicles as the Cybertruck and the Model Y crossover.[2]

While Tesla was strongly leaning toward Austin, Texas, or another location in the right-to-work states of the South, or a Plains state like Oklahoma—Tulsa, for example, made a strong push—the company informed administration officials that Mexico and Canada were also on the table. That prompted an intervention from the Trump administration that led to Musk sitting across from the forty-fifth president, a person familiar with the matter told me.

"You've gotta build here in the United States," Trump said.

Was there anything the administration could do? For Musk, nothing immediately came to mind.

But here was the Trump administration giving Tesla the power to make a direct ask—in this case, working on an arcane federal emissions rule that had been languishing, correcting what Tesla regarded as an Obama-era mistake—as the administration negotiated for Tesla to locate its next factory in its home country. "What the hell are we waiting for?" Trump asked, setting the matter into motion.

In a post taking aim at Musk on Truth Social two years later, Trump revised history: "When Elon Musk came to the White House asking me for help on all of his many subsidized projects, whether it's electric cars that don't drive long enough, driverless cars that crash, or rocketships to nowhere, without which subsidies he'd be worthless, and telling me how he was a big Trump fan and Republican, I could have said, 'drop to your knees and beg,' and he would have done it . . ."[3]

In reality, it was Trump who was asking for the favor, and Musk was happy to give the appearance of obliging.

"SEC, three letter acronym, middle word is Elon's," read the tweet, direct from the CEO of a publicly traded company.[4]

Sitting in his Santa Monica investment office months later, Ross Gerber couldn't believe what he was reading. Gerber, one of Musk's biggest cheerleaders and whose firm had poured millions of dollars into Tesla in hopes of securing a windfall, was now questioning the sanity of the man in charge.

Here was Musk telling the nation's top financial regulator to, in decidedly vulgar terms, take a hike.

"Dangerous," Gerber replied in the comments a minute after Musk's post. "But sooo satisfying," retorted Musk.[5]

The July 2, 2020, tweet broke a period of relative calm—at least by Musk standards. After the $40 million "Funding secured" fiasco, many of Musk's biggest problems had resolved themselves in quick succession. The calls for him to step aside had largely abated, Tesla had solved the Model 3 production bottlenecks and its stock was no longer in freefall, and Musk's legal worries were easing.[6]

After all the antics of 2018, key investors had encouraged him—sometimes publicly—to rein in his behavior. Musk seemed to listen to these moderating forces, Gerber among them. He agreed in 2019 to have his potentially market-moving communications monitored by an approved securities lawyer, for example, a helpless chaperone who would come to be known as a "Twitter sitter." He refrained from tweeting sensitive numbers or inviting regulatory scrutiny through unforced errors.[7] Later in 2019, Musk was found not liable in the defamation suit filed by Unsworth, the Thai cave rescue volunteer he'd called a "pedo guy," erasing another worry.[8]

Tesla's stock had soared in the meantime, quadrupling by the early part of 2020 from where it stood during the depths of Musk's controversies.[9] The market liked a profitable tech company with massive potential, a devoted fan base, and a stable leader.

The COVID-19 lockdowns had put to rest any notion of a new and improved Elon who could remain laser-focused on his business goals. Infuriated and unrestrained, he felt suddenly emboldened to break a cardinal rule of business: picking sides. This was especially problematic in a country tearing itself apart with political polarization. While he was often outspoken to a fault, he had previously hesitated to wade into politics.[10] He simply wanted to build the best and most advanced electric cars and sell them to liberal and conservative Americans alike. Any overtly political stance—particularly from the guy seen hawking luxury green energy cars to California elites—could imperil his whole operation.

Perhaps he had no choice. His patience had worn increasingly thin with a government establishment and left-wing activists he saw as determined to ostracize him and his companies. (It's worth noting that while the Securities and Exchange Commission [SEC] charges technically took place under the Trump administration, Musk directed his ire at the SEC's San Francisco field office, which he saw as uniquely hostile to him.)[11] He took the investigations, regulatory interventions, and enforcement as personal affronts. To Musk, the liberal overreach culminated in Tesla's factory being ordered closed by Bay Area officials.

He would later make clear that he lumped the government's action together with the political attacks, citing "unprovoked attacks by leading Democrats against me & a very cold shoulder to Tesla and SpaceX" when announcing he would be voting Republican in 2022.[12]

Musk appeared to see little distinction between government scrutiny of his companies and the increasing attacks on his business reputation and personal life. Meanwhile, Tesla was expanding its business heavily into Texas and increasingly targeting a new demographic with its offerings, which included a futuristic-looking pickup truck, along with marketing touches like a $50 "Don't Mess with [Tesla]" belt buckle emblazoned with the "T" (Tesla) logo. It didn't help when Democratic officials provided real-time confirmation bias that Musk could weaponize to his millions of followers, as in the case of the "F*ck Elon Musk" tweet from a California state assemblymember following Musk's announcement that he would relocate Tesla's headquarters out of the Golden State.[13]

"Not smart for an elected official," Gerber said in a reply to that official.[14]

If anything, these so-called unprovoked attacks validated—in Musk's mind—his decision to leave.

In a way, Tesla's dominance in electric vehicle sales insulated it from the worst effects of Musk's behavior. Tesla had already saturated the largest US market by far for its product—California—with both the population and political bent to support its massive bet on the future. At this point, how much damage could a hard-right turn really do?

By the end of 2020, Musk had officially moved to Texas, thereby cementing his breakup with the state where he'd made his fortune.[15]

Soon, Musk was showing off a belt buckle and cowboy hat, adopting the faux cowboy persona to match his new digs. Contrary to the combative, unappreciative progressives on the Left, Texas's right-wing politicians like Senator Ted Cruz and Governor Greg Abbott embraced him with open arms.

Musk was entering a new phase of his public life, one where he defined the limits of acceptable behavior and where it seems the only thing worse than being crass and rude was being inauthentic, dishonest—an NPC (a video game term short for "non-player character," i.e., generic and unimportant).[16] "Individuals should always wonder who wrote the software running in their head," he'd later remark. "Don't be an NPC."[17]

He had tried obeying the rules, and where had that gotten him? It was, after all, Musk's defiance of government authority that had gotten the Tesla factory reopened only months earlier. And the SEC had tried to bring Musk to heel—in the tech mogul's view—for a tweet that wasn't even entirely inaccurate. (Musk, as his blog post had made clear, was saying he really had been negotiating with the Saudis about an investment at the time of the "Funding secured" tweet.)

Now, two years after the settlement, Musk was beginning to make clear—in the strongest possible terms—that he saw the SEC's enforcement as unjust.

"He just basically has a complete disdain for any authority period, and he doesn't believe that he should have to answer to any authority," said Gerber in an April 2023 interview with me. "I have a completely different opinion about the hubris of thumbing your nose at the people that could really hurt you."

To Musk, the authority that had emerged was the liberal establishment—the one that powered the mainstream media and regarded him with increasing scrutiny, that dominated the political culture wars seeping into movies and TV shows, and that was reshaping the limits of acceptable speech and humor.

Musk had already essentially told the SEC to fellate him.[18] But it was another tweet sent later in July 2020 that would finally pierce his inner circle.

"Pronouns suck," Musk posted on July 24, a shot at the transgender community and wider society's adoption of gender-inclusive identifiers.[19]

Musk's girlfriend, the singer Grimes, was appalled.

"I love you but please turn off ur phone," she wrote in a since-deleted reply. "I cannot support hate. Please stop this. I know this isn't your heart."[20]

Musk was in the middle of an ideological transformation.

Politically, he had identified as a Democrat for years. He was, after all, the most visible response to climate change the business world could have produced: someone who had not only popularized electric cars but made them *cool* as well. He hastened green technology's transformation from a pipe dream to an inevitability. Musk was hardly a devotee to the Republican causes of the moment: he had made repeated overtures to the Chinese government—increasingly the United States' top competitor on the global stage and the subject of a Trump trade war—in conjunction with his effort to make the world's most populous country a key hub for Tesla manufacturing.[21] Tesla was eyeing Mexico, too, for a new manufacturing plant.[22]

For all of Musk's criticisms of censorship and political overreach, it was rare to see him utter a negative word about China. Meanwhile, he was exerting control over not only the future of car manufacturing but also the United States' space ambitions, often with the help of government contracts and subsidies.[23] On top of that, his start-up Neuralink sought to implant computer chips into people's brains.

As such, it would have been hard to imagine a bigger candidate for right-wing bogeyman than Elon Musk. His climate advocacy wasn't merely passive—in fact, he was such a climate hawk that he had left two of President Trump's advisory councils over the administration's withdrawal from the Paris Climate Accords. (Musk had faced pressure to leave earlier over Trump's travel ban but had opted to stay on then.)[24]

But as was the case for Trump, conservatives seemed willing to trade ideological purity and notions of relatability for the refreshing sight of a person willing to thumb their nose at the establishment. Musk was hardly a blue-collar guy. He was a celebrity dating a famous singer, a tech nerd who had hung out with Kanye West and Joe Rogan, and he commuted between offices via private jet.

Something about his frenetic online posting, however, gave people the impression that Musk was one of them. He lifted memes.[25] He slung impulsive insults.[26] He wasn't afraid to float conspiracy theories, no matter how irresponsible, merely because he'd stumbled on them and found them compelling.

His impulse to shitpost was apolitical ("69 days after 4/20 again ha-ha," Musk wrote on June 28, 2020), but suddenly it was brushing up against his increasing frustration with the Left.[27]

Musk said he had voted Democrat in the 2016 election, casting his ballot for Hillary Clinton.[28] In 2020, he'd do the same for Biden, he said. But on the heels of COVID-19 restrictions and California officials' decision to shut down his factory, his frustration was evident.

"The left is losing the middle," he said that summer.[29]

Musk seemed to see himself as a common-sense voter, a man above partisan politics—similar to a populist presidential candidate who urged the parties to simply work out their differences. He didn't hesitate to align himself with government officials who could help him advance his companies and ambitions, regardless of party. Politics itself was an inconvenience.

"I'm neither anti-conservative nor anti-liberal. Just don't like group think. Ideas should be considered on their own merits," he wrote once.[30]

But of course, by 2020, it was difficult to remain apolitical.

On May 25, George Floyd, a forty-six-year-old Black man and father who lived in Minneapolis was murdered by Minneapolis police officer Derek Chauvin, who pressed his knee into Floyd's neck and back for more than nine minutes as Floyd gasped for breath.

The country erupted in protests and riots, as the anger over Floyd's death spilled into the nation's largest cities. Musk weighed in, writing "#JusticeForGeorge" and urging that the other officers at the scene be charged.[31]

As the protests raged on, so did a sweeping movement for racial justice, heightening public awareness of policing's disproportionate impact on Black communities. The movement soon reached Tesla's front door. That year, companies across the United States decided to honor Juneteenth, the holiday marking the end of slavery.

The morning of the holiday, the same day as a planned protest for racial justice, Tesla's human resources chief Valerie Capers Workman sent an email to the company.[32] "Tesla fully supports Juneteenth for any US employee that wants to take the day off to celebrate, reflect or participate in events that are meaningful to you." It was the next line that struck workers as unusual. "This is an unpaid PTO and excused absence," read the email.[33]

To Tesla workers who had lobbied for better treatment at a company accused of a pattern of racial discrimination and harassment in the past, the message was an insult, in the recollection of a person familiar with their reaction.

Workman, a Black woman, was surprised to have been appointed to the role in the first place. Jerome Guillen, Tesla's former president, had lobbied for her hiring.

She had seen Tesla's shortcomings in dealing with workers, particularly workers of color, and challenged Musk to do things differently. She served as an example of how speaking out could earn Musk's respect and how he didn't simply surround himself with so-called yes-men. Even so, when she was called into a meeting to be told about her promotion, she thought she was being fired.

In mid-2020, however, Workman's name was being signed to a litany of controversial decisions made by upper management, from COVID-19 to racial justice.

Some employees had already arrived at Tesla's facilities that day for work as they read the update, which started off fairly standard.[34] Once they saw how Tesla was treating the holiday—as a concession, almost a favor to workers—it was hard to look at the company the same way.

Nathan Murthy, a software engineer who was working for Tesla at the time, said the period—with the combined effect of the pandemic and Floyd protests—laid bare Musk's feelings on the issues important to his workers; matters they regarded as life-or-death propositions appeared to strike the CEO as mere business inconveniences.

"We saw with definitive proof his true colors," Murthy said. "I don't know if he doesn't want to empathize or if he feels he's just too busy to empathize."

By January 2021, the country was once again in turmoil. As if the pandemic response and racial justice protests hadn't done enough to inject politics into every facet of American life—a climate in which simply the decision to wear a protective facemask or not became a divisive political statement—the outgoing president had refused to acknowledge he'd lost the election.

When thousands of Trump supporters stormed the US Capitol grounds on his behalf, Silicon Valley was suddenly faced with pivotal decisions.[35] Trump had practically fomented an insurrection with social media posts. In the eyes of tech leaders, there wasn't much of a choice.

Twitter and Facebook booted Trump off their platforms.[36]

Musk, no Trump supporter at the time, had made no secret of how he felt about these interventions. A year earlier, during the COVID-19 shutdowns, he had derided Silicon Valley as "Sanctimonious Valley.... Too much the moral arbiter of the world."[37]

Now he hinted at the massive backlash coming against Silicon Valley's seemingly arbitrary content moderation decisions, on the heels of the Trump ban and Twitter's and Facebook's decisions to censor an explosive *New York Post* story about the contents of Hunter Biden's laptop.[38]

"A lot of people are going to be super unhappy with West Coast high tech as the de facto arbiter of free speech," Musk wrote.[39]

Musk's profile, meanwhile, was exploding. He was now the richest person on earth, making him a much easier and more convenient target for left-wing activists that railed against the excesses of billionaires and the massive wealth disparities in American society, those keenly aware of concepts such as greenwashing and who would gladly trade a Mars mission for solving homelessness or, say, ending world hunger.[40] (Musk, for his part, said he would give up Tesla stock to solve world hunger, if the United Nations World Food Programme could outline a clear path for doing so.)[41]

He seemed to take much of the criticism personally. Musk, all the while, demonstrated little self-awareness of his potential to become the type of concentrated center of power he'd previously condemned. He was still operating as if he were the little guy. How could the world's richest person—who'd made his fortune on tech investments, benefiting from years of Wall Street hype and cozy government relationships—credibly argue that it was the tech demigods who had been exerting excessive control? Not him, but *those other guys*.

In a securities filing that year, Tesla announced that Musk and Tesla's chief financial officer Zach Kirkhorn had been granted new titles, as Musk thumbed his nose at the stuffy, straight-laced establishment-rooted culture he sought to dismantle.[42]

Musk would henceforth be officially known as "Technoking of Tesla." His deputy also received an arcane new title: "Master of Coin."

"Elon and Zach will also maintain their respective positions as Chief Executive Officer and Chief Financial Officer," the filing said.

The new titles were said to be "Effective as of March 15, 2021."

Elon Musk was crowned Technoking on the Ides of March.

Tesla's August 2021 omission from the Biden White House's South Lawn event illustrated how Musk's political relationships could turn on a dime.

At the time, Musk was dealing with problems on multiple fronts: inflation was rising, the pandemic-related supply chain woes that had hobbled other automakers were finally catching up to Tesla, and a prounion president suddenly seemed intent on freezing out Tesla and SpaceX.

Tesla's stock declined in the months following Biden's inauguration, as these pressures continued and the Trump administration's historically lax regulatory regime came to an end. Biden's Transportation Department already showed early signs that it would increase scrutiny on Tesla and Autopilot.[43]

That year, some vocal Tesla fans had begun to notice a peculiar trend: the most electric vehicle–friendly administration in history wasn't capitalizing on the most popular EV automaker—and its celebrity CEO—to meet its ambitious goal of making half of US passenger vehicle sales electric, plug-in hybrid, or fuel cell by 2030.

Now Musk was taking notice.

"Is this just because you guys don't like Elon?" a Tesla executive asked when the company wasn't included in the electric vehicle summit on the White House lawn.[44]

That apparent slight, in August 2021, kicked off an increasingly bitter barrage of criticisms of the president. Biden, said Musk, was "biased" against Tesla.[45] The man who had neglected to include his company was "a UAW [sock] puppet" (Musk used the emoji for socks).[46]

But his most biting criticism was reserved for another apparent oversight—this time regarding SpaceX. After the company sent four civilian astronauts into orbit as a charity fundraiser for St. Jude's Children's Research Hospital, Musk floated a theory as to why Biden hadn't yet offered his congratulations.[47]

"He's still sleeping," Musk wrote, a riff on the "sleepy Joe" meme popular with the Right.[48]

The Biden administration, wanting to tout its union-friendly

reputation and keep its distance from a man who was increasingly a political lightning rod, did little to dispel the notion that it was hostile to
Musk. Biden, unlike Trump, never hosted Musk one-on-one at the White
House, though administration officials did meet with him in downtown
Washington—so close to the White House as to make it seem obvious
they were trying to avoid a spectacle—to discuss a Biden charging ini-
tiative.[49]

Though he unleashed on Biden frequently, Musk was much more reserved in his criticism of Republicans, if he jabbed at them at all. Earlier
that month, Tesla faced pressure to protect its employees after a Texas
law banning abortion after six weeks took effect.[50] Musk held his tongue.

But when Governor Abbott took to CNBC and said Musk "consistently tells me that he likes the social policies in the state of Texas," Musk
had to respond.[51] "In general, I believe government should rarely impose
its will upon the people, and, when doing so, should aspire to maximize
their cumulative happiness," Musk wrote. "That said, I would prefer to
stay out of politics."[52] A diplomatic—and safe—statement that reflected
Musk's ability to reasonably disagree and strike a tone of civility.

Weeks later, Rohan Patel was placing a call to the top aide of Senator
Ron Wyden (D-OR). At a time when Tesla was at the height of its valuation, Patel was in the unenviable position of putting out a four-alarm
fire of his boss's making.

Musk had just tweeted a US senator—not just any senator, the chairman of the Senate Finance Committee—a vulgar comment about his
Twitter display photo, or profile picture, in response to a post calling for
a billionaires' tax.[53]

"Why does ur pp look like u just came?" Musk wrote on November 7,
2021.[54]

At Tesla, employees had increasingly begun to arrive at a new conclusion: their boss was a nutcase, according to a person familiar with
the matter, who detailed the fallout from the Wyden tweet. They had
scrambled to respond to one too many episodes like this. In this instance,
Musk's offensive tweet had struck during crucial discussions about the Inflation Reduction Act, President Biden's signature climate bill that was still
being written and which Tesla had been actively engaged in discussions

about.[55] If ever there was a time to fire off the lewdest possible joke about a powerful senator, this was not it.

Tesla's policy team in DC was aghast and began lighting up Patel's phone. This was an emergency. "Can you help us?"

Patel placed the call to Wyden's top aide soon after. He tried to explain, but there wasn't a script for this kind of thing.

"I'm super sorry about this," he said.

The Wyden aide was understanding.

"What the fuck is wrong with your boss?" she asked.

"I don't even know," he replied.

On April 18, 2022, Musk faced a new rejection he blamed on the Left, this time a personal one. That day, Musk's eighteen-year-old daughter Vivian Jenna Wilson, a trans woman, filed paperwork with California Superior Court. She had adopted her mother's maiden name and wanted to have her name change officially recognized.

In the section asking the reason for the name change, Wilson wrote: "Gender Identity and the fact that I no longer live with or wish to be related to my biological father in any way, shape or form."[56]

The Daily Beast captured Musk's public reaction. "She does not want to be a public figure," he told the outlet. "I think it is important to defend her right to privacy. Please don't out someone against their will—it's not right."[57]

The statement read as that of a supportive father. But over the preceding two years, Musk had publicly railed against measures aimed at building inclusive environments for trans individuals. In 2020, a few months after his "pronouns suck" tweet, he wrote: "I absolutely support trans, but all these pronouns are an esthetic [*sic*] nightmare." When some questioned his commitment to LGBTQ rights, Musk pointed to Tesla's 100/100 score on LGBTQ equality in a Human Rights Campaign index.[58]

Behind the scenes, a person in Musk's orbit said, the matter weighed heavily on him. Being disowned as a father turned what Musk had previously regarded as a political crusade into a personal issue. Years later, in a 2024 interview with psychologist Jordan Peterson, Musk removed any doubt as to whether he'd supported Wilson, alleging he'd been duped into signing paperwork for gender-affirming care and arguing that Wilson was "killed by the woke mind virus." He said, "So I vowed to destroy the woke mind virus after that."[59]

Wilson had her say soon after in comments on Threads, Meta's social media site that emerged after Musk's Twitter takeover. She lit into her father as few could have after Musk described her as "not a girl" and described apparent aspects of her childhood that included an early preference for theater and a propensity to describe clothes as "fabulous!" Wilson dismissed these statements as "entirely fake" and an assortment of "gay stereotypes."[60]

"This entire thing is completely made up and there's a reason for this," Wilson wrote. "He doesn't know what I was like as a child because he quite simply wasn't there, and in the little time that he was I was relentlessly harassed for my femininity and queerness." She continued: "As for if I'm not a woman . . . sure, Jan. Whatever you say. I'm legally recognized as a woman in the state of California and I don't concern myself with the opinions of those below me."[61]

Wilson's Threads posts caught fire, and she was suddenly swarmed with thousands of new followers, many of whom expressed support and applauded her bravery for speaking up.

It was her final word on the Peterson interview that she pinned to the top of her profile, visible to more than one hundred thousand followers.

"I look pretty good for a dead bitch."[62]

Meanwhile, as he grappled with his thoughts on transgender ideology, Musk was fending off perceived attacks from another movement: ESG, the push among employees for environmental, social, and governance-rooted investing. Tesla had passed assessments of diversity and LGBTQ inclusion with flying colors, but Musk felt the goalposts had shifted after the pandemic and Floyd protests. His inertia was just the latest attempt by Musk to try to resist sweeping societal change, hoping for the latest wave to blow over.

"I am increasingly convinced that corporate ESG is the Devil Incarnate," he said in April 2022.[63]

After weeks of tweeting about the scourge of ESG, Musk unsurprisingly blew a gasket upon news of the latest indignity: Tesla was being dropped from the S&P 500's ESG Index, a prestige shortlist that directed investors toward environmentally focused and socially conscious companies, over allegations of racial discrimination, among other issues. The allegations included cases such as that of Owen Diaz, an elevator operator who alleged an environment of "daily racist epithets" at the Tesla factory, in a suit that said Black workers faced frequent harassment and a culture "straight from the Jim Crow era." A jury first awarded more than $130 million in damages, but the matter was complicated by a judge's reduction of the initial award, citing it as excessive; the parties later settled.[64]

Musk was enraged over Tesla's removal from the list. As if that wasn't bad enough, an oil company, Exxon Mobil, had made the list. (Musk had a right to be angry about that. Exxon was removed from the list in 2023 and Tesla was restored.)[65]

"ESG," Musk wrote, "is a scam."[66]

"It has been weaponized by phony social justice warriors."

With the approach of the 2024 presidential election, Musk would make a break with the Democratic Party. He believed it was the activist-fueled party, and not him, who had shifted, leaving him and people like him behind. For someone who felt increasingly targeted by the Left, who was exhausted by the perceived infiltration of speech, humor, and corporate governance, there was one clear choice: Florida governor Ron DeSantis (R), the antiwoke crusader who, unlike Trump, demonstrated a commitment to seeing his agenda through.[67]

Musk was soon all in. He privately mobilized behind DeSantis for 2024. "In the past I voted Democrat, because they were (mostly) the kindness party," Musk wrote months before the 2022 midterms. "But they have become the party of division & hate, so I can no longer support them and will vote Republican."[68] Musk declared he had cast his first Republican vote for Mayra Flores, the Texas Republican who won an upset bid for US House in a special election in a Democratic-leaning district.[69]

In June 2022, he tweeted that he was leaning toward DeSantis in the 2024 presidential race.[70] Trump, he said, was simply too old, as was Biden.

"Trump would be 82 at end of term, which is too old to be chief executive of anything, let alone the United States of America," he said, after having earlier noted "it's time for Trump to hang up his hat & sail into the sunset."[71]

He was effusive in his praise for the Florida governor, however, as he pushed his favorite candidate as almost a shoo-in for the job. "If DeSantis runs against Biden in 2024, then DeSantis will easily win—he doesn't even need to campaign," he said.[72]

Earlier in the year, Musk explained his political transformation with a Twitter post showing a cartoon meme created by writer and evolutionary biologist Colin Wright. It depicted three stick figures standing in a line representing the political spectrum.[73] In 2008, the stick figure representing Musk, labeled "me," stood slightly to the left of center. By 2012, the figure representing Musk remained in the same spot, but the center and left had shifted beneath his feet. Musk was edged closer to the center, and the figure termed "my fellow liberal?" raced leftward, extending the left wing farther out in that direction. By 2021, the center had again shifted beneath Musk, placing him on the right of the spectrum, as the "woke-progressive" called him a "Bigot!"

"I strongly supported Obama for President, but today's Democratic Party has been hijacked by extremists," he wrote.[74]

Musk, meanwhile, had also soured on Biden, the president who was pushing major infrastructure and social spending bills as inflation was wreaking havoc on the economy.

"Biden's mistake is that he thinks he was elected to transform the country, but actually everyone just wanted less drama," Musk wrote.[75]

There were plenty of Americans in 2024 who felt alienated by the nation's politics. Musk, though, had money, fame, and power—and other wealthy friends who encouraged him to do something about it. The Left, they said, had gone too far and needed to be reined in.

The latest outrage came when Starlink, Musk's satellite-based internet service that had been launched in Ukraine after Russia's brutal invasion, was allegedly told "by some governments" to block Russian news sources, according to Musk.[76] Musk was defiant, saying it would not do so.

"We will not do so unless at gunpoint. Sorry to be a free speech absolutist," he wrote.[77] It was hardly an unreasonable stance. But to members of Musk's circle, the tech mogul had latched onto the central issue of the times—one that the future of humanity depended on, to put it in terms he could appreciate.

Musk's close friend and confidant, former Tesla board member Antonio Gracias, texted Musk at the time, in March 2022, that he was 100 percent in the right. "To the fucking mattresses no matter what," he wrote in a text message. This "is a principle we need to fucking defend with our lives or we are lost to the darkness."[78]

Musk "loved" the text, appending a heart to it in reply.

It was only later that month that matters truly came to a head.

Musk's favorite social media platform—the one that had booted Trump a year earlier—made another controversial content moderation decision, one that may have altered the course of history: banning Musk's favorite satire site.

Twitter suspended the *Babylon Bee*, a conservative, self-described Christian satire site, after it referred to a transgender woman in the Biden administration, a health official, as "Man of the Year." The site refused to delete the tweet, effectively making the suspension permanent.[79]

Musk's partner, Grimes, had urged him to rethink his tweet about trans-inclusive pronouns. But this time, it was his ex-wife Talulah Riley who seemed to have his ear. Riley, an English actress whose two marriages to Musk had ended in divorce, had kept in contact.

"America is going INSANE," she wrote on March 24, according to text messages revealed in court records. "The Babylon Bee . . . suspension is crazy. . . . It was a fucking joke. Why has everyone become so puritanical?" Then she asked: "can you buy Twitter and make it radically free-speech?"[80]

"Maybe buy it and change it to properly support free speech," Musk wrote back seven minutes later.[81]

Then Musk tapped the "like" button, attaching a thumbs-up to Riley's text asking him to buy the most influential social media website in the world.

7

TESLA VERSUS CHILDREN

We plan to run over the child on Saturday. Mom is on board as we explained how safe it will be."[1]

Omar Qazi, a software engineer living in San Francisco, had grown incensed by what he saw as a misinformation campaign against Tesla. Qazi had found a cause in defending the company online for the past four years after dropping out of Santa Clara University. He became the most prominent in a vocal group of Tesla boosters, shareholders, and Musk superfans who built large followings through their advocacy for what they saw as the auto industry's biggest punching bag. In Qazi's view, Tesla's environmentally friendly vehicles, its lifesaving Autopilot and Full Self-Driving technology—and Elon Musk himself—were under constant attack from a bad-faith campaign led by short sellers. So, one day in late 2022, Qazi decided to take matters into his own hands.

If you had to put your finger on the precise moment the Tesla story jumped the shark, you'd be hard-pressed to find a better one than 2:13 p.m. Pacific time on August 9, 2022.

That was when Qazi took to Twitter with a simple request: to borrow someone's son or daughter so he could launch an approximately four-thousand-pound car in their direction. For science.

"Is there anyone in the Bay Area with a child who can run in front of my car on Full Self-Driving Beta to make a point?" he tweeted under his handle @WholeMarsBlog, an account Elon Musk had used as a sounding board for years. "I promise I won't run them over . . . (will disengage if needed)," he said, adding, "(this is a serious request)."[2]

Two days later, like clockwork, the child was secured.

* * *

Every day, Dan O'Dowd let the top down on his Tesla Roadster and opened up the throttle on the winding roads near Santa Barbara, California. He'd slot the nimble convertible into the corners, riding over the ridge and toward the Pacific Ocean. He'd drive past the park where his kids used to play, past the marina and the palm trees, and make a left toward the fountain.

"Most days," he said, "somebody will stop next to me on the road and say 'what is that car?'"

They would never guess that the man driving it had emerged as Elon Musk's fiercest critic, a man Musk derided as "[batshit] crazy," using emoji icons for the term.[3]

The slight and at-times humorless O'Dowd, a multimillionaire tech entrepreneur, had recently become the chief foe of Qazi and his army of fanboys after taking up a cause of his own: exposing the flaws in Musk's products. He was a relentless critic and a thorn in the side of Tesla evangelists.

O'Dowd, a serious collector and hobbyist who has amassed such artifacts as the world's most valuable private coin collection and a nearly intact Tyrannosaurus rex skull, had also become a sort of foil for the world's richest person in recent years.[4] But he didn't see his conflict with Musk as a personal vendetta. Indeed, it hadn't always been this way. O'Dowd loved the Roadster so much that he owned two of them. He even went to work for Musk in 2014, dispatching a team from his company Green Hills Software to help clean up Autopilot's code, then a bloated mess.

But O'Dowd didn't love Tesla's recent emphasis on making its cars drive themselves, its pursuit of automation. O'Dowd regarded Tesla's Full Self-Driving software as a public menace that should be taken off the roads. Tesla's fans believed they were on the threshold of preventing tens of thousands of annual deaths with the lifesaving technology of the future; its critics saw the company as currently unleashing carnage on the roads, and they believed they could prove it.

Through his public awareness campaign, the Dawn Project, O'Dowd launched a robust crusade against Musk's self-driving bet, pouring more than $10 million into a sweeping operation that included a staff of fifteen, two Tesla test vehicles, and a vast outreach effort that encompasses public relations agencies and lobbyists. The group took out multiple full-page ads in *The New York Times*. In 2023, it ran a Super Bowl commercial that aired in DC and large state capitals showing, among other things, a Tesla plowing into a child-sized mannequin.[5]

O'Dowd, whose net worth was in the hundreds of millions as of 2019, made his career selling operating systems that power safety-critical infrastructure such as large airliners and military jets.[6] He became troubled by the extent to which safety-critical systems relied on internet connections. "I said, 'Oh my goodness, the civilian infrastructure has now become a weapons system for the other guys.'"

Even as an early Tesla fan, he had a premonition about a dystopian future where all this connectivity could lead to disaster. It involved a hacker breaking into Tesla's software and unlocking a type of "God mode" that would allow him to seize control of every Tesla on US roads. The hacker, after gaining control, would instruct all US Teslas to switch to UK mode. Suddenly, the self-driving Teslas would be barreling "at 80 mph the wrong way down the road."

"There'd be millions of people dead," O'Dowd said. "We have to make sure they can't all be hacked."

With the Dawn Project, O'Dowd was already searching for an example of dangerously bad software in action—the type of product that would demonstrate the pitfalls of poorly designed code, connectivity, and public risk—when Full Self-Driving Beta practically fell into his lap.

By 2021, Tesla had released the initial versions of its driver-assistance software intended to operate on city and residential streets. O'Dowd caught wind of the new feature and began watching YouTube videos of people testing the software. What he discovered appalled him.

"The guy's got a video for 10 minutes long and it runs a stop sign [and] does a whole bunch of crazy things," O'Dowd told me in a July 2023 interview. "And the guy says 'well, yeah there's a few glitches.' That's just nuts."

O'Dowd boiled down his focus on Tesla to a simple formula. "How do I make a point?" he asked. "I need a product that is egregiously bad." He could show the risks to power plants and public infrastructure, but he couldn't, for example, demonstrate the fallout from a reactor meltdown.

"[But] I can prove a car is [bad] because I can buy one," he said. "And they let anybody buy one."

So he did. And then he showed—repeatedly—how a Tesla didn't recognize a child-sized mannequin in the road.

"I mean it ran over children," he said. "Can you think of something worse?"

And thus, the stage was set for Qazi's counterexperiment.

It was a corporate restructuring creating a vacuum that led to this collision course.

Tesla's PR staffers faced an impossible task: field and bat down the daily swarm of negative clickbait articles and blog posts, deep investigations from the bigger papers, left-field requests about the habits and behaviors of the CEO, and also somehow get out the positive story about the most successful electric vehicle maker to date. After years of critical coverage culminating in 2018's summer of scandal, Musk began to see the mainstream press that had once built him up as a lost cause, people familiar with the matter told me.

So PR staffers received a directive: don't respond to anything that wasn't positive. Musk had the final say on all of Tesla's public communications—personally approving press releases, blog posts, and statements. But the company continued to get hammered in the press, much to the exasperation of communications operatives who were powerless to change the narrative.

It was only natural that this would soon lead to an erosion of the already-messy daily discourse on Tesla, the most talked-about company on the internet.

Tech journalists, like many business reporters, sometimes have adversarial or contentious relationships with public relations staffers from the companies they cover.

With the decline of traditional newsrooms, PR became an increasingly vital way for companies to tell their stories—with in-house teams that embraced the reach of social media and internet audiences—sometimes eschewing the traditional media altogether. The website *Muck Rack* reported in 2018 that there were then around six public relations professionals for every journalist, citing US Bureau of Labor Statistics data.[7]

But a company's communications staff could also play a vital role for journalists—hand-holding them through product launches, educating reporters on new features and company news, detailing technicalities so they could be translated into print. This was all for the benefit of the reader, but the company was able to get its message out this way too. Under those conditions, perhaps the proliferation of uncritical, hype-based tech coverage fueled by industry blogs, influencers, and niche technology sites in the 2010s and onward—always promoting the next big thing and building up figures like Musk as demigods—should have come as little surprise.

But there was plenty of hard-hitting journalism too.

With the tech giants, the back-and-forth over a story typically followed a pattern: a request to a company for comment was followed by a testy exchange of phone calls and emails where a spokesperson aired disagreements. Ultimately, by publishing day, they would have a grasp of what was going to be reported and what comments of theirs would be included in response. A company spokesperson's tactics in response to a story were limited: picking inane fights over wording, dismissing reporting as "not a story" or unworthy of the publication, or demanding frivolous corrections after the fact. Sometimes, of course, they provided helpful background or talked a reporter out of a tip that wouldn't pan out.

Most of the bluster was theatrical—they knew reporters were going to report the news, but the PR staff had to put up as much of a fight as possible to cover their asses.

For better or worse, Tesla threw this formula out the window.

My conversations with Tesla's PR department sometimes escalated into arguments (I'd like to think they were one-sided), and on at least one occasion, the line went dead at a certain point. These conversations started cordially, but at the flip of a switch, it seemed like someone had reamed the person I'd been speaking with as the possibility of a negative story occurred to them. They would then call back with a series of complaints that could turn personal. When I tried to push back on one such occasion around late 2019, implying that a spokesperson's command of the facts was Trump-ian before the call abruptly ended, I learned how sensitive Tesla was to any criticism—the company could dish it out but couldn't take it.

Tesla's disdain for journalists seemed to be on another level. It was difficult to extract any sort of comment or response from the company.

On the rare occasion they did respond, the answers would drip with snark or arrive in the most difficult possible circumstances. I recall receiving a Tesla response in the dead of the night before publishing, after I hadn't heard from the company all day. The idea seemed to be to provide an answer, no matter how unresponsive to the direct questions asked, and then play the victim once the information wasn't fully reflected in the story.

Meanwhile, Musk seemed to think that the *Post*'s increasingly critical coverage of his company had something to do with its ownership—or, at least, he wanted the public to think so. (The *Post* is owned by Amazon founder Jeff Bezos.)

Several people I spoke with decried Musk's lack of media literacy. Musk was a brilliant product innovator, but his understanding of corporate media, for all its many flaws, was either intellectually lazy or deliberately obtuse. He was willing to believe that the rank-and-file of big media institutions were somehow sicced against him by rival billionaires and Big Oil advertisers. Was it so hard to believe, by contrast, that reporters motivated to report the truth from within powerful and opaque institutions were suddenly focusing their attention on the celebrity CEO of the world's most valuable automaker and a preeminent private space company?

Over time, I began to sympathize with the PR staffers who lit into me when I called with questions for a story. I suspected that if they didn't succeed in talking me out of my line of reporting, they would be in for an earful from Elon.

One former staffer recalled how Musk had made at least two people in the communications department cry. Musk, the person said, would take people individually into a room and berate them, making them feel horrible and incompetent all at once.

Inside the department, staffers had gotten so used to Elon verbally dressing down their counterparts that they developed a strategy: put a shield around those most likely to be the targets of his ire. The staffer recalled how once, when Musk called him into a room to complain about another person's work, he was forced to defend his colleague's job before the CEO. If he had agreed with Musk that their work was substandard, Musk would have likely fired them.

Instead, Tesla's PR staffers closed ranks and delivered sunny reports to the boss, who grew increasingly skeptical of formal communications, in the recollections of people familiar with the matter.

Tesla's abandonment of formal communications kicked off when communications head Dave Arnold, who had featured so prominently in the "Funding secured" episode, left the company in June 2019. In the weeks leading up to the sudden disbanding, his replacement—Tesla director of communications Keely Sulprizio—departed Tesla as well.

Tesla had always had unusually high turnover among company officials in public-facing positions. It was hardly a surprise: the jobs had a tendency to wear people down.

But then all of a sudden, Tesla went entirely quiet.

One day in early 2020, Tesla's public relations staffers were abruptly informed that their department was being disbanded. The news caught many of them off guard, as they fielded sudden phone calls from the company telling them their positions were being eliminated.

Though it wasn't known yet, on my end, the impact was almost immediate. I prodded my usual communications contact there, who wouldn't respond. Calls went unanswered. The pattern continued for months.

By the time news of the directive came down, the fact that Tesla no longer had formal PR was hardly a surprise to the reporters who'd been trying their contacts at the company for months to no avail.[8] But it was a highly unusual step to take for a publicly traded company that relied so heavily on public perception.

Without a public relations department, Tesla stopped official engagement with the mainstream media. There would be no more commenting for stories, inviting the major outlets to product launches, and corporate presentations. Gone, too, would be the rapport that allowed the company to tell its story to the average news consumer.

Instead, Tesla was digging its heels into an approach tailored for the internet age: building an echo chamber of relentlessly positive news, fueled by bloggers and online influencers, who built their names and reputations by feeding the latest dopamine hit to the fanboys: the authoritative word of the company would be replaced with names like Omar Qazi and Sawyer Merritt, a Tesla fan and investor who grew his Twitter (later X) following to more than 750,000 people by trading in company news and scoops.[9]

Anyone who wanted to know the pulse of Tesla at a given moment could readily find out on Elon Musk's Twitter page, after all.[10] The situation seemed similar to the role of the White House communications

office under the Trump administration. Sure, you could gauge the administration's response to the issues of the moment from the press briefings,
but at the end of the day, everything rested on Trump, who could shift the
whole narrative with a spontaneous utterance.

Tesla's PR department had faced turmoil for years, and Musk began
to see it as extraneous—the way he thought advertising was unnecessary,
believing a good product should sell itself. (He'd make this position clear
years later, decrying PR as "Propaganda.")[11]

One afternoon, while working on a piece on Musk balancing his growing celebrity with the vigorous demands on his time, I received an email
from an unexpected sender.

It was Elon Musk.

I had sent him a detailed request for comment on the piece, which
was focused on his frenetic routine and move to Texas.

When I first read Musk's response, I thought I was being trolled. I
double-checked the sender.

Everything checked out.

"Give my regards to your puppet master," Musk had said.[12]

I thought about the irony of a megabillionaire duking it out with another
one of the world's richest people as I slurped down my ramen that night.

Over a year later, Musk commented again for a different story, this
time about his dealings with auto safety regulators.

"For the 100th time, please give my regards to your puppetmaster," he
wrote, this time signing his comment "Elon Musk."[13]

He then followed with a missive about *The Washington Post* charging
readers for its product.

"The Washington Post should change its tagline to 'democracy dies
behind our paywall.' If you're so concerned about democracy, stop forcing
people to pay for (allegedly) important news! Your boss Besos [*sic*] can
certainly afford it, even after buying a support yacht for his yacht."[14]

The commercial opens with a shot of Willow Springs International
Raceway in Rosamond, California, the backdrop for one of the most
talked-about tests in the history of motor vehicle safety.

"Elon Musk says Tesla's Full Self-Driving software is 'amazing,'" O'Dowd says in the ad, quoting Musk. "It will 'blow your mind.' But does it work?"[15]

Almost immediately, a white Tesla Model 3 is shown careening toward a child-sized dummy wearing a red cap. *Crunch*. It slams into the mannequin, whose decapitated head is shown—the red cap is obviously for emphasis—hurtling skyward. Next, the car approaches a mannequin wearing a pink jacket with the same result—the dummy is crunched underneath the car's four-thousand-pound body.

"This happens over and over again," O'Dowd says, as a mannequin in a gray hoodie suffers the same fate.

Suddenly, the camera cuts to O'Dowd, an unassuming silver-haired man in wire frames who could pass as any late-career middle manager.

"I'm Dan O'Dowd. I'm a safety engineer. And Tesla Full Self-Driving is the worst commercial software I've ever seen. Tell Congress to shut it down."

The screen flashes a number for US Congress as a disclaimer reads, "Paid for by The Dawn Project."

Qazi was deeply troubled by what he saw. The Tesla influencer saw O'Dowd's commercial catching fire online—it would garner nearly four hundred thousand views on YouTube alone—and grew frustrated with what he regarded as an unrepresentative hit job of the software he knew so well. A video posted by another Tesla critic, Taylor Ogan, showing the experiment re-created with a Luminar vehicle that did not fail the test as a Tesla Model Y barreled into a mannequin, seemed to add fuel to the fire.[16]

Musk and the fanboys had waged a yearslong battle with short sellers, critics, and naysayers in the press, but during this period, it was O'Dowd whose criticisms had seemed to really get under their skin.

O'Dowd wasn't above criticism himself. The website *Electrek* reported one flaw: the car's center screen showed that the software wasn't on.[17] O'Dowd pointed to extensive documentation to prove it was—releasing raw footage and signed affidavits from those involved in the test showing that the software was activated at the time.

Through his YouTube and Twitter profiles where he is known as

Whole Mars Catalog, Qazi released footage of hours' worth of drives with Full Self-Driving, almost always showing the vehicles performing smoothly with few safety interventions—uninterrupted trips through the winding and chaotic streets of San Francisco, for example, or the dense traffic of Los Angeles. He had extensively documented Tesla's achievement through a relentlessly positive lens, praising successful turns and noncrashes alike as if the cars were babies taking their first steps.

Now O'Dowd was showing the opposite, casting Full Self-Driving as a public menace. And people were paying attention.

In a conversation with me in the summer of 2023, Omar Qazi was candid about his strategy, which aimed to defend Tesla against the daily barrage of negativity that investors and fans dismissed as FUD—fear, uncertainty, and doubt—though they knew they must take it seriously.

"Tesla doesn't advertise FSD or really do a lot of PR," he said. "So it's really this guy and his $10 million sort of FSD smear campaign. . . . We don't have $10 million. Let's just try to make this as sensational as possible. It'll go viral and maybe we can neutralize this thing spreading around that Tesla runs over kids by putting out a video and showing what it'll actually do."

At the very least, it would provide a counterargument—something Tesla was largely failing to do on its own.

Qazi defended his experiment, even as the laughably bad idea spilled into the mainstream press, where articles highlighted the absurdity of the upcoming event. At one point prior to the experiment, San Francisco police sent me a statement discouraging the type of demonstration Qazi intended to put on.

Qazi was determined.

"[This] is completely safe as there will be a human in the car," he wrote, before declaring he'd found someone to participate.[18]

"Okay someone volunteered . . . they just have to convince their wife," he tweeted.[19]

"Many commenters suggested that I should have the car run over me, so I will do that first," he said. "We'll [try] with adults and dummies first. For the kid part they won't need to be in road."[20]

As the criticism of the demo rolled in, Qazi doubled down on Twitter: "I'll run over as many kids as I want and you can't stop me!!" This quip was in response to an open letter published by the technology news website *The Verge* urging him not to go through with it. "Don't. Don't do that," it said. "Really, I would totally just not do that. Don't force a kid to walk in front of your 4,000-pound metal box traveling at god knows what speed just to prove a point to some dummy on Twitter who posted a thing and got you all mixed-up in the head."[21]

If Qazi didn't heed *The Verge*'s plea, he at least planned an interim step before experimenting on real children. He found a child-sized mannequin on Craigslist. When he arrived to pick it up, the owner asked him if he had a store where he planned to display it.

"No, I'm going to try to run it over."

He then proceeded to a discount clothing store to buy an outfit for it.

Qazi described the reaction to his idea in a 2023 interview with me: "Everybody else was getting all worked up. I'm like, 'this is the most normal thing ever.'"

And then he showed up at a house on a picturesque residential street in Alameda, a city in the East Bay where the real-life kids who had been volunteered for Qazi's experiment lived.

Qazi remembers arriving at the house and being shown to a room strewn with toys and children's clothes. The kids noticed the mannequin and the clothes Qazi had bought for it and asked if they could dress it. He handed over the outfit he'd chosen: a turquoise long-sleeve shirt, pajama bottoms, and a baseball cap.

The following section describes events from the ten-minute video posted on YouTube.[22]

It was time to run the tests. Qazi sat in the driver's seat of a gray Tesla Model 3 parked on a quiet residential street with a basketball hoop to his right and facing out toward the road, and a Honda Odyssey minivan parked about two car lengths ahead. It was a cloudless day in a California subdivision lined with mostly single-story homes. The mannequin, wearing a baseball hat and turquoise shirt, was positioned diagonally to the car's left, where the car would meet it once it pulled into the road.

Qazi pulled down twice on the stalk to turn on Autopilot, activating the side-view mirrors, which auto-adjusted into position. And then . . . nothing. The Tesla, seeing the mannequin in the road, wouldn't move at all.

"It won't go," Qazi said.

Time for a second attempt. This time, the mannequin was positioned farther away, beyond the minivan.

Again, Qazi pulled down twice on the stalk to signal the Tesla to move. The car veered left into the road, as a little girl in a pink shirt skipped past on the sidewalk to its right. "All right, the car is proceeding super cautiously," Qazi said, as the car centered itself in the road, opposite the mannequin, maybe about about two car lengths of space between them.

"And it stops. It won't go," he said, the car now facing the mannequin.

Now a third test: the mannequin was placed slightly to the right, so the Tesla would not see it as a roadblock. Again, Qazi pulled down twice on the Autopilot stalk. Suddenly, the Tesla's steering wheel spun itself—no hands in sight—almost fully left, as the car pulled itself into the road at a sharp angle and started to speed up. Now the wheel spun left again, a correction, as the car prepared to maneuver around the mannequin. Now it spun right, the Tesla rocking back into position as it proceeded straight at 15 mph, speeding past the dummy inches to the right of its side-view mirror, straightening itself out again on the open road and hitting more than 25 mph before Qazi deactivated Autopilot.

The Tesla was passing with flying colors.

Qazi, who was making a video of the experiment, later announced, "All right, so far so good" after an initial series of tests, including one with an adult standing in the middle of the road—where the mannequin had been positioned—and later walking in front of the car. "What about with real live kids?"

A man with a chinstrap beard and thick, black-framed glasses strapped himself into the Model 3's driver's seat. Tad Park faced Qazi, who was still recording, and introduced himself as the portfolio manager of VCAR, an autonomous driving fund. He said he had prior experience with Full Self-Driving and believed in the software.

"I trust the system enough . . . that I would trust my kids' lives with them," he said. "So I'm very confident that it's going to detect my kids and then I'm also in control of the wheel so I can brake at any time."

The next shot shows a little girl in a pink shirt standing in the middle of the road, arms crossed and motionless. Her head is concealed.

Qazi recorded from the passenger's seat.

"It sees you! It sees you!" Park yelled to his daughter, a little more than two car lengths in the distance, seeking to reassure her. Then he pulled on the stalk twice, activating Full Self-Driving, alerting the Tesla to proceed in her direction.

At first, the car didn't move.

After a few moments, it began to creep forward at 3 mph, traveling about a car length, aligning the Tesla with the Honda Odyssey parked on the side of the road in front of it and to its right. It came to a halt about a car length and a half from Park's daughter.

"And it stopped," Qazi announced. The girl was perfectly aligned with the car's center screen maybe fifteen feet away from the front bumper. She never flinched.

Now she pranced out of the road to make room for another test.

Park's son, a five-year-old boy whose head was about as far off the ground as a Tesla's side-view mirrors, had been told to cross the road as the car approached in Full Self-Driving (Beta).

Park again started the car moving forward. As it approached a parked Toyota Prius, the boy emerged, wearing a brightly colored shirt and what appears to be a sun hat, skittering into the street. The Tesla courteously halted and let him cross.

Then it proceeded to cruise down the residential street as the child disappeared from view.

"So. It sees kids just fine," Qazi said.

"Yeah. And he's really short," Tad concurred.

In the end, given the limited nature of his experiment, it's unclear what Qazi's test proved, other than the lengths Tesla fanboys were willing to go to defend the company's name.

Qazi admitted to me it was a publicity stunt. It hardly proved that a result like O'Dowd's was impossible, and it involved the participation of real children. And what about the risk of inviting copycat experiments?

"We wanted it to go as viral as [O'Dowd's] video did with his paid advertising," Qazi said in an interview. "People like to write negative things a lot more easily than positive things. If I go in and I go, 'Hey guys we're going to be running this test and I want you guys to cover it,' then most people are going to be like, 'Whatever.' But if I go, 'We're going to try to run over a kid' and somebody wants to write a story about what an asshole you are . . . We ultimately just wanted people to see . . . this isn't actually the situation he painted where it's trying to run over kids left and right."

Sure enough, Qazi's video got traction online. As it began to gather steam, a CNBC reporter reached out to YouTube for comment. YouTube then removed the video in accordance with its policy on "harmful and dangerous" content.[23]

As for Tesla and Musk, they were silent on Qazi's demo. Instead, they turned their attention toward O'Dowd.

That month, the company issued a cease-and-desist letter, signed by its deputy general counsel Dinna Eskin, demanding that the Dawn Project take down the mannequin commercial. Citing the *Electrek* report that Full Self-Driving had not been engaged, the company argued that the commercial misrepresented its software.

"The purported tests misuse and misrepresent the capabilities of Tesla's technology, and disregard widely recognized testing performed by independent agencies as well as the experiences shared by our customers," the letter said. It accused the Dawn Project of "unsafe and improper use" of the software. On the contrary, Tesla argued, it was the Dawn Project that was endangering people. "Your actions actually put consumers at risk," the letter read.[24]

O'Dowd didn't blink. Instead, he poured more money into the project—culminating in the Super Bowl ad campaign that February, where a massive audience was shown a Tesla knocking the head off a child-sized mannequin. A year later, the Dawn Project ran two more Super Bowl ads. The first detailed the aftermath of a horrific crash—just weeks after O'Dowd's commercial showing Teslas mowing down mannequins—in which a seventeen-year-old named Tillman Mitchell was struck by a Tesla allegedly in Autopilot at 45 mph as he was disembarking a school bus in North Carolina, leaving him hospitalized on a ventilator.[25] (NHTSA, through a spokesperson, declined to comment on the North Carolina crash, citing its ongoing investigation.) The other showed footage of a Tesla plowing underneath a semitruck trailer, killing the driver, and speeding past a stop sign and warning lights, killing a young woman who had gotten out of a Chevy Tahoe to stargaze with her partner.[26]

Rohan Patel, Tesla's policy chief in Washington, used the *Post*'s reporting on fatal Autopilot crashes—which later inspired the commercials—as an opening to go on the offensive. Tesla was being crushed in the public messaging department.[27] Its PR strategy—or, really, no-PR strategy—was coming back to bite the company. So he started fighting back.

"Many voices in the media and those who just don't understand the actual data/analytics have demonized Tesla and NHTSA," he said in a post on X. "Whatever their intention, they are on the wrong side of history in creating a misimpression for drivers and the public."[28]

He made no mention of how his boss had played a part in the very "us versus them" dynamic that had landed Patel in the role of fixer.

On the advocacy end, there was O'Dowd, who was in the unique position of having a lot of money and little to lose, though detractors would accuse him of a conflict of interest because of his own software-related work, something O'Dowd denies, saying he is motivated by safety-related worries. He had a track record of deploying safety-critical software and was willing to leverage his fortune for the cause and face the backlash that came with sparring against the world's richest person.

"Why does he not like me? I'm the one person he can't get to," O'Dowd told me of Musk. "I'm the one guy in the world who can stand up to him because I have the money to hire those same armies of lawyers they have. . . . He can't destroy my business . . . can't get to my family . . . I'm the one guy in the whole world, I think, who he can't touch. And that's what kills him.

"And I keep coming," he added when I interviewed him in July 2023.

As regulatory scrutiny and demand and reputational problems piled up over the next few years, Tesla fanboys and investors begged the company to get over its usual aversion to advertising and public relations and start controlling public messaging again. But Musk wouldn't flinch. Super Bowl watchers would see a flood of ads for competing electric vehicles. The only airtime on Tesla came from O'Dowd, whose ads fiercely criticized the company's software and warned the largest television audience of the year of its dangers.

"Boycott Tesla to keep your kids safe," one ad concluded.[29]

8

"THEY OWN THE GOVERNMENT HERE"

Six months after being fired from Tesla in February 2022, John Bernal had flown to Cabo San Lucas, Mexico, seeking a recharge. Bernal, an advanced driver-assistance system test driver for Tesla responsible for evaluating the software's performance, had caught the attention of higher-ups at the company when he posted footage of Tesla's Full Self-Driving software behaving erratically, including the first video-documented crash involving the software the month he was fired.[1] In firing him, Bernal said, Tesla alleged improper use of the Full Self-Driving software he'd gotten through work, which had also helped him build a following on his YouTube channel AI Addict, where he posted his videos.

One day on his trip, after a workout, Bernal told me in a July 2023 interview, he returned to his locker to see his phone screen lighting up. There were dozens of notifications: hordes of missed calls, voicemails, and texts from roommates saying to call them.

As he frantically tried to reach a roommate, he peeked at one of the messages.

"The FBI is here. . . . They're asking for you."

Bernal was convinced he was being pranked.

Then he discovered the voicemail. It was the FBI working with the Department of Transportation. The voice on the other end sternly declared, "We need to speak with you, John."

Bernal briefly wondered whether he should stay in Mexico. Had the antics that got him fired got him into trouble with the government somehow?

Bernal consulted with his attorney. With the lawyer on the line, Bernal then called the FBI back.

He was relieved to hear what came next.

"Oh, you're not in trouble. We're investigating a former employer of yours—not you," Bernal recalled to me.

He flew back to California, and in October, an agent from the FBI field office in San Francisco and a US Department of Transportation official met him at his mother's house in Los Gatos.[2]

There he sat with the federal officials answering questions about their real interest: Elon Musk.

Six years earlier, Tesla released a marketing video that laid out a road map for the company's future ambitions—though it was hardly presented that way.

It began with a black frame. Then white text appeared on the screen, declaring, in all caps: "The person in the driver's seat is only there for legal reasons. He is not doing anything. The car is driving itself."[3]

A Tesla Model X emerged from a garage and a test driver climbed into the driver's seat. The opening riff of the Rolling Stones' "Paint It Black" began to play, the beat building as the SUV started to expertly maneuver itself around the streets of Menlo Park, California, with the driver's hands merely hovering beneath the steering wheel in case the car made a mistake. Along the way, it encountered obstacles such as traffic lights, bicycle lanes, and off-ramps.

The Tesla didn't make a wrong move. It seamlessly navigated the seven-mile route to Tesla's headquarters at 3500 Deer Creek Road in Palo Alto.

When it arrived, the car dropped off the test driver at the door. Then, with no one in the driver's seat, the Tesla maneuvered through the parking lot, stopping to allow a pedestrian to cross in front of it before driving away from the maze of parking spaces.

Finally, it parallel parked itself.

As far as contemporary Teslas' actual on-road performance went, the video was practically a non sequitur. The cars came standard with the driver-assistance system Tesla called Autopilot, but they were hardly self-driving, particularly in the around-town situations documented in the

"Paint It Black" footage. But this early demonstration of the car's capabilities loomed in the background for years.

Three years later, Musk would promise to put one million robotaxis on the road by the following year, 2020.[4]

In the interim, the Tesla's performance in that video raised questions: How had the software performed so flawlessly without driver intervention, so early in the company's pursuit of autonomy? Why couldn't real-life Teslas re-create those successes on the road?

Tesla slowly trickled out new features to drivers in the ensuing years—advancing the capabilities of Autopilot, but hardly in ways that would make their cars self-driving.

It wasn't until 2021 that the reason for the 2016 triumph began to emerge.

In December of that year, *The New York Times* published an exposé.[5]

The *Times* reported that, according to its sources, the route had been premapped, detailed in three dimensions, meaning Tesla had preprogrammed potential obstacles and instructed the car on how to maneuver the complicated route, a level of training not available to typical Autopilot users. Further, the car had actually crashed during filming, which was not shown in the final video. Despite all the meticulous planning and the carefully choreographed driving, the Tesla had hit a chain-link fence.

"At one point during the filming of the video, the car hit a roadside barrier on Tesla property while using Autopilot and had to be repaired, three people who worked on the video said," the *Times* reported.

Later, Tesla's Autopilot chief Ashok Elluswamy would confirm much of the *Times'* reporting as he sat for a deposition in the lawsuit brought by the family of Walter Huang, the Apple engineer who had been killed when his Tesla in Autopilot slammed into a highway barrier in California at a high speed.[6]

The Tesla video was staged, his testimony showed. It was a "demonstration of the system's capabilities," he said, according to Reuters.[7] Musk had not only requested the demo, as Reuters reported; he had overseen the whole operation, even dictating the text that opened the video, *Bloomberg* later reported.[8]

Surely by the time the FBI sat down with Bernal, much of this background was known. But they wanted to know if there was more. Did Tesla's misrepresentations stretch beyond the "Paint It Black" video?[9]

In early 2021, as the fallout from COVID-19 wreaked havoc on the semiconductor supply chain, Elon Musk turned to his Tesla engineers with an order: remove radar from Tesla's vehicles going forward. The chip shortage had decimated production of new vehicles from major automakers—now Tesla was feeling its impacts too.[10] Deleting radar could ease at least one constraint of a computing-heavy component.

Some of Tesla's engineers were taken aback. Tesla was already using a simplified hardware suite that departed from the industry standard in its omission of LiDAR, the laser light-based sensors that rivals such as Waymo and Cruise relied on. They turned to a respected former executive at the company for advice on how to talk Musk out of it, as I reported for *The Washington Post* at the time.

But Musk was undeterred and overruled the engineers, as was reported in the *Post*.[11] It was another instance of Musk strong-arming subject-matter experts in favor of another path, one that would rattle some Autopilot employees so much that they'd end up leaving the company over the issue, a former employee told me. Nonetheless, in May 2021, Tesla announced its cars would no longer be shipped with radar.[12]

To understand the importance of a sophisticated sensor suite that includes redundancies such as radar, consider two different scenarios: in one, a car is traveling down the highway in heavy rain; in the other, the sun is shining brightly in a clear, cloudless sky.

Surprisingly, both scenarios can present problems for automotive cameras. While a raindrop can obscure the front-facing camera, blocking its view, bright sunlight can produce a similar effect, washing out the image. These obstructions can produce "false positives" that can lead to pileups.

For that reason, companies typically equip autonomous vehicles with multiple types of sensors, for redundancy, or "sensor fusion," as it's referred to in the industry. That way, if the camera detects an obstruction, the computer can check the additional sensor to determine whether the hazard is real.

But with supply chain constraints threatening its ability to meet demand, Tesla proceeded down a different path: potentially sacrificing hardware completeness in favor of design rigidity and software simplicity. It rolled out a system it called "Tesla Vision," a camera-only approach championed exclusively by Musk and his deputies.[13]

Sure enough, it was like nothing the industry had ever seen.

Kevin Smith, a vocal Tesla fan and enthusiast who had become one of Elon Musk's de facto Full Self-Driving Beta testers, was excited to try out Tesla's latest update on his way to work.[14]

It was October 24, 2021. The Murfreesboro, Tennessee, resident's excitement soon turned to frustration. He'd been locked out of the software.

At around the same time, he heard from another beta tester. The voice on the other end of the line was screaming: "Do not use it! Do not use it!"[15]

The night before, Teslas that had received the Full Self-Driving version 10.3 update had started to go haywire, slamming on their brakes at highway speeds.

Videos began making the rounds of cars cruising down the highway when Autopilot would jerk nearly to a halt; in some cases, almost causing them to be rear-ended—a phenomenon called phantom braking.

The problem became so bad that Tesla was forced to remotely disable its cars' forward-collision warning and automatic emergency braking functions. The software update had erroneously put thousands of cars at risk.[16]

Within hours, Tesla canceled the update—for those who hadn't downloaded it yet—or reverted the software to the earlier version. Within two days, it decided it had to issue a formal recall, which it filed on October 29.[17] It was a textbook example of the perils of the new connected car era: how an overnight remote update from central command could subject Tesla owners to unanticipated risks.

Musk acknowledged the screw-up in a tweet.

"Seeing some issues with 10.3, so rolling back to 10.2 temporarily," he had written. "Please note, this is to be expected with beta software. It is impossible to test all hardware configs [configurations] in all conditions with internal QA [quality assurance], hence public beta."[18]

Musk's experience building space rockets had seemed to have taught him the value of failure—even of the catastrophic, highly public variety. And one could argue that the beta testers had been informed of the risks and made up their own minds. The only problem was the other people on the road who had not been informed and had not opted in.

People began to ask: Why should those who didn't sign up for it be put at risk? Why should they bear the responsibility of helping to train Tesla's vehicles? Regulators and safety experts pondered the implications.

Ralph Nader, the legendary consumer advocate and presidential candidate, author of *Unsafe at Any Speed: The Designed-In Dangers of the American Automobile* about the auto industry's flagrant disregard of safety standards decades ago, told me that Musk's approach was like nothing he had ever seen. "When he started allowing them on public highways, I said, 'What is going on here?' 'They own the government here.' The state government, federal government . . . I couldn't believe it."

With the lack of clear regulations around advanced driver-assistance systems, Tesla recognized—and exploited—a clear opening: it would be much harder to take Autopilot features away from paying customers once they were already in the hands of hundreds of thousands of users.

For Tesla drivers, the problems didn't end with an errant software update that had to be reversed.

In the months that followed, a growing number of complaints were lodged with NHTSA detailing a phenomenon that users might have previously thought to be isolated: Teslas suddenly jolting them back into their seats, abruptly braking for nonhazards—semitrucks in the opposite lane, for example. In one instance, Tesla owner Ben Morris said his 2021 Tesla Model Y slammed on the brakes on the highway, sending his children's unoccupied booster seats crashing into the car's front row.

"Although my 2017 Model X has phantom braked before, it is very rare, the vision-based system released May 2021 is night and day. We were seeing this behavior every day," he told the *Post* in an email.[19]

Phantom braking complaints had surged, rising to 107 over a three-month span, compared to 34 over the prior twenty-two months.[20]

That opened the floodgates.

Complaints piled into NHTSA as owners had confirmation of the problem that had been illustrated so dramatically by the October 2021 update. In the two weeks that followed the February 2022 *Post* report, NHTSA received around 250 additional reports about phantom braking in Teslas.

Now it had no choice. NHTSA opened an investigation into the phantom braking issue on February 16, 2022, affecting an estimated 416,000 vehicles.[21]

Musk had already taken a shot at the agency over another recall that week, calling NHTSA the "fun police."[22] For the time being, it appeared that regulators might really be closing in.

Despite all of its perceived hiccups, Tesla was riding "Full Self-Driving" to a wave of success in the markets and among the broader public.

More and more, people began to associate Tesla—not the traditional Big Tech companies deploying rolling science experiments—with self-driving.

The major tech companies were years away from unleashing their versions of autonomous vehicles on a wide scale, regulators were hesitant to weigh in one way or the other, and meanwhile, Musk had an enthusiastic group of supporters ready to beta test his software—training it on real-life roads—for free.

The enchantment began in October 2020 when Tesla first put the features into the hands of a select group of beta testers.[23] From there, fanboys and casual enthusiasts alike clamored for access to the release, lured by the Atari-style graphics on the cars' center screens in the early iterations of the software that was going to change the world. (It was hard to say what value the cool center-screen graphics added, but the visualizations that strayed closer to "edutainment" intrigued passengers and gave beta testers a glimpse of what their cars might be seeing, though they were hardly thorough.)

So Tesla implemented a safety test to evaluate whether others should qualify, studying the drivers' habits and scoring them on metrics such as abrupt braking and aggressive turning.[24]

It worked like this: with each release, Tesla lowered the safety threshold from those who maintained a 100, to 99, to 98, and so on.

Interested Tesla drivers practically drove on eggshells for a week, maneuvering as carefully as possible, avoiding speeding or harsh braking, and hesitating to make sudden movements in order to secure access. The safety score system allowed Tesla to slowly release the software to thousands of others with more confidence than a wide release might have given them. Soon, twelve thousand users had access, an exclusive group of supporters posting videos that painted the software in a good light—lest they be bumped. By 2022, Tesla had put Full Self-Driving into the hands of four hundred thousand users—a beta test on public roads that was larger than any autonomous vehicle pilot on earth.

Even so, as the enthusiasts and the broader public gained their coveted access to the software, they quickly learned that Full Self-Driving was far from achieved. Many abandoned the features quickly, finding they didn't make driving any easier; in fact, they sometimes made it more of a hassle, as drivers had to essentially chaperone their Autopilot-in-training through its mistakes.

The truth was that Full Self-Driving had many of the same capabilities as the competitor systems, with way fewer guardrails. And some of the videos used to demonstrate it by influencers such as Qazi—showing flawless journeys between picturesque locations—were staged in one way or another, just like the "Paint It Black" footage that, as Elluswamy's testimony showed, had been smoke and mirrors.

As he sat with federal investigators, Bernal recounted his experience in one of Tesla's most cutthroat departments.

By fall 2020, Tesla was trying to deliver on Musk's "Full Self-Driving" promise at full speed. The company had vastly expanded its staff of data labelers, onboarding hundreds of new workers—community college graduates, animators, aspiring game developers—for $22-per-hour jobs making Elon Musk's vision a reality. Initially, workers were sold on the notion of a fun, upbeat tech environment. By day two, however, the trainings took on a more serious tone.

Tesla had a "celebrity CEO," they were told, in Bernal's recollection, and legions of people wanted to see the company fail. The public must not know what goes on behind closed doors, and only Musk could speak for the company, with rare exceptions. Autopilot was Musk's favorite department, the workers were told, and they were likely to meet him given his regular visits.

That much was true.

Even as he juggled four different companies, Musk always carved out time for Autopilot. He saw the software as crucial to the future of Tesla; the company couldn't justify its valuation as a mere automaker. Musk called Full Self-Driving "the difference between Tesla being worth a lot of money and being worth basically zero."[25]

At rows of desks in a three-story office in San Mateo, the hard work of achieving autonomy was underway.

To call the job monotonous would be an understatement. The newly hired workers were suddenly immersed in a three-dimensional world, the numbers one through eight on their keyboards directing them to any one of a Tesla's eight onboard cameras. Their assignment was to label a ten-second clip. Using their arrow keys, they would flip through each frame of footage—more than thirty per second—and attempt to label three hundred images with pristine accuracy.

Workers sat for hours pinpointing every identifiable object within 150 meters of the vehicle—over and over and over—sometimes identifying five hundred or more objects per clip. And each object had to be labeled in every single frame, even if, say, the same mailbox appeared in each image across the entire clip.

"I probably would have to [make] ten thousand mouse clicks and key-stroke clicks for one clip to get submitted," Bernal said.

Soon, workers began to feel the full weight of Musk's "Full Self-Driving" promise. They were urged to work harder, faster, and more efficiently, as managers interpreted Musk's tweet-length promises as deadlines.

Meanwhile, Musk appeared to grow suspicious of the work-from-home flexibility that so many employers had extended to their staffers after the emergence of COVID-19—despite requiring his labelers to come into the office. That paranoia manifested in workplace surveillance systems, including one called HuMans, which might have drawn parallels to *The Terminator*'s Skynet if it were used in any other environment.[26]

The new software arrived toward the end of 2020 after many of the data labelers had been hired. Suddenly, they found that their computers were running a program that not only logged their keystrokes and mouse clicks; it also placed a timer on their image labeling, according to former Tesla employees.[27]

Workers recounted how if their mouse did not move for an allotted period of time, they could face discipline up to being fired.[28] When a labor group seeking to represent Tesla workers raised the matter, Tesla acknowledged in a blog post that it had been employing time monitoring. It did so "to improve the ease of use of our labeling software," adding that "its purpose is to calculate how long it takes to label an image."[29]

It was only a matter of time before these rigid demands started to take their toll.

"It led to vast amounts of errors," Bernal said. "People started to put quantity over quality."

Months after the surveillance software arrived, one of Musk's rash decisions created another challenge for those beleaguered staffers: without radar, Tesla's data labelers lost the ability to cross-reference sometimes blurry, low-resolution images against another data source. The granularity of the labeling—the level of detail the imagery could provide—was crucial to the whole endeavor. A lack of important context could foul the data set. (Tesla has said that its vehicles without radar have performed equally or better than before in certain measures of safety. "Compared to radar-equipped vehicles, Model 3 and Model Y with Tesla Vision have either maintained or improved their active safety ratings in the U.S. and Europe, and perform better in pedestrian automatic emergency braking [AEB] intervention," it says on its website.[30] In response to a post asking about Tesla's omission of radar, Musk said in 2022, "Only very high resolution radar is relevant.")[31]

Bernal described the internal monologue of a labeler and the sheer insanity of the task they had to take on.

"Is it a human? Is it a car? A truck—[a] dog? Dog with leash? Dog without leash? [Horse?] Human with saddle—no horse?"

For companies researching and deploying autonomous vehicles, San Francisco presented the ultimate test: a hilly labyrinth of narrow streets filled with pedestrians and bicycles, motorcyclists and skateboarders weaving through the commercial vans and box trucks in rush-hour traffic. Cars could encounter the latest cutting-edge wheeled contraption that the tech bros had newly discovered. Each steep hill and neighborhood might have a climate of its own.

For those trying to show off the capabilities of their test cars, Lombard Street, the city's famously winding road, with eight sharp curves down a steep one-block section in Russian Hill, emerged as a sort of proving ground.

But early on, Teslas were struggling to conquer it.

In October 2020, the month Tesla made Full Self-Driving available to key influencers and fanboys, a YouTuber known as Tesla Raj decided to put the software to the test there.

The experiment could hardly have gone worse.

The white Tesla struggled to negotiate the first bend, failing to slow as it approached the apex of the turn, prompting the test driver to intervene. It fared better on the next curve, but as it approached the third one, it failed to follow the road, nearly entering a side pathway.

At one point near the bottom of the hill, the car halted for nearly fifteen seconds as the driver, Tesla Raj, noted the glitching visuals on the screen: "It's tweaking out," he said.

The video amassed more than one hundred thousand views on You-Tube and was picked up by blogs such as *InsideEVs* and *Teslarati*.

Tesla Raj told *Teslarati* that his car "actually almost completed four hairpin turns, but the vehicle ended up not detecting a curb due to a driveway in the area," the blog noted.[32]

Such a problem would have been easier to solve were it not for the unique development approach taken by Tesla. With Full Self-Driving, Musk not only wanted to forgo expensive and complicated hardware and supply chain constraints; he also wanted the software to operate as simply as possible. That meant Full Self-Driving wouldn't rely on the type of high-definition maps used by companies such as Alphabet's Waymo and GM-funded Cruise, meticulously detailed schemas of operating environments that not only told cars to expect stop lights and intersections but also informed them of precise features such as storm drains, painted curbs, and driveways. Those competitor vehicles were confined to premapped operating environments where developers could be confident that they would not encounter much they had not been programmed to expect.

Musk saw this strategy as a crutch. He didn't want Teslas to be confined to elitist enclaves and tech utopias—rather, a Tesla purchased in Manhattan, Kansas, should be equipped to drive itself just as well on local roads as within the New York City borough of Manhattan.[33]

Though most understood that the Full Self-Driving software was still in a test form, mishaps like the one on Lombard Street tended to catch the attention of developers at Tesla overseeing the software—and their managers.

The engineers found themselves with a new assignment: code invisible software barriers over the driveways on Lombard Street, a manual perimeter that acted like bumpers straddling a bowling lane. That way, Tesla could avoid repeating the embarrassment in the future—knowing the importance of conquering this high-profile tourist landmark and proving ground.

Seeing the video clips that featured this extra layer of programming in T-Clips, Tesla's internal archive, Bernal began to feel uneasy.

He knew that wasn't how the software ordinarily worked.

The Lombard Street video was a unique instance of Full Self-Driving's flaws being publicly aired in its early days. During this crucial period when other companies were beginning to showcase and deploy their autonomous technology, key Tesla influencers were reminded of their role when it came to demonstrating the capabilities of Full Self-Driving.

"Please do not ask to be included in early beta releases and then complain," Musk once told a beta tester who had dared to offer feedback.[34]

It was yet another example of Tesla's sensitivity to public criticism and the limitations of Musk's approach to scientific and technical problems: What was the point of a beta test if not to heed and improve on feedback?

For Tesla to build a lead in the race to autonomy, people had to see a version of the software that didn't go haywire on highways, hesitate around windy roads, or crash into bike lane posts. For those who wanted to see Full Self-Driving conquering the roads, embarking on ambitious—and nearly flawless—trips across miles of scenic routes, there was no shortage of footage on Omar Qazi's YouTube page.

The titles of the videos speak for themselves: "Tesla Autopilot FSD Los Angeles to Silicon Valley Zero Interventions."[35] "First Drive with Tesla Full Self-Driving Beta 10.69: 35 minutes with zero takeovers in San Francisco."[36] Qazi's videos attracted large audiences. Hundreds of thousands observed the feats Full Self-Driving could perform as they watched him drive hundreds of miles without having to be nudged to pay attention.

As time went on, however, even Tesla enthusiasts began to question how well the software performed on Qazi's car, given the documented flaws with Full Self-Driving, its seeming inability to operate for extended periods of time without making a mistake that prompted driver intervention. Qazi seemed to be having an altogether different experience than the ordinary Full Self-Driving user.

"I don't think you're lying or exaggerating, but your experience with FSD is not the same as mine, not even close," wrote one skeptic. "That would lead some people to think you are exaggerating."[37]

And in the end, those drives—from the account enthusiastically embraced by Musk, where he sometimes shared news on new releases—were indeed too good to be true.[38]

In my interview with him, Qazi acknowledged that he had a way of circumventing Full Self-Driving's persistent interruptions, but he declined to explain what it was.

At around the time I spoke with Qazi, Kevin Smith, the Tesla fan who'd earlier had trouble with his Full Self-Driving software, posted a video alleging Qazi plugs a device into his car's OBD-II port that sends a recurring signal to adjust its allowed speed in Autopilot mode.[39] That would preempt Full Self-Driving's tendency to ask for driver confirmation to proceed in uncertain moments because the driver is effectively always telling the car to go ahead. (Qazi would all but confirm having turned to such a device around a year later when Tesla took steps to reduce how often it prompted drivers to pay attention—by relying more heavily on the vehicles' in-car camera.)[40]

In December 2024, Qazi confirmed to me that he had used the device to "connect into the Tesla internal communication network . . . and scroll the scroll wheel" that controlled the vehicle's speed in Autopilot mode "up and down at regular intervals."

"This would make the system think the wheel was being held," he said. "I didn't talk about this too much as I didn't want to encourage [people] to try and replicate it. I knew that I was watching carefully and would be ready to take over but didn't want others to abuse it."

Qazi explained his philosophy, telling me: "I believe attentive users like me have a right to circumvent these risks on their own car."

For Bernal, the fact that fanboys were putting their thumbs on the scales in this way was hardly surprising. But it was disheartening to learn that similar behavior was coming from inside the company too.

Soon, the fallout of Musk's rash decision-making was becoming clear to regulators and safety officials.

Teslas were behaving erratically as the company tested its novel vision-based approach on public roads, which resulted in more reports of crashes and near misses involving its driver-assistance system than regulators had ever seen.[41] The number of Teslas on the road was growing by the day, to be sure, but that presented more opportunities for such hazards to unfold; Tesla's share of driver-assistance crashes dwarfed every other automaker on the list.[42] In particular, regulators were alarmed by an emerging trend: the propensity of Teslas to crash into parked emergency vehicles with their emergency lights activated.[43]

Tesla, meanwhile, was shifting its strategy on labeling, increasingly automating those efforts as it struggled to contend with the stockpiles of data its cars were amassing. The company conducted a steep layoff at the San Mateo office in June 2022, cutting more than two hundred jobs and closing the site, *Bloomberg* reported.[44]

In October 2022, the US Department of Justice launched a criminal probe into Tesla's self-driving claims. Prosecutors were looking into Tesla's statements on its driver-assistance technology, sources told Reuters, including whether the company "misled consumers, investors and regulators by making unsupported claims" related to the technology.[45]

Musk, meanwhile, had fully soured on remote work and seemed to cast it as anathema to tech innovation. Musk had already said 2022 was a year of production and execution as opposed to new product launches, but investors were beginning to ask questions about his lagging Full Self-Driving promise and the long-delayed Cybertruck.[46]

In June 2022, Musk ordered his employees at Tesla and SpaceX back to the office.

"If you don't show up, we will assume you have resigned," his email to Tesla workers read. "There are of course companies that don't require this, but when was the last time they shipped a great new product?" he asked.[47]

Some weren't willing to put up with the new mandate and took it upon themselves to leave, I soon learned.

When Qazi asked Musk what he thought about those who considered in-person work an "antiquated concept," Musk replied, "They should pretend to work somewhere else."[48]

9

THE FUN POLICE

For a while, it seemed like nothing could stop the momentum of Elon Musk's self-driving plans—except the pace of technological development itself. Tesla was putting new features on the road faster than any legitimate authority could react. But by 2022, when activists like Dan O'Dowd and safety advocates such as Ralph Nader began publicly decrying how Musk was running roughshod over transportation regulators, the suits in Washington began to notice.

That seeming indifference from the nation's capital had been an affront to Nader and his longtime ally Joan Claybrook, who had lobbied for decades for better motor vehicle regulation, adopting the cause of seat belts, airbags, and basic safety protections that today's drivers and passengers now take for granted when they climb into their three-thousand-pound cars with thick door panels and accordion-like crumple zones. At the time, they faced seemingly insurmountable opposition: corporate executives practically worshipped as gods in Detroit, with a powerful lobby across media and advertising and allies in Washington.

That they had managed to beat the mighty automotive establishment—felling a stubborn and myopic foe, prevailing over a philosophy of deregulation that had swept across American government—was a testament to decades of persistent pressure that had seen its catalyst with the publication of Nader's famous work *Unsafe at Any Speed* in 1965.

Nearly a half-century later, in 2015, Nader, the venerated consumer advocate, and Claybrook, the one-time administrator of the National Highway Traffic Safety Administration (NHTSA) under the Carter administration, had a chance to effect change on the latest auto safety challenge.

Their motives were similar to what they had been in the past, though their foe had evolved, shifting from the auto plants in Detroit to the glass-walled tech hubs of Silicon Valley.

Nader and Claybrook were seated at a long wooden table in the boardroom at Public Citizen, the consumer advocacy nonprofit founded by Nader, in the bustling Dupont Circle neighborhood of Washington, DC. A painting of Robert F. Kennedy hung on the wall and light shone into the windows from Twentieth Street Northwest. Before them was the person with the most power to act on their concerns: Mark Rosekind, the head of the nation's top federal auto safety regulator under President Barack Obama.

Speaking to NHTSA's chief that day, Nader and Claybrook had a new worry: automakers and software developers were piloting experimental and dangerous technologies on public roads, deploying autonomous vehicles and driver-assistance technologies, such as Tesla's Autopilot, with little oversight from the federal government.

They asked Rosekind what he thought about the flood of technology piloting vehicles on American roads.

Rosekind was matter-of-fact in his reply.

"I have a two-word answer," he said, in Nader's recollection. "No data."

Nader and Claybrook were dumbfounded.

By 2016, Tesla had marked a grim milestone, one that could have put its self-driving ambitions at least momentarily on pause. In a blog post headlined "A Tragic Loss," the company announced what it called "the first known fatality in just over 130 million miles where Autopilot was activated."[1]

The crash that killed Joshua Brown was the first of three deadly wrecks over a three-year span that drew attention to the risks of using Tesla Autopilot at a time when the company was ramping up its emphasis on the technology it hoped would one day make self-driving a reality.[2] Brown's vehicle had failed to stop when a tractor-trailer pulled in front of it on US Route 27 in Williston, Florida. Tesla explained that "neither Autopilot nor the driver noticed the white side of the tractor trailer against a brightly lit sky, so the brake was not applied."[3] In the Brown crash, Musk had a parallel conversation with NHTSA to the one he'd have years later with Sumwalt, the National Transportation Safety Board (NTSB) chair.

Musk signaled that he believed officials' intervention would cost lives. In that instance, however, Musk aired another concern that caught the Washington establishment off guard: he was dealing with pressure from short-sellers. The insinuation seemed clear enough: The intervention from safety regulators would play into the hands of those who were betting against Tesla. It was the furthest thing from the regulators' minds. Three years later, Jeremy Banner died in an eerily similar crash that sheared the roof off his car in Delray Beach, Florida.[4] And then there was Walter Huang, the father and Apple engineer who'd bought his Model X SUV as a birthday gift. He was killed in March 2018 when his Tesla in Autopilot slammed into a concrete barrier on US Highway 101 in California.

When the NTSB investigated each crash, it emerged with similar recommendations: limiting Autopilot to conditions and locations for which it was designed to be used, meaning controlled-access highways and generally clear visibility. Some of its harshest criticism, meanwhile, was reserved for NHTSA, the top auto safety regulator, for taking a "hands-off" and "nonregulatory approach to automated vehicle safety," Reuters would report.[5]

Years earlier, Nader and Claybrook had foreseen the consequences of a lax approach to the regulation of driver-assistance systems: companies could be counted on to exploit the regulatory gray area in which their software resided, giving drivers access to features rooted in automation without explicitly crossing the line of officially billing their systems as autonomous.

As far as they were concerned, auto and tech companies' experiments with technology-driven cars were happening currently, with real consequences, on American roads. The lack of data sufficient to adopt new rules, they surmised, was a given—the companies were not going to cough up their most valuable asset without being forced to do so.

"You have subpoena power, you can get all this data," Nader recalled telling Rosekind. In fact, he said, the only way to gather enough data to drive decision-making at the federal level was to fight for it—otherwise, the companies would continue to control the narrative on self-driving and driver-assistance technologies.

"The bad data they're not going to publicize," Nader said. "They'll publicize the good data."

To Nader and Claybrook, NHTSA's soft-handed approach to the most crucial auto safety issue of the twenty-first century was puzzling. Congress had already diminished NHTSA's power through a combination of underfunding and statutory limitations.

"Criminal authority is the thing that really makes the industry behave," Claybrook told me. "Even Musk would behave."

But NHTSA had never really had that authority. Instead, the agency could levy steep penalties and, if needed, make referrals to the US Department of Justice to compel action on the part of automakers.[6]

During the early days of self-driving experimentation, the agency had championed a collaborative—as opposed to adversarial—approach, one rooted in learning and then evaluating the need for any action at the federal level. That went against what Nader and Claybrook knew about auto safety—you had to show the giants who was in charge.

Claybrook had met with Shoichiro Toyoda, the heir of the Toyota Motor Corporation, in 1978 and told him that NHTSA would help him develop an airbag if that was what it took, against fierce opposition from the automotive establishment. She had flown to Japan with three engineers to make a personal appeal to the then-executive VP of the firm, whose footprint had been growing in the United States amid the oil crisis.

"Dr. [Shoichiro] Toyoda told me they didn't know how to develop an airbag. . . . That just completely outraged me," she said.

She turned back to Toyoda.

"I said, 'The engineers at NHTSA are going to show you how,'" she recalled. "I said, 'My engineers will stay here as long as it takes.'"

Toyota, of course, knew exactly how to manufacture a vehicle with airbags—but NHTSA at the time had enough expertise to sniff out the company's plea of ignorance, Claybrook recalled.

Now the agency, hampered by underfunding, was deprived of that sort of institutional knowledge—and gravitas. NHTSA had gradually de-emphasized its focus from auto manufacturers to individual drivers, seeking to improve driver behavior, as noted in a Vanderbilt University Law School publication, which cited the analysis "The Invisible Driver of Policing" in the *Stanford Law Review*.[7] That led to a reliance on pretextual police traffic stops to enforce auto safety, which was "but one example of an administrative agency using criminal law enforcement over regulatory measures to achieve their goals."[8]

"Established with the Department of Transportation in 1970, NHTSA initially used its authority to require auto manufacturers to improve vehicle design," the Vanderbilt Law School write-up said. "In the early 1990s, traffic fatalities were on the rise, along with injury-causing crashes and total crashes. Yet, the political climate dissuaded the agency from a rulemaking focus on auto manufacturers. The agency also faced budget cuts."

Now, in stark contrast to its established purpose, NHTSA even lacked the confidence to properly assess a risk on public roads, in the eyes of the transportation safety advocates. And in Washington, where the climate of deregulation has persisted for decades, there was little political will under the tech-friendly Obama administration to impose restrictions on Silicon Valley.

This ran counter to the approach taken by NHTSA decades before.

"I was extremely aggressive and pushing the companies and putting them on the defense if they opposed putting airbags in their cars because it just didn't make any sense," Claybrook said. "I didn't even think about it," she said of the idea of a collaborative, learning-based approach. "To me the issue was, 'I had the authority to issue this rule, I'm going to issue this rule.'"

Shortly after Nader and Claybrook's meeting with Rosekind, NHTSA took a new approach to driver-assistance features, one that was largely unprecedented in the agency's history of rule-making. Rosekind had grown concerned about the rapid pace of technological development and the potential for automakers to unleash new features on the roads. Knowing the clock was ticking and with elections looming in 2016, Rosekind took his appeal for new safety standards in a different direction.

In March 2016, NHTSA announced it had secured a commitment from twenty automakers, including Tesla, in which they would include automatic emergency braking on nearly all of their vehicles by September 2022.[9] Crucially, as a letter signed by Claybrook highlighted, the agreement did not take the form of an enforceable rule. Rather, as she and other signees alleged, NHTSA had engaged in a "radical departure from the regulatory process enacted by Congress fifty years ago."[10] The message was clear: NHTSA had been neutered, rendered impotent and irrelevant by its inability to establish rules for the burgeoning auto technology industries to follow.

As Claybrook put it, Rosekind "abandoned the authority of his office to issue rules in favor of this voluntary approach."

It was against this backdrop that Tesla and Musk rolled out their "Paint It Black" demonstration touting "Full Self-Driving Hardware on All Teslas," kicking off a yearslong pursuit of making cars already in the hands of thousands of consumers autonomous.

Rosekind's admission that NHTSA didn't have the data it needed may have been excusable in 2015. But six years later, NHTSA was still in the dark, as Tesla was rolling out increasingly sophisticated software to tens of thousands of new vehicles without a second thought.

The Trump administration had done the agency few favors by dawdling—depriving it of a permanent administrator—in the intervening period. Inside the agency during that time, NHTSA's leadership grappled with Tesla's ability to push out technology, in the form of over-the-air updates, faster than regulators could possibly keep up, one former official familiar with the matter told me. Musk's strategy benefited from the lag time between new software's release and efforts to regulate it.

"His business model is [to] be out there doing it before they catch and tell you to stop," the former official told me.

By 2021 NHTSA was still without the data that Rosekind had said years ago was elusive.[11] NHTSA had examined more than a dozen crashes involving Teslas where Autopilot was suspected to have been in use at the time, but it lacked a consistent mechanism for learning of such crashes when they took place.

Dr. Steven S. Cliff, tapped by President Biden to head the agency after four years of inertia during the Trump administration, resolved to obtain that data.

Cliff, who counts a doctorate in chemistry among his extensive academic credentials, came to the agency at a time when questions were swirling around Tesla's marketing of Full Self-Driving as media inquiries were filling the inboxes of press representatives—and Tesla was by far the most asked-about entity under its supervision.

Some of that had to do with Musk and his larger-than-life persona and the media's obsession with his every move. Even so, Tesla seemed to openly exploit the lack of government regulation regarding its technology, baiting officials into action with its audacity.

A key example that would emerge soon after: programming its cars to not fully halt at stop signs, a "rolling stop" feature that violated motor vehicle laws in states across the country. This was the kind of prima facie breach of the rules that a more aggressive NHTSA would present as a slam-dunk case.

Cliff began to realize that Musk's approach to his products was rooted in a laissez-faire philosophy that relied on personal responsibility, entrusting users in a way that effectively cornered regulators in the absence of explicit laws relevant to the tech.

He summed up Musk's outlook as: "Look, you're an adult. I'm not going to babysit you and I have a job to do ... which is, make things that you desire or want or need. And I'm going to trust that you're adult enough to know how to use that product in a way that you deem is safe."

That approach neglected to take into account those who hadn't shelled out tens of thousands of dollars to own one of Tesla's luxury electric vehicles.

"Tesla has decided to take these much greater risks with the technology because they have this sense that it's like, Well, you can figure it out. You can determine for yourself what's safe'—without recognizing that other road users don't have that same choice," Cliff told me for a *Post* story. "If you're a pedestrian, [if] you're another vehicle on the road, do you know that you're unwittingly an object of an experiment that's happening?"[12]

Of course, Tesla loaded its products with disclaimers and disclosures that seemed to be aimed at absolving it of any liability for how customers would use its software. Tesla's Model 3 owner's manual lists conditions under which Autosteer—a key feature of Autopilot—is not intended to operate. They include when "lane markings are excessively worn, have visible previous markings, have been adjusted due to road construction, are changing quickly (lanes branching off, crossing over, or merging), objects or landscape features are casting strong shadows on the lane markings, or the road surface contains pavement seams or other high-contrast lines." Adverse weather could also pose a problem, including circumstances when "visibility is poor (heavy rain, snow, fog, etc.) or weather conditions are interfering with sensor operation." Sunny conditions, too, could prove an impediment, such as when "bright light (such as direct sunlight) is interfering with the view of the camera(s)."[13] Teslas might also be thrown off by following the vehicle in front of them too closely, blocking the view of the cameras.

Another potential obstacle was driving on hills. The problem is immediately clear: if a driver were to disable Autopilot in every instance where it would not perform optimally, using the system might be more trouble than it was worth.

There was also a key warning for the Traffic-Aware Cruise Control system, another feature of the Autopilot suite, that many Tesla owners might have wanted to know beforehand. "Traffic-Aware Cruise Control may react to vehicles or objects that either do not exist, or are not in your lane of travel, causing Model 3 to slow down unnecessarily or inappropriately."[14]

Cliff was unconvinced that the fine print alone would be enough to rein in potential abusers of the system.

On day one, Cliff knew Tesla would become a key focus of his work at NHTSA, a break with years of past administrators (and acting administrators) who had seemingly regarded the Tesla problem as a mere nuisance, a sideshow at best.

Cliff soon learned something that quickly became clear to anybody in Tesla's orbit—the company operated unlike any other auto firm under his purview.

When the Biden White House announced his nomination, Cliff received letters of support from a wide range of respected industry leaders, such as Bill Ford, chairman of the most storied American automaker. He also received a nod of support from Tesla, though it hardly read as one.

One day after his nomination, one of the company's policy officials, a leader charged with managing relationships in Washington, gave him a call. "I just want you to know we're not going to do anything to try and upset your confirmation," he recalled the official telling him.

Cliff was amused by this lack of self-awareness; didn't the person realize that public criticism from a company like Tesla could actually serve to expedite his nomination, showing he was the type of tough leader that Elon Musk's company feared? In any case, while the call didn't cross any lines, the subtext seemed to suggest that Tesla wasn't a company to aggravate.

Meanwhile, he had already started working at NHTSA as acting administrator, with an eye toward the company practically from the start. Unlike his predecessors, Cliff was keen to get to the bottom of the Tesla question.

"I really wanted to understand was there [something] there or is this just: the media is focused on Tesla crashes because of Elon or for whatever reason," Cliff said. "I think what we found was 'no, there was some there, there.'"

In June 2021, NHTSA issued its first major rule on automated features that was directly relevant to Teslas using Autopilot: a standing general order requiring automakers and tech companies to report data on crashes involving self-driving and driver-assistance systems on public roads, disclosing major crashes—such as those with a fatality or serious injury—within one day.[15] Cliff wanted to know what he was dealing with, and requiring the automakers and deployers of self-driving software to produce their data when something went wrong seemed like the best place to start.

Of course, he knew that Tesla would make up a sizeable proportion of the data collected. But he wasn't trying to target any specific company. He simply wanted to solve the problem Rosekind had first identified six years earlier.

"We didn't have the data, so it's like, "Well, how do I gather the data?"" Cliff recalled. "I want it quickly. How do I get it quickly? . . . Well, you could do an order and then you would serve that order to these companies."

Cliff had an idea of what the data might show as far as one particular automaker was concerned, but he kept an open mind.

Tesla had no choice but to comply or risk penalties that could stretch over $100 million and a referral to the Department of Justice.[16]

Even with the data suddenly flowing into his agency, Cliff couldn't have predicted what he'd learn in the coming months about the experiment unfolding on the roads: Tesla was programming its vehicles to break the law. The issues came to his attention as NHTSA reviewed aspects of Tesla's Full Self-Driving Beta feature.[17]

As Tesla's software became more sophisticated in Musk's pursuit of "self-driving," the company soon stumbled into an industry-wide problem: the computers weren't driving like humans would. Cars could be coded to follow instructions, but it was much harder to program them to have common sense. Silcon Valley residents encountering self-driving cars had come across this phenomenon repeatedly over the years—vehicles behaving uncertainly, driving like "geriatrics," or lurching through turns as if following a series of herky-jerky vectors rather than maneuvering in ways that might be second nature to a human driver.[18]

Tesla set out to solve this problem by allowing drivers to select from one of three driving styles when using Full Self-Driving: "chill," "average," or "assertive."[19]

"Chill" mode was already familiar to Tesla drivers who didn't want to sicken their passengers with the cars' punchy acceleration; it offered a smoother launch so cars didn't bolt off the line. For Full Self-Driving users, the "chill" setting would also maintain a healthy cushion of following distance between traffic and limit lane changes.

"Assertive," by contrast, "drives with more urgency," as Tesla put it.[20] Of course, the company wasn't suggesting that users should program their cars to be "assertive" and then kick back and do the crossword.

A neat and concise disclaimer covered Tesla's responsibility in all of this: "Full Self-Driving (Beta) is a hands-on feature. Keep your hands on the steering wheel at all times, be mindful of road conditions and surrounding traffic, and always be prepared to take immediate action. Failure to follow these instructions could cause damage, serious injury or death. It is your responsibility to familiarize yourself with the limitations of Full Self-Driving (Beta) and the situations in which it may not work as expected."[21]

But the intention of "assertive" mode was clear: no longer would the uncertain and hesitant computer-driven car belie its lack of confidence navigating the roads; a Tesla driven in "assertive" mode would behave more like someone late to an appointment in Los Angeles traffic.

Tesla even added a function that would implement rolling stops so its cars wouldn't halt fully at stop signs, treating controlled four-way intersections as mere suggestions.

The blog *InsideEVs* captured the descriptions of "average" and "assertive" modes.[22] In average mode, a Tesla would "have a medium follow distance and may perform rolling stops," it said (it was that last part that caught the attention of regulators). Assertive mode went even further. In that setting, a Tesla would "have a smaller follow distance, perform more frequent speed lane changes, will not exit passing lanes and may perform rolling stops."[23]

Tesla had handed NHTSA its rationale to intervene on a silver platter; this driving practice was generally codified as a moving violation. Confronted with the knowledge that Tesla was directly programming its cars to break traffic laws, Cliff's agency had no choice but to step in.

By that time in early 2022, safety concerns about Tesla were becoming so common that regulators were holding weekly meetings on the status of the various investigations into the company. There was an extensive probe into Teslas' propensity to slam into flashing emergency vehicles and another that looked into drivers' ability to play video games on the car's large center screen while operating their cars, evaluating the "driver distraction potential" of a feature that had once been limited to vehicles in park.[24]

It was during one of these regular briefings in the hybrid days of the post-pandemic workplace when regulators and NHTSA enforcement staff gathered on Zoom that the newly pressing subject came up: Teslas were being programmed to roll through stop signs as if they weren't even there.

Senior executives were dumbfounded at the audacity of programming cars to break the law.

"It was like, 'What?' " Cliff recalled.

His team found the report to be valid, and staffers huddled with lawyers to discuss the relevant laws and settle on an approach for tackling the issue. The legal theory behind going after Tesla on the matter was pretty simple.

"I'm not aware of any state where that's permitted," Russ Martin, senior director of policy and government relations with the Governors Highway Safety Administration, told the *Post* at the time.[25]

Tesla may have been programming its vehicles to act like human drivers, but in the process, the company was introducing what NHTSA saw as a collision risk. The cars could cruise through an intersection at up to 5.6 mph when they should be making complete stops.[26]

NHTSA and Tesla officials met twice in January to discuss the issue, allowing officials to learn more and determine how it could be resolved.[27] And Cliff's agency ultimately advised that the feature was going to lead to a recall. With no reasonable defense, the company agreed to stand down. Even so, Tesla seemed to defend having programmed its vehicles to perform rolling stops, noting in the recall report that the company was "not aware of any collisions, injuries or fatalities related to this condition," which specified that a vehicle must be approaching an all-way stop, with no "relevant moving cars, . . . pedestrians or bicyclists . . . near the intersection" to undertake the maneuver.[28]

Tesla voluntarily agreed to a recall on January 20, 2022, ultimately deciding to address the issue with a software update to some fifty thousand vehicles.[29] (The memory stuck with Musk. "Safety first, then the convenience features," Musk told a customer asking that Teslas be allowed "to break the law at stop signs," in July 2024. "Some of this stuff like the rolling stop is technically illegal, so NHTSA gets upset, but 99% of people do it," Musk wrote.[30] Even so, regulators couldn't stand for haphazard adherence to road laws in automated features; weren't computers supposed to help make the roads safer, in part by following the rules better than humans?)

It wouldn't be the last time Tesla was brought to heel by a process that became NHTSA's most vital tool for bringing a rogue automaker in line.

NHTSA ultimately settled on recalls as the best mechanism to rein in Tesla's excesses because of how the agency's authority was designed. After coming to the agency in 2021, Cliff sought to better understand the tools at his disposal, and he soon realized the power of the recall authority, he told me.

It wasn't the proactive and sweeping regulation that Nader—and even some political officials—sought. And recalls were hardly a way to fully shift the industry's course away from the automation-rooted direction it was taking, either. To his credit, Cliff was also skeptical of choosing this solution: What if the technology ultimately ended up saving lives? But he realized that recalls could at least help the government pump the brakes on developments that put the public at risk.

"You can gather data, you can regulate, you can enforce, or you can use a bully pulpit so to speak," Cliff said. A peer agency, the NTSB, the top federal safety investigator, tended to use the bully pulpit to force compliance given its lack of regulatory authority. NHTSA, meanwhile, was occasionally hamstrung by the necessity of long lead times to gather data, a lack of political will to implement new regulations, and the overwhelming demands on its enforcement team—which led to an at-times reactive posture.

That's where the recalls came in.

"That recall tool is very powerful," Cliff told me. "What Congress knew when they were putting out the [National Traffic and Motor] Vehicle Safety Act together, [is there's] no way they can anticipate every problem that can occur. That's where that recall authority came from."

It was kryptonite to Tesla's rapid development speed, which had for years caught regulators flatfooted.

As Tesla foisted new and unique hazards onto public roads at a rapid clip, NHTSA had found a way to bring the company back to earth.

Five days after publicly dinging Tesla for its rolling stops, NHTSA announced another recall. The agency had learned that Tesla's software-driven cars were sometimes failing to chime to remind their owners to put on their seat belts, a complication of the cars' always-on nature. Tesla explained that the "driver seat belt reminder chimes may fail to reset after sounding a reminder, and may not sound upon the next vehicle start cycle," an issue NHTSA said ran afoul of federal motor vehicle regulations.[31] (Tesla said it remedied the problem by issuing an over-the-air update "that corrects the software error," bringing the vehicles into compliance.)

The very next day, following the notification about seat belt chimes, NHTSA flagged a new issue, announcing on February 2 that certain Tesla models were being recalled because their windshields might not properly defrost.

As an official explained to me at the time, the windshield issue was an example of NHTSA finding a way to use its authority under federal regulations to address problems that sometimes affected owners in other ways.[32]

The core issue of the matter was this: Tesla owners were shivering in their cars. On January 12, less than a month before the recall, the website

Electrek published a story explaining how newly installed heat pumps were struggling to warm the cars' cabins in freezing temperatures.[33]

It was an issue the company claimed to have addressed with a software update a year prior, *Electrek* reported. But now, the site carried the headline: "Tesla Owners Are Again Losing Heat in Extreme Cold as Some Heat Pumps Are Failing Badly."

So it was no coincidence that NHTSA cited the heat pump when announcing a recall on nearly twenty-seven thousand Teslas less than a month later, explaining that a "software error may cause a valve in the heat pump to open unintentionally and trap the refrigerant inside the evaporator, resulting in decreased defrosting performance."[34] It just so happened that the issue had also caused Tesla to run afoul of a federal regulation requiring windshield defogging and defrosting, allowing officials to step in and oversee a fix. Tesla again remedied the matter via an over-the-air software update, it said.

As if three recalls in the span of a week wasn't enough—more, for some models, than had occurred throughout the entirety of the Trump administration—NHTSA posted another announcement that Friday: more than 578,000 Teslas were being recalled. At issue was a feature known as "Boombox."[35]

One concern with early battery-powered vehicles was that people couldn't hear them coming, which proved to be a problem for pedestrians. A federal regulation established in 2016 mandated an "alert sound" at lower speeds, where tire and wind noise alone would not signal that a vehicle was coming.[36] Of course, Tesla wasn't just going to equip its cars with external sound capabilities to comply with federal regulations and call it a day. That would be too sensible—and *boring*.

Since 2020, Tesla had equipped its vehicles with the Boombox feature, which let owners blast external sounds from their cars, such as the jingle of an ice cream truck, fart noises, or prolonged belches, all with a press of the horn.[37]

It was all in good fun.

The only problem was that the quirky noises could drown out a pedestrian warning sound, and a bystander might not immediately associate them with an approaching vehicle—violating the federal regulation that necessitated the external speaker in the first place.[38]

Tesla had to issue an over-the-air update—requiring the car to be in park before the Boombox sounds could be activated.

Musk had kept uncharacteristically quiet as four recalls were issued over eight days. It took a Twitter user's question to flush him out.

Responding on February 12 to a post asking why Tesla recalled Boombox, Musk replied: "The fun police made us do it (sigh)."[39]

Cliff regarded his new moniker as a badge of honor, a sign that his approach was working.

For all the criticism it had invited from activists, Rosekind's collaborative approach eventually bore fruit. By late 2023, each of the automakers that had made the pledge to install automatic emergency braking on the vast majority of their fleets had done so, with some of them—namely, Tesla—meeting the target well before the initial 2022 deadline.[40] The progress culminated in NHTSA's 2024 announcement that AEB must be standard in passenger vehicles by 2029.[41] NHTSA's initial 2016 agreement with the twenty automakers had contained a tacit admission: "NHTSA estimates that the agreement will make AEB standard on new cars three years faster than could be achieved through the formal regulatory process."[42] It wasn't that regulation was impossible. Rather, there was a question of political and institutional will to address safety hazards.

Ralph Nader saw the nuisance that Teslas were becoming, the frequent recalls and investigations and what he regarded as the potential carnage unleashed by Full Self-Driving on public roads. He decided he had to step in. On August 10, 2022, he issued a public statement calling on regulators to act:

"Tesla's major deployment of so-called Full Self-Driving (FSD) technology is one of the most dangerous and irresponsible actions by a car company in decades," Nader said. "This nation should not allow this malfunctioning software which Tesla itself warns may do the 'wrong thing at the worst time' on the same streets where children walk to school. Together we need to send an urgent message to the casualty-minded regulators that Americans must not be test dummies for a powerful, high-profile corporation and its celebrity CEO. No one is above the laws of manslaughter."[43]

10

THE COST OF BUYING TWITTER

Even as the scrutiny from Washington mounted, Tesla was riding a high into the end of 2021. In November of that year, its shares hit a historical peak of more than $400, taking it to a valuation of more than $1 trillion. Investors like Ross Gerber would have been happy to see their celebrity CEO double down on his commitment to the biggest automotive success story of the twenty-first century, but Elon Musk had other ideas.

In the early weeks of 2022, Musk—newly flush with cash from selling billions' worth of Tesla stock to cover a massive tax bill—began an aggressive push to acquire shares of Twitter.[1] At first, he did so quietly, buying a little each day at prices around $32 to $40 per share. But through forty-three transactions beginning on January 31, Musk had begun to accumulate a sizeable stake in the social media platform that he believed held outsized power in the global conversation, as his interactions with his circle showed.

"Given that Twitter serves as the de facto public town square, failing to adhere to free speech principles fundamentally undermines democracy. What should be done?" Musk asked on March 26, following a Twitter poll he'd launched a day earlier where 70 percent of respondents indicated they believed the platform did not adhere to principles of free speech.[2]

"The consequences of this poll will be important. Please vote carefully," he had written on March 25.[3]

Now he was asking another question: "Is a new platform needed?"[4]

It wasn't until April 4 that the endgame became clear. According to a filing with the Securities and Exchange Commission (SEC), Musk now held enough shares to become the company's largest individual shareholder.

His stake of more than 9 percent meant he was serious—enough to be in play for a board seat at least, but the way Musk was talking, his involvement wasn't likely to end there.[5]

As word of Musk's investment started spreading that spring, one conclusion seemed inevitable: Elon Musk was going to buy Twitter. But he wasn't going to do it alone.

Around Silicon Valley, word of Musk's plan to take over the social media site traveled fast. It would be nothing short of a historical first: a practically crowdfunded takeover of the social media site that dominated internet discourse—including media, sports, technology, politics, celebrity gossip, and more—and a chance to buy into a wildly popular service at full maturity, but at the ground floor.

But the cost of doing so was quickly becoming clear. Twitter had been trading at around $40 per share, and now that Musk's involvement was public, it was set to rally. If he wanted to move forward, he would have to leverage some of his valuable stake in Tesla in exchange for the popular and high-profile but barely solvent and chronically mismanaged social media company. Outside investors and analysts had only one question: Why?

"You're giving away caviar to buy a hot dog on the street in New York City," Wedbush Securities analyst Dan Ives described it to *The Washington Post* at the time.[6]

There seemed to be only one explanation for the bid: Musk was buying influence. But even so, why would he encourage the involvement of so many partners who would surely want to recoup their investments?

Yet Musk's emerging partners in the deal could hardly see the risk from the dollar signs flashing before their eyes. They believed their money was safe with the man who was putting rockets in space and making electric cars cool. Many different parties saw an opportunity in the bid: political ideologues on the Right could foist an agenda on a crucial tool of public discourse, Musk's core group of close friends and investors could ride his track record of success to profits, repressive foreign regimes could hold crucial sway over his decision-making, and a new class—a rapidly solidifying group of retail-level investors who saw Musk as either a hero or a useful tool—saw an opportunity to profit off the venture for themselves. This was a chance to buy into Elon Musk's empire.[7]

At the peak of Musk's wealth and fame, the Twitter saga revealed his power transparently—and directly—before the world.

Musk could court billions with a simple text.

"Any interest in participating in the Twitter deal?" he texted his buddy Larry Ellison, the Oracle cofounder whom Musk counted as a close friend.

"Yes," replied Ellison, "of course," followed by a thumbs-up.

"Cool," Musk replied.[8]

A billion had been secured.

Musk similarly courted LinkedIn cofounder Reid Hoffman, a connection from the PayPal days, who was a partner at the venture capital firm Greylock. He explained how he'd receive priority in the deal as "a friend," and that VC money would be welcome.[9]

The Technoking was at work. Old friends and associates appeared from out of the woodwork with their own requests: Would Musk consider their candidate for CEO? Could they get a seat on the board or maybe a position as an adviser? Was he looking for engineers? Even a Saudi prince bowed, as Alwaleed bin Talal Al Saud—initially skeptical, believing that Musk's $54.20 per share price for Twitter was too low—fought "to stay in" the company, rolling over his and Kingdom Holding Company's $1.9 billion stake to become its second-largest shareholder.[10]

Others fawned over their new leader.

"When do I start boss" came one text following the announcement of the deal.[11] It came from someone Musk had asked to serve as a strategic adviser. If anything, the text messages revealed in subsequent court proceedings showed the extent to which the Silicon Valley frat house, eager to score investment gains or influence or both, knew the value of cozying up to the alpha in their ranks. The brown-nosing was bad enough that sites like *TechCrunch* did roundups of the "cringiest" texts in the trove.[12]

Musk was also a sudden sounding board for ideas about new directions that Twitter could take.

Two key advisers wanted him to move the company's headquarters out of San Francisco, which had become the right-wing archetype of a failed Democratic-run city. For the time being, Musk was willing to give San Francisco, which had propelled him to the heights of success, a chance.

Meanwhile, conservatives urged him to immediately restore the banned account of former president Donald Trump.

Musk indicated that he knew that a right-wing Twitter made for a doomed business strategy.

"Twitter is obviously not going to be turned into some right wing nuthouse," he wrote to former Clinton associate Michael Kives, a well-connected cofounder of investment firm K5 Global. "Aiming to be as broadly inclusive as possible. Do the right thing for the vast majority of Americans."[13]

Musk had an answer for everyone, demonstrating his populist appeal.

Ideologically motivated advisers such as David Sacks, Musk's "PayPal Mafia" associate who would emerge as part of the political conscience of his Twitter takeover, could realize their dreams of saving Twitter from left-wing management influence, disgraced Silicon Valley operatives could turn to their pal Elon for a second chance, others could simply make promising investments, while still others could bet on Musk to see their vision of a public square through to fruition.

Some would just join Musk for the ride.

"I REALLY hope you get Twitter," wrote Joe Rogan, the massively popular podcaster who'd increasingly found himself in Musk's circle. "If you do, we should throw a hell of a party." Musk replied with a "100" emoji.[14]

The Twitter investors were hardly a monolith. It wasn't just tech titans like Ellison who wanted in on the deal. Silicon Valley venture capital firms like Andreessen Horowitz and Sequoia were ready to contribute, as was the crypto trading site Binance, which had been founded in China. Joining Alwaleed and Kingdom Holding Company was the Qatar Investment Authority, rounding out more than $2 billion worth of foreign investment in the deal. Jack Dorsey, Twitter's cofounder and former CEO, would roll over an approximately $1 billion stake as well.[15]

For those who wanted in, no matter how close they were to Musk or how important their participation was to the deal, the process of kicking off an investment started the same way: signing a nondisclosure agreement, an increasingly common Musk tool as his profile grew, wielded by his bankers at Morgan Stanley to ensure the silence of all parties involved in the transaction.

Ellison had spoken privately with Musk, and by early May, he was learning what an investment in a Musk-run Twitter would look like. For the price of a cool $1 or $2 billion, he would be entrusting Musk with total control over the company. Musk would step in, at least temporarily, as Twitter CEO.

Like other investors, Ellison would have no direct power over internal decision-making or rights to a seat on a private Twitter board.

But in exchange for his money, Musk was promising a steep return on his investment. This would be achieved through a mix of cost cutting and aggressive monetization. Musk would seek to replicate the successes of Tesla, where he charged star teams of engineers to solve difficult problems, and cut out the bloat that he regarded as an impediment to the mission of a "free speech" platform.

This was the deal that ignited an all-out feeding frenzy across Silicon Valley, one that stretched deeper into New York investment banking, the Arab oil economy, crypto, and even the music industry, where Musk's team had secured funding from record mogul Sean "Diddy" Combs.[16]

Although Musk is often regarded as the richest person on earth, his finances are famously illiquid, meaning they are tied up in the stock of his companies—namely, Tesla, the company in which he held around a 20 percent stake at the time of his Twitter bid.[17] Each sale of that stock had the potential to erode investor confidence, meaning Musk couldn't easily convert his stock to spendable currency.

Take, for example, the most significant haul of cash to find its way into Musk's coffers during this period: the sale of more than $15 billion worth of stock in 2021 as Musk faced a massive upcoming tax bill.

The Wall Street Journal detailed the impact on Tesla's stock of a string of sales that had publicly commenced when Musk launched a Twitter poll on whether to sell.

"Tesla's shares slumped after Mr. Musk began his selling last month," the *Journal* wrote. "The stock, which closed up 7.49% on Wednesday at $1,008.87, is down more than 17% from the day Mr. Musk took the Twitter poll."[18]

In other words (and for lack of better ones), Musk was cash-poor, and the allocation of his assets has not shifted significantly as of this writing, even as his fortune has ballooned.

And that was before accounting for his loans. Buried inside Tesla's financial filings is a peculiar disclosure, one that likely wouldn't fly for most corporate CEOs, but it served as legal boilerplate for Musk.

"We are not a party to these loans, which are partially secured by pledges of a portion of the Tesla common stock currently owned by Mr. Musk," Tesla said. "If the price of our common stock were to decline substantially, Mr. Musk may be forced by one or more of the banking institutions to sell shares of Tesla common stock to satisfy his loan obligations if he could not do so through other means. Any such sales could cause the price of our common stock to decline further."[19]

Musk had pledged massive amounts of his Tesla stock—at times, more than half—as collateral to secure loans.[20] That tied his fate to Tesla's stock performance in more ways than one and put him in a bind when it came to dipping into his "crown jewel," as one analyst put it to me for a *Post* story, to make the Twitter purchase possible.

It was a vicious cycle: every time Musk put Tesla money toward Twitter, he risked an erosion of investor confidence, potentially driving down the price of Tesla shares. If Tesla shares fell by enough, bankers could come calling, asking him to sell shares—or perhaps pledge more collateral—to secure his loans. The more Tesla was collateralized, or the more its fate was tied to Twitter, the more reason for investors to question whether the electric car company's sky-high valuation was justified.

Musk was playing a dangerous game. That's where his friends and longtime associates came in, floating vast sums of money, tens or hundreds of millions, even billions, to cover the bill. His Morgan Stanley bankers Michael Grimes and Kate Claassen did the heavy lifting while Musk courted investors over the phone.

Faced with this barrage of wealth being thrown his way, Musk had to draw the line somewhere. When his banker Michael Grimes inquired about a potential investment from Sam Bankman-Fried, the now-disgraced founder of crypto exchange FTX, Musk sent a prescient reply.

"Does Sam actually have $3B liquid?" he asked.[21]

In the early months of 2022, Musk had largely accumulated his Twitter shares for around $35, which eventually netted a stake of around 9 percent in the company. But wanting to move fast in April 2022, he floated a final price well above the market rate, what he called his "best and final offer," which doubled as a weed joke: $54.20 per share.[22]

Musk was adamant that his offer was more than fair.

"I am not playing the back-and-forth game," he told Twitter's then-chair, according to an SEC filing. "I have moved straight to the end."[23]

His offer of $54.20 was "a high price and your shareholders will love it," he said over the phone, though he would have to reconsider his position as a shareholder if it were turned down. "This is not a threat, it's simply not a good investment without the changes that need to be made."

Musk was making an argument that it wasn't enough to have mere influence over Twitter through a minority stake, even if it was enough to secure a board seat; he'd need to be at the wheel.

An April 20 filing with the SEC, made public the following day, outlined how Musk planned to execute his bid to buy Twitter for that price. He had secured a commitment of $13 billion in financing from Morgan Stanley and other banks in addition to a $12.5 billion margin loan against his own wealth. That constituted more than $25 billion in borrowing to fund the operation.[24]

The balance was going to be covered by Musk, the filing said, through an equity commitment. Musk was going to commit approximately $21 billion of his money—largely derived from shares in Tesla—to the purchase of Twitter. For notoriously spending-averse Musk, who has couch-surfed with friends at crucial periods in his life, that type of financial commitment was a tall order. But it seemed the pursuit of "free speech" was worth it.[25]

Musk was essentially giving Twitter an IOU stating that he was good for the rest of the money, and they could proceed with a transaction on that basis. He would have to hand over the $21 billion—or its equivalent in equity—at closing.[26]

Musk was massively wealthy by any measure, and his behavior funding his Twitter stake outlined how such large sums can beget fortunes of their own. He had been accumulating his Twitter stake for weeks, but by delaying the disclosure—which would have been required when he became a 5 percent investor on March 14, as revealed in a later filing—he benefited from buying Twitter shares at a lower price than he likely would have had his involvement been public. The *Post* quantified how much he had netted by doing so: $156 million.[27]

As the *Post* wrote: "After his disclosure, Twitter's share price rose roughly 30 percent and is now above $50 per share."

"Was he ignorant or knowledgeable that he was violating securities law?" asked David Kass, a University of Maryland finance professor, the paper went on to report.

The Wall Street Journal reported in May that the SEC was investigating Musk over the late disclosure, in a matter that is yet to be resolved at the time of this writing in early 2025.[28] Musk publicly blasted the SEC's attempt to settle the case, which examined potential securities fraud, in December 2024, posting a letter in which his attorney asked whether the probe might be politically motivated.[29]

As he sought backers for Twitter, Musk soon went from pitch mode to closing, turning informal conversations about theoretical interest in his Twitter bid into real investments. For anyone ready to move forward, Jared Birchall, the manager of his family office, would be in touch with details about the next steps. After further vetting, Musk's bankers from Morgan Stanley would swoop in with nondisclosure agreements, as the parties got down to brass tacks over confidential information such as revenue projections for Musk's Twitter and finalized their commitment.

Musk was impressed by the machine.

"The Morgan Stanley deal team is truly excellent and I don't say such things lightly," Musk texted Reid Hoffman on April 28.[30]

The results of Musk's aggressive funding push soon became clear: a regulatory filing made public on May 5 demonstrated the power of his network and the soft influence he wielded even with adversaries. Musk detailed more than $7 billion in financing from various sources, including the sovereign wealth fund of Qatar, his friend Ellison, Binance—a crypto firm founded in China—and Silicon Valley venture capital firms Andreessen Horowitz and Sequoia Capital.[31]

Securing the commitment from Saudi prince Alwaleed bin Talal Al Saud was a particularly significant coup, given Musk's history with the Kingdom of Saudi Arabia; the negotiations that had led him to falsely say he had "Funding secured" to take Tesla private; and Prince Alwaleed's previous public questioning of Musk's Twitter offer, which had led to a public spat.[32]

"I don't believe that the proposed offer by @elonmusk ($54.20) comes close to the intrinsic value of @Twitter given its growth prospects," read a post from the prince's account on April 14. "Being one of the largest & long-term shareholders of Twitter, @Kingdom_KHC & I reject this offer."[33]

Musk had two questions for the prince of a nation that had recently been implicated in the execution and dismembering of journalist Jamal Khashoggi.

"How much of Twitter does the Kingdom own, directly & indirectly?" Musk asked that same day. "What are the Kingdom's views on journalistic freedom of speech?"[34]

A key Musk deputy, Omead Afshar, was taken aback by the weight of the prince's interjection, according to text messages revealed in court proceedings.

"Who knew a Saudi Arabian prince had so much leverage and so much to say about twitter," Afshar wrote on April 15.[35]

Still, within weeks, the one-time adversaries were inexplicably parties in a private takeover of Twitter. Alwaleed told me in a 2024 interview that he merely objected to Musk's asking price, believing it to be too low.[36] He said no formal influence or concessions—for example, the ability to exert political pressure on the platform—were awarded to secure his involvement in the deal.

This new batch of funding, which practically erased any questions about the seriousness of Musk's bid, would allow Musk to cut his margin loan, perhaps the biggest financial risk of the funding plan, in half. Of course, the funding arrangements raised important questions: What kind of private data would the financial commitment allow repressive regimes such as Saudi Arabia to receive in exchange for their investors' participation? Would the Qatari regime receive access to private data about Twitter users, and could China pressure Binance to hand over confidential information?

On May 5, a post from Prince Alwaleed showed how effectively Musk had subdued an adversary—or perhaps vice-versa, given how little was known about the provisions securing their participation.

"Great to connect with you my 'new' friend @elonmusk," read the post on the prince's Twitter feed, complete with a handshake emoji, appended as an amicable conclusion to their earlier thread. "I believe you will be an excellent leader for @Twitter to propel & maximise its great potential."[37]

As Tesla's stock took repeated hits in the days after Musk's Twitter acquisition deal, the reality of the risk—and the danger it posed to his entire empire—seemed to dawn on him.

Tesla's stock lost nearly 30 percent of its value between the time that Musk's investment in Twitter became public and the days in mid-May when Musk and his team were furiously lining up funding for the takeover.[38] Just six months after the peak of more than $400 per share in November 2021, Tesla was now trading around $250.

Musk had to do something to calm investors, lest the bottom fall out on the key source of his wealth.

In the days before his takeover, Musk had pledged to eliminate a key source of Twitter frustration: automated and inauthentic accounts peddling crypto scams and other online rubbish on the platform. It was a fair target, a persistent thorn in the side of users, although Musk's experience as such a high-profile user may have exacerbated the problem on his end.

"If our twitter bid succeeds, we will defeat the spam bots or die trying!" Musk tweeted on April 21.[39]

Days earlier, he had been texting with Jason Calacanis, a Silicon Valley investor with whom he'd become close. Calacanis noted the ease with which Musk could fix the problem.

"You could easily clean up bots and spam and make the service viable for many more users," Calacanis, who later declined an interview for this book, wrote on April 14. "Removing bots and spam is a lot less complicated than what the Tesla self driving team is doing," he added.[40]

The interaction highlighted the bizarre impulse of Musk's associates to butter him up to achieve their aims, something Musk surely recognized but hardly objected to. This was most prominently displayed in a text from CBS anchor Gayle King, who courted Musk for an interview that same day.

"ELON!" she wrote. "You buying twitter or offering to buy twitter," she continued, "Wow! Now Don't you think we should sit down together face to face this is as the kids of today say a 'gangsta move' I don't know how the shareholders turn this down . . . like I said you are not like the other kids in the class . . ."[41]

Musk "loved" the text, attaching a heart to the message.

Appealing to Musk's ego was not a bad idea; the strategy was so effective that even regulators had used it in the past, as when they sought to convince him to implement a crucial fix to battery fires prompted by debris puncturing Teslas' undercarriage.

"Wait, you can't solve this?" an NHTSA staffer asked, in a former official's recollection, as I reported for the *Post*, prompting Musk to come back with a solution the following day.[42]

But Twitter repeatedly insisted that spam wasn't as big of a problem as Musk had made it out to be, and there may have been merit to the argument. The impression from some internally was that Musk's experience of the platform, as a celebrity power user with tens of millions of devoted fans, was wholly different from the typical tweeter's. His replies were littered with crypto scams seeking to prey on the enormous engagement he generated and catch users off guard, perhaps through accounts impersonating Musk himself.

On May 2, a week after Musk's deal to buy the site was announced, Twitter disclosed an internal finding that spam accounts made up fewer than 5 percent of its monetizable daily active users.[43]

That was hardly Musk's experience.

It was bad enough that Musk was being roundly criticized for turning a minor investment into a Twitter ownership bid and putting Tesla at risk. Tesla was facing a rout on the public markets. The Dow Jones index had taken a massive hit over the past few weeks, proving Musk's Twitter bid to have been overpriced and ill-timed.

Now Twitter management was potentially lying to him?

Musk had to do something.

Faced with the Twitter report on spam and bots, Musk found his answer.

"Twitter deal temporarily on hold pending details supporting calculation that spam/fake accounts do indeed represent less than 5% of users," Musk tweeted on May 13, sending Twitter's stock price falling and Tesla's relatively unaffected.[44]

Musk's timing was convenient. Given the circumstances of the announcement—a falling market, extreme pressure on Tesla's stock, and a growing recognition that Musk was overpaying, few thought of the spam and bot issue as the mere hiccup Musk presented it to be. The tweet read as a potential exit ramp.

But Musk said he was still trying to see the deal through.

"Still committed to acquisition," he tweeted two hours later.[45]

"It's going to look really foolish if you walk away and prove others (incl me) right who said you weren't serious and were looking for a way out," read one reply.[46]

In the background, a group of Silicon Valley investors and power players were trying to find their way into a deal they had little business being a part of. A day earlier, an email from Calacanis hit inboxes around the Valley. The message, labeled "CONFIDENTIAL," carried the subject line "Twitter Interest."

"We are now collecting interest to invest in Twitter, with Elon Musk's plan to take it private," it read.[47] "If you are interested in investing please complete the form below—we are giving priority to Qualified Purchasers."[48] The last line referred to, essentially, big-time investors.

Calacanis was floating a Special Purpose Vehicle (SPV), an entity created to support Musk's Twitter bid, which would pool the commitments of a group of wealthy investors contributing a minimum of $250,000 each to have a collective stake in Musk's Twitter acquisition.

Around Silicon Valley, these SPVs were popping up left and right as individual investors with little influence over Musk on their own saw a way to potentially cash in and hold a stake in the deal of the century.

It seemed like a hustle if there ever was one. Given Twitter's uninspiring track record as a seller of ads—the key driver of social media revenue—the financial upside was not immediately obvious. Were they simply leveraging their proximity to Musk?

By mid-May, as Calacanis was hawking his new investment vehicle, Musk seemed to sniff out a potential opportunist.

"What's going on with you marketing an SPV to randos," he wrote to Calacanis on May 12, according to text messages revealed in court proceedings. "This is not ok."[49]

Calacanis frantically replied that he had solicited more than $100 million in commitments.

"Just wanted to support the effort," he said.

"Morgan Stanley and Jared [Birchall] think you are using our friendship not in a good way," Musk replied. "This makes it seem like I'm desperate. Please stop."

"Only ever want to support you," Calacanis told Musk.

"Morgan Stanley and Jared are very upset," said Musk.

A short while later, Calacanis said he cleaned up the matter with Birchall, and Musk "liked" his text, quashing any beef for the time being.

But Musk was right that moves by Calacanis and other aspiring partners had made him look desperate at a time when he didn't need to be, given the commitments he'd lined up. To any neutral observer, it seemed like Musk was scraping the bottom of the barrel for funding. It was no coincidence that suddenly, Silicon Valley was leaking like a sieve and rumors of new funding were swirling left and right.

Within a few days, as I was looking into the latest developments regarding the deal, I caught wind of another SPV that had managed to obtain confidential information in Musk's bid.

Stonks, a crowdfunding investment start-up, was gauging investor interest in the Twitter deal. It was a way for smaller investors, perhaps those who didn't meet the "Qualified Purchaser" threshold, to get a slice of Musk's Twitter. And it was proving to be attractive to its audience; the start-up, a platform to bring interested parties together, managed to find $20 million worth of investor interest in the deal, though it was quick to say investors had not firmly committed that amount.[50]

More important to me, the start-up had secured confidential information on Musk's financial projections for the privately run Twitter, which showed that Musk's team expected to generate $16.8 billion from advertising in year five—a massive increase from Twitter's total revenue of just over $5 billion the previous year. Stonks knew all about his plans for the site too: Musk, it said, planned to reduce "headcount and costs across a bloated organization," while bolstering Twitter's ads business and emphasizing subscription plans, payments, and the creator economy. Crucially, it said Musk's Twitter planned to more than triple its revenue over a five-year period.[51]

Reporting in late May on the Stonks deck, as I called it, I discovered additional critical information: Musk was upping his equity commitment in the Twitter deal to $33 billion, eliminating his margin loan entirely, as a financial filing would later reflect.[52]

All from a deck that included a disclaimer that could have come straight out of the show *Silicon Valley*.

"Nothing is certain: while Stonks is obviously a fan of Elon, you could still lose everything if you YOLO on this investment," it announced, using shorthand for the saying "you only live once."

For each of Musk's equity investors, there was the promise of prestige and influence; the perks of proximity to the world's most famous businessman; and, if things panned out, perhaps even a financial reward. But for a select few, there was an additional benefit.

Each of Musk's equity investors filed a confidential agreement with his bankers that spelled out the terms of their commitment. I learned that those agreements contained a clause for major investors: those who exceeded a $250 million threshold would earn information rights in the new company, meaning they would be entitled to confidential financial data and other nonpublic materials. It was barely consolation for the financial commitments that someone like Ellison was making. I had talked to enough investors to know a return on investment was the primary motivation for most.

But it was perhaps no coincidence that three of the parties with foreign ties invested amounts above the $250 million threshold: Binance at $500 million, a subsidiary of Qatar's sovereign wealth fund at $375 million, and Saudi prince Alwaleed and the holding company he chaired at nearly $2 billion.[53]

There was one other relevant detail, as mentioned in the *Post* story in November 2022: the US government claimed that Saudi officials had previously sought personal information on Twitter users.[54] Now a Saudi prince had bought his and the Kingdom's way into information on the newly private Twitter, all by converting an existing stake into the new venture to be run by Elon Musk. Alwaleed, in a conversation with me, said he received the same set of business information available to investors, and his motives were purely financial.[55]

11

EXIT PLAN

Elon Musk was getting cold feet. The task of talking the world's richest person off the ledge fell to Parag Agrawal, a man who'd risen to the post of Twitter CEO barely six months earlier.[1]

Agrawal had been plucked from relative obscurity within Silicon Valley by Twitter's longtime chief executive Jack Dorsey to lead the company through the transition from founder to handpicked successor. But even among some Twitter staff, Agrawal was relatively unknown, an engineering and technical expert who lacked the wunderkind reputation of a Mark Zuckerberg or a trusted understudy role like Tim Cook. He was seen as a transitional leader who could take the reins of a now-mature Twitter—one that had grown complacent in its lackluster financial performance under Dorsey's part-time leadership.[2] He could bring a needed dose of stability, while remaining true to the vision of those before him.[3]

Agrawal was, as one article in *The Washington Post* put it, "relatively uncontroversial."[4]

On May 16, after Musk announced the deal was "on hold,"[5] Agrawal tried reasoning with him. To date, their relationship had not exactly blossomed. It was only a month earlier that Musk had challenged Agrawal's work ethic over text message and pledged to make an offer to take Twitter private, instead of taking a seat on the company's board. This time, Agrawal approached Musk the old-fashioned way, on Twitter.

"Let's talk about spam. And let's do so with the benefit of data, facts, and context," he tweeted.[6] "First, let me state the obvious: spam harms the experience for real people on Twitter, and therefore can harm our business. As such, we are strongly incentivized to detect and remove as much spam as we possibly can, every single day. Anyone who suggests otherwise is just wrong," he added.[7]

In a fifteen-tweet thread, Agrawal detailed why spam was not easy to distinguish from authentic posts and how the tactics used by bad-faith users evolve.[8] He noted the increasing sophistication of those who used Twitter for coordinated bad-faith campaigns and made the point of stating that Twitter suspends more than half a million spam accounts daily. Agrawal went on to explain that he didn't believe Twitter's methods for detecting spam and bots could be performed externally—by a third party, for example, someone who could check Twitter's work. The overall message was that Twitter had a grasp on the problem, with the benefit of internal data only it could possess, and it was carrying out its task to the best of its ability—even if its methods were not perfect.

Musk's reply was short: a poop emoji.[9] It gained more than fifty thousand "likes," far more than any of the tweets in Agrawal's thread. (Never mind Musk's nondisparagement clause in his deal to buy Twitter.[10])

"So how do advertisers know what they're getting for their money?" Musk tweeted minutes later. "This is fundamental to the financial health of Twitter."[11]

Twitter staff seemed to take Musk's complaints about the prevalence of spam and bots personally. The company maintained a site integrity team that answered to Twitter's head of site integrity Yoel Roth (promoted to head of trust and safety that month). Their job was to see that the conversation on Twitter was organic and human-driven, rather than a bot-fueled hellscape of misinformation, propaganda, and impersonation. That was on top of the coordinated, state-sponsored efforts to hijack the public conversation that were a constant threat to the site.

Musk, in painting Twitter as overrun by bots, was describing a version of the site that essentially negated the results of that hard work.

It was true, though, that Twitter was becoming a different place than the organic haven for micro-updates on the world, followers' lives, sports, and politics that it had been in its early days.

The conversation on Twitter had been shifting—and the quality of the conversation appeared to be eroding. Internal slides first reported by Reuters showed that Twitter counted only two key areas of growth:

cryptocurrency and NSFW (not safe for work—an acronym associated with nudity and adult content), in addition to the Japanese animation style known as anime.[12] Twitter's traditional strongholds such as world news, entertainment, and liberal politics were on the decline, as was another topic that had previously signaled the health of the platform: the Kardashians.

Current "Heavy Tweeters," the slides suggested, were more likely posting about the latest Bitcoin boom-bust cycle or speculating about the next crypto crash. For all the sudden and promising new interest from hawkers of decentralized currency, there was a clear catch: these clusters, the slides said, tended to be "spammy."

If Musk had wanted a site that represented the pulse of the public conversation, capturing the wide range of topics spanning the day's events, he may have missed his window.

Among the rank-and-file staff—contrary to the broader media and tech worlds—the spam issue wasn't dismissed as a thinly veiled ruse to exit a bad deal, though many shared that belief. Twitter had extensively studied interactions with Musk, one of its most powerful users, who invited engagement unlike any other account on the site. It should come as no surprise, then, that workers were tasked with getting to the bottom of whether Musk's skepticism was warranted.

For them, one possible explanation emerged above all others: spam and bots *were* a problem on Twitter, one faced acutely by power users with the pull of Elon Musk. Musk, in fact, had made the crucial mistake of taking his experience as representative of the typical user on the site. Musk was projecting his experience of Twitter onto the rest of the user base.

In April 2022, as the public was still processing the news of Musk's initial investment in Twitter, he decried the "crypto scam accounts that twitter constantly shows as 'real' people in everyone's feed."[13]

This wasn't a new issue for Musk. More than two years before his Twitter bid, in February 2020, he complained about the sudden surge in spam posts.

"The crypto scam level on Twitter is reaching new levels," he wrote. "This is not cool."[14]

Even then—well before President Trump was banned from the platform and before the *Babylon Bee* suspension prompted a crisis that only

Musk could solve—Musk argued that Twitter spam was an issue with profound implications for both the site's users and society more generally.

"Report as soon as you see it. Troll/bot networks on Twitter are a *dire* problem for adversely affecting public discourse & ripping people off," Musk posted in 2020. "Just dropping their prominence as a function of probable gaming of the system would be a big improvement."[15]

The problem was that Musk had an experience like no one else on Twitter—the replies to his posts were flooded with crypto scams, impersonators, and armies of bots that sought to exploit vulnerable users sifting through his replies—some of whom were desperate to be noticed by their hero. Musk was at the cross section of too many internet subcultures to count, not just the Tesla fanboys and space enthusiasts but also a cryptocurrency coin with a Shiba Inu dog as its mascot (Dogecoin) and an underground group of crypto hawks who thought Musk was the founder of Bitcoin, to name a few. It was easy to see how he could conclude that the site was a cesspool of spam and bots.

"I remember people on our team thinking he's having a very personal experience unique to him on the platform," a former Twitter employee told me at the time.[16]

The question was whether that experience held true for those who didn't have tens of millions of followers or a business empire whose value rivaled the GDP of many countries.

Musk's image as a genius had been practically unimpeachable until this point. It wasn't hard to see why: How many people possessed the knowledge and public platform to question his approach to auto manufacturing, to literal rocket science, against a backdrop of unfettered success?

But the saga over spam and bots provided a clue into Musk's thought process on an issue that dozens of researchers studied regularly and millions of web users experienced on a daily basis.

For anyone who suspected that Musk, while a genius, might just be intellectually lazy or even openly hostile to legitimate expertise, the unfolding drama over crypto scams provided what looked like concrete proof.

Data scientists may have been digging into the issues Musk was raising, but Musk didn't return their attention to detail, their capacity for nuance, their penchant for rigorous methodology. The day he announced that the deal was "on hold," Musk told his Twitter followers he would be running his own test to get to the bottom of whether spam and bot accounts made up fewer than 5 percent of Twitter users.

"To find out, my team will do a random sample of 100 followers of @twitter," he wrote, adding, "I invite others to repeat the same process and see what they discover."[17]

A subsequent reply expanded on this seemingly crude methodology.

"How are [you] defining random?" a Musk fan asked. "How will you select them."[18]

"Ignore first 1000 followers, then pick every 10th," replied the richest person on earth. "I'm open to better ideas."[19]

Musk—a man with practically unlimited resources at his disposal, access to top engineers and data scientists, was turning to randos on Twitter to help solve his problems.

"If we collectively try to figure out the bot/duplicate user percentage, we can probably crowdsource a good answer," Musk added in another tweet.[20]

Twitter wasn't blameless. Its figures relied on crude calculations and private data unviewable by the public—so much so that Agrawal suggested an external analysis would be all but impossible.[21]

But employees were adamant that Musk's accusations of undercounting spam and bots were off base.

Weeks after the deal was announced, the conversation around Twitter headquarters had shifted from skepticism about Musk's intentions to abject disbelief over his lazy approach to analysis.

The reactions reflected a common pattern: Musk was publicly regarded as a brilliant thinker, a genius. But when he delved into a person's specific area of expertise, they began to realize he might be out of his depth. This had happened in small ways at Tesla and in its dealings with auto safety officials, spilled into public view with the case of the Thai cave rescue and COVID-19. And now it was happening with Twitter.

Twitter employees increasingly suspected that Musk's ignorance of the inner workings of their platform must be part of some grand strategy, a ploy to exit the deal.

But time and time again, his outrageous public statements were revealed to illuminate his true thinking. Musk can be brazen, insensitive, combative, and childish, but he is rarely accused of masking his true feelings on a subject.

Despite all the research devoted to spam and bots internally, research that found Musk's concerns about fake accounts were valid—even if only in his experience—workers found the prevailing notion hard to shake: this was a 4-D chess game aimed at wriggling out of the deal.

In fact, both things could be true: Musk had a hunch based on flawed thinking and then devoted significant monetary and human resources to proving it.

Behind the scenes, according to a person familiar with the matter, Musk's lawyers engaged researchers to run the actual data on his suspicions, an effort that went beyond sampling one hundred random accounts. By early June, however, that effort had run into its first major hurdle: Twitter appeared suddenly reluctant to hand over a set of data—data that had otherwise been available to purchase by around two dozen companies—that could shed light on its spam claims.[22]

The apparent impasse over access to the data not only raised the question of what Twitter might have to hide; it threatened the completion of the deal itself.

A letter from Musk's lawyers on June 6 made as much clear, carrying the strongest language to date that Musk might, in fact, have to back out of the $44 billion deal.[23] For Twitter, the argument to withhold the data was flimsy, given how widely it had been distributed, even to those who weren't planning on spending tens of billions to acquire the site. But there was a legitimate concern that handing the data to Musk's team might subject it to bad-faith attacks—and twisting of its numbers—from a group that had already arrived at its conclusion and had no plans to consummate the deal.

Musk's lawyers were adamant, however, that the data must be handed over.

"If Twitter is confident in its publicized spam estimates, Mr. Musk does not understand the company's reluctance to allow Mr. Musk to independently evaluate those estimates," the June 6 letter said. "This is a clear material breach of Twitter's obligations under the merger agreement and Mr. Musk reserves all rights resulting therefrom, including his right not to consummate the transaction and his right to terminate the merger agreement."[24]

It worked. On June 8, the *Post* reported that Twitter planned to comply with Musk's request for the firehose, handing over a data stream of more than five hundred million daily tweets, aiming to comply within days.[25]

As the Twitter negotiations stretched into summer with no clear resolution, bankers who had been in regular contact with Musk's camp suddenly stopped hearing from his deputies. And they weren't rushing to resume the discussions.

It looked like the weight of the $44 billion mistake he had just made began to dawn on Elon Musk.

Musk had lined up billions of dollars' worth of funding to back the deal—securing commitments from longtime associates and key investors who were ironclad supporters of his agenda. But smaller institutions had entered talks on the deal when it looked much more promising. Now that Musk was expressing doubts, and the market had clearly spoken, some of Musk's institutional investor support seemed to be fraying.

Musk's team, meanwhile, struggled to reconcile the massive trove of data it had received from Twitter with the company's public statements about spam and bots. The more his researchers dug into the "firehose," the more their trust in Twitter's statements eroded—and the more of a legal case they had. Twitter had argued that an external analysis of the spam and bot problem was infeasible; Musk's team now had the internal data it needed to make its case.

Musk revealed the concern at a tech conference in Miami, the All-In Summit hosted by Calacanis and a fellow group of podcasters.[26]

"It's a material adverse misstatement if they, in fact, have been vociferously claiming less than 5 percent of fake or spam accounts but in fact it is four or five times that number," Musk said.[27]

That carefully worded legalese did not simply translate to "major screw-up"; rather, it was a reference to a clause in the merger contract that Twitter and Musk signed upon agreeing to the deal. The contract included a $1 billion termination fee, though Musk's legal and financial consequences could stretch far beyond that figure if he walked away.[28] Think of how much damage Twitter's brand had taken since Musk began sparring with its executives online.[29]

But Musk could legitimately exit the deal, contractually speaking, in case of a "material adverse effect" (note the similarity to Musk's claim of a "material adverse misstatement").

If, for example, the value of the company were materially different from what Twitter had represented at the time of the deal—if, say, its ad base was significantly smaller than Musk had been led to believe because of overinflated user numbers—Musk might have an exit ramp.[30]

July 7 delivered a bombshell: Musk's team concluded once and for all it couldn't trust Twitter's numbers, which put the deal in jeopardy. *The Washington Post* carried the ominous headline, accompanied by an "exclusive" tag: "Elon Musk's deal to buy Twitter is in peril."[31]

The news sent the financial and tech worlds into a frenzy. Suddenly, major media, tech platforms, and financial institutions were grappling with the possibility of an imminent reversal on the deal—an about-face of epic proportions.

Outlets including tech publication *The Verge*, gaming site *IGN*, Utah's *Deseret News*, right-wing politics site *Daily Wire*, *The Daily Mail*, and the vaunted *New York Times* carried stories about the potential implications.

"It's looking more like Elon Musk could bail on buying Twitter," *The Verge* declared.[32] "Is Elon Musk's $44B Twitter deal about to implode?" asked the *Deseret News*.[33]

The New York Times added the reporting the following day, leading with the ominous declaration that "Elon Musk may be preparing for the next chapter in his Twitter takeover journey: court," with a headline that announced: "Twitter is ready for a legal battle to force Elon Musk to buy the company."[34]

Some journalists criticized the *Post*'s scoop, saying the paper had provided unverified coverage of Musk's claims about Twitter's calculations being bogus.[35] In my view, it wasn't the meat of his team's conclusions on Twitter's spam problem that were most crucial at this phase—those claims would soon be raised in court—it was their impact on the deal.

The next twenty-four hours would determine whether our scoop was another incremental development in intractable, frankly irritating, back-and-forth or the moment the deal fell apart.

Of course, there had been no sudden turning point; the skepticism had been slowly building over the previous few weeks. Musk's team had examined the information in Twitter's firehose and emerged unconvinced. Twitter had been touting a user base of 238 million monetizable daily active users, referring to the set that could see and interact with ads—in other words, humans. But that figure was actually closer to 170 million, Musk's team claimed. And the majority of ads were shown to a subset of users that was minuscule by comparison—fewer than 16 million, less than 7 percent of the figure Twitter was touting as its ad base.[36]

They were buckling down for a long and messy legal battle. The effort to undo the Twitter deal had a new name in Musk's circle: Project Y.

On Friday, July 8, Musk filed a new disclosure with the Securities and Exchange Commission (SEC).

The line that blew up the deal was hardly poetry: "On July 8, 2022, the Reporting Person's advisers sent a letter to Twitter (on the Reporting Person's behalf) formally notifying Twitter that the Reporting Person is terminating their merger agreement."[37]

And with that, a $44 billion transaction, one of the biggest tech mergers in history, was off.

A letter from Musk's team rattled off a laundry list of accusations: stonewalling data requests, supplying "incomplete information" and ignoring them, and ultimately failing to reconcile Twitter's estimates on spam and bots with the findings of his researchers.

"Mr. Musk is terminating the Merger Agreement because Twitter is in material breach of multiple provisions of that Agreement, appears to have made false and misleading representations upon which Mr. Musk relied when entering into the Merger Agreement, and is likely to suffer a Company Material Adverse Effect (as that term is defined in the Merger Agreement)," the letter read.[38]

Musk was making it clear he wanted a clean exit from the deal.

But Twitter wasn't going to let him go easily. Company executives had seen their names dragged through the mud, Twitter's market valuation was being called into question, and a $44 billion acquisition by a raving tech demagogue suddenly seemed like the best way forward. The roles had reversed: the Twitter board that had once adopted a "poison pill" to stave off Musk was now willing to go to war for him to buy the site.[39]

Twitter's board chairman, Bret Taylor, made clear where the fight would land everyone involved.

"The Twitter Board is committed to closing the transaction on the price and terms agreed upon with Mr. Musk and plans to pursue legal action to enforce the merger agreement," he tweeted that afternoon. "We are confident we will prevail in the Delaware Court of Chancery."[40]

It took all of a weekend for Twitter to fire the next shot. It came in the form of a 241-page legal document historic for its blunt assessment of the ride Musk had taken Twitter executives on over the previous three months.

"In April 2022, Elon Musk entered into a binding merger agreement with Twitter, promising to use his best efforts to get the deal done. Now, less than three months later, Musk refuses to honor his obligations to Twitter and its stockholders because the deal he signed no longer serves his personal interests."[41] That opening salvo set the stage for a damning assessment of Musk's behavior over the last few months.

"Having mounted a public spectacle to put Twitter in play, and having proposed and then signed a seller-friendly merger agreement, Musk apparently believes that he—unlike every other party subject to Delaware contract law—is free to change his mind, trash the company, disrupt its operations, destroy stockholder value, and walk away," the document continued.

The lawsuit was practically dripping with contempt for Twitter's prospective owner, suggesting that an amicable resolution was no longer possible.[42]

Further, it made no secret of Musk's motives for exiting the deal—at least in the eyes of company officials. The stock market had fallen, and Musk's wealth had declined by more than $100 billion from November 2021 highs, it said, citing *The Wall Street Journal*.

"So Musk wants out." Musk's "exit strategy," meanwhile, was "a model of hypocrisy," of "bad faith," it argued. Musk, it said, must be compelled to complete the deal.[43]

Lauren Pringle's life was about to change. The University of Pennsylvania Law School graduate had recently uprooted her life to become the editor in chief of a small publication in Delaware called the *Chancery Daily*. In its exhaustive effort to chronicle the goings-on of an obscure but powerful court in a small state, it punched well above its weight. Pringle had been monitoring the unfolding drama over the acquisition of Twitter for weeks, knowing the case was likely to end up in the court whose work she meticulously documents.

But on July 12, Pringle knew she had to dig out the nearly one-foot pile of legal documents and other assorted detritus that had accumulated on her glass-topped desk. The corporate battle of the century was on in the Delaware Court of Chancery.

She remembers thinking, "This is my Super Bowl."

In early August, I was pursuing a new line of reporting on Twitter's spam and bot claims when a message appeared in my inbox from a name I didn't recognize. It included a document filed under seal.[44]

Elon Musk's counterclaim against Twitter, which had landed in my inbox, was heavy on data; it also included a clear argument about the motivations of Musk's adversary. Twitter, it alleged, had been playing a "months-long game of hide-and-seek to attempt to run out the clock before the Musk Parties could discern the truth."

The company's financial disclosures, it said, "contain numerous, material misrepresentations or omissions that distort Twitter's value and caused the Musk Parties to agree to acquire the company at an inflated price. Twitter's Complaint, filled with personal attacks against Musk and gaudy rhetoric more directed at a media audience than this Court, is nothing more than an attempt to distract from these misrepresentations."

Musk accused Twitter of misleading the SEC in its financial disclosures—of feeding the top securities regulator overly optimistic assessments of its monetizable user base. Twitter's employees had been on the money with their blunt assessment of Musk's spam and bot claims: Musk, in simple terms, was accusing Twitter of fraud.

"The more Twitter evaded even simple inquiries, the more the Musk Parties grew to suspect that Twitter had misled them," the counterclaim alleged.

Musk's team detailed its calculations: the proportion of accounts eligible to receive ads was far lower, it alleged, than Twitter had publicly claimed. And those seeing the majority of ads were practically minuscule, from a relative standpoint.

"What limited information has come to light proves Twitter's disclosures about the number of false or spam accounts are false," the counterclaim said. "The Musk Parties' preliminary analysis shed light as to why Twitter has stonewalled—Twitter did not want the Musk Parties (or the market) to discover that Twitter has been misleading investors regarding its 'key metric.' As a long bull market was coming to a close, and the tide was going out, Twitter knew that providing the Musk Parties the information they were requesting would reveal that Twitter had been swimming naked."

The stage was set.

The responsibility of sorting out this epic corporate drama fell to Delaware Chancery Court chancellor Kathaleen McCormick, a relatively new appointee to that role on the bench but one who already commanded the respect of the courtroom with her clear writing and sound reasoning. It soon became clear that McCormick, an energetic Harvard graduate who had earned a law degree from Notre Dame, would have little patience for any antics Musk and his lawyers might bring to the courtroom. She was known for her meticulous approach, capacity for fairness, and reputation for quick-witted, sometimes cutting, comments from the bench.

Pringle, editor in chief of the *Chancery Daily* and an attorney in Delaware herself, thought McCormick was the perfect person for the job. McCormick, who worked for a legal aid organization before venturing into private practice, had worked hard to get to her post.[45] She did not seek the limelight, nor did she evade it. McCormick could handle a case of this magnitude and had the presence of mind to know her rulings would be widely read, meaning they must be clear and accessible to a general audience. And that played to her strengths.

Her defining trait was her writing, which was far from the bloated legalese one might expect from convoluted court opinions. Her sentences were direct, with active verbs and clear-cut analogies. Pringle appreciated McCormick's clarity and attention to detail.

McCormick, she said, could see the signal through the noise, a key requirement in a court of equity—as was a keen sense of right and wrong.

Little did anyone know that in Washington, another matter was brewing that threatened to blow the case open before it started.

12

LIFELINE

On the morning of August 23, 2022, Elon Musk seemed to be in a good mood, though there were plenty of reasons why he might not have been. He and his team had taken repeated lashings in the markets, the media, and the Delaware Chancery Court. In the early days of the proceedings, Chancellor Kathaleen McCormick's patience was tested by a legal team whose arguments had thus far not proven compelling.

It all began with what looked like an attempt at stalling, a fishing expedition: Musk's lawyers sought to spend the next seven months gathering relevant data and more than fifty depositions in preparation for trial. McCormick took umbrage with the insinuation that her court could not resolve the dispute more quickly. The February 2023 trial date requested by Musk's team, McCormick said, "underestimates the ability of this court to quickly process litigation." Further, the delay "threatens irreparable harm to the sellers and to Twitter."[1]

McCormick's cutting replies from the bench reflected the steep uphill climb Musk faced to exit the Twitter deal. Musk had to convince the court that a material adverse effect had occurred; in essence, that circumstances had changed so much since he agreed to the deal—perhaps based on his new claims about spam and bots—that Twitter's value had been decimated.

McCormick's first major decision granted Twitter the expedited timeline it was seeking—an October trial date—dealing Musk's team a setback only days into the proceedings.

But the attorneys didn't need McCormick's sharp-witted replies from the bench to remind them of the unlikely odds. The consensus had already emerged: Musk's case was dead in the water.

But that August morning, Musk had been handed a lifeline.

CNN and *The Washington Post* revealed that a whistleblower, Peiter "Mudge" Zatko, had gone to federal regulators with claims that Twitter had concealed "extreme, egregious deficiencies" in its cybersecurity practices and spam-fighting efforts. The complaint also reached Congress.[2]

Zatko was Twitter's former head of security. A portion of his allegations specifically addressed the spam and bot claims made by Musk. He accused his former employer of "lying about Bots to Elon Musk" and alleged that Twitter was not incentivized to accurately tally the proportion of spam and bot accounts on the site.[3] Zatko had compiled a list of allegations that were altogether damning—not just for the trial but for Twitter itself.

Essentially, Zatko claimed that Twitter had been deceiving federal regulators for years about its security and privacy practices and misleading its board about actions it was taking in response to Federal Trade Commission (FTC) requirements; he also accused the company of a range of offenses including fraud and materially inaccurate financial filings. The complaint alleged that Twitter's merger documents with Musk contained "fraudulent misrepresentations" based on, for example, Twitter's statements that it was in compliance with applicable laws and didn't have the type of security vulnerabilities that would constitute a "Material Adverse Effect."[4]

This was a bombshell. Finally—finally—it looked like things were going Musk's way.

The fallout for Twitter was swift, as detailed in Musk's legal arguments soon after. The company's stock slid by more than 7 percent as "investors learned of the serious undisclosed risks" that jeopardized the deal and the Senate Judiciary Committee scrambled to set up a hearing to collect Mudge's testimony.[5]

"You could feel the vibe shift from Musk's [side]," said Pringle, who noted that "you could frequently tell how Musk was feeling about everything."

The Mudge case, where Musk embraced unauthorized leaks of Twitter's internal information, illustrated a particular irony for Musk. As the leader of Tesla, he had exhibited no tolerance of whistleblowers. Those suspected of bringing concerns about the company to light were fired or subjected to well-documented attempts to destroy their lives, as in the case of a former Tesla employee named Martin Tripp.[6]

Suddenly, Musk was singing a different tune.

At 8:52 a.m. Pacific time, Musk tweeted a cartoon of Jiminy Cricket, a character from the animated film *Pinocchio*, featuring the phrase "give a little whistle" from the movie.[7]

"Take the straight and narrow path and if you start to slide," the song went, "give a little whistle."

"And always let your conscience be your guide."[8]

The subtext was obvious, but Musk erased any doubt by posting a screenshot of *The Washington Post*'s findings on Twitter. Never mind the irony that—according to a one-time member of his circle—he believed there was a mainstream media conspiracy to oppose him, fueled by factors including Big Oil advertising revenues. Now Musk was sharing a screenshot with a *Washington Post* banner at the top of the page, complete with the slogan "Democracy Dies in Darkness."[9]

He was particularly interested in a passage from one of the stories that revealed Twitter had an internal tally of what was called "spam prevalence," something it had declined to share with the broader public.

"So spam prevalence *was* shared with the board, but the board chose not disclose that to the public . . ." he wrote.[10]

Musk's team were eager to introduce the new evidence in court—and use it to bolster their case to delay the trial. They seized on the momentum within a day, invoking the whistleblower complaint and arguing that Twitter should be required to disclose detailed data on its spam and bot tallies.[11] A day later, McCormick granted their plea to access additional data, despite characterizing their request as "absurdly broad."[12]

In early September, with the October trial date rapidly approaching, the lawyers took to Delaware Chancery Court to press their case on two additional points before McCormick: amending their counterclaim to include the Mudge revelations and delaying the trial.[13]

They presented a novel argument: Musk couldn't have discovered the information revealed by Zatko over the course of ordinary due diligence because Twitter had intentionally sought to conceal it. (A common criticism of Musk's approach in the Twitter deal was that by rushing to buy

Twitter at a generous cost, he had effectively waived due diligence. Musk's team claimed they had in fact conducted diligence by asking Twitter, for example, to detail its "tech debt" and "strategy for data centers."[14] Twitter was not forthcoming about the Mudge allegations in its answers, Musk's new counterclaim alleged.)

McCormick wasn't amused by the lawyers' arguments and issued one of her signature rebukes. "We'll never know, right?" she said. "Because the diligence didn't happen."[15]

McCormick had already expressed frustration with Musk's lawyers over what appeared to be gaps in Musk's text messages handed over as part of discovery. In one case, a conversation being reviewed as part of the process did not seem to flow naturally to the next message.

"Assuming that Musk's response was not telepathic," McCormick wrote, it appeared to be missing, causing a gap in the text message records.[16]

Musk's legal arguments were a constantly shifting mess—latching onto one finding and then another—but that was better than having insufficient grounds for his team's position. Still, the Musk team's antics were clearly wearing on McCormick. At one point, she admonished them for altering the scope of a discovery request for messages from Twitter.

"In this highly expedited case, there is no time for 'just kiddings,'" McCormick wrote.[17]

After that early September hearing, McCormick issued a split decision on the key matters before the court. Musk's team could indeed amend their counterclaims to include the Zatko allegations, but the trial would proceed as planned for October 17, a little over a month away.

The outcome of the case still felt uncertain despite Musk's seeming breakthrough. Tabulating the actual number of spam and bot accounts on Twitter was always going to be an inexact science. And even if Mudge's claim that Twitter had lied to Musk proved to be true, there was still the question of whether Twitter's actions were egregious enough to sink the value of the platform on their own.

Some weren't convinced. Amid the flood of media coverage about the Mudge claims—which, perhaps frustratingly to those who saw a groundbreaking whistleblower revelation with massive cybersecurity implications, was dominated by the implications for Musk-Twitter—a chorus of skeptics emerged, predicting they would do little to move the needle on Musk's case.

"The Twitter Whistleblower Doesn't Help Elon Musk's Case Much," read a headline on *Bloomberg*, drawing on columnist Matt Levine, who had consistently given Musk's team needed doses of reality during the ordeal.[18] Levine's argument,[19] supplemented by a Twitter thread from Tulane University law professor Ann Lipton, was that Musk could certainly make a case based on the issues raised by Mudge—but it would be a new case.[20] Levine argued that Mudge's claims explicitly rebutted the argument put forward by Musk by painting Twitter's figures as accurate but the metric itself as flawed.

That didn't help Musk very much, in Lipton's estimation.

Twitter's active user metric being a "concocted measure to goose exec" pay was "not a basis to get out of the deal if Twitter's actual disclosures are accurate," she wrote.[21]

In an interview with me, Lipton said she immediately recognized the whistleblower complaint for what it was.

"It wasn't a securities problem. It was a 'Twitter, you're running your business badly' problem," she said. "Because he framed it as a disclosure problem, that gave it sort of the hook for Musk to seize on it."

Twitter had committed a damning series of errors, but was that enough to get out of the deal? Levine, like Lipton, was unconvinced.

"If Twitter was bad at safeguarding user data, did that violate the law (including in particular its 2011 settlement with the Federal Trade Commission over user data)? Were Twitter's securities filings misleading because they didn't disclose all of its security vulnerabilities? When all this stuff comes out, will that cause a 'material adverse effect' on Twitter's business, which will let Musk get out of the deal? Meh, I don't know," he wrote. "Even if these claims are true, and even if they are evidence of fraud or material adverse effect, they are not evidence of anything that Musk has been complaining about."[22]

But even this ambivalence was a step forward for Musk's troubled case.

Few thought Musk was going to get away without paying at least $1 billion (and likely more). But with the Mudge revelations, Musk had the prospect of a less damaging outcome, while he was otherwise facing certain defeat. Pringle knew Musk would try to use the new claims for leverage.

"It all was just sufficiently tangential to the actual legal issues [that it] was pretty clear right from the jump it wasn't going to have an impact on the case," she said. "But it was also clear that Musk was going to do everything in his legal power to try to make it a distraction."

What followed was a swarm of legal justifications for exiting the deal.

"It was really like a throw spaghetti against the wall and see what sticks kind of approach," Pringle said.

It was the kind of attack Levine had foreshadowed in his analysis of the Mudge claims.

"Musk would have to, like, send Twitter a new termination letter saying 'never mind about the bot stuff, now I'm terminating the deal because of the security vulnerability stuff,'" Levine wrote. "But he could do that, why not. He's not limited to the excuses he's already tried; if people keep finding him new excuses to get out of the deal, he can try those too. Maybe one will work."

As luck would have it, that's exactly what Musk's team ended up doing. On August 29, *Bloomberg* reported, Musk filed a new termination letter. "On August 23, 2022, the Washington Post published a whistleblower report [in which Peiter Zatko] alleges far-reaching misconduct at Twitter—all of which was disclosed to Twitter's directors and senior executives, including Parag Agrawal—that is likely to have severe consequences for Twitter's business," it read.[23]

The letter went on to allege, among other things, that Twitter was defying its FTC obligations under the 2011 consent decree, that it was vulnerable to cyber threats, and it had "acquiesced to demands made by the Indian government," all issues raised by the Mudge complaint.[24]

All of this was not even really necessary, Musk's team argued, because it had terminated the deal a month earlier—but the court should know in any case. It's not like this sudden new basis to terminate the deal was somehow more justified than the previous one. That would make it sound like Musk's claims about spam and bots were a half-baked justification for exiting, while a real reason had emerged in the meantime.

"Although the Musk Parties believe this termination notice is not legally necessary to terminate the Merger Agreement because they have already validly terminated it pursuant to the July 8 Termination Notice, the Musk Parties are delivering this additional termination notice in the event that the July 8 Termination Notice is determined to be invalid for any reason," the letter read.

That wasn't the end of Musk's swing-for-the-fences strategy. Days later, on September 9, his team filed a new termination letter—with yet another new argument.[25]

This time, they argued that Twitter had breached its contract with Musk by issuing a severance payment to Zatko, who would later emerge as the whistleblower, after the deal had already been made. One provision of the contract did indeed prohibit Twitter from making severance payments except those "in the ordinary course of business consistent with past practice."

It was unclear how Twitter's June 28 payment of $7.75 million to Mudge and his attorneys constituted standard practice, although the Musk team's contention that this apparent breach "cannot be cured" seemed equally irreconcilable. Musk's letter argued that he had only learned of the payment on September 3 when Twitter issued a filing detailing the agreement in court.

The new letter seemed to indicate that they had found something that might enable them to get out of the deal.

"Defendants are thus not required to close . . . and have an additional basis to terminate the Merger Agreement if the Musk Parties' termination of the Merger Agreement pursuant to the July 8 Termination Notice and the August 29 Termination Notice is determined to be invalid for any reason. . . . For the avoidance of doubt, these bases are in addition to, and not in lieu of, the bases for termination identified in the July 8 Termination Notice and the August 29 Termination Notice."

By this point, the termination notices were pouring in.

"It smacked of desperation by the time we had a third termination letter," Pringle, the editor in chief of the *Chancery Daily*, told me.

Musk's team publicly filed its updated counterclaim—encompassing the Mudge allegations—on September 15. It contained sweeping allegations against the site Musk had once hoped to take over.

As CNN reported, quoting the counterclaim, Musk's side alleged that Mudge's claims "have revealed that the misrepresentations regarding mDAU [monetizable daily active users] were only one component of a broader conspiracy among Twitter executives to deceive the public, its investors, and the government about the dysfunction at the heart of the company."[26]

The new counterclaim spelled out just how much Mudge's allegations had transformed Musk's case. It characterized a series of "stunning events" that had called into question not just Twitter's claims on spam and bots but also the integrity of the platform itself. If this new line of thinking was to be believed, Musk was purchasing damaged goods.[27]

"Needless to say, the newest revelations make undeniably clear that the Musk Parties have the full right to walk away from the Merger Agreement—for numerous independently sufficient reasons," the new complaint read. "In short, the Musk Parties and Twitter's many other investors were sold a different company than the Twitter that actually exists—one that was more valuable, more popular, more secure, and more compliant with governing law," it argued.

It was hard to imagine a more fitting venue for this epic battle between a desperate corporate behemoth and a recalcitrant business tycoon than the Delaware Court of Chancery, an arcane, somewhat parochial body that reflected the colonial roots of the American legal system but was tailor-made to handle the business disputes of the modern era.[28] This was among the key draws—the other being a friendly tax environment—that led a disproportionate number of businesses to incorporate in Delaware. The Chancery Court was a court of equity, not of law, meaning it strove to devise a fair solution to such disputes, in some cases absent clear legal direction, while taking into account that "equity does not act where there is an adequate remedy at law."[29]

The Court of Chancery had broad discretion to force action on the part of those who appeared before it—something most courts of law shied away from. In this case, Twitter was asking it to order "specific performance" by Musk, simply for Musk to *perform* the action of closing the deal he'd agreed to with his $44 billion purchase. That fell right within the Court of Chancery's purview.

"It's an affirmative injunction versus a negative injunction" (such as a financial penalty), Pringle told me.

There was only one problem: the Court of Chancery was largely based on a shared understanding of right and wrong, something that seemed to have frayed from the fabric of American society in recent decades as political polarization took hold and the population stratified into disparate online echo chambers. Chancery cases, Pringle told me, were not as reliant on precedent as those in a court of law.

And critics had emerged, most notably the Delaware Supreme Court, that suggested such a model was not predictable enough to sort out the business disputes before it, Pringle told me. In any case, none of that was going to be solved before the matter of Twitter's ownership was settled.

In the summer and early fall of 2022, this strange court in Delaware was essentially going to serve as a referee in an intractable showdown between parties that it appeared increasingly could not stand one another.

Musk and Twitter engaged in a series of discovery disputes—as Twitter pushed for access to Musk's private communications, which had appeared incomplete—and Musk's legal team pressed the social media company for internal metrics.[30]

At one point, unresolved disputes between Twitter and Musk pushed the court to another measure, the appointment of a special discovery master who could take some of the burden off the judge by determining whether certain documents met the bar for privilege, such as attorney-client communications.[31] This relieved McCormick of a time-intensive task while also insulating her from materials that might not end up factoring into the case. It was an additional—albeit not especially uncommon—step, one that showed just how complicated discovery between Twitter and Musk had become.

Aside from discovery disputes, September brought a flurry of deposition notices involving prominent names connected to the case: Jack Dorsey, Parag Agrawal, Mudge.

But one name loomed above all others: Elon Musk's.

He wasn't eager to testify. In late September, he managed to delay the matter until October.[32]

It soon became clear that Musk would prefer that the deposition not happen at all.

Still, it had seemed like the stage was set for trial. Reporters reserved flights and booked hotel rooms in Wilmington, Delaware, during the third full week of October. We knew that a settlement could happen just before the trial began—or even, say, before a crucial day of testimony.

And then something strange happened.

On October 4, a *Bloomberg* story announced that Elon Musk planned to proceed with the Twitter deal at the original price of $54.20 per share.[33] A filing with the SEC confirmed the report.

Musk was willing to follow through with the deal, provided his debt financing was in place and the trial was stayed, allowing the parties to close.[34] Twitter had reservations, particularly over the question of Musk's financing.

Was this just another ploy? Would he claim his funding had fallen through?

What had caused the turnabout by the Musk team? Musk was slowly coming to terms with the fact that he was going to lose. His team started to recognize that his chances of prevailing were minimal, and a series of procedural losses in court had made that abundantly clear.

The October 4 *Bloomberg* story on Musk's reversal captured his team's sense of oncoming defeat.

"Musk's legal team was getting the sense that the case was not going well, as Judge Kathaleen St. J. McCormick sided repeatedly with Twitter in pretrial rulings, according to one person familiar," it said.[35] Despite the Mudge allegations, the story said, Musk's side worried it would not be able to prove that the damage to Twitter was sufficient to wiggle out of the deal.

It seemed the best move for him was to cut his losses and retain what little leverage he had left.

But the move came so suddenly, so unexpectedly, that Twitter was understandably skeptical. Its lawyers took to court seeking assurances. In a filing responding to Musk's offer, they likened the newest development to a promise of "trust us, we mean it this time."[36]

Musk's side wanted to suspend the trial, but Twitter—which had been pushing for the deal to close—suddenly wasn't ready to surrender. The roles had reversed—again.

Ultimately, McCormick agreed to delay the trial to November so Twitter and Musk could close. Musk's team said it could come through by October 28.[37] There was a caveat, of course: Were the billions of dollars' worth of debt financing Musk was reliant on still in place? Musk's attorneys said the notion that Musk wouldn't be able to come up with the money was "baseless speculation," the Associated Press reported.[38]

But with the judge agreeing to a trial delay, the ball was now in Musk's court.

"We look forward to closing the transaction at $54.20 by October 28th," Twitter's spokesman told the *Post*.[39]

There was only one outstanding question to resolve: Were the banks still invested? The equity commitments from Musk's friends and partners were still in place. But what about the $12.5 billion "headache," as *Bloomberg* referred to it, the massive loan that banks led by Morgan Stanley had agreed to take on?[40]

Musk had collected his debt commitments well before a market downturn cast a shadow over the deal, tanking Twitter's valuation and cratering his own fortune. It wouldn't have come as a surprise to learn the banks were backing out. The *Post* learned that one firm in talks to participate in the deal, Apollo Global Management, was no longer involved.[41]

Musk's April commitments, however, had left him in a unique position of leverage: he had secured loans on terms that might no longer be available. If he lost at trial, he might have to purchase Twitter with substantially less help, which would put a much larger dent in his net worth.

Whether the banks would pony up should hardly have been a question, given that their financing was laid out in a debt commitment letter, and the term of the commitment had been extended from an October 20 deadline to the following April, making the money good for a full year from the deal's announcement.[42]

It didn't help that the banks were silent on whether the money was still in place. At the time, the *Post* tried getting in touch with Musk's bankers directly only to be rerouted to corporate communications, who had little to say. It was entirely possible that they needed to figure out how to line up more than $12 billion in time for the October 28 deadline.

Those involved with the Twitter deal weren't the only people holding their collective breath. Tesla investors had celebrated Musk's potential exit, which promised to put an end to the bleeding. Now he was back in.

"Many of us are done with this," one told me in August of that year. "I love Elon. But to put lots of money into this broken venture . . . $44 bil error."

Now they were despondent.

This was a "nightmare," the person said as Musk reentered. "Hope it ends soon."

For Twitter employees, however, the nightmare was only beginning.

As the closing date approached, they learned that Musk had told investors he was planning to cut Twitter's workforce by up to 75 percent, reducing its head count from seventy-five hundred to around two thousand.[43] To be sure, Twitter had already planned extensive layoffs, and Musk's offer was regarded as a "golden ticket" for a company that had been expected to shed a quarter of its workforce in any event. (Musk was openly acknowledging by now that he was overpaying.)

But a layoff of three-quarters of the staff was unimaginable.

"What's he gonna replace it with, AI?" a corporate governance expert asked the *Post*.[44]

In internal chat rooms, Twitter employees channeled anger and worry into gallows humor.

The countdown to the deal marched on.

A *Wall Street Journal* story on October 21 showed the banks were treading carefully, holding on to their debt in the deal instead of selling it amid a cooling market. It was significant that they were making plans for the debt at all.[45]

On the morning of October 26, Elon Musk showed up at Twitter headquarters in San Francisco straining under the weight of a porcelain sink. The message was not subtle. Musk, clad in all black wearing a short-sleeved T-shirt, posted a tweet with the nine-second clip: "Entering Twitter HQ—let that sink in!" it read.[46] Musk changed his Twitter bio to read "Chief Twit."[47] Musk's public entrance into Twitter HQ and his embrace by the workers inside practically erased the remaining logistical questions about whether the deal was going to proceed.

He spent the day holding meetings with Twitter executives. Musk was hardly given a hero's welcome, but neither was he decried as a conqueror. For all the controversy his likeness had invited, he retained his allure to tech workers in Silicon Valley, even those who would be sacrificed to his plans for the company.

At one point, as his biographer Walter Isaacson posted, Musk held court among the Twitter staff and surrounded himself with a cadre of workers at the company coffee bar.[48]

Twitter's Slack channels lit up again as workers posted videos of Musk touring the office, the tech titan declaring at one point: "This is a sweet office."[49]

In another clip, the *Post* reported, Musk was surrounded by about twenty-five people who asked him questions—pressing ones, such as: Did he really plan to fire 75 percent of the staff?

Musk said he didn't.[50]

By the time the case neared its end, *Chancery Daily* editor in chief Lauren Pringle had become a bona fide social media star—at least as far as legal influencers were concerned. She had grown *Chancery Daily* from a small Twitter following to one of around twenty thousand users, encompassing the Silicon Valley power players; the tech media; the country's best legal minds; and, most crucially, many Twitter employees.

The quick resolution of the case, with no trial after all, left a void—an anticlimax to the battle that had thus far contained everything.

Everyone was tired. The lawyers on both sides were tired. The players in the lawsuit were exhausted by the relentless back-and-forth. Even McCormick had tapped out of a complicated discovery dispute that preceded the trial with her appointment of a special master. Reporters on the story had been running on fumes.

Now, in one fell swoop, the case was resolved. Suddenly, Pringle found herself grappling with what came next. The daily drumbeat of legal updates would suddenly seem so mundane.

"There was nothing," she said in our interview. "I was leaving behind [a] complete vacuum after the case ended. . . . I know I used to do something. What was my life about? I have to rebuild that floor and furniture . . . in my life."

On McCormick's docket, meanwhile, another trial loomed—one that would decide the fate of Elon Musk's 2018 Tesla pay package. Though few knew it at the time—they just thought Musk had gotten himself into a financially disastrous pickle—the turnabout that led to Musk buying Twitter would prove to be one of the most significant developments not just of the internet era but of the cultural and media landscapes in the twenty-first century as well. At a time of mass polarization and entrenched political division, Musk was being handed the keys to arguably the most influential political messaging tool in existence.

13

"I JUST WANT TO MAKE TWITTER FUN AGAIN"

The Elon Musk era at Twitter began with a series of firings.

At 3:50 p.m. on October 27, Vijaya Gadde, Twitter's head of legal, public policy, trust, and safety, officially signed a certificate to complete the Twitter merger. It took around ten minutes for Musk to implement his first order: cleaning house.[1]

Within minutes, four top executives each received an email from a member of Musk's family office. Twitter CEO Parag Agrawal, chief financial officer Ned Segal, general counsel Sean Edgett, and Gadde—the face of Twitter's content moderation strategy who had just executed the deal—were all told they had been terminated.[2]

Edgett was on site, and Musk's security was instructed to escort him out of the building.[3] Gadde soon found her access to company systems cut off.[4]

Musk took to Twitter at 8:49 p.m., issuing a succinct confirmation of his takeover on the platform he now owned: "The bird is freed."[5]

At Twitter's art deco headquarters on 1355 Market Street on Friday, the day after Musk seized control, an unusually large number of employees showed up in person to make an appearance for a management team that had expressed its disdain for remote work and the old regime that had hired them. The printers hummed, spitting out lines of computer code.[6] Amid the commotion, internal message boards went quiet, as workers sat in fear of posting anything that could be used as a pretext to fire them.

That day, a cryptic message hit some engineers' calendars, instructing them to stand by: they should prepare to account for their last thirty to sixty days' work. "Please be ready to show your recent code," read the invitation. "Please come prepared with code as a backup to review on your own machines with Elon."[7]

Musk had yet to introduce himself to his new employees since becoming Twitter's owner.

Led by his personal lawyer Alex Spiro, Musk's trusted advisers huddled in the "war room," a conference room with a long, raw-edge wooden table, the second-floor nerve center of the operation, and enjoyed the spoils. Over catered food, coffee deliveries, and clear glass cylinders of Voss water, they drew up their plans to slash the company in half. The sterile boardroom was strewn with toys; Musk's two-year-old had been on site.[8]

Spiro was an odd choice to head up a social media company, even in the interim. A brash celebrity lawyer who had made his name representing NBA players and rappers such as Meek Mill and Jay-Z, Spiro had little experience operating in such a famously relaxed workplace as Twitter's.

It was hardly a good sign for thousands of Twitter employees that the rocket and automotive executive's personal lawyer was making key decisions on how the company should operate. Further, the coders found their work scrutinized in a way it hadn't been before. As instructed, after they provided their code, a handpicked group of engineers from Tesla, the stars from Musk's Autopilot team, began to review it.[9] Senior managers had been told to rank their employees in order of value to their teams. Soon, unexpected names began appearing in Twitter's internal directory. Investors David Sacks and Jason Calacanis were listed as staff software engineers, a sign that Musk was giving loyalists positions in the company.[10]

As Musk brought in trusted deputies from companies including Tesla, Neuralink, and The Boring Company, one former employee recalled that he had never seen anything like it.

"Do they have a day job?" he remembered thinking. It "doesn't seem to be right that they can just come in from a different company and have that authority."

There had been at least one sign that Musk might be extending an olive branch to the company's employees. He met with Twitter's trust and safety head Vijaya Gadde amid the takeover, engaging in discussions about the future of the company, and Gadde told her team it had been a productive discussion, the *Post* reported.[11]

But Musk's immediate firing of top executives when he took over removed any notion of cooperation.

Musk was used to navigating companies through crises—production snags for Tesla's Model 3, for one, at a time when Tesla's survival was at stake—and the situation at Twitter carried a similar urgency. But perhaps the only major departure from his past approach was the extent to which he'd appeared to become desensitized to the toll of job cuts on workers—and the backlash they could spur. He'd already been prone to "rage firings."[12] Now he was in charge of a company-wide reorganization.

Musk's advisers saw Twitter as a bloated organization that could operate at a fraction of its size; its workforce, they recommended, should be reduced from around seventy-five hundred to two thousand and include around fifty star engineers who pursued major initiatives. They viewed staff in policy and communications and marketing as nonessential to the core function of the website.

Musk's efforts to create a team of stars went on for weeks, through numerous rounds of job cuts, an ultimatum, and a late-night code review that had remote workers flying out to San Francisco, luggage in hand, to try to woo the new boss.

That summer, as the Twitter takeover was being set into motion, Musk's team pitched his plan for reshaping the company to investors. One line in particular stuck out: "Resize cost base by right-sizing headcount across all functions (~2,100 employees) and by streamlining infrastructure, real-estate, marketing, contracting / consulting," and more.

Another key tenet of the plan was equally critical: "Make Twitter trusted and transparent."

There was only one person listed on Twitter's post-closing executive leadership team. And his title hadn't yet been decided.

"Elon Musk
"Head of []"

On November 1, as the team led by Alex Spiro finalized the layoff plans, Elon Musk was just one rectangle in a Zoom grid, trying to calm a group of activists in New York City who were a crucial bridge to gaining the trust of Twitter's advertisers.[13]

Musk had joined a video call with the civil rights activists in an effort to assure a skeptical audience that his vision for the company wouldn't be a disaster to their agendas. Musk, who had been planning to meet with advertisers in New York that week, sat before a wallpaper background of the New York City skyline, with the Empire State Building peeking out.

Rashad Robinson, president of the racial justice organization Color of Change, recalled that Musk appeared in a black T-shirt and gold chain, looking tired and a bit disheveled, like it had been a long few days.

For years, civil rights leaders including the National Association for the Advancement of Colored People (NAACP) president Derrick Johnson had preached the harms of misinformation and unfettered online hate speech to any social media executives who would listen.[14] They were cognizant of the potential network effects of online rabbit holes and echo chambers. Dylann Roof, the perpetrator of the Charleston church massacre, had sought out swarms of hateful online misinformation before carrying out the murder of nine Black worshippers in 2015.[15]

But as the concerned heads of groups including the NAACP and Anti-Defamation League gathered on Zoom to hear him out, Musk had a simple mantra for his plans for his latest acquisition.[16]

"I just want to make Twitter fun again," Musk said, in Robinson's recollection, reciting the mantra at least twice on the call.

It was, in a way, quintessential Musk: an attempt to divorce himself from any political ideology.

To those participating in the call, the consequences of all the fun were quickly becoming clear. Days after taking control of the most influential social media site on earth in a $44 billion acquisition, Musk had plunged Twitter into crisis. His takeover had triggered an immediate spike in hate speech on the platform, and his sudden firings of key executives had eroded confidence in the company's content moderation strategy.[17] But perhaps the most damaging blow was an unforced error from Musk himself.

Early on the Sunday morning following his takeover, Musk decided to share a link from the *Santa Monica Observer*, a right-wing conspiracy site peddling a bogus rumor about a brutal attack on Paul Pelosi, the husband of Nancy Pelosi, who was serving as Speaker of the House at the time. Paul Pelosi had been assaulted by an intruder wielding a hammer, who had used the weapon to strike the eighty-two-year-old on the head, leaving him hospitalized with a skull fracture.[18] Musk, less than seventy-two hours after taking over Twitter, decided to use the platform to promote a crackpot theory from the *Santa Monica Observer* that the incident might have been a meetup with a male prostitute gone awry.[19]

"There is a tiny possibility there might be more to this story than meets the eye," Musk wrote in a tweet reply to Hillary Clinton that day, October 30, amid the outpouring of support for Paul Pelosi. Musk linked to the article that questioned the official narrative, with such ironclad sourcing as "IMHO."[20]

By the time Musk deleted the tweet, it was too late. Even Musk's investors, like Ross Gerber, were furious. "You can't be the president of twitter and not know that's a bullshit paper," Gerber told me. "People were calling me. Imagine how many people were calling him!"

That was part of how Musk ended up in a virtual face-to-face with leaders such as Robinson, trying to assuage their concerns that Twitter might become a cesspool of hate. They hardly believed him. For one, Musk's arguments were flimsy, Robinson said, like someone trying to convince you that "running a kitchen during a dinner rush in New York City is easy to do because they cook for their friends."

This wasn't an isolated incident. Data from the Network Contagion Research Institute research had shown that use of the N-word on Twitter had spiked nearly 500 percent in the hours after Musk's takeover,[21] and a news report in *Bloomberg* said Twitter had internally limited some access to its content moderation tools.[22]

To Robinson, Musk's attitude reflected a general feeling that the collective concerns of the civil rights leaders were valid, that Musk was on their side, that getting these problems addressed would be no big deal. While finding him conciliatory and agreeable overall, Robinson recalls him seeming a bit casual in his commitments.

Back at Twitter, Musk's intense demands for quick progress on new initiatives were being felt by the engineers, many of whom were still unsure of their status and felt the need to prove themselves. Days into his Twitter takeover, Musk had tasked his key engineers and product heads with delivering a new version of Twitter Blue, the company's paid subscription service. Musk saw subscriptions as a key moneymaker for a site with the addictive qualities of Twitter. Maybe it was the fog of war, but a technologist of Musk's caliber should have seen the obvious problem: users did not want to be charged for features that used to be free.

Setting aside their doubts, top engineers found themselves sacrificing their weekends and adopting a twelve-hour workday to meet their new boss's demands.

Perhaps the most visible manifestation of Musk's new internal hustle culture came when a Twitter employee posted a picture of his boss, Esther Crawford, Twitter's director of product management, curled up in a silver sleeping bag wearing an eye mask as she rested on the floor of the office.[23] Musk had made a repeated point of reminding people how he'd slept at the Tesla factory during the height of the company's Model 3 challenges.

Now Crawford was replicating that sacrifice for the boss, in a way many saw as performative.

"When your team is pushing round the clock to make deadlines sometimes you #SleepWhereYouWork," Crawford wrote in a tweet that quickly made the rounds online, as users mocked the try-hard attitude and Crawford's seemingly earnest adoption of Musk's mission.[24] Crawford was hardly the bad guy in all this, but her tweet had struck in time for peak outrage given the looming layoffs.

"Since some people are losing their minds I'll explain: doing hard things requires sacrifice (time, energy, etc)," she wrote in a series of tweets. "We are less than 1wk into a massive business & cultural transition. People are giving it their all across all functions."[25]

For many Twitter employees, no amount of hard work would have sufficed. But Crawford had the right idea.

Musk's playbook for extracting the most out of his workers was decidedly old school, littered with touches that would today be derided as *performative*—some of which stood in direct contrast to the ethos of a company that offered benefits like a monthly "day of rest."[26] Employees were expected to work late nights and long hours in person and demonstrate their commitment through their passion for the challenge before them—channeling Musk in their intense focus on a big problem that needed solving. At Tesla and SpaceX, employees were motivated by the challenge of making vehicles autonomous and putting humans on Mars. They were expected to find novel and unexplored methods to do so and reject the orthodox approaches if necessary. At a company where workers were persistently on edge, distrustful of the management, and not aligned with the vision, Musk expected blue badges to command the same level of urgency.

The results of that approach would speak for themselves.

The Thursday after Musk took over, Twitter sent out an all-staff email.

Earlier in the week, it still seemed like the job cuts might be tamer than expected. As the silence and information vacuum dragged on, skeptics started to wonder if Musk might be reevaluating. He called a *New York Times* report about potentially laying off workers before a November 1 stock vesting deadline "false."[27]

Musk, speaking to workers shortly before taking over the company, dismissed a report claiming he planned to lay off 75 percent of the staff, telling them he had no such intentions.[28]

On the Monday following Musk's takeover, the *Post* reported that the first round of layoffs would target about a quarter of the company.[29] Tuesday came and went. Then Wednesday. By Thursday, workers had spent a full week waiting for the other shoe to drop.

Then suddenly, their email inboxes began lighting up all at once.

"Team," the message began.

This was it.

"In an effort to place Twitter on a healthy path, we will go through the difficult process of reducing our global workforce on Friday. We recognize that this will impact a number of individuals who have made valuable contributions to Twitter, but this action is unfortunately necessary to ensure the company's success moving forward." The email continued: "By 9AM PST on Friday Nov. 4th, everyone will receive an individual email with the subject line: Your Role at Twitter. Please check your email, including your spam folder."[30]

Employees being retained would be notified via internal email. Those being let go would receive a message in their personal inbox.

That was how Elon Musk introduced himself to his new company.

The message, the Musk team's first official communication with its new staff, was signed: "Twitter."

The civil rights leaders were pleasantly surprised when Musk accepted terms they had set forth, including:[31]

- Twitter would not restore accounts that had been booted for violating its rules until after the coming US midterm elections, meaning Trump—banned after the January 6 Capitol riot—would not immediately get his account back
- Twitter would employ a transparent process for restoring previously banned accounts
- Twitter would make efforts to "combat hate & harassment," in Musk's words, in part by forming a content moderation council that included civil rights groups and those with "widely divergent views" overall; it was geared at protecting those who "face hate-fueled violence"
- Twitter's existing election integrity policies would continue to be enforced
- Those who had been locked out of Twitter's content moderation tools would have their access restored[32]

Musk had also agreed to tweet about the event, but when hours passed without a tweet, Color of Change's Rashad Robinson began to smell a rat. He'd had more than one experience in which a CEO would say one thing in the room and then suddenly vanish.

"When we left that meeting and nothing had been tweeted, I was like . . . 'not interested,'" he said. "I've led enough advertiser campaigns, boycott campaigns, where there's a window where people are paying attention. And companies and CEOs always try to slow-walk you—creating situations where you don't say anything, they don't say anything, but they benefit from the silence."

So Robinson was all the more shocked when he woke up around 4:30 a.m. Eastern time to find Musk had tweeted shortly after midnight, listing the groups he'd met with and detailing "how Twitter will continue to combat hate & harassment & enforce its election integrity policies," including listing the terms.[33]

As his notifications exploded from being tagged by Musk, Robinson went back to bed—relieved, at the very least, that the terms were now public.

On Thursday night, some employees found themselves locked out of their internal tools. Hundreds would awaken on Friday morning to find their access to email, Slack, and other work applications cut off.

The scale of the job cuts was a signal that Musk's earlier reassurances had merely been lip service.

By Friday morning, the civil rights groups were calling for a boycott. Brands including General Motors, General Mills, and Volkswagen paused their spending on Twitter. In addition to the civil rights groups, Musk had met that week with leaders from WPP, a powerful advertising agency whose influence could swing hundreds of millions of dollars' worth of spending. That effort, too, had failed.[34]

"It is immoral, dangerous, and highly destructive to our democracy for any advertiser to fund a platform that fuels hate speech, election denialism, and conspiracy theories," Derrick Johnson, the NAACP's president who had met with Musk earlier in the week, said in a statement.[35]

Robinson said Musk had no intention of following through. "He just got on the phone and he told us things he was unwilling to actually do," Robinson said. "The wheels were in motion while he was on the phone. You don't make that level of layoffs without those wheels being in motion."

Musk was dismayed. He had done his best to make peace with the activists, agreeing to their demands and even bringing them into the fold. Now they were targeting his company openly.

"Twitter has had a massive drop in revenue, due to activist groups pressuring advertisers, even though nothing has changed with content moderation and we did everything we could to appease the activists," he tweeted that morning. "Extremely messed up! They're trying to destroy free speech in America."[36]

Now they had to pay.

"It's time to stop appeasing the activists because they will stop at nothing to hurt Twitter regardless of what you do," wrote one right-wing commentator in Musk's replies.[37]

"You're right," Musk said.[38]

Twitter closed its offices on Friday, wary of the potential for sabotage by outgoing employees.[39] That meant even those who remained at the company couldn't swipe in to say a final goodbye to their departing colleagues.

On Slack, the workplace messaging app, workers watched in horror as their colleagues dropped off like flies.[40] Internal groups lit up with salute emojis and blue hearts as departing workers informed their colleagues of their fate.[41] An outpouring of grief soon played out on Twitter itself, where #TwitterLayoffs became the country's top trending hashtag and #LoveWhereYouWorked became a rallying cry of departing employees.[42] The layoffs were conducted with little regard for workers' personal situations—or, as time would show, for the health of Twitter itself. Those laid off, the *Post* reported, "included a product marketer who's eight months pregnant, a creative director who spent more than a decade at the company and the former vice president of engineering who promised to help others who need assistance."[43] Musk later admitted to being perhaps overzealous with the layoffs. "Desperate times call for desperate measures," he told CNBC in 2023. "There's no question that some of the people who were let go probably shouldn't have been let go. . . . This is not to say that 'hey everyone who was let go from Twitter is somehow terrible' or something. We have to, with very little information, get the headcount expenses and the nonpersonnel expenses down to where we're at least break-even."[44]

Those remaining at the company didn't immediately receive the reassurance they'd been promised. And so they sat, refreshing their emails, waiting for news of their fate. Finally, on Friday, hours after the layoffs had begun, they received an email informing them they'd been spared. Written again in the voice of God, signed "Twitter," the email informed the staff of what their leader had been up to over the past few days.

"Throughout the last week, Elon has spent time with a number of employees, customers, partners, policymakers and Twitter users," it read. "He is looking forward to communicating with everyone about his vision for the company soon."[45]

* * *

After laying off half of the company, Musk was ready to officially introduce himself. On November 9, at 11:39 p.m., he sent the following email:[46] "Sorry that this is my first email to the whole company, but there is no way to sugarcoat the message," it read. "Frankly, the economic picture ahead is dire, especially for a company like ours that is so dependent on advertising in a challenging economic climate. . . . Without significant subscription revenue, there is a good chance Twitter will not survive the upcoming economic downturn."[47]

Morale was already low. Now Musk was giving Twitter's version of a malaise speech. And though he was realistic about the challenges—many of which preceded him—rallying workers to solve Twitter's economic challenges might be hard from his perch as one of the richest people on earth.

His next point would be an even harder sell.

"Starting tomorrow (Thursday), everyone is required to be in the office for a minimum of 40 hours per week," read the message. "Obviously, if you are physically unable to travel to an office or have a critical personal obligation, then your absence is understandable."

Workers who'd missed the email shortly before midnight awoke the next day frazzled, scrambling to get to Twitter's downtown headquarters. They didn't want to give management any excuse to target them in what they assumed would be another round of job cuts.

Meanwhile, Musk's signature product was ready.

Musk had taken aim at Twitter's blue check mark badges, but it wasn't clear if his qualms were with the "verified" designation itself—intended less as a signal of notoriety than a symbol of authenticity—or those who possessed it. Nonetheless, Musk began to decry the checks as a "lords & peasants system."[48]

His solution: grant anyone access to the coveted blue check—for a mere fee of $8 a month. Musk was going to free the check mark from the grasp of media elites, celebrities, and status-obsessed snobs and shift the "power to the people!"[49]

The problem was that Musk had just laid off many of those responsible for implementing product rollouts at Twitter, not to mention a risk mitigation team whose importance would soon become abundantly clear.

Musk promised a spate of new features to those willing to pay. Crucially, those who subscribed to Musk's version of Twitter would have their tweets prioritized in a list of replies, and their names would pop up first when other users searched for them.[50]

But soon after the new features launched that Wednesday, it was apparent that something had gone wrong. Twitter was suddenly flooded with impersonators.[51] They targeted politicians, celebrities, and public figures—even Musk himself. Someone set up a fake account purporting to be NBA superstar LeBron James requesting a trade to another team.

But perhaps the biggest blow came when an account purporting to be pharmaceutical company Eli Lilly triumphantly declared, "We are excited to announce insulin is free now."[52]

The fake tweet caused a panic at the real company, the *Post* reported, as executives scrambled to respond. The tweet remained online for more than six hours; Twitter staff who would have taken it down were no longer employed. The $330 billion giant with an advertising budget in the hundreds of millions ultimately paused its spending on the social media site over the fiasco. It had shed more than $15 billion in value during the fallout.

Twitter employees were flummoxed by how to respond to the sudden wave of impersonators. Musk's team had rushed out the blue check marks without addressing their compatibility across Twitter's content moderation tools. That meant that even Twitter staffers sometimes couldn't tell real accounts from fake ones.

Something had to be done. If brand trust was in question before, now it was on the verge of disappearing entirely.

By November 10, the day after the rollout of Musk's signature feature, Twitter hit pause, telling employees it was suspending the feature to "help address impersonation issues."[53]

Musk's first product rollout at Twitter had been an unmitigated disaster.

That same day, workers scrambled to join Musk's first all-hands meeting with the staff. Employee Slack channels lit up with tough questions for the new boss: "What's the motivation? Work hard or get fired?" read one.

The hot-button issue that day was Twitter's remote work policy, and

Musk was in no mood to entertain debate. What if workers chose not to show up in person?

"Resignation accepted," Musk said.[54]

Musk, seemingly rattled by the extent of his first week's blunders, dug in on his vast experience leading tech companies, even if they weren't social media powerhouses. As questions swirled around the issue of privacy, for example, Musk said Tesla had vast experience in that realm. All Tesla's vehicles are connected and outfitted with cameras providing a complete picture of their surroundings, he said, but the company goes to great lengths to ensure they don't capture more than they should—footage from the last half-mile of people's trips, for example, isn't stored the way other trip data might be, given the potential to reveal sensitive details about someone's home location or travel destinations.[55]

The larger message was that the issues at Twitter weren't new to Musk. This echoed his reassurances to the civil rights groups. Robinson, president of Color of Change, described his attitude as: "Hey guys, there's no problem here, come on."

But at any hint of a challenge to his plans, Musk's demeanor could shift 180 degrees.

Former employees recalled a town hall meeting early in Musk's tenure when an engineer questioned Musk about his effort to position Twitter as an all-encompassing suite of services—including payments, subscriptions, social media—a catch-all that he termed "X, the everything app."[56] He asked how Twitter would create that kind of service when every one of its competitors who had sought to do so had failed. The all-encompassing model had worked in China, where WeChat was dominant, but the type of service Musk was envisioning had yet to take hold in the US, where antitrust laws have increasingly targeted social media companies.

"Don't you know a lot of our peers have tried this?" the engineer asked, as recollected by one former employee. "It didn't work."

Musk sighed.

"I've already answered that question," he said in the person's recollection. "Why are you asking this? It'll work."

He signaled for the next question.

"He always felt he was the smartest guy in the room," the former employee said. "He was extremely confident in his own views. I didn't get a sense he was willing or able to incorporate that and change his view."

14

"WELCOME TO LEVEL 2 OF HELL"

Late one evening shortly after Elon Musk took over Twitter, head of trust and safety Yoel Roth ventured from his desk in the San Francisco office where he had worked for seven years to grab some dinner. Taking a seat on a second-floor sofa, Roth began running down a set of data on child safety at Musk's request.

Antonio Gracias, one of Musk's most trusted associates approached.

"What are you doing?" he asked.

Roth replied that he was obtaining data on child safety.

"Why are you doing that?" Gracias countered.

Because people have concerns about it, Roth said, taken aback by the inquisition.

Gracias continued. "Who told you to do that? . . . Why are you doing it?"

Again Roth answered.

Gracias paused.

"Well . . . why are you doing it *here*?"

Gracias's tone was sufficiently disdainful that Roth decided to pick up and relocate. As far as Roth was concerned, he had simply sought a moment's comfort while working to satisfy his boss's orders well after normal hours, and it was unreasonable to be forced to justify himself to a strange man with no formal role at the company.

Gracias, who had similarly put off Tesla's Jerome Guillen with his comments toward factory workers, was starting an important role at Twitter as Musk's chief deputy—managing financial matters, cost cutting, and layoffs. His attitude toward the head of trust and safety embodied what Twitter's rank-and-file feared in their new bosses.

So Twitter employees were not surprised when an email arrived at precisely midnight on November 16. It carried a cryptic subject line: "A Fork in the Road."

My phone buzzed at 12:04 a.m.

"Elon just sent an email to the whole company giving us an ultimatum via Google Form," the person told me.

In the days leading up to the midnight email, Twitter had been hemorrhaging advertisers and gutting its ranks, while pushing away power users with sweeping changes aimed at monetizing the platform.

Against this backdrop of internal discord, Yoel Roth had been plotting his resignation. Among his key considerations that month was his personal security. As an executive responsible for content moderation at Twitter, Roth faced vicious online attacks, including threats to his safety. In response, Twitter's corporate security had decided to place a round-the-clock guard outside his home in El Cerrito.

Suddenly, however, lawyer Alex Spiro had bad news: Twitter was pulling Roth's personal security. It was a casualty of cost cutting, Musk's lawyer told Roth. But he made sure to punctuate the revelation with a note of reassurance.

"I have clients that are much more famous than you," he said, in the recollection of a person familiar with the exchange. "You're going to be fine."

Not entirely reassuring.

That Thursday, Musk held his first all-hands meeting with staff in what was regarded as a disastrous introduction to a company not yet sold on its new owner.

To add to the turmoil, that was the moment when Roth, who had stayed on to serve as Twitter's head of trust and safety—in a promising sign of continuity for advertisers—abruptly quit. He timed his resignation email to hit Musk's inbox while he was speaking to the staff so Musk wouldn't be able to react in haste.

The timing carried another important benefit: Roth could exit the building without being escorted out by security.

But among Musk and his circle, Roth's resignation quickly triggered a crisis.

Suddenly, messages began pouring in—from Musk's top adviser Jared Birchall and lawyer Alex Spiro—trying to convince him to stay.

Birchall and Roth talked by phone for nearly an hour, as Birchall made an unsuccessful bid to keep Roth on board, raising, among other subjects, his compensation. Musk was, of course, still occupied with his address to the staff.

But at around 3 p.m., as Twitter staff and the media were digesting news of the all-hands, Roth received a Signal message.

It was Musk.

"Do you have a moment to talk?" he asked. "It would mean a lot if you would consider remaining at Twitter."

The seven-year Twitter veteran had carefully thought out every aspect of the resignation, including how to de-escalate the situation. He knew the risks of making an enemy of Musk, so he decided to pinpoint the three key reasons behind his decision to leave, tailoring his script around the personal career risks and blowback he faced, instead of indicting Musk's leadership.

He messaged Musk back around two hours later. I'll call you shortly, Musk said.

The call came at 5:22 p.m.

"It would mean a lot to me if you stayed," Musk said. "I really feel like we're doing important work. . . . Is there anything that will change your mind?"

Roth had been the liaison between Musk's Twitter and the Twitter of old. Without him, the institutional knowledge—and willpower—to recognize and correct a potential catastrophic mistake in the making was depleted. The trust and safety team, responsible for content moderation on the site, had warned of the potential disastrous implications of rushing out Musk's revamped Twitter Blue, for example.

But after their warnings went unheeded, some of the survivors started to question the usefulness of remaining there.

As a result of Musk's failure to listen, the launch was a catastrophe on nearly every front—not merely because of the flood of impersonators but from a pure business standpoint as well. Only around 150,000 users opted to pay for Twitter Blue, just 0.06 percent of the company's user base, a figure that would bring in only $14.4 million in annual revenue.[1]

"Punting relaunch of Blue Verified to November 29th to make sure that it is rock solid," Musk said in a tweet earlier in the afternoon, before he issued his midnight email to Twitter staff.[2]

In his phone call with Musk, Roth highlighted Blue as a central factor in his decision to leave. Frenetic product development, he said, was "setting fire" to Twitter's brand equity; Blue was rushed out the door and faltered in all the predicted ways, something that affected Roth's reputation and credibility.

The layoffs and return-to-office orders, meanwhile, had taken such a steep toll on morale that Roth would face challenges leading a deflated—and depleted—staff, rife with holes in key positions. Meanwhile, Twitter was battling dueling impulses: to slim down, trim the budget, and eliminate staff, while embarking on ambitious new product launches at the same time. Roth recognized Twitter's immediate cashflow needs, but the whiplash-inducing strategy didn't make sense.

Musk stood down.

"I understand," he said. "I wish that you would stay but I understand your decision."

"Thank you. I appreciate you hearing me out," Roth said. "I want you to know I am rooting for your success, and I am rooting for Twitter's success."

"Thanks," Musk said and then hung up.

In the dark days of March 2020, after the COVID-19 pandemic forced much of the Bay Area into lockdown, I found myself on a quiet stretch of San Francisco on the edge of the Outer Mission district, picking up a gaming laptop I had bought off Craigslist. The seller and I chatted a bit, and he mentioned that he worked at Twitter. We exchanged phone numbers.

Two years later, I found myself staring at a message from the same number, though I couldn't remember who it was.

Normally, this would have been an odd hour to receive a work-related text, but in the weary-eyed days of November 2022, I immediately knew where the conversation was headed.

"So . . . big news incoming about Twitter," the person said.

* * *

The Chief Twit, to his credit, didn't beat around the bush.

"Going forward, to build a breakthrough Twitter 2.0 and succeed in an increasingly competitive world, we will need to be extremely hardcore. This will mean working long hours at high intensity. Only exceptional performance will constitute a passing grade," Musk wrote in the November 16 email. "Twitter will also be much more engineering-driven. Design and product management will still be very important and report to me, but those writing great code will constitute the majority of our team and have the greatest sway. At its heart, Twitter is a software and servers company, so I think this makes sense."[3]

It was the next part of the email that made me question whether I was being roped into a hoax.

"If you are sure that you want to be part of the new Twitter, please click yes on the link below," Musk wrote, followed by a link to a Google Form. "Anyone who has not done so by 5pm ET tomorrow (Thursday) will receive three months of severance," he continued. "Whatever decision you make, thank you for your efforts to make Twitter successful. Elon."

The email was unambiguous. Musk was issuing an ultimatum aimed at consolidating his power within the company, getting rid of troublemakers and perceived pencil pushers and, presumably, cutting down on leaks. And he was stealthily conducting a layoff of hundreds.

Twitter employees had sporadically begun discussing the bizarre late-night email on Slack. Many were adamant they would not sign.

"Anyone who signs it is signing their work-life balance away," the employee told me. "As if he didn't already take it from us. It's like 'welcome to level 2 of hell' . . . the mood and morale in the office is unbelievably bad."

And that was before thousands would wake up to find out that their boss had demanded they commit to an "extremely hardcore" Twitter or leave the company.

By eight o'clock that morning, Twitter employees were processing the news en masse.

"I just got up," one told me. "Saw the email and I'm delighted to know I have the option to leave. I'm not committing to hardcore Twitter."

The sentiment was widespread.

Twitter employees rightly asked: What was in it for them? What was Musk offering in response to their commitment to stay and pledge fealty to the new regime?

But among the staffers, one captive group emerged. Sure, there were the stragglers among the bunch—careerists or the stray Musk loyalist. But it was the workers from overseas, software engineers on visas tied to their employment, who were suddenly on the hook.

If they didn't sign the loyalty pledge, they could be out of a job and on a plane back to India or China. Those who were locked in constituted a sizeable proportion of the staff, one that was consistently left without a voice in the process when contrasted with the steep resistance—through the press, social media, and public condemnation—to Musk's actions among the broader Twitter workforce.

By Thursday, the day their answers were due, Twitter employees were making their stance abundantly clear. By several estimates, more than one thousand staffers opted against signing the pledge, a higher number than anticipated. Musk was prompted to make concessions: easing a return-to-the-office order and even drawing up plans to ask some staffers back.[4]

All the while, Twitter's internal Slack channels were lighting up with employees posting "goodbye salute" emojis, the unofficial symbol of the Twitter resistance. Again, the hashtag #LoveWhereYouWorked flooded social media.[5] This time, employees publicly aired their farewells online—what did they have to lose?

The hashtag #RipTwitter emerged as a top Twitter trend as users prepared for the inevitable fallout: glitches, momentary breakdowns, and then widespread outages that would leave the site unusable.

If Musk's team didn't intervene, Twitter would be left in shambles. Key teams, core to the functioning of the site, were completely gutted, with only one or two, or sometimes zero, staffers handling critical systems.

"It will continue to coast until it runs into something, and then it will stop," a former employee said, according to the *Post*.[6]

For a site with few key staffers at the helm of critical functions, the prognosis was grim.

"Every mistake in code and operations is now deadly," said a former engineer who'd newly departed the company.[7]

Musk had sent a frantic series of emails attempting to save face, some of which even landed in the inboxes of those who'd refused to sign his pledge.[8]

At the same time, he was trying to assemble his all-star team of engineers from among the loyalists. He directed employees who "actually write software" to attend a summit where they would meet him for a code review. Those who were not in the office were expected to rectify that, and those who were out of town—for personal travel, for example— were expected to buy flights back. All of this reflected exactly the sort of shoot-from-the-hip ethos that wouldn't be tolerated from anyone at lower levels. At one point, for example, Musk emailed workers asking for screenshots of their recent code. Then he followed up with his expectation that they make their way to Twitter's headquarters in person unless it was an emergency or they could not physically do so. Within minutes, there was a third request that workers fly out to San Francisco. Finally, a fourth said doing so was not ultimately required, the *Post* reported.[9]

A photo posted on Twitter showed Musk gathered with engineers after 1:00 a.m., with Musk boasting: "Just leaving Twitter HQ code review." Staffers flashed peace signs and thumbs-ups in another photo showing them in sweatshirts, sweatpants, and baseball caps, sitting on an office table, as if participants in a late-night hackathon.

What the photo didn't show was hordes of other workers, many of them the immigrant staffers dependent on visas, who were flying in overnight to meet Musk by Saturday morning, when he had promised to be there.

One former staffer recalled seeing some of them roll into the tenth floor with carry-on luggage in tow early that morning, clearly desperate to keep their jobs. But Musk failed to show.

"You had people on that floor waiting around all day for a guy who told them to come and he never showed up," the former staffer recounted.

Musk's dual roles as head of Tesla and Twitter—and his open exchange of resources between the companies—were brought into stark relief that week, as he appeared in Delaware Chancery Court to defend the $56 billion pay package he had received from Tesla's board years earlier, after investors sued alleging a flawed compensation process.[10]

Among those who came to his defense was former Tesla board member Antonio Gracias, whose current role at Twitter highlighted a fundamental truth of Musk-world.[11] Musk's fiduciary duty might ordinarily have been to his Tesla shareholders; as far as the in-group was concerned, there were hardly any clear lines between publicly and privately traded companies, between board and management, between business and personal. And Musk counted Gracias as a close friend.

Now, at the Tesla shareholder trial, Musk was defending his behavior as CEO of another company, Twitter. And with the Tesla stock still reeling from his $44 billion Twitter takeover, he was speaking to a different audience than he had for much of the previous two weeks: angry Tesla shareholders.

He was ready to placate them and, when asked, freely admitted that Tesla employees were taking on work at Twitter.[12]

"There's an initial burst of activity needed post-acquisition to reorganize the company," Musk said in court, according to Reuters. "But then I expect to reduce my time at Twitter."[13]

The Tesla staff at Twitter, *The Washington Post* reported, were conducting work there in a "voluntary" capacity, "after hours," "a minor thing," Musk said.[14]

The arrangement certainly raised eyebrows among critics, investors, and at least one US government official.[15] And their concerns were valid: investors were furious with Musk for disrupting Tesla's roaring momentum with this Twitter distraction, one that had no discernible payoff.

"We're in literally the best part of the company's history and it's being totally demolished by Twitter," investor Ross Gerber would later tell me.[16]

Suddenly, Senator Elizabeth Warren (D) began asking questions on behalf of those bruised investors. In a letter to Tesla board chair Robyn Denholm, Warren raised the issue of "whether Mr. Musk is funneling Tesla resources into Twitter," citing a CNBC report that Musk had brought in more than fifty Tesla employees, a majority of them from the Autopilot team, to perform work at Twitter.[17]

The Warren letter alleged "misappropriation of Tesla resources" and cast doubt on Musk's assertion that the Twitter work was just a "voluntary thing." Another CNBC report cited a Tesla employee: "Most would also feel it was impossible to turn down a direct request from Musk without later facing poor performance reviews or other consequences."[18]

Days earlier, Warren had publicly urged tax code changes to rein in "freeloading" billionaires such as Musk. (Musk would later say he faced a tax bill worth more than $11 billion in 2021[19] and "paid more income tax than anyone ever in the history of Earth for 2021 and will do that again in 2022.")[20]

"Please don't call the manager on me, Senator Karen," he said, throwing up a "prayer hands" emoji.[21]

Shortly after the Twitter takeover and around two weeks before his resignation, Yoel Roth received a text message from a Tesla employee. It wasn't unusual to hear from the Tesla staffer, who was managing Twitter's security procedures during the transition. But the request that night struck Roth as overstepping his bounds. He was being ordered to reinstate the *Babylon Bee*.[22]

The *Bee*, which calls itself a "Christian news satire" site, was suspended in 2022 after declaring Biden administration health official Dr. Rachel Levine, a transgender woman, its "Man of the Year."

The *Bee*'s tweet promoting its article violated Twitter's policy on misgendering, and the site was required to delete the tweet before regaining its account, something its leadership refused to do.[23]

The suspension had caught the attention—and ire—of Musk in the days leading up to his initial investment in Twitter. It was the rallying cry on which ex-wife Talulah Riley had helped encourage Musk to buy Twitter.

Now, with Musk at the helm, a Tesla employee was ordering Twitter's head of trust and safety to restore the account and one other: that of psychologist Jordan Peterson, who had been banned after referring to actor Elliot Page by the name Page used before transitioning; Peterson's tweet decried the removal of Page's breasts by a "criminal physician."[24]

Roth soon found himself at a meeting with Musk's attorney, Alex Spiro, in the second-floor conference room, where he raised the matter.

"I don't understand why this is a violation," Spiro said, noting that the *Bee*'s tweet was satirical, according to a person familiar with the exchange. It was a matter on which reasonable people could disagree.

But Roth quickly pointed Spiro to Twitter's policy of explicitly prohibiting that sort of behavior. He explained why it would pose an issue to make individual exceptions to the rules—from a consistency standpoint—without overhauling the policy entirely.

That was a decision that Spiro was powerless to make.

"We need to talk to Elon about this," Spiro said, according to the person with knowledge of the exchange.

Around an hour later, Spiro and Roth huddled in a U-shaped kitchen on Twitter's second floor. After Musk arrived, Roth told him that he had been asked to reinstate the banned accounts. And he quickly explained why that would pose an issue, given Twitter's policy on misgendering.

Musk floated a solution.

"What about this idea of a presidential pardon?" he said, according to a person familiar with the matter. "A presidential pardon is a thing in the Constitution. Can't I just do a presidential pardon?"

Roth was concerned that an exception might ignite a user backlash and erode trust, given the lack of consistency in the application of Twitter's policies. He raised that concern with Musk.

Then why not allow everyone to post that kind of content? That would constitute a change of policy, Roth said. Musk followed that reasoning.

The tweets in question were "not cool," he said, but they didn't rise to the level of "sticks and stones," referring to violent threats. The rules should reflect that.

Roth agreed that there should be distinctions among different types of objectionable content.

Musk suggested the idea of punishments, including search limitations, preventing certain objectionable tweets from appearing in users' timelines, the type of visibility restrictions Roth himself had advocated at times.

The men agreed, and soon after, Musk was pulled elsewhere.

But by Friday, November 18, with Roth out and the world watching Twitter melt down, Musk announced the surprise reinstatement of two previously banned accounts: *The Babylon Bee* and Jordan Peterson, along with that of comedian Kathy Griffin, who had been banned after changing her name and profile picture to match Musk's in violation of Twitter's parody rules.[25]

"New Twitter policy is freedom of speech, but not freedom of reach,"

Musk said. "Negative/hate tweets will be max deboosted & demonetized, so no ads or other revenue to Twitter."

Throughout Musk's highly tumultuous and chaotic Twitter takeover, there were many moments that called into question his business acumen, management style, and strategic vision. But now, with his seeming mismanagement of Twitter spilling into public view, his intellectual capacity was being directly challenged. Did Elon Musk really know what he was talking about?

That was the question that drove Ian Brown to confront the world's richest person over a live audio chat during one heated moment in December 2022.

Brown probably didn't expect to be called a moron and a jackass in return or dismissed as a nobody. But a month of policy failures and public embarrassments was finally boiling over as the former Twitter employee posed a simple question to Musk.

It happened over Twitter Spaces, the live-audio feature that Musk was quickly turning into the app's marquee offering, where thousands could tune into an open-ended conversation with the richest person on earth—where he and many other high-profile celebrities, politicians, and newsmakers would begin to take questions. He would interact directly with listeners, though speakers were screened by the host, who had the power to boot them if needed.

On Spaces, Musk was insistent that Twitter's code base—the computer code that powers the whole website—needed a complete rewrite. The following interaction played out over the same Twitter Spaces.

Brown, a former senior engineering manager at Twitter, wanted to know what Musk really knew about the company's code.

"I think, frankly, if you want to have a really high velocity of features I think we'll just need to do a total rewrite of the whole thing," Musk said, according to audio captured of the Twitter Spaces interview and posted to the site now known as X.[26]

"Wait, seriously, a total rewrite, that's your prediction for velocity?" Brown interjected, insinuating that Musk's plan would hardly make things more efficient.

The host of Twitter Spaces, a software developer named George Hotz, who had secured a brief internship at Musk's Twitter, posed the question simply: "Revolution or reform?"

"You can either try to amend the crazy stack that exists or rewrite it," Musk said.

Brown wasn't convinced that Musk knew what that meant.

"When you say crazy stack, like, what do you mean? Break it down," he said.

Musk grew agitated. He hadn't signed up for an interrogation.

"Come on, buddy, come on," Brown said over laughter in the background as Musk hesitated.

"Who . . . who are you?" Musk shot back.

"What do you mean who am I?" Brown answered, while Hotz pleaded for civility. "You're in charge of the servers and programming, whatever. Like, what is the stack, Elon? Come on, man. Take me from top to bottom. What does the stack look like right now? What's so crazy about it? What's so abnormal about this stack versus every other large-scale system on the planet, buddy. Come on."

"Amazing," Musk shot back. "Wow. You're a jackass. . . . What a moron."[27]

The backdrop of Musk's frustrations was a month and a half of failures on nearly every front. In the run-up to his ill-fated acquisition, Musk had famously asked, "Is Twitter dying?"[28] Now it looked like it really might be. The blunders that followed his initial weeks at the helm—when a handful of mistakes might have been forgivable—were among the most destructive of his tech career, and they happened in rapid sequence: banning an account that tracked the location of his private jet, booting the journalists who reported on the fiasco, and rolling out a new policy that prohibited promotion of outside social media sites, an attempt to knee-cap the competition that rapidly backfired when one launched a rival platform. By the end, Musk would agree to step down as Twitter CEO.

It began in mid-November, as the moderating forces slowly disappeared from Musk's circle.

The departures of Yoel Roth and hundreds of others following Musk's ultimatum had consolidated Musk's power and accelerated Twitter's descent into yet another fiefdom. Suddenly, decisions that had previously been subjected to a deliberative process—whether a board or an executive team—were handed to a committee of one. He was increasingly isolated and consumed by conspiracy theories inside his tenth-floor office, believing Twitter's previous management was incompetent, maybe criminally so, and the only solution was to air Twitter's dirty laundry in public.

Suddenly, priorities shifted inside Twitter's Market Street headquarters. Musk allies were now deputized to sift through internal systems for evidence of malfeasance—for signs, for example, that Twitter was a left-aligned organization doing the bidding of the US government; that its staff was aligned against Musk; that its previous management, including its former head of trust and safety, had allowed child sex abuse material to flood the site.[29] That fishing expedition culminated in what Musk termed the "Twitter Files," a trove of documents "on free speech suppression" motivated by a long-standing grievance about Twitter restricting the distribution of a *New York Post* story detailing leaked materials from a laptop that belonged to Hunter Biden, son of the then-presidential candidate.[30]

"The public deserves to know what really happened . . ." Musk wrote on November 28.[31]

Investors wanted Musk to focus on making money, selling ads, driving subscriptions, and executing the ambitious product changes he had been promising. Having believed that Musk had the potential to make Twitter revolutionary in the manner of Tesla or SpaceX, they were hardly content to see it turn into a mere museum piece.

They wanted a return on their investment.

Meanwhile, Twitter was becoming the ultimate expression of Musk's penchant for putting cronies and loyalists in charge, people who had a hard time saying no and neglected to question his lack of technical expertise or social media experience. It was around this time that some in Silicon Valley began to see Musk as a charlatan, a successful entrepreneur posing as an engineering genius.

Inside the company, an unlikely coterie of advisers was drawing up draconian budget cuts—targeting and slashing expenses that would have been previously unthinkable. These advisers included his confidant, Antonio Gracias, as well as Steve Davis, the president of Musk's tunneling firm The Boring Company, an entrepreneur who had previously owned a bar and a frozen yogurt shop in Washington, DC.[32]

Basic requests suddenly flowed through Davis, who emerged as the executor of Musk's wishes and the slasher in chief. The strategy was hardly sophisticated. Twitter alone would determine its budget—bills be damned—and anything it couldn't afford (or hadn't planned to cover) would simply go unpaid, as reporting from *The New York Times* illuminated that month.[33] The internal justification for this line of thinking was that Musk wasn't responsible for the commitments made under the previous management team. First, Musk ordered $1 billion in infrastructure-related cuts, according to Reuters[34]—an amount equivalent to a fifth of Twitter's 2021 revenue—which meant that data centers and services responsible for keeping the site running were suddenly liable to be shut down. Musk would not waste time in seeing them dismantled. Meanwhile, as the *Times* reported, Twitter stopped paying rent on its San Francisco office and locations around the world.[35]

As key advertisers like Apple pulled back their Twitter campaigns and new product ideas such as Twitter Blue flopped, Twitter burned through money.[36] The clock was ticking on the company's first interest payment on Musk's debt, quarterly installments that would add up to around $1 billion annually.[37]

But during that time, Musk turned his attention to something else: vengeance.

The self-dubbed "Chief Twit" occupied a tenth-floor office, a spare conference room where he was insulated from criticism; protected by yes-men; and, most importantly, shielded from employees who increasingly regarded him with contempt. Those seen as possessing an inadequate level of "hardcore" energy—pragmatists who had signed the pledge but didn't believe its message—were regarded with suspicion.

One high-up executive recounted to me the bizarre sequence of events that played out after he was called up to the tenth floor to meet Musk.

Those about to meet with Musk were advised to follow a rigid set of instructions. First, they were to wait in a staging room of the large conference area he occupied. There, they could wait for minutes or hours to be called into the office—at Musk's whim. Once inside, they were told, they should let Musk wrap up whatever he was doing before proceeding into their discussion or meeting. They should remember to let Musk speak first.

The executive recalled how he was kept waiting for about ninety minutes before being called into Musk's office. He entered the space to find the Twitter leader occupied with what appeared to be a YouTube video on his phone.

Ten minutes of strained silence ensued.

Musk finally surfaced, said, "How are you doing?" followed by a brief update and exchange of pleasantries. The briefing was light on details.

All of a sudden, Musk said, "Thank you," shook the executive's hand, and returned to watching his video.

Amid all the chaos and upheaval in San Francisco invited by the transition to Musk's management team, Twitter's New York–based information security team wanted to brief Musk about the state of play in its world.

Twitter was under a decade-old FTC consent decree governing its handling of user data, which had stemmed from the hacks of high-profile accounts under the Obama administration, including the then-president's own. Musk needed to understand the stringent rules under which Twitter was required to operate.[38]

So a meeting was arranged with Musk in the company's San Francisco office. Musk's budget cuts were already hitting hard in New York—what must it be like clear across the country at headquarters? In New York, the austerity showed up in the most basic ways; Red Bull and M&Ms were no longer on offer. Twitter mugs gave way to paper cups. Soon, the coffee was gone entirely.

Perhaps more important than the disappearance of sugary snacks was the brain drain that began filtering down the company's ranks. Once again, the question of preserving institutional knowledge became paramount. Musk's team had to understand what it was dealing with as far as the FTC was concerned.

When they arrived to brief Musk, the security employees found him gregarious and reassuring—he gave the impression that he was on top of everything.

Twitter's chief information security officer, Alan Rosa, made a point of emphasizing the importance of the consent decree. "Look, this order that we signed is a bit aggressive," he told Musk. "It's not your run-of-the-mill average consent order."

"Yeah," Musk said, in one person's recollection. "I know all about this. I'm aware of it."

The meeting ended on favorable terms, as Musk appeared to understand the importance of complying and seemed familiar with the topic of discussion, if a bit light on the details as usual.

But within minutes, an email arrived from one of Musk's staffers that signaled to at least one executive that Musk may not be in full command of the FTC order.

Could they pass along a copy of that consent decree when they had a chance?

At the end of November, Elon Musk took to Twitter to promote the company's latest work under his leadership—not a new product or feature but the trove of documents he depicted as a bombshell, an unambiguous revelation of how intertwined Big Tech and government had become, with aligning interests in suppression of free speech on partisan grounds.

"The Twitter Files on free speech suppression soon to be published on Twitter itself. The public deserves to know what really happened," he wrote.[39]

The first batch was published within days, detailing Twitter's internal scrambling over the *New York Post*'s Hunter Biden laptop story and the ultimate decision to limit its spread on the site. But there was only one problem: the findings were largely underwhelming for many of Musk's supporters, even the ardent conservatives among them.[40] The batch of documents, for example, fell well short of showing that Twitter acted at the behest of the government or Democratic politicians, as right-wing figures had insinuated. Instead, they showed Twitter's internal process for fielding content moderation requests from political officials—including the Trump White House and Biden campaign. The journalist who revealed the documents, Matt Taibbi, wrote: "Both parties had access to these tools."[41] Still, he continued, "This system wasn't balanced. It was based on contacts. Because Twitter was and is overwhelmingly staffed by people of one political orientation, there were more channels, more ways to complain, open to the left (well, Democrats) than the right."[42]

The revelation of the process itself was interesting, a fascinating look under the hood of a social media company with vast influence. Still, a consensus soon emerged that the Twitter Files hadn't gone far enough.

Meanwhile, security staff auditing the company's logs had discovered a far more widespread pattern of self-interested maneuvering. Contractors deputized by Musk had been digging through old emails, looking for dirt. This clandestine group had been charged with searching for Twitter employees actively disagreeing with Musk, speaking ill of the company's new leader.

But things came to a head one afternoon in December, when Musk wrote to an IT subordinate, Alex Stillings, with a bizarre order to let an outsider raid Twitter's internal systems.

"Alex, please give Bari full access to everything at Twitter," he wrote over Signal, in a message I obtained. "No limits at all."[43]

The message revealed how unrestrained Musk had become. He wanted to essentially onboard former *New York Times* columnist Bari Weiss to Twitter, giving a journalist the same access to email, internal messages, private user data, and documents that a senior employee would have.

This raised antennae inside the company's IT department, to say the least—employees were aghast to discover how broad Musk's fishing expedition was becoming. They were reluctant to grant the wide access he was requesting.

Their concerns had nothing to do with politics. They were well aware of the federal consent decree that governed Twitter's protection of private user data. Musk hadn't even managed to earn their trust as CEO yet—they certainly weren't willing to break the law on his behalf.

"These guys did amazing damage," a former employee later recalled of Musk's trusted circle of deputies. "They are basically bullying their way to getting 'super god' access to these things. All they're doing is they're witch hunting for Elon, so they can find people talking [about him] so they can fire them."[44]

As it turned out, their skepticism and quick thinking ended up saving Musk from another headache.

A letter from FTC chair Lina Khan to Republicans in Congress detailed that the saga had played out exactly as employees described to me at the time. "Longtime information security employees at Twitter intervened and implemented safeguards to mitigate the risks," it said, according to *The Washington Post*. "The FTC's investigation confirmed that staff was right to be concerned, given that Twitter's new CEO had directed employees to take actions that would have violated the FTC's Order."[45]

* * *

The same month as the Twitter Files fishing expedition, Musk's attorney, Alex Spiro, departed Twitter. Spiro and Musk had not been seeing eye to eye. Musk's frustration with Spiro had grown amid a series of controversies invited by a smooth talker with a high tolerance for risk. Musk took issue with Spiro's initial decision to keep Twitter's deputy general counsel James A. Baker, a former FBI lawyer, on board in a prominent role where he had influence over the Twitter Files. After learning about his role in reviewing the documents and vetting the release of a trove intended to show a vast government conspiracy, Musk decided to fire Baker, as *The New York Times* reported.[46] (Baker and Rosa, the chief information security officer, were both fired within hours of each other that December.)

Spiro would win his way back into Musk's good graces in due time, as a key Tesla trial loomed in January.

The "free speech" philosophy that drove Musk's initial pursuit of Twitter was increasingly at odds with his desire for control over the platform's discourse. Any suspicions that his free speech commitment wasn't iron-clad would only be confirmed by later actions, such as his high-profile cancelation of a deal with television host Don Lemon after a testy interview with Musk, for example.[47] People were quick to point out that Lemon was only the latest journalist to be lured in and then spurned by the promises of the man who'd called himself a "free speech absolutist."

But at the time of Musk's takeover, many were willing to take him at his word. Musk alleged that commitment to the philosophy had been exemplified in a November 6 tweet when he wrote, "My commitment to free speech extends even to not banning the account following my plane, even though that is a direct personal safety risk."[48]

It took a little more than a month for him to violate that commitment on its face, a lasting scar on his claims of free speech absolutism.

On December 14, Jack Sweeney, a college sophomore at the University of Central Florida, woke up to find his popular Twitter account @ElonJet had been banned.[49]

The account, which synthesized public data to publish the real-time location of Musk's Gulfstream plane, had amassed hundreds of thousands of followers, generating concerns—many legitimate—about doxxing and the security of high-profile public figures.

Now it was wiped off the internet as Musk's site claimed it "broke the Twitter rules."[50]

The background for the suspension soon became clear. That night, as the backlash against Musk's ad hoc decision-making mounted, Musk posted a tweet to explain himself—baselessly accusing Sweeney of aiding in a stalking attempt on him and his toddler.

"Last night, car carrying lil X [Æ A-Xii] in LA was followed by crazy stalker (thinking it was me), who later blocked car from moving & climbed onto hood," he wrote. "Legal action is being taken against Sweeney & organizations who supported harm to my family."[51]

Musk did not follow through on that claim, Sweeney told me in December 2024.

In the wake of the incident, where a member of Musk's security team confronted an alleged stalker at a South Pasadena, California, gas station, according to a news report, Musk turned his attention to journalists who had been covering the jet-tracking account's suspension.[52]

More than a half dozen journalists, high-profile reporters with large followings, soon faced the same fate as Sweeney—they were banned from Twitter with little recourse. They included my colleague Drew Harwell. In posting a thread on the developing situation, Harwell had tagged @ElonJet, apparently now a capital offense—at least in Twitter terms.[53] Internally, Twitter employees soon discovered how their platform was being used to settle the CEO's personal vendettas. One of my colleagues and I discovered that the suspensions were tagged with labels that marked them, in one case, "direction of Elon," and in others, "direction of Ella," referring to Twitter's new head of trust and safety, Ella Irwin.[54]

Two Musk tweets soon erased any doubt about who was behind the decision to boot Harwell and the other journalists.

"Same doxxing rules apply to 'journalists' as to everyone else," he wrote, referring to posting a person's real-time location, something the journalists had not done.[55] In some cases, the journalists, like Harwell, had linked to the now-suspended @ElonJet account.[56]

Musk apparently saw a different version of the events.

"They posted my exact real-time location, basically assassination coordinates, in (obvious) direct violation of Twitter terms of service," Musk said.[57]

The Washington Post later revealed that police did not see a connection between the jet-tracking account and the alleged stalker.[58] Sweeney and the journalists had seemed to be made out as scapegoats anyway.

Ultimately, at the time, Twitter alone enacted a policy that classified Sweeney's activity as doxxing, meaning he could not post the location of Musk's jet in real time, instead having to do so with a one-day delay—making competitors such as Instagram and Mastodon the new source of relevant information on Musk's whereabouts. The journalists were restored, on the condition they delete their offending tweets.[59]

Twitter was starting to seem less useful. Even some of Musk's allies were souring on the direction the platform was heading with his ad hoc decision-making.

Even friendly journalist Bari Weiss, who had recently detailed her Twitter Files findings in a series of threads,[60] broke with Musk over his arbitrary bans and highlighted the inconsistency in his positions,[61] drawing his ire.[62]

"If someone messed with my baby or my family I'm sure I'd change the rules and ban the jet account, too," she posted. "But last month you said you were leaving it up to show your commitment to free speech. So doesn't it make sense that people would be confused?"[63] (More than a year later, her fellow Twitter Files journalist Matt Taibbi would admit Musk "proved to be very disappointing on the free speech issue.")[64]

But for those who objected to Musk's arbitrary policies on acceptable posting, the final nail in the coffin was still to come.

On December 18, Elon Musk took in the World Cup final with Jared Kushner and the CEO of Qatar's investment authority, a Twitter investor. On the same day, the social media site rolled out a surprise new policy: "free promotion" of other social media sites was no longer allowed; no longer could users rely on Twitter to push alternatives such as Facebook, Instagram, or Truth Social, which was cofounded by former president Donald Trump.[65] The policy, enacted as prohibited competitors such as Mastodon and Post were gaining traction, prompted an immediate backlash.[66] People had put up with Musk's erratic decision-making for months, but for Twitter power users—even those who had relentlessly supported Musk—this was a bridge too far. The policy violated not only Musk's commitment to free speech but also the basic principles of the open internet.

Twitter, under Musk's new policy, would be erecting a firewall between itself and other social media networks. Critics attacked the new policy—not just the usual cohort of Musk-haters but also Silicon Valley names who had been in Musk's corner. Paul Graham, a programmer and writer with a popular Twitter handle, promoted his Mastodon account and was soon suspended. That created a wave of criticism of its own.

"This is the last straw," Graham wrote, linking to Twitter's new policy, before his account was suspended.[67]

Meanwhile, George Hotz, the developer who'd been hired for an internship at Twitter, tweeted a link to his Instagram account.

"If saying that is banned, this isn't somewhere I want to be anymore. That's so far from free speech," he wrote.[68]

The new policy even came to the attention of Edward Snowden, the famed National Security Agency whistleblower, as big an advocate of transparency and an open internet as anyone online.

"[This] is a bad policy and should be reversed," Snowden wrote.[69]

Amid the furor, Musk outlined his thinking in a series of tweets.

"Twitter should be easy to use, but no more relentless free advertising of competitors. No traditional publisher allows this and neither will Twitter," he wrote.[70] "Casually sharing occasional links is fine, but no more relentless advertising of competitors for free, which is absurd in the extreme," he added.[71]

But now the usual swarm of criticism of Musk's actions was gaining a foothold in the mainstream. Twitter users were in open revolt.

Musk issued a rapid succession of tweets aiming to calm the backlash.

"Paul's account will be restored shortly," he wrote at 6:15 p.m. Eastern time, reversing the ban on a handle that had promoted a competing social media site.[72]

Then Musk did something rare: he apologized.

"Going forward, there will be a vote for major policy changes. My apologies. Won't happen again," he said at 6:17 p.m. Eastern time.[73]

Musk appeared to be in a dour mood that evening. Three minutes later, he would issue a stern declaration, his strongest since taking over the site he hadn't wanted to buy for $44 billion he didn't have in hand. Musk's impulsive decision-making was finally catching up to him. His tweet would make that much clear.

"Should I step down as head of Twitter?" he wrote at 6:20 p.m. "I will abide by the results of this poll."[74]

Musk was increasingly turning to an unscientific method—the Twitter poll, an informal survey of respondents on a social media site—to drive his decision-making. Polls had featured in several high-profile decisions— whether to reinstate the account of former president Donald Trump;[75] whether to restore thousands of other previously banned accounts;[76]even, a year earlier, whether to sell 10 percent of his Tesla stock[77] in the face of a massive tax bill,[78] giving him a hefty chunk of cash in the months before he pursued Twitter. In theory, the method was foolproof. While any Twitter user could vote in the polls, they were most likely to show up in the time-lines of those who followed Musk or were in his proximity. That meant that Musk's massive following produced a self-selecting group of sycophants who could read between the lines and produce the result Musk wanted.

And in general, the polls always went the way Musk hoped. Take, for example, the question of selling stock. Musk's phrasing hinted at the desired result: "Much is made lately of unrealized gains being a means of tax avoidance, so I propose selling 10% of my Tesla stock," he wrote,[79] adding in a later tweet, "I will abide by the results of this poll, whichever way it goes."[80]

Overwhelmingly, the 3.5 million respondents supported the stock sale by a margin of around 58 to 42.

The only problem was when Musk sold a chunk of his stock only days later, a filing revealed that more than $1 billion worth of the sales was preplanned, suggesting he had used his Twitter sounding board as a trial balloon for decisions that had already been made.[81] The poll merely served as a record of public validation or, perhaps, in Tesla's case, to quell any shock to the public markets.

But in mid-December, as Musk's moves were becoming increasingly erratic and unpopular, even his canned Twitter polls turned against him. Users voted by a wide margin of around 59 to 41, for example, to immediately restore the journalists Musk had suspended following the alleged stalking incident.[82]

Musk responded in characteristic fashion, smearing them as he let them back onto the site.

"The people have spoken," he wrote on December 16. "Accounts who doxxed my location will have their suspension lifted now."[83]

After launching his poll on whether to step down as CEO, Musk went eerily, uncharacteristically quiet. The twelve-hour Twitter survey garnered more than a million votes per hour on average, capturing real-time public sentiment as it went viral, finding its way onto the feeds of users who'd previously had no reason to engage with Musk's content.

Now they had a personal say in whether the CEO who had wrought so much havoc on the site over the past few days would remain in charge.

"Those who want power are the ones who least deserve it," Musk tweeted amid the voting.[84]

And users voted in droves; the poll amassed millions of responses, more than 17.5 million votes overall.

By Monday morning, the results were in, though they had hardly ever been in question. Users had overwhelmingly voted that Musk should step down—by a 15-point margin, 57.5 percent to 42.5 percent.

Now all eyes turned to Musk.

But the Twitter CEO, a prolific user of the website who sometimes posted multiple times per hour, was nowhere to be found. The markets liked what they saw that morning; Tesla, which had been battered by Musk's Twitter acquisition, was up slightly on the news that Musk may step down.[85]

But as the day wore on with no response from Musk, Twitter's future was no clearer than before he'd launched the poll. Some floated a simple explanation: Musk had been flying back from Qatar, where he had watched the World Cup, and lacked a stable internet connection. It would have been much more believable had he not pioneered the Starlink-based internet that he provided to the front lines of the war in Ukraine.[86] At times Musk even conducted live audio chats from his plane over Twitter Spaces.

No, Musk had simply gone silent—whether shell-shocked by the results or helpless to craft a proper response.

He finally emerged at 6:27 p.m. Eastern time, roughly twelve hours after the poll's conclusion.[87] But not to acknowledge the results. Rather, Musk was finally ready to cast doubt on the reliability of Twitter polls as a decision-making tool. First, he replied, "Interesting" to a thread that alleged the poll had been flooded with "deep state bots" voting against him.[88]

Less than fifteen minutes later, Musk tweeted again—this time to publicly agree with a user who suggested Twitter should restrict policy-related polls to paying users.[89]

It took him until the following day to firmly acknowledge the results.

"I will resign as CEO as soon as I find someone foolish enough to take the job!" he wrote at 8:20 p.m. ET on December 20, exactly two days and two hours after putting his fate in the hands of Twitter users. "After that, I will just run the software & servers teams."[90]

But Musk was hardly chastened. It was during this period that he made an impulsive decision that might have exposed Twitter to more risk than any previous misstep, betting on its ability to withstand his aggressive cost cutting. It's become a popular meme that Musk fired three-fourths of Twitter's workforce and the site continued to function just fine. But those who perpetuate it neglected the state of Twitter after Musk's takeover. The site was crippled by outages—multiple major breakdowns prompted by small tweaks in code—and bogged down by glitches to key features. Twitter was unable to meet the moment when major global events relied on it.[91]

In the following days, Musk ordered the company's largest data center to shut down. Biographer Walter Isaacson detailed the operation, in which Twitter managers were asked about moving computer servers to Portland to save the company $100 million per year. Musk was dissatisfied with the projected six-to-nine-month timeline.[92]

He scrounged together a ragtag team that would move the servers over the approaching Christmas holiday and in the days that followed, relying on a semitruck, moving vans, and Apple AirTags to track the equipment.

As Isaacson explained: "Other workers at the facility watched with a mix of amazement and horror. Musk and his renegade team were rolling servers out without putting them in crates or swaddling them in protective material, then using store-bought straps to secure them in the truck."[93]

Musk would come to regret dismantling the data center as Twitter became increasingly sensitive to minute changes, resulting in a "brittle" environment, as Musk termed it—a site prone to outages.[94] (One such outage occurred three days after Christmas.[95]) Most famously, in an episode Isaacson pointed out, Twitter's live-streamed launch of Ron DeSantis's presidential campaign—Musk's preferred candidate at one point—was a colossal failure.[96] During that announcement, Musk struggled to maintain a conversation with a candidate who dropped off the call because of the apparent overload on Twitter's servers.

"All right, I'd like to welcome Governor DeSantis for the—" Musk began, his own audio cutting out, as I reported in the *Post*. "This is unfortunate; we've never seen this before." In the background, a voice announced, "There's so many people."[97]

"In retrospect, the whole Sacramento shutdown was a mistake," Musk told his biographer, Isaacson. "I was told we had redundancy across our data centers. What I wasn't told was that we had seventy thousand hardcoded references to Sacramento," he said, implying that large portions of Twitter's computer code were programmed specifically to rely on the data center he'd scrapped. "And there's still shit that's broken because of it."[98]

As Musk continued to float conspiracy theories about Twitter's departed executives, some found the fallout of the online harassment he invited seeping into their real lives.

Yoel Roth, the departed head of trust and safety, was now living with his husband, a social worker, in a temporary apartment in Oakland—they had removed their belongings from their home and placed them in storage while they waited for the heat to die down.

But by January, they decided to list their house, a renovated Craftsman in El Cerrito. The allegations Musk and his followers were fueling about Roth's views and approach to content moderation, accelerated by the Twitter Files, had made it practically impossible for Roth and his partner to ever feel comfortable at that address again. Roth was facing threats in his Twitter direct messages and emails from online harassers who had discovered his home address.

He and his partner disclosed that they were leaving the property because of safety concerns, causing at least two prospective buyers to back out. In the end, the house they'd bought and fixed up years earlier—their primary asset, which they'd poured the entirety of Roth's Twitter savings into—sold at a loss.

If rumors of Twitter's imminent demise were exaggerated, problems with its ability to remain functional during periods of peak demand certainly persisted.

During the 2024 presidential election, Musk hosted a Spaces chat with former president Donald Trump, the candidate he'd endorsed only minutes after an assassination attempt earlier in the summer. Despite having almost two years to work out the kinks, Musk experienced an almost exact repeat of the DeSantis announcement fiasco, as X's servers couldn't handle the load and the start of the interview had to be delayed.

This time, Musk blamed a "massive distributed denial of service" attack for the technical issues, referring to a type of targeted action by hackers or spammers to bring the site down, announcing, once the event had gotten going, that it had "saturated all our data lines."[99] He did not provide evidence for the claim. He turned back to a free speech argument.

"As this massive attack illustrates, there's a lot of opposition to people just hearing what President Trump has to say," he said.

With hundreds of thousands tuned in, Trump appeared to take X's servers crashing as a positive sign, congratulating Musk for "breaking every record in the book."

15

"CAN ELON MUSK DO WHATEVER HE WANTS AND NOT FACE THE CONSEQUENCES?"

In January 2023, Elon Musk sat before a jury in a San Francisco courtroom. He looked tired.

The situation that had brought everyone there was familiar. It was Musk's first full day of testimony in the federal shareholder trial over his 2018 "Funding secured" tweet. From my vantage point among the members of the press, facing Musk from across the room, I saw a man struggling, perhaps sick of discussing this particular subject; the color had disappeared from his face.

It didn't help that he was shifting in his seat and complaining of back pain.

"I had trouble sleeping last night so unfortunately I am not at my best," he said from the witness stand.

Musk had famously slept in the Tesla factory during particularly challenging times. The situation at Twitter was apparently bad enough that he had to sleep on the floor there too.[1]

Nonetheless, the absurdity of this billionaire's sleeping arrangements certainly struck some as a performance. Around that time, according to a person familiar with the matter, Musk's good friend and fellow billionaire Larry Ellison urged him to stay at his Pacific Heights mansion, essentially a glass-enclosed paradise with sweeping views of the Bay Area and the Golden Gate Bridge, located a short jaunt from Twitter HQ.

"Larry offered him his home," the person told me, urging him, "Listen, why sleep on the Twitter floor if you can drive ten minutes, have your driver [drive you] ten minutes," to Twitter?

"It's kind of theatrical rather than real . . . like you have a car and a driver and three guards, you get in the car, you can be on the phone, text, whatever, so you don't waste a minute. You get home and you go to a nice bed."

But perhaps Musk's refusal to sleep in comfort was part of the strategy. Musk made for a compelling, even sympathetic witness as he testified about everything from his emigration to Canada, to working through college and accruing student loan debt, to his SpaceX ambitions. In a room full of stuffy lawyers, the world's richest person was the everyman.

Musk was at his most compelling when asked by his attorney Alex Spiro what his childhood was like.

Musk paused. All he could muster was a two-word answer.

"Not good.

"I don't think a few sentences would describe it," he added.

I found myself feeling bad for him. This was a man who spent his childhood being bullied—and who could never shake that framework from his mind. He could sell you on the idea that he was still being picked on—now it was just the system in the role of playground bully.

Everyone in that courtroom was transfixed.

Trials can be a drag—and witnesses, particularly experts, can drone on for hours while doing little to keep the jury engaged. Not so with Musk. He was amusing on the witness stand—charming and even funny at points.

It was the plaintiffs' attorney, a taciturn character, who elicited perhaps the biggest laugh of the trial when he referred to Musk as "Mr. Tweet," which he called a "Freudian slip."[2]

Musk seized on the opening.

"Mr. Tweet," Musk conceded, was "probably an accurate description." (He would soon change his Twitter display name to Mr. Tweet.)

Musk, from the witness stand, also seemed able to spin practically anything into a believable story. That included his 2018 statement, which he referred to as "the infamous tweet," that had landed everybody in this courtroom.[3] A refresher: Musk tweeted, "Am considering taking Tesla private at $420. Funding secured." Tesla's stock popped with that news, jumping by nearly 11 percent, as the inflated price Musk hinted at suddenly seemed within reach before the claim came crashing down— culminating in the SEC suing Musk for fraud.[4]

In the courtroom, though, Musk was nonchalant about the whole thing.

"Just because I tweet something does not mean people believe it or will act accordingly," he said.

"Can Elon Musk do whatever he wants and not face the consequences?"

That was the question on the mind of attorney Nicholas Porritt as he turned to the jury in the San Francisco federal court.

"This is about rules," Porritt told them. "This is about applying rules to billionaires like Elon Musk."[5]

Half a decade later, Musk's offense in the "Funding secured" saga seemed almost tame in light of his indiscretions in the years that followed. Among the people who suffered the most from the fallout were Wall Street investors and short sellers, not exactly sympathetic characters. But it was clear Musk had done something wrong—boneheaded, really—and this mistake had cost him tens of millions of dollars and his position as board chairman of Tesla. Judge Edward Chen had already ruled that Musk's claim of "Funding secured" was untrue.[6] The open question was whether investors had relied on that claim to make trades and whether it was material to the market moves that lost them money.

Plaintiff Timothy Fries testified that he had lost $5,000 in the subsequent frenzy, buying Tesla shares on the belief that they would soon be worth far more because he thought that Tesla was going private. He eventually sold his fifty shares—purchased at $370 each—at a loss, *The Wall Street Journal* reported.[7]

"I felt that I lost money due to a misrepresentation," he said, according to my *Washington Post* story that included his testimony.[8]

Glen Littleton, the key plaintiff and class representative, claimed to have lost far more: in excess of $3.5 million. But unlike Fries's smaller bet, Littleton's losses seemed to have come from a miscalculation in a sophisticated operation that involved vast sums of money. Littleton, Spiro argued, was "betting." And the evidence showed why. He had sent an email to his stockbroker referring to Musk's tweet as a "rumor," saying, according to Spiro's closing remarks, he had "heard about this 'Am considering' rumor" and decided to make trades based on it.

Spiro characterized this as a "maybe/maybe-not he was gambling on."[9]

The way Littleton's investment was designed, the seventy-one-year-old would have benefited if Tesla had surpassed the $420 per share that Musk said he'd secured, according to *Fortune*.[10] But it became clear that wasn't going to happen anytime soon, and Littleton was forced to sell.

Littleton seemed like an exorbitantly rich guy, and Musk and his lawyer painted him and his peers out to be the villains of the story. That's where the one final piece of red meat came in: short sellers—traders who took the opposite approach to Littleton and stood to gain if Tesla *didn't* meet the $420 target. Musk and Spiro successfully portrayed these plaintiffs as people who would benefit from Tesla's failure. Musk, then the richest person on the planet, had skillfully laid out a David versus Goliath dynamic that somehow cast him as David.

"A bunch of sharks on Wall Street wanted Tesla to die very badly," Musk told the jury. "I believe short-selling should be made illegal. It is a means for, in my opinion, bad people on Wall Street to steal money from investors. Not good."[11]

Spiro, too, called out the short sellers in his closing argument.

People "who were betting against Tesla and were shorting Tesla want bad things to happen to Tesla," he said. "And anybody who was shorting Tesla at this time didn't do very well."[12]

In January 2023, nearly five years after Musk's tweet that raised doubts about his leadership at Tesla—only part of a series of scandals that threatened to dethrone Musk from his role at the company—the billionaire entrepreneur was absolved in the matter once and for all. Musk was found not liable; the jury didn't buy the plaintiff's argument that "Funding secured" was material to the investors' losses.

After the case, plaintiffs' attorneys embraced one another, sitting in an almost funereal silence.

I found Porritt despondent when I spoke with him. He was a serious man who prided himself on his preparation.

"We're just disappointed," he said. "I don't think this is the sort of conduct we expect from the CEO of a large public company. . . . I think we presented a very good case and I think we presented the case as well as we could.

"I imagine he's pleased," he added.

He was.

"Thank goodness, the wisdom of the people has prevailed!" Musk tweeted. "I am deeply appreciative of the jury's unanimous finding of innocence in the Tesla 420 take-private case."[13]

Spiro, his attorney, said simply, "The jury got it right."[14]

Musk liked a tweet calling Spiro—the man who helped him beat the "pedo guy" defamation lawsuit and now "Funding secured"—an "absolute legend."[15] As reported in the *Post*, "It continues a string of verdicts in Musk's favor, from the shareholder lawsuit over Tesla's purchase of embattled solar energy company SolarCity, and Musk's defamation lawsuit over calling a Thai cave rescue volunteer a 'pedo guy.'"[16]

After the trial, reporters spoke to one of the jurors, who explained the result of the two hours of deliberation.

"I thought a lot of times it seemed disorganized," he said of the cases against Musk. The juror praised the Musk side's "very, very effective witnesses," including longtime Tesla board member Antonio Gracias, who said Musk's posts were made in the interest of disclosing pertinent information to shareholders.[17]

In the end, the juror said, the case against Musk simply "didn't land."[18]

One day near the conclusion of the trial, I sat in the hallway outside the courtroom waiting for Musk to emerge. The doors swung open, and Musk, flanked by multiple security guards, rushed out. We made brief eye contact, then Musk turned and stared straight ahead.

I had a question. Musk had locked his Twitter account in the preceding days in an apparent effort "to test whether you see my private tweets more than my public ones."[19] As events over the next few weeks would show, Musk seemed preoccupied with his Twitter account's reach.

"Mr. Musk," I asked, "why did you make your Twitter private?"

Before he could answer, I spotted a hand waving in my direction. One of Musk's security guys was making a "zip it" motion as if to shush me.

Musk and his team proceeded down the long corridor and disappeared from sight. Never mind how compelling a witness he could be—outside of the courtroom, Elon Musk was Elon Musk: the richest man on earth. He was a man who required an entourage for a trip to the bathroom.

* * *

There were numerous court cases and trials over the period that could have provided insight into how Musk dealt with the onslaught of new public attention to his empire, including the accompanying assortment of overzealous, litigious, and—a favorite target of his—class-action plaintiffs. The federal shareholder trial over "Funding secured" was particularly instructive as a window into how he managed to escape the litany of consequences stemming from one of his more egregious public actions, at least one of the more indefensible ones.

As it turned out, the answer to Porritt's question—"Can Elon Musk do whatever he wants and not face the consequences?"—seemed self-evident.

The shareholder suit in San Francisco was a federal jury trial involving aggrieved shareholders of Musk's largest and most important asset, Tesla. The company's shareholders had alleged Musk's false statements cost them millions.[20] It was a deeply personal matter to Musk—a matter of pride— and it involved so many of his closest allies. It took place as Musk was in the throes of the chaotic Twitter takeover. Musk, as he admitted, may not have been at his best. But he presented as a vulnerable, flawed, and human witness, complaining of back pain and laboring under the weight of his Twitter obligations.

Perhaps emboldened by the legal victory in "Funding secured," Musk only became more erratic in the weeks that followed.

The website Platformer soon reported that Musk had boosted his own tweets to the top of Twitter feeds after his engagement figures during the Super Bowl disappointed him.[21] "Yes, Elon Musk created a special system for showing you all his tweets first," the headline blared. A *Washington Post* analysis backed up that finding, showing Musk's tweets had declined to an average of 137 million views per day, before spiking to around 400 million per day "after his posts were artificially boosted."[22]

This news put Musk on the defensive. He decried the reporting in the *Post* and other outlets,[23] attributing the issue to a bug.[24]

But examples of Musk using Twitter as a vehicle for his self-interest abounded—from his bans of journalists who posted about the account tracking his private jet, to stripping his foes in the media of blue verification check marks as part of his business push to make users pay $8 a month for that privilege, to his crackdown on the wave of impersonators—an effort I learned commenced only after workers were shown examples of people posing as Musk.[25]

Musk seemed to be catering the user experience on the platform toward himself while also losing sight of what might be best for his businesses. On a Tesla earnings call, the *Post* reported, he was asked about the prospect that his vocal political tweets could affect Tesla's brand.[26] He pointed to his Twitter following.

"Let me check my Twitter account. So I've got 127 million followers," Musk said. "It continues to grow quite rapidly. That suggests that I'm reasonably popular."[27]

Then he doubled down, underscoring the extent to which the world might be witnessing what happens when its most influential business leader becomes trapped in a filter bubble of his own making.

"I might not be popular [with] some people but for the vast majority of people, my follower count speaks for itself," Musk said.

(A year later, Musk would again display his penchant for over-indexing the importance of Twitter engagement when Don Lemon asked him about his baseless claims that diversity, equity, and inclusion initiatives could be responsible for lowered safety standards in the airline industry. "You've repeatedly said that there's no evidence that standards are being lowered—and watch the replies showing all the evidence that it is," Musk said, as Lemon pushed back that social media replies were not the same thing as evidence.[28])

It had been nearly two months since Musk had promised to appoint a permanent CEO. On Twitter, Musk posted jokes instead.

He tweeted a photo of his Shiba Inu, Floki, sitting at a desk before a miniature laptop and a page that described his new title. "The new CEO of Twitter is amazing," he wrote on Valentine's Day.[29]

Musk's continued occupation with running a social media site was taking a toll elsewhere too. The consequences for Tesla, whose fate he had tied to Twitter, were real. Amid the pressure from shareholders, Musk said his search could take until the end of the year.[30]

From the looks of it, his investors didn't have that long. Tesla's valuation—and Musk's net worth—had peaked toward the end of 2021 as postlockdown consumer spending was high and demand for Tesla's vehicles shot through the roof. Musk was worth more than $300 billion at the time.[31] He had really done it: taken Tesla from an upstart manufacturing outfit—one that more closely resembled an automotive skunkworks operation than a Fortune 500 company—to a blue chip tech juggernaut worth more than a trillion dollars.

What happened next was a bloodbath worthy of the record books—literally—as Musk would become memorialized in Guinness World Records for the largest loss of a personal fortune ever recorded.[32]

On the other side of Musk's zenith were new worries about inflation, the global chip shortage, and the effect of Russia's war in Ukraine. These trends offered at least a partial explanation for why Tesla's valuation began to tumble back to earth—though it was still in the stratosphere—by early March.

But once Musk started accumulating Twitter shares, the descent was steep. The chart of Tesla's performance between Musk's peak and the Twitter debacle roughly a year later could rival even the steepest mountain range. The drop was practically vertical. There was no overstating how much the market hated what Musk was doing, even amid other factors such as demand concerns.[33]

Tesla's valuation wasn't just slashed in half—by the bottom, the company was trading at around a quarter of what it had been worth a little more than a year earlier.

There was only one man who could stop the bleeding, and he had evidently been sleeping on a couch on the seventh floor of Twitter's headquarters.[34] This was the same floor where, *Forbes* had reported, the conversion of some office space into actual bedrooms prompted San Francisco city officials to investigate potential code violations.[35]

His dog, Musk maintained almost two months after his initial pronouncement, was in charge.

"I did stand down," he told a BBC interviewer, as I reported in the *Post*. "I keep telling you, I'm not the CEO of Twitter. My dog is the CEO of Twitter." He repeated his point for emphasis. "I said I would appoint a new CEO, and I did, and it's my dog."[36]

Wall Street didn't buy it. Say what you will about the market, it would never punish a dog this way.

By May, Musk was finally ready to appoint a permanent CEO. There had been rumors swirling for months about potential candidates. Each time a person emerged, however, it seemed like their chances sunk the moment their name leaked to the media.

This time, however, word came directly from Musk.

"Excited to announce that I've hired a new CEO for X/Twitter. She will be starting in ~6 weeks!" he wrote. "My role will transition to being exec chair & CTO, overseeing product, software & sysops."[37]

The woman who would take over, Linda Yaccarino, was in some ways unlike any job candidate Musk had ever appointed to such a prominent role—and in others, a perfect fit for the gig. A seasoned advertising executive from NBCUniversal, Yaccarino was just what Twitter needed to turn around its fortunes—someone who could restore trust with the company's decimated ad base and serve as an antidote to Musk's lightning rod personality. But like many of Musk's picks, she wasn't powerful enough in the space to, say, force him out—or rein him in. That push-and-pull power dynamic would become especially relevant over the coming months. Yaccarino was being brought in to do a critically important job—restoring Twitter's trust and therefore its revenue—but could Musk tone down his inflammatory behavior long enough to let her?

Musk formally announced Yaccarino as the new CEO the following day.

"Obviously, bringing on Linda allows me to devote more time to Tesla, which is exactly what I will be doing!" Musk wrote in another tweet.[38]

While announcing his new hire, he mentioned something else that caught everyone off guard.

"Looking forward to working with Linda to transform this platform into X, the everything app."[39]

Musk made good on that promise by July, officially changing the name of the platform to a single letter, one that had intrigued him for practically his whole career, thereby bookending his technological pursuits. It was a puzzling business move. For all of its financial woes, Twitter's strength as a brand was undeniable; the ubiquitous name immediately evoked a unique shade of blue, its unmistakable bird icon. It had even brought new terms into the lexicon. Nobody had to explain that a "tweet" wasn't a bird sound. (By contrast, news articles would have to reference a tweet with the clunky "a post on X, the site formerly known as Twitter.")

Wasn't Musk torching the company's brand value even further?

"Twitter was acquired by X Corp both to ensure freedom of speech and as an accelerant for X, the everything app. This is not simply a company renaming itself, but doing the same thing," he wrote in a post on X, the site formerly known as Twitter. "The Twitter name does not make sense in that context, so we must bid adieu to the bird."[40]

And Musk had an answer for the doubters.

"X will become the most valuable brand on Earth. Make [*sic*] my words," he wrote.[41]

To really drive home the renaming, the company erected a giant pulsing X sign atop its San Francisco headquarters, like a Bat-Signal looming over the city streets below, one with the side effect of disturbing the sleep of senior citizens, as was discussed in the introduction.

At first, said Christopher J. Beale, a journalist in his forties who had observed the nightly light show from the balcony of his thirteenth-floor apartment, the sign "looked kind of cool." But Beale began to understand the problem as the new logo washed his living room in bright white as he tried to watch television at 10:30 one night, the light eventually becoming inescapable. He relocated to his bedroom, where the light crept through the reduction blinds.

Beale began to film from his balcony.

The latest monument to tech decadence began pulsing, then soon started strobing. Beale's apartment started to feel like the Mid-Market neighborhood's hottest nightclub.

The apparent lack of a permit had prompted San Francisco to investigate the matter. The sign came down a few days later, dismantled amid a flood of complaints, including "concerns about its structural safety and illumination," the Associated Press reported.[42]

16

AUTOPILOT GROUNDED

It had been nearly half a decade since Walter Huang was killed in a crash involving Tesla's Autopilot as he drove to work on US 101. In the meantime, in 2021, the National Highway Traffic Safety Administration (NHTSA) had begun requiring manufacturers such as Tesla to quickly report any serious crashes involving their driver-assistance systems.

Former NHTSA administrator Steven Cliff had a hunch about what would happen when the agency began asking for that information. But he wasn't certain. By 2022, the data were in—and the results were unequivocal: Teslas posed a unique hazard on the roadways, with hundreds of crashes, far exceeding figures from mainstream automakers that had taken more cautious approaches with their driver-assistance features.[1]

By 2023, Teslas in Autopilot mode had been involved in 736 reported crashes since 2019, far more than any other automaker, including many of the better-known German, Japanese, and American brands subject to the order. There had been seventeen fatal incidents and five serious injuries, the *Post* reported.[2]

NHTSA had been stymied by fears of stifling potential lifesaving innovation, bailed out by political chaos in Washington, and hampered by a lack of data.

But by the end of the year, the agency would finally take unprecedented action to rein in Tesla. It was the type of broad intervention that officials like Jennifer Homendy and Robert Sumwalt had been seeking for years as they saw the consequences of Tesla's experiment play out.[3]

* * *

In 2023, the Cybertruck arrived, but Elon Musk's promise of a robotaxi had yet to manifest.

Musk had spent years telling Tesla owners that their cars were essentially able to drive themselves.[4] At some point, they began to believe it.

The dynamic was dramatically illustrated on a rural highway in North Carolina that March in an incident that revealed yet another new danger of the unfolding experiment with automation on public roads. A man named Howard Yee had allegedly affixed steering wheel weights to his Tesla Model Y in an apparent effort to defeat so-called nags—alerts reminding Autopilot users to keep their hands on the wheel. Ideally, Yee's car would have been cruising down the road on its own at 45 mph, sensing that his hands were on the wheel and guiding him along without the pesky intervention of safety nannies.[5] This was the way of the future.

The only problem was that seventeen-year-old Tillman Mitchell was coming home from school at the same time that afternoon. The teenager stepped off the bus—with its stop sign out and its warning lights flashing—only to be met by Yee's car barreling down the road. Mitchell was thrown into the windshield before flying upward, landing facedown in the road.

His great-aunt was blunt about the severity of the collision that left Mitchell on a ventilator, with a fractured neck and broken leg.

"If it had been a smaller child," she told me, "the child would be dead."[6]

The crash demonstrated so many of the problems with Tesla's approach to Autopilot at once: the cars' apparent struggle to identify stopped vehicles with flashing warning lights, a segment of a customer base that had been lulled into inattentive complacency, the risks of a company accountable to so few turning the real world into an open test lab for unfinished technology.

I was struck by the irony of all this happening on a rural road thousands of miles away—clear across the country—from where Tesla's engineers were developing their tech, insulated from the consequences. The fact that it had happened only weeks after Dan O'Dowd's Super Bowl commercial and not long after Omar Qazi's experiment of sending actual children into the path of his Tesla in Full Self-Driving mode, was just plain sad.

To Steven Cliff, NHTSA had to be methodical—its findings bulletproof and inarguable. Securing Tesla's buy-in was also essential, or a crucial safety intervention could become mired in court battles, a legacy of the recall system on which NHTSA staked so much of its authority.

Tesla, never one to back down from a fight, would have to be presented with findings so indisputable that the company would be convinced that pushing back wasn't worth the hassle.

In the end, Cliff said, NHTSA had a strong case bolstered by more than two years of data. Tesla had proven itself to be different from the other automakers and companies using driver-assistance technology. Competitors existed in a space where their cars had high levels of control accompanied by high levels of driver monitoring. Their tech was a hassle to use outside of the locations and conditions for which it was designed.

Autopilot wasn't. Many of the fatal crashes were occurring in cross traffic, far from the controlled-access highways for which the features were designed. Owners were using Tesla's driver-assistance features on surface streets, sometimes with deadly consequences.[7]

"Tesla has developed a system that is so convenient that it lulls the driver into the assumption the vehicle actually is driving itself," Cliff told me in December 2023. "It's not."

What made Tesla's system special?

"Tesla's system is unique in that it has a high level of control, low level [of] driver monitoring," Cliff said.

Evidently, that was a disastrous recipe.

For years, the media had been reporting on cases where Teslas slammed into stationary or otherwise massive objects at high speeds, resulting in horrific destruction—cars that were barely recognizable husks, roofs sheared off by the underside of trucks, vehicles charred to bits from the ensuing battery fires.[8] The pattern was typically similar: a driver who'd been distracted—thought to be playing a game on their iPhone, in one case, watching a video in another—as their vehicle hurtled down the road in Autopilot at speeds up to 70 mph.

In December, the *Post* published a story that documented eight separate fatal or serious crashes involving Autopilot on roads for which the software hadn't been designed.[9] A few days later, NHTSA announced Tesla's largest-ever recall, partly an effort to address precisely the problem the *Post* had laid out in its story.[10] The agency, which had been investigating Teslas' repeated crashes with parked emergency vehicles while in Autopilot over a two-year probe, had presented its findings to the company in a tense series of meetings beginning two months earlier.

"In those meetings, Tesla 'did not concur' with the agency's safety analysis but proposed several 'over-the-air' software updates to make sure drivers who engage Autopilot keep their eyes on the road," the *Post* reported.[11]

The result was a massive coup for federal regulators—a voluntary recall that would change the behavior of more than two million vehicles on the road. Tesla was recalling nearly every car it had ever built.

Unlike a traditional automotive recall, which requires owners to bring their vehicles to dealerships for maintenance, Tesla could use its software capability to update its fleet remotely—an early advantage that other major automakers have been slow to adopt. This convenience led some to dismiss the weight of what had happened. Rohan Patel, Tesla's policy chief, characterized it as an "improvement," as if the idea had been hatched out of thin air.[12] (In fact, Tesla had been fighting against making such an improvement for years.) The problem with this framing was that it negated the involvement of federal officials in securing Tesla's buy-in. Repeatedly checking the company's homework to make sure it was complying with federal regulations was a resource-intensive undertaking that diverged heavily from the self-certification model expected of automakers.

And while the nature of the action was sweeping and dramatic, the fix itself seemed tame—it added "controls and alerts" to ensure drivers were paying attention while using Autopilot, "additional checks" when using the software outside the intended areas such as controlled-access highways, and the suspension of the key Autosteer feature for repeat scofflaws who failed "to demonstrate continuous and sustained driving responsibility."[13] In other words, the action comprised a handful of common-sense measures that Tesla had neglected to add until it was compelled to do so by indisputable findings about its software's performance.

The fixes were far from perfect. For one, now that Tesla's driver monitoring had proven to be flawed, officials in Washington didn't trust the company to make its own fix, as the voluntary recall model prescribed. And when a *Washington Post* columnist tested the software update, which included the additional warnings and messages, his Tesla blew through two stop signs.[14]

Still, Tesla fans were already feeling the impact of the changes. *The Wall Street Journal* reported drivers said they were irritated by the persistent nags that were intended to reprimand them if they failed to pay attention, but which they said had run amok.

One driver put it succinctly: "I didn't think my car would be bullying me so much."[15]

17

THE TECHNOKING HAS NO CLOTHES

Who really controlled Tesla?

In January 2024, Chancellor Kathaleen St. J. McCormick of the Delaware Court of Chancery set out to resolve that $56 billion question once and for all.

Six years after Musk was handsomely rewarded with the most generous compensation package ever recorded—exceeding the distant runner-up, Musk's 2012 pay package—McCormick was tasked with deciding the most crucial matter that still loomed over his empire.

If Musk had controlled Tesla and leveraged his relationships with beholden and otherwise conflicted board members to secure a record-breaking payout for himself, depriving shareholders of the knowledge of his extensive ties, the entire package could be in jeopardy. An unfair process—one overseen by a CEO who exerted dictatorial control, for example—would scuttle Musk's big payday.

As to that key question—was Musk really in control?—McCormick laid out the stakes.

"This decision dares to 'boldly go where no man has gone before,'" she wrote.[1]

The evidence was damning. She listed a number of factors that worked against Musk, from workers' description of him as a "tyrant"—someone who "fires people 'on a whim'"—to his intimate involvement in financial and operational matters, to operating on his "own set of rules at Tesla" where, for example, "no one at Tesla could review his email account without permission except when legally required," to the title he gave himself in 2021 "without first consulting with the Board": Technoking, "a position he compared to being a monarch."[2]

"Truly, the avalanche of evidence on this point is so overwhelming that it is burdensome to set out in prose," McCormick wrote.

Musk was in control.

And his board was clearly conflicted. Investors weren't given a fair rundown of those conflicts, which would have allowed remaining shareholders to partake in an "informed vote," the other way to ensure fairness.

McCormick was tongue-in-cheek about the process's shortcomings.

"In the final analysis, Musk launched a self-driving process, recalibrating the speed and direction along the way as he saw fit," she wrote.

That left the verdict.

"The plaintiff is entitled to rescission."

Translation: Elon Musk's gargantuan $56 billion payday was no more. The vessel that had enabled some of Musk's most ambitious bets—leveraging his Tesla stake for loans, selling billions' worth of shares to buy Twitter, always with the assurance that there was more stock around the corner—could vanish.

To add insult to injury, the person who wrote the decision was the same judge who'd presided over the Twitter takeover, the case in which Musk had overpaid for a $44 billion social media site under the duress of a certain courtroom defeat.

Elon Musk was livid.

"Never incorporate your company in the state of Delaware," he wrote on X, the first in a series of posts that might accurately be described as a meltdown if they had been written by anyone else.[3]

Soon, he turned his attention to McCormick. "She has done more to damage Delaware than any judge in modern history," he wrote.[4]

To Musk, the decision was outrageous: he'd opted against taking a salary and now was being punished for it.

"The judge in Delaware who improperly rescinded my comp literally earns more than I do," he wrote.[5]

Tesla fanboys shared his fury. Musk had hit every ambitious

milestone of a compensation package that deprived him of a salary—against odds that some said were impossible. Now he was being punished for it?

The decision fueled weeks of resentment aired over X. Musk ultimately made the same decision he'd made during the COVID-19 shutdowns—pick up and move to a friendlier state.

Musk turned to his usual playbook: a Twitter poll. He asked whether Tesla should move its state of incorporation to where its headquarters now resided.

In the poll, 87 percent of more than one million respondents said that yes, Tesla should change its incorporation to Texas.[6]

"The public vote is unequivocally in favor of Texas!" Musk wrote. "Tesla will move immediately to hold a shareholder vote to transfer state of incorporation to Texas."[7]

Musk soon announced that SpaceX had incorporated in Texas.[8] Neuralink, meanwhile, moved to Nevada, news outlets reported.[9]

Alexandra Merz, a Tesla shareholder who'd amassed a following of tens of thousands under the handle TeslaBoomerMama, rallied support for a new shareholder vote that would once again award Musk the $56 billion package that had been taken from him.[10] Musk's fans online were calling for him to be given the billions he felt he was owed. Musk personally thanked Metz[11] as the measure passed overwhelmingly, along with another to relocate Tesla's incorporation from Delaware to Texas.[12]

The shareholder vote alone did not overturn the decision, which remained in McCormick's hands. But it sent a clear message. Musk's support remained ironclad, and the cost of beating him was often self-defeating—he wasn't going to put up with losing; instead, he was going to pick up his ball and go home, where he felt appreciated. By the end of the year, McCormick had issued a new ruling in light of the shareholder vote—this time standing by her original decision. The defendants' team "got creative with the ratification argument," McCormick wrote, but they "have no procedural ground for flipping the outcome of an adverse post-trial decision based on evidence they created after trial."[13]

McCormick awarded legal fees of $345 million—payable in Tesla stock or cash—to the plaintiffs' side. The plaintiffs' attorneys expressed hope the matter would end there, but said if not, "we look forward to the privilege of defending the Court's thoughtful and well-grounded opinions on appeal to the Delaware Supreme Court."[14]

Tesla pledged to appeal. And Musk fumed, calling McCormick an "activist."[15]

The costliest tweet of Musk's career may not have been "Funding secured" after all.

On November 15, 2023, weeks after the horrific events of October 7, Elon Musk decided once again to respond to a tweet promoting a crackpot interpretation of current events—evidently, the fallout of promoting conspiracy theories related to the attack on Paul Pelosi two years before had taught him nothing.

Musk took to X that afternoon to respond to a baseless claim that "Jewish communities have been pushing the exact kind of dialectical hatred against whites that they claim to want people to stop using against them."[16] The poster's general argument was that Jewish Americans—whose politics generally trend progressive—had encouraged the country to be flooded by immigrants who were now mobilizing against them and were thus responsible for the antisemitism they faced in rising numbers. It was a nonsense claim, not to mention an apparent strawman attack against the hordes of pro-Palestine protesters who had mobilized after Israel's massive military response that had killed tens of thousands in Gaza.

Musk gave it a full-throated endorsement.

"You have said the actual truth," he wrote in response to the tweet.[17]

He doubled down less than two hours later, expanding on his initial thought.

"The ADL [Anti-Defamation League] unjustly attacks the majority of the West, despite the majority of the West supporting the Jewish people and Israel," Musk wrote. "This is because they cannot, by their own tenets, criticize the minority groups who are their primary threat. It is not right and needs to stop."[18]

A few minutes later, amid the growing furor over his remarks, Musk tried to clarify.

"You [are] right that this does not extend to all Jewish communities, but it is also not just limited to ADL," he wrote in response to a post objecting to his use of generalizations.[19]

Musk was trying to play clean-up, but it was already too late. Many were still processing the devastation of the October 7 attack in Israel and the horrors of the subsequent ground invasion in Gaza, as corporate entities carefully navigated the crisis through canned and measured statements.

Musk was operating from a different playbook.

The day after Musk's antisemitic tweet, the nonprofit Media Matters posted a report alleging that ads for major companies such as Apple and IBM had appeared next to pro-Nazi content on X.[20] Many users had been up in arms about Musk's antisemitic post, and now the bottom was going to fall out. By this point, you can guess the pattern: Apple, IBM, and Disney were among the major advertisers who pulled their ads from the platform.[21]

Musk couldn't hide his disgust. He called Media Matters "pure evil."[22] X vigorously denied the claims, alleging that the Media Matters test was manipulated to produce a desired result—and that in almost every case, authentic users had not seen the ads next to the offensive content in question. Soon after, they launched a lawsuit, which Media Matters decried as "frivolous."[23]

But the damage was already done.

Ross Gerber read Musk's remarks in horror as investors scrambled to pull their money out of Tesla.

"It offended so many of my clients," he said.

On X, he lit into Musk—whom he'd supported through so many of his trials and controversies, whom he backed even through his absurdly misguided pursuit of Twitter. No more.

"It takes a lifetime to build a reputation, and a day to lose it," Gerber wrote.[24] On investing in Tesla, he wrote, the "party seems to be ending for now."[25]

Musk blocked him soon after.

Deep down, Gerber knew he could no longer reason with the man.

"People get too big, think they're too smart, and they stop listening to the people who've been helping them for ten years," Gerber said in an interview with me in January 2024. "I'm sorry I'm not coming to you to kiss your ass. I'm an equal."

Privately, he lobbied Yaccarino to have Musk unblock him over direct messages on X. Yaccarino did not engage. She did, however, make an effort to placate Gerber on one point—showing how Musk's extreme positions sometimes left her on the defensive, playing clean-up for the actions of the owner.

The Anti-Defamation League (ADL), Yaccarino told Gerber in a private message, "is one of the best."

It was a far cry from Musk's stated position that "the ADL unjustly attacks the majority of the West"[26] and should be renamed the "Defamation League."[27]

For Musk, the loss of an ally like Gerber—someone who regularly praised him and Tesla on CNBC and had become a de facto public face of a company without a PR department—was significant.

This became abundantly clear when he had to turn to investors with requests that required the sort of backing he'd had in the glory days, when Tesla was the envy of the tech and auto worlds, when Musk was comfortably the richest man in the world and was infallible in the eyes of investors—before he'd risked it all with Twitter. That was what happened in January 2024, when he came to Tesla investors to ask for 25 percent control of the company as a condition for making artificial intelligence bets within the company.

"I am uncomfortable growing Tesla to be a leader in AI & robotics without having ~25% voting control," he wrote. "Unless that is the case, I would prefer to build products outside of Tesla."[28]

Some saw it as a shakedown. Musk had been in the driver's seat at Tesla before making a series of unforced errors and boneheaded tweets, before he became consumed with grievance politics, before he divided his fan base and emerged as one of the most polarizing figures on earth.

"Let's just go back two years," Gerber told me. "Everything was great two years ago. Stock's at $400, life is great for Elon. He's king of the world."

But being the Technoking had its downsides.

"You've got somebody who thinks he's Caesar, or thinks he's Napoleon, who thinks he can do no wrong," Gerber said.

Elon Musk had one answer for the advertisers who had left X over the furor he'd ignited with his antisemitic tweets.[29] It would leave the audience in stunned silence.

Musk was furious about the advertiser boycott that had threatened his company's fortunes and, ultimately, its survival. He was not prepared to take responsibility for it. "What this advertising boycott is going to do is it's going to kill the company," he would say later when the headlines were already being written. "And the whole world will know that those advertisers killed the company."[30]

He was visibly indignant that day at *The New York Times'* DealBook Summit, shortly after returning from a visit to Israel that many saw as an effort to make amends.[31] Anyone expecting him to have been mellowed by the trip was sorely disappointed.

CNBC anchor Andrew Ross Sorkin asked Musk about the perception that his Israel trip was an "apology tour," citing advertisers' response. Musk quickly erased any doubt about the question.[32]

"If somebody's gonna try to blackmail me with advertising, blackmail me with money?" he began, his tone escalating with each word.

He turned toward the audience so nobody would mistake the words that would spill out of his mouth next.

"Go fuck yourself."

The audience was silent, apart from a few nervous chuckles. What seasoned advertising executive Linda Yaccarino must have been thinking at that moment was anyone's guess.

"But—" Sorkin interjected.

Musk interrupted, raising his arms and gesticulating as he dragged out each word for emphasis.

"Gooo. Fuck. Yourself."

Elon Musk tweeted as his empire burned. The early weeks of 2024 found him posting relentlessly about "illegals" and decrying wokeness in every form. He seemed to be inured to the criticism and fallout around Tesla's stock, which was being pummeled, threatening the very fortune that he used to propel his planet-saving ambitions. His behavior drew the ire of even his most ardent fans. He couldn't accelerate the transition to renewable energy if he became a political lightning rod; he would just be another polarizing and divisive figure in the geopolitical arena, a demagogue.

Musk did not care.

X's valuation was also in the gutter, worth around a quarter of what Musk had paid for it by some estimates.[33] Tesla had fallen nearly 30 percent since the beginning of the year, trimming tens of billions off its valuation. Musk had been stripped of his $56 billion pay package, the one that helped him become the richest man on earth. Every Tesla with Autopilot had been recalled over safety concerns. Investors were beyond tired of Musk's antics cutting into their fortunes and began questioning his bid for more control.[34] On top of that, the Cybertrucks were beginning to rust.[35]

Musk, meanwhile, was spending much of his time railing against the surge of migrants entering the country and what he perceived to be anti-white racism—ranting on the social media platform many thought he was burning to the ground with his reputation in tow. Not only was Musk unconcerned with the potential fallout to his companies and personal image; he also saw the acclaim of his hard-won followers—sycophants who'd purchased the blue check marks he hawked, opportunists who had exploited his sudden interest in their political extremism—as a sign of his broadening popularity. Remember when he said, "My follower count speaks for itself?"

There is little disagreement on one point: the Musk of today is distracted from the pursuits that had once won him admiration around the world. He is fueled by grievance. He believes he is being treated unfairly. He is consumed by the same extremist politics that have overtaken the political right wing, as a supposed counterweight to the identity politics of the Left. He believes he is in an existential fight.

But the warning signs of this erratic behavior have long been present. Recall Musk's reaction to the National Transportation Safety Board—the mistaken sense that Tesla was being singled out. Look at Tesla's board and the foundation established after "Funding secured," which could have been a reset but instead ensured that a key source of oversight would instead serve as a rubber stamp. Look at how he justified unleashing the Autopilot and Full Self-Driving experiments on public roads. To his credit in the latter case, he acknowledged that there would be deaths or injuries in the meantime—but somehow, they were necessary to achieve the promised land of full autonomy.

For some, it took the shift into politics to finally expose Musk's delusions of grandeur. Regardless, the important question at this stage is who gave him this monopolistic power over such life-and-death decisions? And was it a mistake not to restrain it before the logic extended to other arenas?

"The woke mind virus is either defeated or nothing else matters," Musk wrote in 2022.[36] Indeed, this argument propelled him years later to fight back against someone ostensibly in his corner, an advocate of Tesla's Full Self-Driving technology named Chuck Cook, who was annoyed at his overt shift into political grievance and the seeming lack of moderating forces around him.[37]

"Chuck labors under the illusion that western civilization is not at risk, when it clearly is," Musk wrote. "If America falls, nothing else matters, not stocks, not properties, nothing. All civilizations eventually fall, as history shows, but we want this one to last as long as possible."[38]

The basic scam here was that nearly any behavior could be justified under the moral cloak of averting "civilizational risk." Musk managed to convince the masses that small sacrifices—to decorum, to accountability, even to safety—must be tolerated in pursuit of something greater.

Why would anyone want to work for a man like this? A former Tesla executive I spoke with in summer 2023 explained the appeal to me succinctly. "When Elon gets on the stage and says, 'This thing is going to happen'—whether it's occupying Mars, whether it's in 2012, 2013, telling us, 'Tesla will be the largest company in the world,' there's never a doubt in his mind. In many ways that's really, really contagious.

"It's so addicting for engineers," the person continued. "You look behind you and every day you're accomplishing things that you could have sworn were impossible."

It wasn't unlike what another one of Musk's former deputies told me years earlier—that Musk's goals were like religious pursuits.

The seduction of that environment—and its immense rewards—can also lure those same otherwise smart people into a trap, one whose

AFTERWORD

Back in the mid-1990s, Elon Musk was a start-up founder in his twenties, working illegally under a student visa to bring a phone book–style directory online with his company, Zip2.[1] One day, Derek Proudian, a partner with one of the start-up's key investors, stopped by Zip2's Cambridge Avenue offices to grab lunch with its precocious founder, who'd already blown away his eventual financial backers with his unrelenting drive to be successful, Proudian recalled to me nearly thirty years later.

Walking to lunch that afternoon, Proudian was preoccupied with the company's priorities: bringing in engineers to scale the product, conducting a search for a chief executive, capitalizing on what he thought might be a $10 billion industry.

Musk was thinking bigger. "It's going to be global," he said, in Proudian's recollection. Zip2 was "going to be the biggest company ever."

"Well, maybe it'll be the biggest company ever," Proudian said. "Right now, we're focused on the Yellow Pages. We're not getting a whole lot of traction with these small businesses."

Musk's mind was elsewhere.

"I have bigger visions," he said.

Proudian tried to interject, hoping to redirect the conversation.

"No—you don't understand," Musk cut in. "I'm the reincarnation of the spirit of Alexander the Great."

What?

Proudian had to bring him back to earth. "What if you swing for the fences and you strike out?"

destructive effects are not alien to other industries, including mine: to conflate work with pain.

"Working for Elon is pain guaranteed," the former executive told me. It was only time to leave once the pain exceeded the rewards, a lesson so many have learned over the years, leading to the kind of rapid turnover seen only among the executive ranks of Musk-run companies.

To Musk, the mission was everything; those who weren't fully on-board were simply obstacles to be overcome.

"And what that means is people who he works with sometimes are disposable unless they're supportive to the mission," the former executive told me.

Those who might be expected to create the kind of friction other-wise known as accountability—say, internal naysayers, corporate boards, regulators—must be circumvented or, worse, defeated at all costs.

That left the question of why. Why was Musk so determined to solve all of the problems of a complicated, chaotic, and otherwise dysfunctional world? What did he get out of it?

As I gathered reporting for this book, one conversation with another former Tesla official in 2023 stuck with me. The official recounted how he had tried to reason with Musk about his ambitions of settling on Mars but found him undeterred by reason and logic.

"Why go to Mars?" he asked Musk.

"We need to be a multiplanetary species, so mankind survives a big meteorite hitting the Earth," he recalled Musk as saying.

The former Tesla official retorted that—sidestepping the question whether "to survive as mankind" was important—"the mean time be-fore [the] next big impact is a couple of hundred million years." In that context, it didn't matter if we went to Mars now or in twenty thousand years. "And in twenty thousand years, it will be a piece of cake to go to Mars—so why go now with this super immature technology of ours of the year 2000, instead of waiting for the technology of the year 20,000?"

That was the end of their conversation. The former Tesla official came away with the conclusion that Musk wanted to be the one to accomplish the feat. He tied that perspective to Musk's personality and said the be-havior fits a pattern.

"[It] is always about saving the world, anything below that is not worth the attention," he told me.

"I've got the samurai spirit," Musk declared. "I'd rather commit sep-puku than fail."

That day, Musk saw the roadblock as a peer's limited thinking, his realism. Today, his thinking seems to suggest, incompetence at the federal level—the abandonment of meritocracy, in favor of mediocrity—is the obstacle between him and his ultimate goal.

The presidential campaign of 2024 was a Musk gamble of galactic proportions, perhaps the only pivot that could have landed him with responsibility bigger than his business empire could afford him. By the time of the election, Musk had become convinced that this new foe stood in the way of his ambition to propel humanity to Mars, the same pursuit that motivated his bet on his massive pay package from Tesla, that had evidently driven his acquisition of Twitter in his effort to defeat the "woke mind virus," the one that represented SpaceX's north star.[2]

"Unless we stop the slow strangulation by overregulation happening in America, we will never become a multiplanetary civilization," he said,[3] before adding, "Unless something is done about strangulation by overreg-ulation, humanity will never reach Mars."[4]

And when the dust settled, Musk had sided with the winning party and become "first buddy" to the incoming president.[5]

At the time of this writing in December 2024, Elon Musk appears to have secured the power necessary to challenge the bureaucrats and oppressive regulations that have been holding him back. In appointing Musk and Vivek Ramaswamy to co-lead the new Department of Government Efficiency (DOGE), the Trump administration appears to have given him the opportunity to reshape the government while perhaps putting Musk's own ambitions for autonomous vehicles on a glide path. And while there are questions about how much authority Musk's quasi-agency will actually have, his influence on Trump—after pouring more than $275 million toward seeing him and other Republicans elected through a super-PAC, the America PAC—is clear.[6]

Days before the official announcement of the role, Musk had elevated a call for "defanging" agencies that had investigated him and his busi-nesses, including the SEC and FTC.[7] Now he had the blessing of the most powerful person in the world, who outlined a vision to "slash excess regulations, cut wasteful expenditures and restructure Federal Agencies," and believes he has a mandate to carry it out.[8]

Musk's entrance into politics—and governance—is a predictable outcome. At any time in Musk's history, given the scale of the gambles he has made with his fortune and power, he has variously seemed to be utterly in command or on the verge of total destruction. But one thing remains: he is inevitable.

However, now that he has reached a new plateau of power, the stakes have shifted. He is no longer limited to recklessly gambling with one of his companies' bottom lines, or the livelihoods of his workers. He is poised to apply his existential thinking to our society as a whole, exerting his influence on the foundational rules and regulations—such as norms around conflicts of interest—that hold us together. Protecting those conventions and the order they are intended to bring is hardly Musk's concern—as evidenced by the chapters of this book—especially if upholding them results in the continuation of the slow march to humanity's destruction that he believes has already begun.

Musk and his acolytes have made clear that they are comfortable with imposing a short-term "hardship" on Americans, including an economic and market downturn, in pursuit of their ultimate goal.[9] One of Musk's closest allies said the DOGE would require a "collective sacrifice."[10]

That only leaves the question—to what end? What is the collective sacrifice *for*, if not Musk's clearly stated goal of putting humans on Mars? And what has Musk done for the public at large to earn that kind of loyalty from the millions he is asking to take the plunge with him? Some may argue that his business achievements merit that sort of leap of faith, but it is an immense amount of power to give someone who is unaccountable to the public, by any measure.

And what if this publicly stated goal—the noble ambition to extend the reach of humanity—masked another worry?

Going into the election, Musk had seemed to sense danger. He felt he had everything on the line. Musk made no secret of how he saw the stakes—both for the country and for himself personally.

"I view this election as a turning point, like a fork in the road of destiny that is incredibly important. You know I've not been politically active until this election," he told podcaster Joe Rogan. "And the reason I've been politically active this election is because I think if we don't elect

Trump, I think we will lose democracy in this country. We will lose the two-party system," Musk said, while explaining his unfounded theory that the Democrats in power were "importing vast numbers of" undocumented migrants into swing states as part of an elaborate conspiracy to hold the Electoral College in perpetuity.

But as with all his political activism, Musk cheekily hinted he had a personal stake as well.

"If he loses, man, you're fucked, dude," Tucker Carlson told him during an October 2024 interview.

"If he loses, I'm fucked," Musk agreed. "How long do you think my prison sentence is going to be? Will I see my children? I don't know."[11]

It was meant to be a light-hearted moment, but it hinted at what Musk felt he had on the line. At the time, Musk's companies—and in certain cases, Musk himself—faced scrutiny from the Department of Justice, the SEC, the FTC, federal transportation regulators, and the Federal Communications Commission, just to name a few, and his PAC's unconventional methods of voter outreach were raising some early eyebrows as well.[12]

But as he often did, he was projecting those personal worries onto humanity itself, suggesting that the endless labyrinth of regulatory intervention stifled human potential as a whole, by slow-rolling and interfering with matters that were ultimately existential.

Indeed, "survival," as we laid out in the introduction, "is the organism's ultimate value, the 'final goal or end to which all [its] lesser goals are the means,' and the standard of all its other values: 'that which furthers its life is the good, that which threatens it is the evil,'" according to the *Stanford Encyclopedia of Philosophy*, outlining a core tenet of Ayn Rand's philosophy.[13]

When Musk declared himself Alexander the Great around thirty-odd years ago, it felt like a one-off from a brash founder like any other in Silicon Valley. But as the election loomed, Proudian, one of the first Silicon Valley power brokers to recognize Musk's spirit but also his stubbornness, suddenly thought: "Oh, shit," he told me.

Now he had begun to see his experiences with Elon Musk through a new lens. Strange outbursts and spontaneous, one-off utterances—that he had brushed off as hubris or the brashness of maladjusted youth—started to take on a new meaning.

"I thought the market forces would control Elon," Proudian said, adding later that he "didn't take it that seriously when he was a twenty-three-year-old entrepreneur who didn't have two nickels to rub together.

"I am really concerned because I know how smart this guy is and I know how much money he has and I know how ruthless he is and it's playing out in front of my eyes."

We should all heed that concern. It's unfashionable to admit now—but Musk's record of firings and his zealous deletion of once-normal business principles has emanated far beyond his business empire.

So many who have worked closely with Musk have emerged with the same sort of impression as Proudian, as *Hubris Maximus* demonstrates time and again: that Musk, however misguided he may be at times, is unyielding.

Some have lost sleep in connection with Musk's hubris; others have lost their lives believing in his company's promise. Whatever the harm in connection to something bigger, it matters greatly. People have lost their lives believing in his technological promises; others have seen their lives upended or careers destroyed; still others have faced potential financial ruin from believing in him.

Whether Musk's latest forays into the political realm ultimately achieve their stated goals, or his relationship with the Trump administration deteriorates at some point along the way, he has consistently shown a taste for opportunist behavior and a disregard for limiting collateral damage in the pursuit of his goals, and the stakes have never been higher.

Even if DOGE is a big success—by his own standards—history has shown that he's unlikely to be satisfied; the pattern shows he'll continue to seek more power and responsibility, to go all-in on the next moon shot. And if it isn't, and his "samurai spirit" calls him to commit seppuku rather than admit failure, he very well might take a lot of us with him next, before dusting himself off and trying again.

ACKNOWLEDGMENTS

I owe a debt of gratitude to far too many people to count, but I will do my best to name them all here.

First and foremost, I am deeply thankful to all those who spoke with me, often more than once—sometimes at odd hours—as I gathered reporting and fact checking and nudged them repeatedly with inquiries to tell this story in as comprehensive a way as possible. This includes those with whom I've at times, by the nature of my position, had adversarial relationships. I admire their appreciation of—and commitment to—the truth.

Many of my interviews were conducted on background, where sources provided a variety of reasons for withholding their names—most often to candidly discuss sensitive, nonpublic information or, in some cases, for fear of retribution. A fair number of my sources were willing to speak with me only to ensure I had my facts straight. Their help with getting the story right is greatly appreciated. Background sources were vital in helping to tell the stories about internal events at Tesla, Musk's dealings with Washington and his Twitter takeover. The Twitter chapters, and in particular chapter 14, relied heavily on trusted sources who spoke on the condition of anonymity to candidly discuss internal matters. In most circumstances, unless otherwise noted, quotes left unattributed in the text were said to me in interviews or other direct correspondence.

I've detailed Musk's hostility to the press, the way online troll armies have upended people's lives, and the blowback some have faced for speaking out. With that in mind, I take the commitments made to my sources extremely seriously. I am in awe of their courage and endlessly grateful.

The existing scholarship on Musk, Twitter, and Tesla has also proven exceptionally helpful. Each of the books below delves exhaustively into its topic, be it Twitter, Tesla, or Musk himself:

- *Ludicrous: The Unvarnished Story of Tesla Motors* by Edward Niedermeyer
- *Elon Musk* by Walter Isaacson
- *Elon Musk: Tesla, SpaceX, and the Quest for a Fantastic Future* by Ashlee Vance
- *Insane Mode: How Elon Musk's Tesla Sparked an Electric Revolution to End the Age of Oil* by Hamish McKenzie
- *Power Play: Tesla, Elon Musk, and the Bet of the Century* by Tim Higgins
- *Character Limit: How Elon Musk Destroyed Twitter* by Kate Conger and Ryan Mac
- *Battle for the Bird: Jack Dorsey, Elon Musk, and the $44 Billion Fight for Twitter's Soul* by Kurt Wagner
- *Extremely Hardcore: Inside Elon Musk's Twitter* by Zoë Schiffer

With thanks always to the reporters who doggedly cover Musk every day and a particular shoutout to my peers and predecessors on the Tesla beat who took Musk seriously from the beginning: Lora Kolodny, Dana Hull, Russ Mitchell, Linette Lopez, Drew Harwell, Tim Higgins, Charley Grant, Ed Niedermeyer, Rebecca Elliott, Neal Boudette, and so many others. None of us could have predicted where the story would take us.

To Jada Chin, thank you for supporting me with every aspect of the book, from helping me stay organized to serving as a sounding board for ideas, and putting up with all that was required to ensure this project was on track during the biggest year of our lives. You never let me doubt myself. I can't wait to marry you later this month.

To my parents, Sabah and Firasat Siddiqui, you are an unending source of inspiration with your values, work ethic, and the example you provide—of unwavering generosity to those around you and a fierce commitment to what is right. Thank you for everything.

Thanks to all those involved in the production and editing of *Hubris Maximus*, with particular gratitude to my editor Tim Bartlett and to Kevin Reilly, who guided me through every step of the process and worked tirelessly to make it better with exactly the temperament—and urgency—this writer demanded.

Jane Dystel believed in the project—and in me—from the moment I called her with a book pitch in mind. She has my unending gratitude. Thanks to Reed Albergotti, Nitasha Tiku, and Ed Niedermeyer for taking seriously my idea from the beginning.

Thanks to my *Washington Post* colleagues current and former, including Cameron Barr, Liz Seymour, Lori Montgomery, Christina Passariello, and Evelyn Larrubia for their understanding as I took leave to complete work on this project and juggled book deadlines during this process.

Laura Stevens was the perfect editor at the right time for a newspaper reporter chronicling Musk's rise. Thanks to Rachel Lerman, Trisha Thadani, Elizabeth Dwoskin, Cat Zakrzewski, Drew Harwell, Gerrit De Vynck, and so many of my fellow reporters who provided support and enriched the public's understanding of Musk and his companies. Thanks also to my former editors on the local desk, Mike Semel and Victoria Benning, for helping me launch my career at an institution I revere.

Thanks to Kenneth J. Silver, Diane Dilluvio, Gabrielle Gantz, Michelle Cashman, Laura Clark, Lizz Blaise, Young Lim, Omar Chapa, and Steve Wagner as well for their work on *Hubris Maximus*. Ben Kalin, who provided fact checking, was not only wonderful to work with, he was a calm and level-headed presence at a critical time.

Faraaz Siddiqui and Zahra Fatima: Thank for showing me what relentless drive, persistence, and belief in your values looks like. Thanks also for your apartment, which was a second office. My grandmother Bushra Yousuf provided encouragement and prayer (badly needed), and Imaan Yousuf read an early draft of my book pitch and provided feedback. Thank you. My grandfather Dr. Abdul Yousuf is always in my heart.

Mariam Quraishi provided guidance on an industry with which I was largely unfamiliar.

Thanks also to my new family—Steve and Sabrina Chin, and Elsa Chin, for always checking in on how I am holding up and trying to get the best out of me.

Last, none of this would be possible without my mentors and writing coaches over the years—in particular, Joe Starita, Scott Winter, and Dean Hume. Thank you.

NOTES

Introduction

1. @elonmusk, X, November 21, 2023. https://x.com/elonmusk/status/1726989224073896365.
2. @elonmusk, X, January 29, 2021. https://x.com/elonmusk/status/1355068728128516101.
3. "SEC: Musk's misleading statement caused significant market confusion and disruption," *CNBC*, September 27, 2018. https://www.youtube.com/watch?v=tNJhUTeTsa4.
4. *Joe Rogan Experience*, September 7, 2018. https://www.youtube.com/watch?v=ycPr5–27vSI.
5. "Ayn Rand," *Stanford Encyclopedia of Philosophy*, June 8, 2010. https://plato.stanford.edu/entries/ayn-rand/#WhatEthiWhyDoWeNeedIt.
6. @elonmusk, X, June 5, 2022. https://x.com/elonmusk/status/1533410745429413888; @elonmusk, X, December 13, 2022. https://x.com/elonmusk/status/1602734819225571328.
7. @elonmusk, X, May 19, 2022. https://x.com/elonmusk/status/1527356085090545664.
8. "Ayn Rand," *Stanford Encyclopedia of Philosophy*.
9. @elonmusk, X, May 19, 2022. https://x.com/elonmusk/status/1824637108570521983.
10. Faiz Siddiqui, "How auto regulators played mind games with Elon Musk," *Washington Post*, March 27, 2022. https://www.washingtonpost.com/technology/2022/03/27/tesla-elon-musk-regulation/.
11. Ashlee Vance, *Elon Musk: Tesla, SpaceX, and the Quest for a Fantastic Future* (New York: Ecco, 2015).
12. @elonmusk, X, June 15, 2018. https://x.com/elonmusk/status/1007665949044928517.
13. Lisa Napoli, "Compaq Buys Zip2 to Enhance Altavista," *New York Times*, February 17, 1999. https://www.nytimes.com/1999/02/17/business/compaq-buys-zip2-to-enhance-altavista.html; @elonmusk, X, April 2, 2021. https://x.com/elonmusk/status/1378139804647313411.
14. Sergei Klennikov, "8 Innovative Ways Elon Musk Made Money Before He Was a Billionaire," *Money*, August 8, 2017. https://money.com/8-innovative-ways-elon-musk-made-money-before-he-was-a-billionaire/.
15. Marc Fisher, Christian Davenport and Faiz Siddiqui, "Elon Musk, the Twitter deal and his quest to save 'all life on Earth,'" *Washington Post*, May 14, 2022. https://www.washingtonpost.com/business/2022/05/14/musk-twitter-deal-legacy/.
16. @elonmusk, X, July 29, 2022. https://x.com/elonmusk/status/1553029208057810945.
17. Faiz Siddiqui, "Tesla is like an 'iPhone on wheels.' And consumers are locked into its ecosystem," *Washington Post*, May 14, 2021. https://www.washingtonpost.com/technology/2021/05/14/tesla-apple-tech/.
18. @pkafka, X, April 7, 2023. https://x.com/pkafka/status/1644440081720045598.
19. Sanj Atwal, "Elon Musk suffers worst loss of fortune in history amid "market madness," Guinness World Records, January 6, 2023. https://www.guinnessworldrecords.com/news

/2023/1/elon-musk-suffers-worst-loss-of-fortune-in-history-amid-market-madness
-731988.

20. Faiz Siddiqui, "Twitter brings Elon Musk's genius reputation crashing down to earth," *Washington Post*, December 24, 2022. https://www.washingtonpost.com/technology/2022 /12/24/elon-musk-twitter-meltdown-tesla/.

21. Kate Conger, Tiffany Hsu and Aaron Krolik, "Twitter Barred Them. What Happened When Elon Musk Brought Them Back?," *New York Times*, October 12, 2024.

22. @elonmusk, X, July 2, 2020; Jacob Kastrenakes and Mia Sato, "Elon Musk tells advertisers: 'Go fuck yourself,'" *The Verge*, November 29, 2023. https://www.theverge.com/2023/11/29 /23981928/elon-musk-ad-boycott-go-fuck-yourself-destroy-x.

23. Faiz Siddiqui, "Musk's Twitter investors have lost billions in value," *Washington Post*, September 1, 2024.

24. Alexander Saeedy and Dana Mattioli, "Elon Musk's Twitter Takeover Is Now the Worst Buyout for Banks Since the Financial Crisis," *Wall Street Journal*, August 20, 2024. https:// www.wsj.com/tech/elon-musks-twitter-takeover-is-now-the-worst-buyout-for-banks -since-the-financial-crisis-3f4272cb.

25. @munster_gene, X, December 30, 2024. https://x.com/munster_gene/status/18738536 18430087460

26. Tom Krisher and Bernard Condon, "Tesla sales dropped 1.1% in 2024, its first annual decline in a dozen years," *AP*, January 2, 2025. https://apnews.com/article/tesla-sales-2024 -drop-electric-vehicles-69af17c4e606625694af8293db25b2f3.

1. Elon Musk's War Against Washington

1. Faiz Siddiqui, "Tesla sued by family of Apple engineer killed in Autopilot crash," *Washington Post*, May 1, 2019. https://www.washingtonpost.com/technology/2019/05/01/tesla -sued-by-family-man-killed-autopilot-crash/.

2. "Witness Group Attachment 2-Family Response to Request for Information," Huang, et al. v Tesla Inc., National Transportation Safety Board, March 20, 2019.

3. "Accident Report: Collision Between a Sport Utility Vehicle Operating With Partial Driving Automation and a Crash Attenuator Mountain View, California," NTSB, March 23, 2018. https://www.ntsb.gov/investigations/AccidentReports/Reports/HAR2001.pdf.

4. Michael Laris, "Tesla running on 'Autopilot' repeatedly veered toward the spot where Apple engineer later crashed and died, federal investigators say," *Washington Post*, February 11, 2020.

5. Faiz Siddiqui and Trisha Thadani, "In 2018 crash, Tesla's Autopilot just followed the lane lines," *Washington Post*, April 7, 2024. https://www.washingtonpost.com/technology/2024 /04/07/tesla-autopilot-crash-trial/.

6. Accident Report, NTSB, March 23, 20178.

7. Ibid.

8. Ibid.

9. Tom Krisher, "11 more crash deaths are linked to automated-tech vehicles," AP, October 18. 2022. https://apnews.com/article/technology-business-traffic-government-and -politics-a16c1aba671f10a5a00ad8155867ac92.

10. @elonmusk, X, December 27, 2020. https://x.com/elonmusk/status/13431127525129 46176

11. "The Atlantic Meets the Pacific: Exploring the Mind of an Entrepreneur–Elon Musk & James Fallows," November 11, 2011. https://www.uctv.tv/shows/The-Atlantic-Meets-the -Pacific-Exploring-the-Mind-of-an-Entrepreneur-Elon-Musk-James-Fallows-22483.

12. Marc Fisher et al, "Elon Musk, the Twitter deal and his quest to save 'all life on Earth.'" https://www.washingtonpost.com/business/2022/05/14/musk-twitter-deal-legacy/.

13. Faiz Siddiqui, "How auto regulators played mind games with Elon Musk," *Washington Post*, March 27, 2022.

14. @elonmusk, X, October 19, 2021. https://x.com/elonmusk/status/1450653942938054656.

15. Faiz Siddiqui, "NTSB 'unhappy' with Tesla release of investigative information in fatal crash," *Washington Post*, April 1, 2018. https://www.washingtonpost.com/news/dr-gridlock/wp /2018/04/01/ntsb-unhappy-with-tesla-release-of-investigative-information-in-fatal-crash/.

16. Drew Harwell, "Elon Musk's highflying 2018: What 150,000 miles in a private jet reveal about his 'excruciating' year," *Washington Post*, January 29, 2019. https://www .washingtonpost.com/business/economy/elon-musks-highflying-2018-what-150000-miles -in-a-private-jet-reveal-about-his-excruciating-year/2019/01/29/83b5604e-20ee-11e9 -8b59-0a28f2191131_story.html.

17. Brian Fung, "The technology behind the Tesla crash," *Washington Post*, July 1, 2016. https:// www.washingtonpost.com/news/the-switch/wp/2016/07/01/the-technology-behind-the -tesla-crash-explained/.

18. Ibid.

19. Michael Laris, "No defect found in Tesla 'Autopilot' system used in deadly Florida crash," *Washington Post*, January 19, 2017. https://www.washingtonpost.com/local/trafficandcommuting /no-defect-found-in-tesla-autopilot-system-used-in-deadly-florida-crash/2017/01/19 /36e4fa7c-de65-11e6-ad42-f3375f271c9c_story.html.

20. Bloomberg, "The Tesla Autopilot Crash Investigation: A Timeline," *Fortune*, April 14, 2018. https://fortune.com/2018/04/14/tesla-autopilot-crash-investigation-timeline/.

21. Lauren Botchan, "Wife of Tesla crash victim speaks out: 'I just want this tragedy not to happen again to another family'," *ABC News*, April 11, 2018. https://abcnews.go.com/US /wife-tesla-crash-victim-speaks-tragedy-happen-family/story?id=54392855.

22. Dana Hull and Ryan Beene, "A Timeline of the Tesla Autopilot Crash Investigation," *Bloomberg*, April 12, 2018. https://www.bloomberg.com/news/articles/2018-04-12/a-timeline -of-the-tesla-autopilot-crash-investigation.

23. Lora Kolodny, "Federal agency says it booted Tesla from crash probe, but Tesla says it withdrew and will complain to Congress," *CNBC*, April 12, 2018. https://www.cnbc .com/2018/04/12/ntsb-revokes-tesla-status-as-a-party-to-crash-investigation.html.

24. David Shepardson, "Biden to tap No. 2 official to head U.S. auto safety agency," Reuters, October 20, 2021. https://www.reuters.com/business/autos-transportation/exclusive-biden -tap-no-2-official-head-us-auto-safety-agency-source-2021-10-19/.

25. Matt McFarland, "Tesla's latest Autopilot feature is slowing down for green lights, too," CNN Business, April 28, 2020. https://www.cnn.com/2020/04/27/tech/tesla-autopilot -stoplight/index.html.

26. Fred Lambert, "Tesla Twitter tries to 'cancel' Biden's NHTSA safety adviser over criticism of Autopilot / FSD Beta," *Electrek*, October 20, 2021. https://electrek.co/2021/10/20/tesla -twitter-tries-to-cancel-biden-nhtsa-safety-advisor-critics-autopilot-fsd/.

27. David Shepardson, "UPDATE 1-Veoneer says Cummings to resign from board after NHTSA appointment," Reuters, October 25, 2021. https://ca.finance.yahoo.com/news/1 -veoneer-says-cummings-resign-171151660.html.

28. "Missy Cunnings is fighting to make sure you don't read this petition," *Whole Mars Catalog*, November 21, 2021. https://wholemars.net/2021/11/21/missy-cummings-is-fighting-to -make-sure-you-dont-read-this-petition/.

29. @elonmusk, X, https://x.com/elonmusk/status/1450653942938054656.

30. @elonmusk, X, March 21, 2024. https://x.com/elonmusk/status/1770669199612170277.

31. @Safety, X, March 20, 2024. https://x.com/Safety/status/1770647182279921840.

32. @elonmusk, X, https://x.com/elonmusk/status/1486809727963123716.

33. Trisha Thadani, Rachel Lerman, Imogen Piper, Faiz Siddiqui and Irfan Uraizee, "The final 11 seconds of a fatal Tesla Autopilot crash," *Washington Post*, October 6, 2023. https://www .washingtonpost.com/technology/interactive/2023/tesla-autopilot-crash-analysis/.

34. Andrew J. Hawkins, "Tesla's 'Full Self-Driving' software is starting to roll out to select customers," *The Verge*, October 21, 2020. https://www.theverge.com/2020/10/21/21527577 /tesla-full-self-driving-autopilot-beta-software-update

35. Faiz Siddiqui, "How auto regulators played mind games with Elon Musk," *Washington Post*, March 27, 2022. https://www.washingtonpost.com/technology/2022/03/27/tesla-elon-musk-regulation/.

36. Faiz Siddiqui, "Tesla owners can now request 'Full Self-Driving,' prompting criticism from regulators and safety advocates," *Washington Post*, September 25, 2021. https://www.washingtonpost.com/technology/2021/09/24/tesla-full-self-driving/.

37. Ibid.

38. @elonmusk, X, September 25, 2021. https://x.com/elonmusk/status/1441837997645729794; https://www.teslarati.com/tesla-fair-chance-ntsb-chief-comments/.

39. @JenniferHomendy, X, October 22, 2021. https://twitter.com/JenniferHomendy/status/1451524796689358860.

40. Faiz Siddiqui, "NTSB chair expresses concern over Tesla 'inaction' on safety recommendations in letter to Elon Musk," *Washington Post*, October 25, 221. https://www.washingtonpost.com/technology/2021/10/25/tesla-ntsb-musk/.

2. A "Difficult and Painful Year" and a Handsome Reward

1. Tornetta et al. v. Musk et al., Post-Trial Opinion, January 30, 2024. https://corpgov.law.harvard.edu/2024/02/01/tesla-musk-case-post-trial-opinion/.

2. Ibid.

3. Ibid.

4. Tesla Annual Report 2017, United States Securities and Exchange Commission, February 22, 2018.

5. Ibid.

6. Dan Mangan, "Judge throws out Elon Musk's $56 billion Tesla pay package," *NBC News*, January 30, 2024.

7. Post-Trial Opinion, Richard J. Tornetta et al. v. Elon Musk et al., January 30, 2024.

8. @elonmusk, X, October 12, 2018. https://x.com/elonmusk/status/1050812486226599936.

9. Post-Trial Opinion, Richard J. Tornetta et al. v. Elon Musk et al., January 30, 2024.

10. Jena McGregor, "These Tesla investors want even bigger changes on its board," *Washington Post*, November 1, 2018. https://www.washingtonpost.com/business/2018/11/01/these-tesla-investors-want-even-bigger-changes-its-board/.

11. Tesla Schedule 14A Information, United States Securities and Exchange Commission, March 21, 2018. https://www.sec.gov/Archives/edgar/data/1318605/000119312518035345/d524719ddef14a.htm.

12. "Post-Trial Opinion," Tornetta v. Musk, January 30, 2024. https://courts.delaware.gov/Opinions/Download.aspx?id=359340.

13. Alexandria Sage and Ross Kerber, "Tesla shareholders approve CEO Musk's $2.6 billion compensation plan," Reuters, March 21, 2018. https://www.reuters.com/article/idUSKBN1GX0C0.

14. Lora Kolodny, "Tesla stock drops as Elon Musk gives bizarre earnings call," *CNBC*, May 2, 2018. https://www.cnbc.com/2018/05/02/tesla-stock-drops-as-elon-musk-gives-bizarre-earnings-call.html.

15. Mark Matousek, "Elon Musk just apologized to the analyst whose questions he called 'boring' and 'boneheaded' last quarter," *Business Insider*, August 1, 2018. https://www.businessinsider.com/elon-musk-apologizes-to-analyst-on-tesla-q2-earnings-call-2018-8.

16. @elonmusk, X, November 4, 2016. https://x.com/elonmusk/status/794578375415238656.

17. Emily Glazer, "Elon Musk Has Used Illegal Drugs, Worrying Leaders at Tesla and SpaceX," *Wall Street Journal*, January 6, 2024. https://www.wsj.com/business/elon-musk-illegal-drugs-e826a9e1.

18. Elon Musk, *Don Lemon Show*, March 18, 2024. https://www.youtube.com/watch?v=hhsfjBpKiTw.

19. @elonmusk, X, June 6, 2017. https://x.com/elonmusk/status/872260000491593728.

20. Lindsey Bever, "Get more sleep, Arianna tells Elon. It's not an 'option,' he tells her in 2:30 a.m. tweet," *Washington Post*, August 20, 2018. https://www.washingtonpost.com/technology /2018/08/20/get-more-sleep-arianna-tells-elon-its-not-an-option-he-tells-her-am-tweet/.

21. @elonmusk, X, August 19, 2018. https://twitter.com/elonmusk/status/1031111742103 814144.

22. Andrew Hawkins, "Elon Musk admits at trial that he ignored pleas to stop tweeting," *The Verge*, January 20, 2023. https://www.theverge.com/2023/1/20/23564629/elon-musk -twitter-testimony-securities-fraud-trial.

23. Grace Kay and Sindhu Sundar, "Read the email billionaire Ron Baron sent Elon Musk telling him to stop tweeting when angry: 'Get an ice cream cone. Just don't use Twitter', *Yahoo! Finance*, March 10, 2023. https://www.yahoo.com/lifestyle/read-email-billionaire-ron -baron-094200707.html.

24. In re Tesla Inc. Securities Litigation Document 639.

25. "Saudi Arabia's sovereign fund builds $2bn Tesla stake," *Financial Times*, August 7, 2018. https://www.ft.com/content/42ca6c42-a79e-11e8-926a-7342fe5e173f.

26. Ibid.

27. @elonmusk, X, August 7, 2018. https://x.com/elonmusk/status/1026872652290379776 ?lang=en.

28. David Gelles, James B. Stewart, Jessica Silver-Greenberg and Kate Kelly, "Elon Musk Details 'Excruciating' Personal Toll of Tesla Turmoil," *New York Times*, August 16, 2018. https:// www.nytimes.com/2018/08/16/business/elon-musk-interview-tesla.html.

29. @elonmusk, X, June 18, 2018. https://x.com/elonmusk/status/1008906087611883521.

30. @elonmusk, X, June 18, 2018. https://x.com/elonmusk/status/1008906087611883521.

31. Lora Kolodny, "Tesla production briefly halted by paint shop fire in Fremont factory," *CNBC*, April 5, 2018. https://www.cnbc.com/2018/04/05/tesla-production-briefly-halted -by-paint-shop-fire-in-fremont-factory.html.

32. Christian Davenport and Faiz Siddiqui, "How Elon Musk went from sleeping in the factory to being on the cusp of launching a crew into space," *Washington Post*, February 21, 2020. https://www.washingtonpost.com/technology/2020/02/21/how-elon-musk-went-sleeping -factory-being-cusp-launching-crew-into-space/.

33. United States Securities and Exchange Commission vs. Elon Musk, Complaint, September 27, 2018. https://www.sec.gov/files/litigation/complaints/2018/comp-pr2018-219.pdf.

34. Ibid.

35. Ibid.

36. Ibid.

37. Drew Harwell and Renae Merle, "Tesla suspends share-trading after Elon Musk tweets he wants to take the carmaker private," *Washington Post*, August 7, 2018. https://www .washingtonpost.com/technology/2018/08/07/teslas-elon-musk-tweets-he-wants-take -carmaker-private/.

38. "Nasdaq 5200 Series: 5205. The Applications and Qualifications Process," Nasdaq Listing Center, March 12, 2009. https://listingcenter.nasdaq.com/rulebook/Nasdaq/rules/Nasdaq %205200%20Series/ten%20minutes/EQUALS/.

39. SEC complaint.

40. @elonmusk, X, August 7, 2018. https://twitter.com/elonmusk/status/10268942285410 71360.

41. Faiz Siddiqui, "Musk, defending 'Funding secured' statement, downplays impact of tweets," *Washington Post*, January 20, 2023. https://www.washingtonpost.com/technology/2023/01 /20/elon-musk-tesla-trial/.

42. @elonmusk, X, January 30, 2024. https://x.com/elonmusk/status/1752532343993323742.

43. "Report of Investigation Pursuant to Section 21(a) of the Securities Exchange Act of 1934: Netflix, Inc., and Reed Hastings," SEC, April 2, 2013. https://www.sec.gov/litigation /investreport/34-69279.htm.

44. Faiz Siddiqui, "Elon Musk found not liable in federal trial over 'Funding secured' tweet," *Washington Post*, February 3, 2023. https://www.washingtonpost.com/technology/2023/02 /03/elon-musk-tesla-verdict/.

45. Dave Michaels, "SEC Probes Tesla CEO Musk's Tweets," *Wall Street Journal*, August 8, 2018. https://www.wsj.com/articles/sec-has-made-inquiries-to-tesla-over-elon-musks-taking -private-tweet-1533757570.

46. Kalman Isaacs et al., vs Elon Musk and Tesla, Class Action Complaint, August 10, 2018.

47. David J. Lynch and Drew Harwell, "Saudi oil money may give Elon Musk the private Tesla of his dreams," *Washington Post*, August 13, 2018. https://www.washingtonpost .com/business/economy/saudi-oil-money-may-give-elon-musk-the-private-tesla-of-his -dreams/2018/08/13/5a00a234-9f2c-11e8-83d2-70203b8d7b44_story.html.

48. Ibid.

49. Armani Sayed, "Everything We Know About the Death of Duangphet Phromthep—One of 12 Boys Rescued from a Thai Cave in 2018," *Time*, February 16, 2023. https://time.com /6256167/duangphet-phromthep-dies-thai-rescue-cave/.

50. Drew Harwell, "Elon Musk's 'pedo' attack rattles Tesla investors: 'This thing is unraveling,'" *Washington Post*, July 16, 2018. https://www.washingtonpost.com/technology/2018/07/16 /elon-musks-pedo-attack-rattles-tesla-investors-this-thing-is-unraveling/; @elonmusk, X, July 4, 2018. https://x.com/elonmusk/status/1014509856777293825.

51. @elonmusk, X, July 7, 2018. https://x.com/elonmusk/status/1015657378140704768.

52. @elonmusk, X, July 9, 2018. https://x.com/elonmusk/status/1016443130017505280.

53. Muktita Suhartono and Julia Jacobs, "Elon Musk Defends His Rejected Mini-Sub Plan for Thai Cave," *New York Times*, July 10, 2018. https://www.nytimes.com/2018/07/10/world /asia/elon-musk-thailand-cave-submarine.html.

54. Helier Cheung and Tessa Wong, "The full story of Thailand's extraordinary cave rescue," BBC, July 13, 2018. https://www.bbc.com/news/world-asia-44791998.

55. Jackie Wattles, "Elon Musk makes unfounded accusation against Thai cave rescuer," *CNN*, July 16, 2018. https://money.cnn.com/2018/07/15/technology/elon-musk-thai-cave-rescue /index.html.

56. Ibid.

57. Avi Selk, "Thai cave rescuer considers suing Elon Musk over deleted 'pedo' tweets," *Wall Street Journal*, July 16, 2018. https://www.washingtonpost.com/news/worldviews/wp/2018 /07/15/elon-musk-insisting-he-helped-in-thai-cave-rescue-calls-actual-rescuer-a-pedo/.

58. Meagan Flynn, "Elon Musk claims 'pedo guy' is actually a South African insult that doesn't mean pedophile," *Washington Post*, September 17, 2019. https://www.washingtonpost.com /nation/2019/09/17/elon-musk-pedo-guy-thai-cave-rescue-lawsuit/.

59. Helen A.S. Popkin, "Elon Musk's 'Pedo Guy' Tweet Isn't Defamation, Jury Rules," *Forbes*, December 6, 2019. https://www.forbes.com/sites/helenpopkin/2019/12/06/elon-musks -pedo-guy-tweet-isnt-defamation-jury-rules/?sh=5cecf01834b0.

60. Shweta Ganjoo, "Is Elon Musk losing it, he just called the diver who rescued 12 Thai boys pedo," *India Today*, July 16, 2019. https://www.indiatoday.in/technology/news/story/is-elon-musk -losing-it-he-just-called-the-diver-who-rescued-12-thai-boys-pedo-1287286-2018-07-16.

61. Meagan Flynn, "Elon Musk claims 'pedo guy' is actually a South African insult that doesn't mean pedophile," *Washington Post*, September 17, 2019. https://www.washingtonpost.com /nation/2019/09/17/elon-musk-pedo-guy-thai-cave-rescue-lawsuit/.

62. Avi Selk, "Thai cave rescuer considers suing Elon Musk over deleted 'pedo' tweets," *Washington Post*, July 16, 2018. https://www.washingtonpost.com/news/worldviews/wp/2018 /07/15/elon-musk-insisting-he-helped-in-thai-cave-rescue-calls-actual-rescuer-a-pedo/.

63. Grace Kay and Sindhu Sundar, "Read the email billionaire Ron Baron sent Elon Musk telling him to stop tweeting when angry: 'Get an ice cream cone. Just don't use Twitter," *Business Insider*, March 10, 2023. https://www.businessinsider.com/tesla-investor-ron -baron-email-elon-musk-dont-tweet-angry-2023-3.

64. Unsworth vs. Musk, Plaintiff's Statement of Genuine Disputes in Opposition to Defendant's Motion for Summary Judgement, October 28, 2019. https://www.plainsite.org/dockets/download.html?id=285066911&z=db38aaa2.

65. Gene Munster, "An Open Letter to Elon Musk," July 17, 2018. https://deepwatermgmt.com/an-open-letter-to-elon-musk/.

66. Unsworth vs. Musk, Plaintiff's Statement of Genuine Disputes in Opposition to Defendant's Motion for Summary Judgement, October 28, 2019.

67. Jackie Wattles, "Lawyer: We're 'finalizing' a libel lawsuit against Elon Musk over 'pedo' tweet," CNN Money, August 29, 2018, https://web.archive.org/web/20211010181502/https://money.cnn.com/2018/08/29/news/elon-musk-libel-lawsuit-vern-unsworth/.

68. Ryan Mac, Mark Di Stefano and John Paczkowski, "In A New Email, Elon Musk Accused A Cave Rescuer Of Being A 'Child Rapist' And Said He 'Hopes' There's A Lawsuit," BuzzFeed News, September 4, 2018. https://www.buzzfeednews.com/article/ryanmac/elon-musk-thai-cave-rescuer-accusations-buzzfeed-email.

69. Unsworth vs. Musk, Plaintiff's Statement of Genuine Disputes in Opposition to Defendant's Motion for Summary Judgement, October 28, 2019.

70. Ibid.

71. Mac, et al., "In A New Email, Elon Musk."

72. Unsworth vs. Musk, Plaintiff's Statement of Genuine Disputes in Opposition to Defendant's Motion for Summary Judgement, October 28, 2019.

73. Ryan Mac, "The Cave Rescuer Suing Elon Musk Claims The Tesla CEO Fabricated Pedophilia Claims Against Him," BuzzFeed News, October 8, 2019. https://www.buzzfeednews.com/article/ryanmac/unsworth-reply-elon-musk-fucking-idiot.

74. Ryan Smith, "Who Is Richard Tornetta? Thrash Metal Drummer Who Took Down Elon Musk," Newsweek, January 31, 2024. https://www.newsweek.com/elon-musk-lawsuit-56-billion-richard-tornetta-delaware-pay-deal-court-1865638.

75. "Elon Musk Charged With Securities Fraud for Misleading Tweets," SEC, October 1, 2018. https://www.sec.gov/newsroom/press-releases/2018-219.

76. "Elon Musk Settles SEC Fraud Charges; Tesla Charged With and Resolves Securities Law Charge," SEC, October 2, 2018. https://www.sec.gov/news/press-release/2018–226.

77. Ibid.

78. Mark Matousek, "A Tesla without Elon Musk as CEO is a good thing: Gene Munster," Business Insider, September 28, 2018. https://www.businessinsider.com/tesla-without-elon-musk-as-ceo-would-be-good-thing-gene-munster-2018-9.

79. Ibid.

80. Christian Davenport, "NASA to launch safety review of SpaceX and Boeing after video of Elon Musk smoking pot rankled agency leaders," Washington Post, November 20, 2018. https://www.washingtonpost.com/business/2018/11/20/nasa-launch-safety-review-spacex-boeing-after-video-elon-musk-smoking-pot-rankled-agency-leaders/.

81. Lora Kolodny, "Robyn Denholm replaces Elon Musk as Tesla's board chair," CNBC, November 8, 2018. https://www.cnbc.com/2018/11/08/robyn-denholm-will-replace-elon-musk-as-teslas-board-chair.html.

82. Sara Salinas, "Tesla's pick for a new chairwoman is boring, but that's exactly what the company needs," CNBC, November 8, 2018. https://www.cnbc.com/2018/11/08/tesla-chairwoman-robyn-denholm.hml.

83. Elizabeth Lopatto, "If James Murdoch is the new Tesla chairman, that's bad news for Elon Musk," The Verge, October 12, 2018. https://www.theverge.com/2018/10/12/17965382/tesla-chairman-james-murdoch-board-director-rumors-elon-musk.

84. "Elon Musk." 60 Minutes, December 9, 2018.

85. Tornetta v. Musk: Post-Trial Opinion, January 30, 2024. https://corpgov.law.harvard.edu/2024/02/01/tesla-musk-case-post-trial-opinion/.

86. Ibid.

87. Tim Levin, "Uber CEO: CEOs are paid too much," *Business Insider*, July 16, 2021. https:// www.businessinsider.com/ceo-salary-pay-uber-dara-khosrowshahi-overpaid-executive -compensation-2021-7.

88. Emily Peck, "The fight over Apple CEO Tim Cook's $99M pay package," *Axios*, February 18, 2022. https://www.axios.com/2022/02/18/apple-tim-cook-pay-package-iss.

89. Kirsten Grind, Emily Glazer, Rebecca Elliott and Coulter Jones, "The Money and Drugs That Tie Elon Musk to Some Tesla Directors," *Wall Street Journal*, February 3, 2024. https:// www.wsj.com/tech/elon-musk-tesla-money-drugs-board-61af9ac4.

90. Sissi Cao, "Who is Tesla's New Chair Robyn Denholm, the Australian Woman Replacing Elon Musk?," *Observer*, November 8, 2018. https://observer.com/2018/11/robyn-denholm -elon-musk-tesla-chair/.

91. *60 Minutes*, December 9, 2018.

92. Faiz Siddiqui, "How auto regulators played mind games with Elon Musk, *Washington Post*, March 27, 2022. https://www.washingtonpost.com/technology/2022/03/27/tesla-elon -musk-regulation/.

93. "Post-Trial Opinion," Tornetta v. Musk, January 30, 2024. https://courts.delaware.gov /Opinions/Download.aspx?id=359340.

3. Up in Smoke

1. "Still on Top: Ford F-Series Retains Title of Best-Selling Truck for 46th Consecutive Year; Overall Best-Seller for 41st," Ford, January 3, 2023. https://media.ford.com/content /fordmedia/fna/us/en/news/2023/01/03/ford-f-series-is-americas-best-selling-truck-and -vehicle-once-ag.html.

2. Aaron Holmes, "People are saying the 'cybergirl' who introduced Elon Musk at Tesla's Cybertruck unveiling was girlfriend Grimes—here's the evidence," *Business Insider*, November 22, 2019. https://www.businessinsider.com/grimes-elon-musk-cybertruck-unveil -as-cybergirl-2019-11.

3. "People are saying the 'cybergirl' who introduced Elon Musk at Tesla's Cybertruck unveiling was girlfriend Grimes—here's the evidence," *Business Insider*, November 22, 2019. https://www.businessinsider.in/slideshows/miscellaneous/people-are-saying-the-cybergirl -who-introduced-elon-musk-at-teslas-cybertruck-unveiling-was-girlfriend-grimes-heres -the-evidence/slidelist/72192271.cms.

4. "2014 Chevrolet Silverado Pickup debut," December 13, 2012. https://www.youtube.com /watch?v=XIej-CbknYo.

5. Ibid.

6. Sean Szymkowski, "GM Banks $17,000 Profit Per Pickup On Average," *GM Authority*, August 10, 2018. https://gmauthority.com/blog/2018/08/gm-banks-17000-profit-per-pickup -on-average/.

7. Greg Gilmore, "Mazda Designer Von Holzhausen Bolts for Tesla," *Autoweek*, August 4, 2008. https://www.autoweek.com/news/a2043726/mazda-designer-von-holzhausen-bolts-tesla/

8. Faiz Siddiqui, "Tesla's new 'Cybertruck' promised unbreakable windows. They broke onstage," *Washington Post*, November 22, 2019. https://www.washingtonpost.com/technology/2019/11 /21/america-loves-pickup-trucks-can-elon-musk-win-drivers-over-with-tesla-cybertruck/.

9. Tim Higgins and Heather Somerville, "Tesla Unveiled a Bulletproof Pickup. Then the Window Broke," *Wall Street Journal*, November 22, 2019. https://www.wsj.com/articles /tesla-unveiled-a-bullet-proof-pickup-then-the-window-broke-11574444427.

10. Naomi Tajitsu, "Tesla's cybertruck launch takes hit as 'shatterproof' windows crack," Reuters, November 22, 2019. https://www.reuters.com/article/markets/teslas-cybertruck -launch-takes-hit-as-shatterproof-windows-crack-idUSL3N2821Y8/.

11. Vivian Ho, "Elon Musk's net worth plunges $768m in a day after cybertruck fiasco," *Guardian*, November 22, 2019. https://www.theguardian.com/technology/2019/nov/22/elon-musk -net-worth-tesla-cybertruck.

12. Galen Gruman, "Steve Jobs' Wi-Fi meltdown at WWDC," *InfoWorld*, June 7, 2010. https://www.infoworld.com/article/2297843/steve-jobs-wi-fi-meltdown-at-wwdc.html.
13. Helena Andrews-Dyer, "Dave Chappelle brings Elon Musk onstage at comedy show and boos abound," *Washington Post*, December 12, 2022. https://www.washingtonpost.com/arts-entertainment/2022/12/12/dave-chappelle-elon-musk-booed/; Faiz Siddiqui, "Twitter repeatedly crashes as DeSantis tries to make presidential announcement," *Washington Post*, May 24, 2023. https://www.washingtonpost.com/technology/2023/05/24/elon-musk-ron-desantis-2024-twitter/.
14. Andrews-Dyer, "Dave Chappelle brings Elon Musk onstage at comedy show and boos abound," *Washington Post*, December 12, 2022. https://www.washingtonpost.com/arts-entertainment/2022/12/12/dave-chappelle-elon-musk-booed/.
15. @elonmusk, X, November 22, 2019. https://twitter.com/elonmusk/status/1198090787520598016.
16. @elonmusk, X, November 24, 2019. https://twitter.com/elonmusk/status/1198772995021406209.
17. Jason Torchinsky, "Tesla's Claim That Cybertruck Can Pull 'Near Infinite Mass' Is Hilarious Bullshit," *Autopian*, January 4, 2023. https://www.theautopian.com/teslas-claim-that-cybertruck-can-pull-near-infinite-mass-is-hilarious-bullshit/.
18. Carmen Reinicke, "'Looks weird . . . like, really weird': Wall Street isn't sold on Tesla's new Cybertruck design. Here's what 7 analysts think about the electric pickup," *Business Insider*, November 22, 2019. https://markets.businessinsider.com/news/stocks/tesla-cybertruck-analyst-reaction-live-demo-wall-street-puzzled-appearance-2019-11-1028712126.
19. Brett Smith, "Why Tesla's weird new Cybertruck could be a hit," *CNN Business Perspectives*, November 29, 2019. https://www.cnn.com/2019/11/29/perspectives/cybertruck-tesla-elon-musk/index.html.
20. @elonmusk, X, November 26, 2019. https://x.com/elonmusk/status/1199526897887195136.
21. Fred Lambert, "Exclusive: Tesla Cybertruck reaches 1.5 million pre-orders—Can it live up to the hype?," *Electrek*, November 22, 2022. https://electrek.co/2022/11/22/tesla-cybertruck-million-pre-orders-live-up-to-hype/.
22. @elonmusk, X, May 3, 2021. https://twitter.com/elonmusk/status/1389102532706848768.
23. Benjamin Spillman, "It's big, loud and secretive: We got a tour of Tesla's Gigafactory and here's how it works," *Reno Gazette Journal*, December 10, 2018. https://www.rgj.com/story/news/2018/12/10/reno-sparks-nevada-tesla-gigafactory-factory-model-3-sedan-jobs/2211115002/.
24. Ibid.
25. Kyle Field, "Tesla Model Y To Share ~76% Of Parts With Model 3, Be Built At Gigafactories," *Clean Technica*, January 31, 2019. https://cleantechnica.com/2019/01/31/tesla-model-y-to-share-76-of-parts-with-model-3-built-at-gigafactories/.
26. Fred Lambert, "Tesla reduces Model Y prices, now starts below $50,000," *Electrek*, July 11, 2020. https://electrek.co/2020/07/11/tesla-model-y-price-drop/; Fred Lambert, "Tesla Model Y roof allegedly falls off brand new car—turning it into a convertible," *Electrek*, October 5, 2020. https://electrek.co/2020/10/05/tesla-model-y-roof-fall-off/.
27. Hamza Shaban, "Tesla to unveil Model Y crossover SUV March 14," *Washington Post*, March 4, 2019. https://www.washingtonpost.com/technology/2019/03/04/tesla-unveil-model-y-crossover-suv-march/.
28. Sean O'Kane, "Elon Musk is driving Tesla's Cybertruck prototype around Los Angeles," *The Verge*, December 9, 2019. https://www.theverge.com/2019/12/9/21002684/elon-musk-driving-cybertruck-footage-photos-nobu; "Jay Leno's Garage," *CNBC*, May 23, 2020.
29. "Tesla delays Cybertruck production due to supply chain constraints; new timeline is vague," *Electrek*, January 26, 2022. https://electrek.co/2022/01/26/tesla-delays-cybertruck-production-new-timeline-uncertain/.

30. Faiz Siddiqui, "Elon Musk says Tesla will not produce a new vehicle model in 2022, renews prediction on Full Self-Driving," *Washington Post*, January 26, 2022. https://www.washingtonpost.com/technology/2022/01/26/tesla-elon-musk/.

31. @elonmusk, X, September 29, 2022. https://twitter.com/elonmusk/status/1575508498430820352.

32. Hamza Shaban, "Elon Musk: Tesla has moved from 'production hell' to 'delivery logistics hell'," *Washington Post*, September 17, 2018. https://www.washingtonpost.com/technology/2018/09/17/elon-musk-tesla-has-moved-production-hell-delivery-logistics-hell/.

33. Faiz Siddiqui and Rachel Lerman, "Elon Musk's role at Tesla questioned as Twitter occupies his attention," *Washington Post*, December 16, 2022. https://www.washingtonpost.com/technology/2022/12/15/elon-musk-tesla-twitter/.

34. Tim Stevens, "Waiting for Cybertruck: Some Tesla Customers Have Lost Faith During the Long Road to Production," *The Information*, August 19, 2023. https://www.theinformation.com/articles/waiting-for-cybertruck-some-tesla-customers-have-lost-faith-during-the-long-road-to-production.

35. @MKBHD, X, November 30, 2023. https://x.com/MKBHD/status/1730332614039368051.

36. Nik Berg, "World's Best-Selling Car Is the Tesla Model Y," *Hagerty*, January 26, 2024. https://www.hagerty.com/media/news/the-worlds-best-selling-car-is-the-tesla-model-y/.

37. @jimfarley98, X, December 12, 2023.

38. Bryan Hood, "Cybertrucks Aren't Rusting, It's 'Surface Contamination,' Tesla Engineer Says," *Robb Report*, February 22, 2024. https://robbreport.com/motors/cars/tesla-engineer-says-cybertrucks-isnt-rusting-1235519993/.

39. Brad Anderson, "Tesla Cybertruck's 'Guillotine' Panels Can Chop Off Carrots, But What About Your Fingers?," *Carscoops*, January 27, 2024.https://www.carscoops.com/2024/01/you-definitely-dont-want-to-get-your-finger-stuck-in-the-tesla-cybertruck-heres-why/.

40. @aaronjcash, X, April 20, 2024. https://x.com/aaronjcash/status/1781734760215408922.

41. JerryRigEverything, "How far can the CYBERTRUCK tow 11,000lbs in Freezing Weather?," YouTube, January 19, 2024. https://www.youtube.com/watch?v=yk_u9fbkoKM; WhistlinDiesel, "WhistlinDiesel Cybertruck Durability Test #1," YouTube, August 2, 2024, https://www.youtube.com/watch?v=PK_EJ3DyiiA; WhistlinDiesel, "Cybertruck Frames are Snapping in Half," August 22, 2024, https://www.youtube.com/watch?v=_scBKKHi7WQ.

42. TechRax, "How Deep Can Tesla Cybertruck Drive in Water? -Wade Mode Test," YouTube, February 20, 2024. https://www.youtube.com/watch?v=4lKAEHMvvxg.

43. Hyunjoo Jin, Norihiko Shirouzu and Ben Klayman, "Exclusive: Tesla scraps low-cost car plans amid fierce Chinese EV competition," Reuters, April 5, 2024. https://www.reuters.com/business/autos-transportation/tesla-scraps-low-cost-car-plans-amid-fierce-chinese-ev-competition-2024-04-05/.

44. @elonmusk, X, February 28, 2024. https://x.com/elonmusk/status/1762716007913652650.

4. The Mind-Killer

1. Chuck Squatriglia, "Tesla's Got the Factory, Now It Needs to Fill It," *Wired*, October 28, 2010. https://www.wired.com/2010/10/teslas-got-the-factory-now-it-needs-to-fill-it/.

2. Faiz Siddiqui, "The Bay Area ordered millions to shelter in place. Elon Musk had Tesla employees report to work anyway," *Washington Post*, March 19, 2020. https://www.washingtonpost.com/technology/2020/03/18/bay-area-ordered-millions-shelter-place-elon-musk-had-tesla-employees-report-work-anyway/.

3. David Close, "NBA suspends season after Jazz center Rudy Gobert tests positive for coronavirus," *CNN*, March 12, 2020. https://www.cnn.com/2020/03/11/us/nba-season-suspended-spt-trnd/index.html; Sandra Gonzalez, "Tom Hanks and Rita Wilson diagnosed with coronavirus," *CNN*, March 12, 2020.

4. "Order of the Health Officer of the County of Alameda Directing All Individuals Living in the County to Shelter at Their Place of Residence Except That They May Leave to Provide

or Receive Certain Essential Services or Engage in Certain Essential Activities and Work for Essential Businesses and Governmental Services; Exempting Individuals Experiencing Homelessness from the Shelter in Place Order but Urging Them to Find Shelter and Government Agencies to Provide It; Directing All Businesses and Governmental Agencies to Cease Non-Essential Operations at Physical Locations in the County; Prohibiting All Non-Essential Gatherings of Any Number of Individuals; And Ordering Cessation of All Non-Essential Travel," March 16, 2020. https://www.acgov.org/documents/Final-Order -to-Shelter-In-Place.pdf.

5. "Governor Gavin Newsom Issues Stay at Home Order," March 19, 2020. https://www.gov .ca.gov/2020/03/19/governor-gavin-newsom-issues-stay-at-home-order/.

6. @elonmusk, X, March 14, 2020. https://twitter.com/elonmusk/status/1239031946962 808832.

7. Faiz Siddiqui, "The Bay Area ordered millions to shelter in place. Elon Musk had Tesla employees report to work anyway," *Washington Post*, March 19, 2020. https://www.washingtonpost .com/technology/2020/03/18/bay-area-ordered-millions-shelter-place-elon-musk-had-tesla -employees-report-work-anyway/; California Coronavirus deaths, John Hopkins University of Medicine, March 10, 2023. https://coronavirus.jhu.edu/region/us/california.

8. @elonmusk, X, September 12, 2023. https://x.com/elonmusk/status/1701767282509 111307.

9. Faiz Siddiqui, "Tesla to suspend operations at California factory following local intervention amid coronavirus outbreak," *Washington Post*, March 19, 2020. https://www .washingtonpost.com/technology/2020/03/19/tesla-factory-closes-coronavirus/.

10. @elonmusk, X, September 12, 2023. https://x.com/elonmusk/status/1701767282509 111307.

11. @elonmusk, X, March 6, 2020. https://x.com/elonmusk/status/1236029449042198528.

12. @elonmusk, X, March 19, 2020. https://twitter.com/elonmusk/status/1240758710646 878208.

13. Fred Lambert, "Elon Musk says 'coronavirus panic is worse than virus itself' in email to Tesla employees," *Electrek*, March 17, 2020. https://electrek.co/2020/03/17/elon-musk -tesla-coronavirus-panic-email/.

14. @elonmusk, X, March 16, 2020. https://x.com/elonmusk/status/1239650597906898947.

15. @elonmusk, X, March 20, 2020. https://x.com/elonmusk/status/1241054739921428480.

16. Faiz Siddiqui, "The return of erratic Elon Musk: During coronavirus, Tesla CEO spreads misinformation and over-promises on ventilators," *Washington Post*, April 29, 2020. https:// www.washingtonpost.com/technology/2020/04/29/musk-tesla-coronavirus/.

17. Reed Albergotti and Faiz Siddiqui, "Ford and GM are undertaking a warlike effort to produce ventilators. It may fall short and come too late," *Washington Post*, April 4, 2020. https:// www.washingtonpost.com/business/2020/04/04/ventilators-coronavirus-ford-gm/.

18. Neal E. Boudette, "Inside Tesla's Audacious Push to Reinvent the Way Cars Are Made," *New York Times*, June 30, 2018. https://www.nytimes.com/2018/06/30/business/tesla-factory -musk.html.

19. Faiz Siddiqui, "Elon Musk launches into expletive-laden rant, calling quarantine measures 'fascist,'" *Washington Post*, April 29, 2020. https://www.washingtonpost.com/technol ogy/2020/04/29/tesla-earnings-2020/

20. Faiz Siddiqui and Josh Dawsey, "Tesla's Elon Musk receives support from Trump as he reopens factory in defiance of county order," *Washington Post*, May 12, 2020. https://www .washingtonpost.com/technology/2020/05/11/musk-tesla-factory/.

21. Ibid.

22. Faiz Siddiqui, "The return of erratic Elon Musk: During coronavirus, Tesla CEO spreads misinformation and over-promises on ventilators," *Washington Post*, April 29, 2020. https:// www.washingtonpost.com/technology/2020/04/29/musk-tesla-coronavirus/.

23. Lora Kolodny, "Tesla cancels plans to bring workers back to US car plant this week,"

CNBC, April 27, 2020. https://www.cnbc.com/2020/04/27/tesla-cancels-plans-to-bring -workers-back-to-us-car-plant-this-week.html.

24. Tesla, Inc. (TSLA) Q1 2020 Earnings Call Transcript, *The Motley Fool*, April 30, 2020. https://www.fool.com/earnings/call-transcripts/2020/04/30/tesla-inc-tsla-q1-2020 -earnings-call-transcript.aspx.

25. Ibid.

26. "Tesla Q1 2020 Earnings Call (audio)," April 29, 2020. https://www.youtube.com/watch ?v=vEvXfHHEdNc.

27. @elonmusk, X, April 29, 2020. https://twitter.com/elonmusk/status/1255380013488189440.

28. @elonmusk, X, May 1, 2020. https://twitter.com/elonmusk/status/12562395541487 24737; Anna Almendrala, "Elon Musk Buys Gene Wilder's Former House in Bel Air For $6.75 Million," *HuffPost*, November 4, 2013. https://www.huffpost.com/entry/elon-musk -gene-wilder-house_n_4215105; @elonmusk, X, May 1, 2020. https://x.com/elonmusk /status/1256256494447636480; @elonmusk, X, May 4, 2020. https://x.com/elonmusk /status/1257508900812713984.

29. @elonmusk, X, May 1, 2020. https://x.com/elonmusk/status/1256239815256797184; Rachel Lerman, "Now all he needs is a throne: Elon Musk assumes title of Technoking of Tesla," *Washington Post*, March 15, 2021. https://www.washingtonpost.com/technology /2021/03/15/technoking-elon-musk-tesla/.

30. Rachel Lerman, "Elon Musk's baby name isn't just weird, it may be against California regulations," *Washington Post*, May 8, 2020. https://www.washingtonpost.com/technology/2020 /05/08/musk-grimes-baby-name/.

31. @elonmusk, X, May 9, 2020. https://x.com/elonmusk/status/1259159878427267072.

32. "Identifying Critical Infrastructure During COVID-19," Cybersecurity & Infrastructure Security Agency, March 19, 2020. https://www.cisa.gov/topics/risk-management /coronavirus/identifying-critical-infrastructure-during-covid-19.

33. Taryn Luna and Phil Willon, "Gov. Gavin Newsom says reopening California will begin this week amid coronavirus crisis," *Los Angeles Times*, May 4, 2020. https://www.latimes .com/california/story/2020-05-04/california-reopening-coronavirus-gavin-newsom -phases-begin-retail-pickup.

34. Matt Kawahara, "Alameda County's health officer resigning to take top state epidemiology job," *San Francisco Chronicle*, June 30, 2020. https://www.sfchronicle.com/news/article /Alameda-County-s-health-officer-resigning-to-15375534.php.

35. @elonmusk, X, May 9, 2020. https://twitter.com/elonmusk/status/1259162367285317633.

36. @LorenaGonzalez, X, May 9, 2020. https://twitter.com/LorenaSGonzalez/status/1259287 879177531392; @elonmusk, X, May 10, 2020. https://twitter.com/elonmusk/status/1259 638112688304129.

37. "Getting Back to Work," Tesla, May 9, 2020. https://www.tesla.com/blog/getting-back-work.

38. The Tesla Team, "Getting Back to Work," Telsa.com, May 9, 2020. https://www.tesla.com /blog/getting-back-work.

39. @elonmusk, X, May 11, 2020. https://twitter.com/elonmusk/status/1259945593805221891.

40. Faiz Siddiqui and Josh Dawsey, "Tesla's Elon Musk receives support from Trump as he reopens factory in defiance of county order," *Washington Post*, May 12, 2020. https://www .washingtonpost.com/technology/2020/05/11/musk-tesla-factory/.

41. Julian Glover, "Elon Musk says Fremont Tesla plant restarting prod," *ABC 7 News*, May 11, 2020. https://abc7news.com/tesla-elon-musk-fremont-factory/6172737/

42. Faiz Siddiqui and Josh Dawsey, "Tesla's Elon Musk receives support from Trump as he reopens factory in defiance of county order," *Washington Post*, May 12, 2020.

43. Faiz Siddiqui, "Tesla gave workers permission to stay home rather than risk getting covid-19. Then it sent termination notices," *Washington Post*, June 25, 2020. https://www .washingtonpost.com/technology/2020/06/25/tesla-plant-firings/.

44. Ibid.

45. Faiz Siddiqui, "Hundreds of covid cases reported at Tesla plant following Musk's defiant reopening, county data shows," *Washington Post*, March 24, 2021. https://www.washingtonpost.com/technology/2021/03/12/hundreds-covid-cases-reported-tesla-plant-following-musks-defiant-reopening-county-data-shows/.

46. Faiz Siddiqui, "The return of erratic Elon Musk: During coronavirus, Tesla CEO spreads misinformation and over-promises on ventilators," *Washington Post*, April 29, 2020. https://www.washingtonpost.com/technology/2020/04/29/musk-tesla-coronavirus/.

47. Faiz Siddiqui, "Tesla fires three more, overriding guidance allowing workers to stay home during pandemic," *Washington Post*, July 1, 2020. https://www.washingtonpost.com/technology/2020/07/01/tesla-plant-firings/.

48. Faiz Siddiqui, "Hundreds of covid cases reported at Tesla plant following Musk's defiant reopening, county data shows," *Washington Post*, March 24, 2021. https://www.washingtonpost.com/technology/2021/03/12/hundreds-covid-cases-reported-tesla-plant-following-musks-defiant-reopening-county-data-shows/.

49. Sergei Klebnikov, "Tesla Is Now The World's Most Valuable Car Company With A $208 Billion Valuation," *Forbes*, June 30, 2021. https://www.forbes.com/sites/sergeiklebnikov/2020/07/01/tesla-is-now-the-worlds-most-valuable-car-company-with-a-valuation-of-208-billion.

50. Lora Kolodny, "Tesla moves Automotive president Jerome Guillen to lead trucking business," *CNBC*, March 15, 2021. https://www.cnbc.com/2021/03/15/tesla-president-of-automotive-jerome-guillen-named-to-lead-trucking.html.

51. Rebecca Elliott, Emily Glazer and Tim Higgins, "Elon Musk Made Unusual Request in Falling Out With Top Tesla Lieutenant," *Wall Street Journal*, November 11, 2022. https://www.wsj.com/articles/elon-musk-made-an-unusual-request-in-fallout-with-a-top-lieutenant-11668140888.

52. Tesla: Form 8-K, United States Securities and Exchange Commission, June 3, 2021. https://www.sec.gov/Archives/edgar/data/1318605/000156459021031976/tsla-8k_20210603.htm.

53. Rebecca Elliott, Emily Glazer and Tim Higgins, "Elon Musk Made Unusual Request in Falling Out With Top Tesla Lieutenant," *Wall Street Journal*, November 11, 2022. https://www.wsj.com/articles/elon-musk-made-an-unusual-request-in-fallout-with-a-top-lieutenant-11668140888.

5. Arms Race

1. Faiz Siddiqui and Greg Bensinger, "As IPO soars, can Uber and Lyft survive long enough to replace their drivers with computers?," *Washington Post*, March 29, 2019. https://www.washingtonpost.com/technology/2019/03/29/even-with-ipo-billions-can-uber-lyft-survive-long-enough-replace-their-drivers-with-machines/.

2. "Elon Musk says had once reached out to Apple for acquiring Tesla," Reuters, December 22, 2020. https://www.reuters.com/article/us-apple-autos-elon-musk-idUKKBN28W2KF.

3. Fred Lambert, "Tesla (TSLA) bonds were oversubscribed by $300 million, $1.8 billion raised for Model 3 production," *Electrek*, August 11, 2017. https://electrek.co/2017/08/11/tesla-tsla-bonds-oversubscribed-model-3-production/; "Elon Musk says had once reached out to Apple for acquiring Tesla," Reuters, December 22, 2020; https://www.reuters.com/article/us-apple-autos-elon-musk-idUKKBN28W2KF; @elonmusk, X, July 30, 2021. https://x.com/elonmusk/status/1421150913075503112.

4. Brad Jones, "An Investor Wants Tesla and Uber to Merge, with Musk as CEO," *Futurism*, August 22, 2027. https://futurism.com/an-investor-wants-tesla-and-uber-to-merge-with-musk-as-ceo.

5. Michael J. de la Merced and Kate Conger, "Uber Is Said to Aim for I.P.O. Valuation of Up to $100 Billion," *New York Times*, April 10, 2019. https://www.nytimes.com/2019/04/10/technology/uber-ipo.html; Faiz Siddiqui, "Self-driving Uber vehicle strikes and kills pedestrian,"

Washington Post, March 19, 2018. https://www.washingtonpost.com/news/dr-gridlock/wp/2018/03/19/uber-halts-autonomous-vehicle-testing-after-a-pedestrian-is-struck/.

6. Steve LeVine, "What it really costs to turn a car into a self-driving vehicle," *Quartz*, March 5, 2017. https://qz.com/924212/what-it-really-costs-to-turn-a-car-into-a-self-driving-vehicle.

7. Faiz Siddiqui, "Tesla floats fully self-driving cars as soon as this year. Many are worried about what that will unleash," *Washington Post*, July 17, 2019. https://www.washingtonpost.com/technology/2019/07/17/tesla-floats-fully-self-driving-cars-soon-this-year-many-are-worried-about-what-that-will-unleash/.

8. Kirsten Korosec, "Tesla plans to launch a robotaxi network in 2020," *TechCrunch*, April 22, 2019. https://techcrunch.com/2019/04/22/tesla-plans-to-launch-a-robotaxi-network-in-2020/.

9. Vikas Khare and Ankita Jain, "Predict the performance of driverless car through the cognitive data analysis and reliability analysis based approach," *Advances in Electrical Engineering, Electronics and Energy*, Volume 6, 2023. https://www.sciencedirect.com/science/article/pii/S2772671123002395.

10. @elonmusk, X, January 13, 2022.

11. Aaron Mok, "Tesla owners who just want a normal steering wheel on their Model S and Model X get their wish," *Business Insider*, January 7, 2023. https://www.businessinsider.com/tesla-offers-round-steering-wheel-option-yoke-replacement-complaints-2023-1.

12. "Autopilot and Full Self-Driving (Supervised)," Tesla. https://www.tesla.com/support/autopilot.

13. "Early Estimate of Motor Vehicle Traffic Fatalities in 2022," NHTSA, April 2023. https://crashstats.nhtsa.dot.gov/Api/Public/ViewPublication/813428.

14. @elonmusk, X, July 31, 2021. https://x.com/elonmusk/status/1421573785988309002.

15. Faiz Siddiqui, "How auto regulators played mind games with Elon Musk," *Washington Post*, March 27, 2022. https://www.washingtonpost.com/technology/2022/03/27/tesla-elon-musk-regulation/.

16. Drew Harwell, "As Elon Musk promises 'full self-driving,' experts worry Tesla is 'using consumers as guinea pigs'," *Washington Post*, June 11, 2018. https://www.washingtonpost.com/news/the-switch/wp/2018/06/11/elon-musk-promises-full-self-driving-tesla-soon-despite-autopilot-crashes/.

17. "Part 573 Safety Recall Report," NHTSA, February 15, 2023. https://static.nhtsa.gov/odi/rcl/2023/RCLRPT-23V085-3451.PDF.

18. Piede Wang, "Research on Comparison of LiDAR and Camera in Autonomous Driving," *Journal of Physics: Conference Series*, 2021. https://iopscience.iop.org/article/10.1088/1742-6596/2093/1/012032.

19. @elonmusk, X, March 27, 2022. https://x.com/elonmusk/status/1508167534821793792.

20. Victor Luckerson, "Steve Jobs Totally Dissed the Stylus 8 Years Before Apple Pencil," *Time*, September 10, 2015. https://time.com/4029142/steve-jobs-stylus/.

21. Faiz Siddiqui, "Tesla is putting 'self-driving' in the hands of drivers amid criticism the tech is not ready," *Washington Post*, October 22, 2020. https://www.washingtonpost.com/technology/2020/10/21/tesla-self-driving/.

22. Faiz Siddiqui, "What self-driving cars can't recognize may be a matter of life and death," *Washington Post*, November 11, 2019. https://www.washingtonpost.com/technology/2019/11/11/what-self-driving-cars-cant-recognize-may-be-matter-life-death/.

23. @Tesla_AI, X, October 4, 2024. https://x.com/Tesla_AI/status/1842143130302177380.

24. Trisha Thadani, Rachel Lerman, Imogen Piper, Faiz Siddiqui and Irfan Uraizee, "The final 11 seconds of a fatal Tesla Autopilot crash," *Washington Post*, October 6, 2023. https://www.washingtonpost.com/technology/interactive/2023/tesla-autopilot-crash-analysis/.

25. Soo Youn, "Tesla sued for 'defective' Autopilot in wrongful death suit of Florida driver who crashed into tractor trailer," *ABC News*, August 1, 2019. https://abcnews.go.com

/Technology/tesla-sued-defective-autopilot-wrongful-death-suit-florida/story?id
=64706707.

26. @elonmusk, X, August 20, 2019. https://twitter.com/elonmusk/status/1163903521701
294081.

27. Andrej Karpathy bio, https://karpathy.ai/.

28. @elonmusk, X, May 23, 2019. https://twitter.com/elonmusk/status/1131746784315727872.

29. @elonmusk, X, August 20, 2019. https://x.com/elonmusk/status/1163903521701294081.

30. Isobel Asher Hamilton, "Tesla cars can now drive themselves to their owners with 'Smart Summon' but video shows the feature wreaking havoc," *Business Insider*, October 1, 2019. https://
www.businessinsider.com/teslas-smart-summon-feature-is-wreaking-havoc-2019-10.

31. @TeslaJoy, September 27, 2019. https://x.com/TeslaJoy/status/1177766546921287680.

32. "Tesla Enhanced Summon in WalMart Traffic + CRAZY REACTION," Inside Tesla,
September 29, 2019. https://www.youtube.com/watch?v=-dfpnL9OpzM&t=168s.

33. Isobel Asher Hamilton, "Tesla cars can now drive themselves to their owners with 'Smart
Summon' but video shows the feature wreaking havoc," *Business Insider*, October 1, 2019.

34. @elonmusk, X, October 2, 2019. https://twitter.com/elonmusk/status/11795206220045
88544.

35. @elonmusk, X, October 12, 2019. https://twitter.com/elonmusk/status/11830827645154
14016.

36. @elonmusk, X, October 11, 2019. https://x.com/elonmusk/status/1182823556830253056.

37. Jameson Dow, "Tesla CEO Elon Musk talks self driving; $1,000 price increase coming
Nov. 1," *Electrek*, October 11, 2019. https://electrek.co/2019/10/11/tesla-self-driving-price
-increase-1000-november-1/.

38. @elonmusk, X, June 21, 2023. https://x.com/elonmusk/status/1671703741626499075;
@Tesla_AI, X, September 3, 2024. https://x.com/Tesla_AI/status/1830868721641939445.

39. Michael Laris, "Tempe police release video of moments before autonomous Uber hit pedestrian," *Washington Post*, March 21, 2018. https://www.washingtonpost.com/news/dr-gridlock
/wp/2018/03/21/tempe-police-release-video-of-moments-before-autonomous-uber-crash/.

40. Heather Somerville, "Homeless Arizona woman killed by Uber self-driving SUV was
'like everyone's aunt'," Reuters, March 20, 2018. https://www.reuters.com/article/us-autos
-selfdriving-uber-victim/homeless-arizona-woman-killed-by-uber-self-driving-suv-was
-like-everyones-aunt-idUSKBN1GW36P.

41. Michael Laris, "Pedestrian in self-driving Uber crash probably would have lived if braking
feature hadn't been shut off, NTSB documents show," *Washington Post*, November 5, 2019.
https://www.washingtonpost.com/local/trafficandcommuting/pedestrian-in-self-driving
-uber-collision-probably-would-have-lived-if-braking-feature-hadnt-been-shut-off-ntsb
-finds/2019/11/05/7ec83b9c-ffeb-11e9-9518-1e76abc088b6_story.html; Michael Laris,
"U.S. oversight of self-driving cars falls short, NTSB says in review of Uber death," *Washington Post*, November 19, 2019. https://www.washingtonpost.com/local/trafficandcommuting
/us-oversight-of-self-driving-cars-falls-short-ntsb-says-in-review-of-uber-death/2019/11
/19/6e583448-0a3f-11ea-97ac-a7ccc8dd1ebc_story.html;

42. Daniel Wu, "A self-driving Uber killed a woman. The backup driver has pleaded guilty,"
Washington Post, July 31, 2023. https://www.washingtonpost.com/nation/2023/07/31
/uber-self-driving-death-guilty/.

43. Brian Fung, "What to know about Uber's months of crises," *Washington Post*, June 21, 2017.
https://www.washingtonpost.com/news/the-switch/wp/2017/04/18/from-deleteuber-to
-hell-a-short-history-of-ubers-recent-struggles/; Mike Isaac, "What You Need to Know
About #DeleteUber," *New York Times*, Jan 31, 2017. https://www.nytimes.com/2017/01/31
/business/delete-uber.html.

44. Susan Fowler, "Reflecting on one very, very strange year at Uber," Susanjfowler.com, February 19, 2017. https://www.susanjfowler.com/blog/2017/2/19/reflecting-on-one-very
-strange-year-at-uber.

45. Anita Balakrishman, "Here's the full 13-page report of recommendations for Uber," CNBC, June 13, 2017. https://www.cnbc.com/2017/06/13/eric-holder-uber-report-full-text.html.

46. Eric Newcomer, "In Video, Uber CEO Argues With Driver Over Falling Fares," *Bloomberg*, February 28, 2017. https://www.bloomberg.com/news/articles/2017-02-28/in-video-uber-ceo-argues-with-driver-over-falling-fares.

47. Travis M. Andrews and Sarah Larimer, "'I must fundamentally change and grow up': Uber CEO Travis Kalanick's big apology," *Washington Post*, March 1, 2017. https://www.washingtonpost.com/news/morning-mix/wp/2017/03/01/i-must-fundamentally-change-and-grow-up-uber-ceo-travis-kalanicks-big-apology/.

48. Elizabeth Dwoskin, "Uber founder Travis Kalanick resigns as CEO amid a shareholder revolt," *Washington Post*, June 21, 2017. https://www.washingtonpost.com/business/technology/2017/06/21/cecb34bc-564e-11e7-ba90-f5875b7d1876_story.html.

49. Cade Metz and Kate Conger, "Uber, After Years of Trying, Is Handing Off Its Self-Driving Car Project," *New York Times*, December 7, 2020. https://www.nytimes.com/2020/12/07/technology/uber-self-driving-car-project.html.

50. Alex Hern, "Uber execs including Travis Kalanick 'went to escort/karaoke bar'," *Guardian*, March 27, 2017. https://www.theguardian.com/technology/2017/mar/27/uber-execs-including-travis-kalanick-went-to-escortkaraoke-bar.

51. Faiz Siddiqui, "Tesla sells 'Self-Driving' cars. Is it fraud?," *Washington Post*, July 11, 2024. https://www.washingtonpost.com/technology/2024/07/11/elon-musk-tesla-full-self-driving/.

52. "Defendants Tesla, Inc., Tesla Lease Trust, And Tesla Finance Llc's Opposition To Plaintiffs' Motion For Preliminary Injunction And Provisional Class Certification," In Re Tesla Advanced Drive Assistance Systems Litigation, United States District Court Northern District of California, Oakland Division, April 5, 2023. https://driveteslacanada.ca/wp-content/uploads/2023/04/https-ecf-cand-uscourts-gov-doc1-035123009755.pdf.

53. Ibid.

6. "To the F_____ Mattresses"

1. Faiz Siddiqui, "Tesla engaged in unfair labor practices, must reinstate fired worker and scrub Elon Musk tweet, NLRB says," *Washington Post*, March 25, 2021. https://www.washingtonpost.com/technology/2021/03/25/tesla-nlrb-ruling/.

2. Tom Krisher, "Tesla picks Texas site for second US vehicle assembly plant," *Washington Post*, July 22, 2020. https://www.washingtonpost.com/climate-environment/tesla-picks-texas-site-for-second-us-vehicle-assembly-plant/2020/07/22/182379c4-cc64-11ea-99b0-8426e26d203b_story.html.

3. @realDonaldTrump, Truth Social, July 12, 2022. https://truthsocial.com/@realDonaldTrump/posts/108636743295734643.

4. @elonmusk, X, July 2, 2020. https://twitter.com/elonmusk/status/1278764736876773383.

5. Ibid.

6. Christian Davenport and Faiz Siddiqui, "How Elon Musk went from sleeping in the factory to being on the cusp of launching a crew into space," *Washington Post*, February 21, 2020. https://www.washingtonpost.com/technology/2020/02/21/how-elon-musk-went-sleeping-factory-being-cusp-launching-crew-into-space/.

7. Bryan Logan, "One of Tesla's largest shareholders is urging Elon Musk to simmer down and focus after a tumultuous few weeks," *Business Insider*, July 12, 2018. https://www.businessinsider.com/large-tesla-shareholder-baillie-gifford-rebukes-elon-musk-urges-him-to-focus-2018-7; Faiz Siddiqui, "Elon Musk and the SEC resolve dispute over the Tesla CEO's tweets," *Washington Post*, April 26, 2019. https://www.washingtonpost.com/technology/2019/04/26/elon-musk-sec-resolve-dispute-over-teslas-ceos-tweets; Christian Davenport and Faiz Siddiqui, "How Elon Musk went from sleeping in the factory to being on the cusp of launching a crew into space," *Washington Post*, February 21, 2020. https://

www.washingtonpost.com/technology/2020/02/21/how-elon-musk-went-sleeping
-factory-being-cusp-launching-crew-into-space/.

8. Lora Kolodny, "Elon Musk found not liable in 'pedo guy' defamation trial," *CNBC*, December 6, 2019. https://www.cnbc.com/2019/12/06/unsworth-vs-musk-pedo-guy-defamation
-trial-verdict.html.

9. Christian Davenport and Faiz Siddiqui, "How Elon Musk went from sleeping in the factory to being on the cusp of launching a crew into space," *Washington Post*, February 21, 2020.https://www.washingtonpost.com/technology/2020/02/21/how-elon-musk-went
-sleeping-factory-being-cusp-launching-crew-into-space/.

10. @elonmusk, X, February 4, 2017. https://twitter.com/elonmusk/status/8279283667119
67745.

11. @elonmusk, X, April 25, 2022. https://x.com/elonmusk/status/1518569260523659266.

12. @elonmusk, X, May 30, 2022. https://x.com/elonmusk/status/1531297810758389760.

13. @LorenaSGonzalez, X, May 9, 2020. https://x.com/LorenaSGonzalez/status/125928787
9177531392.

14. @GerberKawasaki, X, May 10, 2020. https://x.com/GerberKawasaki/status/125946969
8686578690.

15. Heather Somerville, "Elon Musk Moves to Texas, Takes Jab at Silicon Valley," *Wall Street Journal*, December 8, 2020. https://www.wsj.com/articles/elon-musk-to-discuss-teslas
-banner-year-despite-pandemic-silicon-valleys-future-11607449988.

16. @elonmusk, X, December 30, 2022. https://twitter.com/elonmusk/status/16089391905
48598784.

17. @elonmusk, X, April 6, 2023. https://x.com/elonmusk/status/1644036581466992658.

18. @elonmusk, X, July 2, 2020. https://x.com/elonmusk/status/1278764736876773383.

19. Sinéad Baker, "Grimes told Elon Musk to turn off his phone and that she 'cannot support hate' in a now-deleted tweet, after he tweeted that 'pronouns suck'," *Business Insider*, July 25, 2020. https://www.businessinsider.com/grimes-tells-musk-cannot-support-hate-after-he
-tweets-pronouns-2020-7.

20. Ibid.

21. Jeanne Whalen, David J. Lynch and Gerry Shih, "Trump's stunning decision to escalate trade wars with China and Mexico signals a turning point for U.S. policy," *Washington Post*, June 1, 2019. https://www.washingtonpost.com/business/economy/trumps-stunning
-decision-to-escalate-trade-wars-with-china-and-mexico-signals-a-turning-point-for-us
-policy/2019/05/31/d1e28270-83da-11e9-95a9-e2c830afe24f_story.html .

22. "There was never any intention to bring Tesla plant to Mexico, says," *CENoticias Financieras English*, December 16, 2020.

23. Jason Lalljee, "Elon Musk is speaking out against government subsidies. Here's a list of the billions of dollars his businesses have received," *Business Insider*, December 15, 2021. https://
www.businessinsider.com/elon-musk-list-government-subsidies-tesla-billions-spacex
-solarcity-2021-12.

24. Philip Rucker and Jenna Johnson, "Trump announces U.S. will exit Paris climate deal, sparking criticism at home and abroad," *Washington Post*, June 1, 2017. https://www.washingtonpost
.com/politics/trump-to-announce-us-will-exit-paris-climate-deal/2017/06/01/fbcb0196
-46da-11e7-bcde-624ad94170ab_story.html.

25. Dan Robitski, "Elon Musk Just Got Majorly Called Out for Stealing Memes," *The__Byte.*, May 7, 2021. https://futurism.com/the-byte/elon-musk-stealing-memes.

26. Luc Olinga, "Elon Musk Picks High-Stakes Fight with Sen. Elizabeth Warren," *The Street*, December 20, 2022. https://www.thestreet.com/technology/elon-musk-picks-high-stake
-fight-with-senator-elizabeth-warren.

27. @elonmusk, X, June 28, 2020. https://x.com/elonmusk/status/1277359833721655302.

28. @elonmusk, X, May 30, 2022. https://x.com/elonmusk/status/1531297810758389760.

29. @elonmusk, X, July 27, 2020. https://x.com/elonmusk/status/1287818109651431427.

30. @elonmusk, X, July 31, 2012. https://twitter.com/elonmusk/status/230507510929440768.
31. @elonmusk, X, June 1, 2020. https://x.com/elonmusk/status/1267409179339296768.
32. Sean O'Kane, "Tesla employees are holding a Juneteenth rally at the company's California factory," *The Verge*, June 18, 2020. https://www.theverge.com/2020/6/18/21296239/tesla-employees-juneteenth-protest-black-lives-matter-fremont-factory.
33. Lora Kolodny, "On the morning of Juneteenth, Tesla tells employees they can take the day off unpaid," *CNBC*, June 19. 2020. https://www.cnbc.com/2020/06/19/tesla-tells-employees-they-take-juneteenth-off-unpaid.html.
34. Ibid.
35. Olivia Rubin, Alexander Mallin and Will Steakin, "7 hours, 700 arrests, 1 year later: The Jan. 6 Capitol attack, by the numbers," *ABC News*, January 6, 2022. https://abc7.com/jan-6-insurrection-us-capitol-riot/11428976/.
36. Gerrit De Vynck and Rachel Lerman, "YouTube suspends Trump, days after Twitter and Facebook," *Washington Post*, January 13, 2021. https://www.washingtonpost.com/technology/2021/01/12/trump-youtube-ban/.
37. @elonmusk, X, April 27, 2020. https://x.com/elonmusk/status/1254921937714905092.
38. Emma-Jo Morris and Gabrielle Fonrouge, "Smoking-gun email reveals how Hunter Biden introduced Ukrainian businessman to VP dad," *New York Post*, October 14, 2020. https://nypost.com/2020/10/14/email-reveals-how-hunter-biden-introduced-ukrainian-biz-man-to-dad/.
39. @elonmusk, X, January 11, 2021. https://twitter.com/elonmusk/status/1348688644173934593.
40. @elonmusk, X, October 31, 2021. https://x.com/elonmusk/status/1454808104256737289.
41. @elonmusk, X, October 31, 2012. https://x.com/elonmusk/status/1454808104256737289.
42. Tesla Form 8-K, United States Securities and Exchange Commission, March 15, 2021. https://www.sec.gov/Archives/edgar/data/1318605/000156459021012981/tsla-8k_20210315.htm.
43. Faiz Siddiqui, "The government helped Tesla conquer electric cars. Now it's helping Detroit, and Elon Musk isn't happy," *Washington Post*, September 15, 2021. https://www.washingtonpost.com/technology/2021/09/15/tesla-biden-administration/.
44. Josh Dawsey, Eva Dou and Faiz Siddiqui, "How Elon Musk came to endorse Donald Trump," *Washington Post*, July 29, 2024. https://www.washingtonpost.com/technology/2024/07/29/musk-trump-endorsement-immigration/.
45. Edward Ludlow and Mark Gurman, "Elon Musk Says Biden Administration Is 'Biased' Against Tesla," *Bloomberg*, September 28, 2021. https://www.bloomberg.com/news/articles/2021-09-28/musk-says-biden-administration-is-biased-against-tesla.
46. @elonmusk, X, October 31, 2021. https://x.com/elonmusk/status/1454926841467256835.
47. Christian Davenport, "SpaceX makes history by launching Inspiration4, first all-civilian crew, to orbit," *Washington Post*, September 15, 2021. https://www.washingtonpost.com/technology/2021/09/15/spacex-launch-civilian-flight/.
48. @elonmusk, X, September 19, 2021. https://twitter.com/elonmusk/status/1439665626914635783.
49. Nandita Bose, David Shepardson and Raphael Satter, "Exclusive: Tesla's Musk meets top Biden officials on EVs in Washington," Reuters, January 27, 2023. https://www.reuters.com/business/energy/elon-musk-meets-top-biden-admin-officials-discuss-electrification-goals-2023-01-27/.
50. Amer Phillips, "What to know about the Texas abortion law," *Washington Post*, April 21, 2022. https://www.washingtonpost.com/politics/2021/09/01/texas-abortion-law-faq/.
51. Lora Kolodny and Kevin Breuninger, "Elon Musk declines to address Texas abortion law directly after Gov. Greg Abbott's comments," *CNBC*, September 2, 2021. https://www.cnbc.com/2021/09/02/texas-abortion-law-elon-musk-reacts-to-gov-greg-abbotts-comments.html.

52. @elonmusk, X, September 2, 2021. https://x.com/elonmusk/status/1433474893316722691.
53. @RonWyden, X, November 6, 2021. https://x.com/RonWyden/status/14571101759328 46080
54. @elonmusk, X, November 7, 2021. https://x.com/elonmusk/status/145749743847498138.
55. "Inflation Reduction Act Guidebook," WhiteHouse.gov. https://www.whitehouse.gov /cleanenergy/inflation-reduction-act-guidebook/.
56. "Daughter Files to Change Last Name . . . No Longer Wants to 'Be Related' to Him," *TMZ*, June 20, 2022. https://www.tmz.com/2022/06/20/elon-musk-daughter-name-change -transgender-court-filing/.
57. Dawn Ennis and Pilar Menendez, "Elon Musk's Daughter Disowns Him and Files to Ditch His Name," *Daily Beast*, June 20, 2022. https://www.thedailybeast.com/elon-musks -daughter-files-to-ditch-his-last-name.
58. @elonmusk, X, December 16, 2020. https://twitter.com/elonmusk/status/1339255372 956176384.
59. @jordanbpeterson, X, July 22, 2024. https://x.com/jordanbpeterson/status/1815427698 703090085.
60. @elonmusk, X, July 22, 2024. https://x.com/elonmusk/status/1815519696424161361.
61. @vivllainous, Threads, July 25, 2024. https://www.threads.net/@vivllainous/post/C91x FT8yhWo.
62. @vivllainous, Threads, July 23, 2024. https://www.threads.net/@vivllainous/post/C9xj MJIygVN.
63. @elonmusk, X, April 3, 2022. https://x.com/elonmusk/status/1510485792296210434.
64. Ross Kerber and Hunjoo Yin, "Tesla cut from S&P 500 ESG Index, and Elon Musk tweets his fury," Reuters, May 19, 2022. https://www.reuters.com/business/sustainable -business/tesla-removed-sp-500-esg-index-autopilot-discrimination-concerns -2022-05-18/; Faiz Sidduiqi, "Jury orders Tesla to pay more than $130 million in dis- crimination suit, which alleged racist epithets and hostile work environment," *Washington Post*, October 5, 2021. https://www.washingtonpost.com/technology/2021/10/04/tesla -discrimination-case/.
65. "S&P Dow Jones Indices Announces April 2023 Rebalance of the S&P 500 ESG Index," S&P Dow Jones Indices, April 21, 2023. https://www.spglobal.com/spdji/en/documents /indexnews/announcements/20230421–1463609/1463609_s&p500esgindexreview-apr -2023.pdf.
66. @elonmusk, X, May 18, 2022. https://twitter.com/elonmusk/status/15269581100232 45829.
67. @elonmusk, X, April 29, 2023. https://x.com/elonmusk/status/1652223973739098114.
68. @elonmusk, X, May 18, 2022. https://x.com/elonmusk/status/1526997132858822658.
69. @elonmusk, X, June 15, 2022. https://twitter.com/elonmusk/status/15369739653941 57569.
70. @elonmusk, X, June 15, 2022. https://x.com/elonmusk/status/1536976484446904320.
71. @elonmusk, X, June 11, 2022. https://x.com/elonmusk/status/1546679818959278081; @ elonmusk, X, July 11, 2022. https://x.com/elonmusk/status/1546669610509799424.
72. @elonmusk, X, June 11, 2022. https://x.com/elonmusk/status/1546679818959278081.
73. @SwipeWright, X, March 3, 2024. https://x.com/SwipeWright/status/1764426510255 948195.
74. @elonmusk, X, April 28, 2022. https://twitter.com/elonmusk/status/1519852213698 502656.
75. @elonmusk, X, May 12, 2022. https://twitter.com/elonmusk/status/15248834828366 23373.
76. @elonmusk, X, March 5, 2022. https://x.com/elonmusk/status/1499976967105433600.
77. Ibid.
78. Matt Novak, "Read Elon Musk's Private Texts with Joe Rogan, Jack Dorsey, Larry

Ellison, and More," *Gizmodo*, September 30, 2022. https://gizmodo.com/elon-musk-texts-joe-rogan-larry-elllison-dorsey-twitter-1849600155.

79. "Twitter Suspends The Babylon Bee," *The Babylon Bee*, March 22, 2022. https://babylonbee.com/news/twitter-has-shut-down-the-bee.

80. Dana Hull and Lisa Fleisher, "Musk's Texts Over Twitter Deal Included Ex-Wife Talulah Riley," *Bloomberg*, October 4, 2022. https://www.bloomberg.com/news/articles/2022-10-04/musk-s-texts-over-twitter-deal-included-ex-wife-talulah-riley.

81. Will Oremus, Elizabeth Dwoskin, Sarah Ellison and Jeremy B. Merrill, "A year later, Musk's X is tilting right. And sinking," *Washington Post*, October 27, 2023. https://www.washingtonpost.com/technology/2023/10/27/elon-musk-twitter-x-anniversary/.

7. Tesla versus Children

1. @WholeMarsBlog, X, August 11, 2022. https://x.com/WholeMarsBlog/status/1557790148435140609.

2. @WholeMarsBlog, X, August 9, 2022. https://x.com/WholeMarsBlog/status/1557112809132945408.

3. @elonmusk, X, August 25, 2022. https://x.com/elonmusk/status/1562839680747388934.

4. @RealDanODowd, X, March 12, 2022. https://x.com/RealDanODowd/status/1502784004927508485.

5. Gerrit De Vynck and Faiz Siddiqui, "One of Tesla's biggest critics is funding a Super Bowl ad against it," *Washington Post*, February 11, 2023. https://www.washingtonpost.com/technology/2023/02/11/tesla-super-bowl-ad/.

6. Gerrit De Vynck, "The tech CEO spending millions to stop Elon Musk," *Washington Post*, November 13, 2022. https://www.washingtonpost.com/technology/2022/11/13/dan-odowd-challenges-tesla-musk/.

7. Mike Schneider, "There are now more than 6 PR pros for every journalist," *Muck Rack*, September 6, 2018. https://muckrack.com/blog/2018/09/06/there-are-now-more-than-6-pr-pros-for-every-journalist.

8. Aleda Stam, "Tesla reportedly eliminates PR department," *PRWeek*, October 6, 2020. https://www.prweek.com/article/1696519/tesla-reportedly-eliminates-pr-department.

9. @SwayerMerritt, X. https://twitter.com/SawyerMerritt.

10. Michael Strong, "Tesla's Public Relations Team Gets the Ziggy," *The Detroit Bureau*, October 6, 2020. https://www.thedetroitbureau.com/2020/10/teslas-pubic-relations-team-gets-the-ziggy/.

11. @elonmusk, X, April 10, 2023. https://x.com/elonmusk/status/1645565105256513540.

12. Faiz Siddiqui, "Elon Musk moved to Texas and embraced celebrity. Can Tesla run on Autopilot?," *Washington Post*, February 23, 2021. https://www.washingtonpost.com/technology/2021/02/23/musk-tesla-texas/.

13. Faiz Siddiqui, "How auto regulators played mind games with Elon Musk," *Washington Post*, March 27, 2022. https://www.washingtonpost.com/technology/2022/03/27/tesla-elon-musk-regulation/.

14. Simon Alvarez, "Tesla's Elon Musk slams paywalled news in recent media critique," *Teslarati*, March 28, 2022. https://www.teslarati.com/tesla-elon-musk-slams-paywalled-news/.

15. "Test Track—The Dangers of Tesla's Full Self-Driving Software," *Dan O'Dowd Media*, August 9, 2022. https://www.youtube.com/watch?v=nHIgawTRCv8.

16. Andrew J. Hawkins, "An open letter to the Tesla fan who wants to run over a kid to prove a point," *The Verge*, August 12, 2022. https://www.theverge.com/2022/8/12/23302850/tesla-full-self-driving-child-crash-open-letter.

17. Fred Lambert, "Tesla self-driving smear campaign releases 'test' that fails to realize FSD never engaged," *Electrek*, August 10, 2022. https://electrek.co/2022/08/10/tesla-self-driving-smear-campaign-releases-test-fails-fsd-never-engaged/.

18. @WholeMarsBlog, X, August 9, 2022. https://x.com/WholeMarsBlog/status/15571347 27428993024.
19. Ibid.
20. @WholeMarsBlog, X, August 11, 2022. https://x.com/WholeMarsBlog/status/15577 90148435140609
21. Andrew J. Hawkins, "An open letter to the Tesla fan who wants to run over a kid to prove a point," *The Verge*, August 12, 2022. https://www.theverge.com/2022/8/12/23302850/tesla -full-self-driving-child-crash-open-letter.
22. @WholeMarsBlog, X, August 14, 2022. https://x.com/WholeMarsBlog/status/155887 6752062976000.
23. Lora Kolodny, "YouTube removes video by Tesla investors using kids in FSD Beta test," *CNBC*, August 19, 2022. https://www.cnbc.com/2022/08/19/youtube-removes-video-by -tesla-investors-using-kids-in-fsd-beta-test.html.
24. Faiz Siddiqui and Gerrit De Vynck, "Tesla demands removal of video of cars hitting child size mannequins," *Washington Post*, August 25, 2022. https://www.washingtonpost.com /technology/2022/08/25/tesla-elon-musk-demo/.
25. Faiz Siddiqui and Jeremy B. Merrill, "17 fatalities, 736 crashes: the shocking toll of Tesla's Autopilot," *Washington Post*, June 10, 2022. https://www.washingtonpost.com/technology /2023/06/10/tesla-autopilot-crashes-elon-musk/.
26. Trisha Thadani, Faiz Siddiqui, Rachel Lerman and Jeremy B. Merrill, "Tesla drivers run Autopilot where it's not intended—with deadly consequences," *Washington Post*, December 10, 2023. https://www.washingtonpost.com/technology/2023/12/10/tesla-autopilot-crash/.
27. Faiz Siddiqui, "'Boycott Tesla' ads to air during Super Bowl," *Washington Post*, February 11, 2024. https://www.washingtonpost.com/technology/2024/02/11/tesla-super-bowl-ads/.
28. @rohanspatel, X, December 13, 2023. https://x.com/rohanspatel/status/173490608 8984584689.
29. Faiz Siddiqui, "'Boycott Tesla' ads to air during Super Bowl," *Washington Post*, February 11, 2024. https://www.washingtonpost.com/technology/2024/02/11/tesla-super-bowl-ads/.

8. "They Own the Government Here"

1. Lora Kolodny, "Tesla fired an employee after he posted driverless tech reviews on You-Tube," *CNBC*, March 17, 2022. https://www.cnbc.com/2022/03/15/tesla-fired-employee -who-posted-fsd-beta-videos-as-ai-addict-on-youtube.html.
2. Faiz Siddiqui, "Tesla sells 'Self-Driving' cars. Is it fraud?," *Washington Post*, July 11, 2024.
3. Lakshmi Varanasi, "Tesla faked a 2016 video promoting its self-driving technology, according to a senior company engineer's deposition testimony," *Business Insider*, January 17, 2023. https://www.businessinsider.com/tesla-faked-video-in-2016-promoting-self -driving-technology-report-2023-1.
4. Rob Stumpf, "Tesla Network Promises One Million Robotaxis on the Road by 2020," *The Drive*, April 23, 2019.
5. Cade Metz and Neal F. Boudette, "Inside Tesla as Elon Musk Pushed an Unflinching Vision for Self-Driving Cars," *New York Times*, December 6, 2021. https://www.nytimes.com /2021/12/06/technology/tesla-autopilot-elon-musk.html.
6. Hyunjoo Jin, "Tesla video promoting self-driving was staged, engineer testifies," Reuters, January 18, 2023. https://www.reuters.com/technology/tesla-video-promoting-self-driving -was-staged-engineer-testifies-2023–01–17/.
7. Ibid.
8. Dana Hull and Sean O'Kane, "Musk Oversaw Video That Exaggerated Tesla's Self-Driving Capabilities," *Bloomberg*, January 19, 2023. https://www.bloomberg.com/news/articles /2023–01–19/elon-musk-directed-tesla-autopilot-video-saying-car-drove-itself-tsla.
9. "How Elon Musk knocked Tesla's 'Full Self-Driving' off course," *Washington Post*, March 19, 2023. https://www.washingtonpost.com/technology/2023/03/19/elon-musk-tesla-driving.

10. "Supply chain issues and autos: When will the chip shortage end?" J.P. Morgan, April 18, 2023. https://www.jpmorgan.com/insights/global-research/supply-chain/chip-shortage.
11. Faiz Siddiqui, "How Elon Musk knocked Tesla's 'Full Self-Driving," *Washington Post*, March 19, 2023. https://www.washingtonpost.com/technology/2023/03/19/elon-musk-tesla-driving/.
12. Ibid.
13. "Tesla Vision Update: Replacing Ultrasonic Sensors with Tesla Vision," Tesla.com, October 10, 2024. https://www.tesla.com/support/transitioning-tesla-vision.
14. Faiz Siddiqui, "Tesla's recent Full Self-Driving update made cars go haywire. It may be the excuse regulators needed," *Washington Post*, November 11, 2021. https://www.washingtonpost.com/technology/2021/11/08/tesla-regulation-elon-musk/.
15. Ibid.
16. Ibid.
17. "Part 573 Safety Recall Report," NHTSA, February 15, 2023. https://static.nhtsa.gov/odi/rcl/2023/RCLRPT-23V085-3451.PDF.
18. @elonmusk, X, October 24, 2021. https://twitter.com/elonmusk/status/1452345284483235841.
19. Faiz Siddiqui and Jeremy B. Merrill, "Tesla drivers report a surge in 'phantom breaking'," *Washington Post*, February 2, 2022. https://www.washingtonpost.com/technology/2022/02/02/tesla-phantom-braking/.
20. Ibid.
21. "ODI Resume: Unexpected Brake Activation," NHTSA, February 16, 2022. https://static.nhtsa.gov/odi/inv/2022/INOA-PE22002-4385.PDF.
22. @elonmusk, X, February 12, 2022. https://x.com/elonmusk/status/1492667516275105792.
23. Faiz Siddiqui, "Tesla is putting 'self-driving' in the hands of drivers amid criticism the tech is not ready," *Washington Post*, October 22, 2020. https://www.washingtonpost.com/technology/2020/10/21/tesla-self-driving/.
24. "Tesla tempted drivers with 'insane' mode and now is tracking them to judge safety. Experts say it's ludicrous," *Washington Post*, October 10, 2021. https://www.washingtonpost.com/technology/2021/10/10/tesla-full-self-driving/.
25. Faiz Siddiqui, "Tesla issues recall of cars with 'Full Self-Driving' over crash risk" *Washington Post*, February 16, 2023. https://www.washingtonpost.com/technology/2023/02/16/tesla-full-self-driving-recall/.
26. Grace Kay, "What it's like working at Tesla's Autopilot labeling facilities, where your keystrokes and bathroom breaks are tracked," *Business Insider*, September 3, 2024. https://www.businessinsider.com/tesla-autopilot-fsd-labeling-facilities-jobs-2024-9.
27. Ibid.
28. Faiz Siddiqui, "How Elon Musk knocked Tesla's 'Full Self-Driving' off course," *Washington Post*, March 19, 2023. https://www.washingtonpost.com/technology/2023/03/19/elon-musk-tesla-driving/.
29. The Tesla Team, "In Response to False Allegations," Tesla.com, February 16, 2023. https://www.tesla.com/blog/in-response-false-allegations.
30. "Tesla Vision Update: Replacing Ultrasonic Sensors with Tesla Vision," Tesla.com. December 5, 2024. https://www.tesla.com/support/transitioning-tesla-vision.
31. @elonmusk, X, February 5, 2022. https://x.com/elonmusk/status/1489841690601041924.
32. Simon Alvarez, "Tesla FSD beta takes on San Francisco's famed Lombard Street and its 8 hairpin turns," *Teslarati*, October 30, 2020. https://www.teslarati.com/tesla-fsd-beta-lombard-street-test-video/#google_vignette.
33. @Tesla_AI, X, October 4, 2024. https://x.com/Tesla_AI/status/1842143130302177380.
34. @elonmusk, X, August 23, 2022. https://x.com/elonmusk/status/1562157209513066501.
35. Whole Mars Catalog, "Tesla Autopilot FSD Los Angeles to Silicon Valley Interventions," YouTube, January 4, 2021. https://www.youtube.com/watch?v=XPrsRM2cxGs.
36. Whole Mars Catalog, "First Drive with Tesla Full Self-Driving Beta 10.69: 35 minutes

with zero takeovers in San Francisco," YouTube, August 21, 2022. https://www.youtube.com/watch?v=jCTssX2VdKA.

37. @ValueAnalyst1, X, June 1, 2023. https://twitter.com/ScottBeck68/status/1664290716669837317.

38. @elonmusk, X, https://x.com/elonmusk/status/1668877942141640704.

39. Kevin Smith, "Omar Cheats?!? Tesla FSD Beta Chat," YouTube, July 6, 2023. https://www.youtube.com/watch?v=tW4S0vk_-i8.

40. @WholeMarsBlog, X, June 7, 2024. https://x.com/WholeMarsBlog/status/1799276775912153403.

41. Faiz Siddiqui, "How Elon Musk knocked Tesla's 'Full Self-Driving,'" *Washington Post*, March 19, 2023. https://www.washingtonpost.com/technology/2023/03/19/elon-musk-tesla-driving/.

42. Faiz Siddiqui and Jeremy B. Merrill, "17 fatalities, 736 crashes: The shocking toll of Tesla's Autopilot," *Washington Post*, June 10, 2023. https://www.washingtonpost.com/technology/2023/06/10/tesla-autopilot-crashes-elon-musk/.

43. "ODI Resume: Autopilot & First Responder Scenes," NHTSA, June 8, 2022. https://static.nhtsa.gov/odi/inv/2022/INOA-EA22002–3184.PDF.

44. Edward Ludlow and Dana Hull, "Tesla Cuts 200 Autopilot Workers as California Site Closes," *Bloomberg*, June 28, 2022. https://www.bloomberg.com/news/articles/2022-06-28/tesla-lays-off-hundreds-of-autopilot-workers-in-latest-staff-cut.

45. Mike Spector and Dan Levine, "Exclusive: Tesla faces U.S. criminal probe over self-driving claims," Reuters, October 27, 2022. https://www.reuters.com/legal/exclusive-tesla-faces-us-criminal-probe-over-self-driving-claims-sources-2022–10–26/.

46. Faiz Siddiqui, "Elon Musk says Tesla will not produce a new vehicle model in 2022, renews prediction on Full Self-Driving," *Washington Post*, January 26, 2022. https://www.washingtonpost.com/technology/2022/01/26/tesla-elon-musk/.

47. Rachel Lerman, Faiz Siddiqui and Christian Davenport, "Elon Musk tells Tesla, SpaceX workers to go back to office or go away," *Washington Post*, June 1, 2022. https://www.washingtonpost.com/technology/2022/06/01/elon-musk-tesla-office/.

48. @elonmusk, X, June 1, 2022. https://twitter.com/elonmusk/status/1531867103854317568.

9. The Fun Police

1. Jacob Bogage, "Tesla driver using autopilot killed in crash," *Washington Post*, June 30, 2016. https://www.washingtonpost.com/news/the-switch/wp/2016/06/30/tesla-owner-killed-in-fatal-crash-while-car-was-on-autopilot/.

2. Michael Laris, "Fatal Tesla crash tied to technology and driver failures, NTSB says," *Washington Post*, February 25, 2020. https://www.washingtonpost.com/local/trafficandcommuting/ntsb-says-driver-in-fatal-tesla-crash-was-overreliant-on-the-cars-/autopilot-system/2017/09/12/38e5f130–9730–11e7–82e4-f1076f6d6152_story.html.

3. Jacob Bogage, "Tesla driver using autopilot killed in crash," *Washington Post*, June 30, 2016. https://www.washingtonpost.com/news/the-switch/wp/2016/06/30/tesla-owner-killed-in-fatal-crash-while-car-was-on-autopilot/.

4. Hamza Shaban, "Tesla Model 3 Autopilot was active before deadly collision, federal investigators say," *Washington Post*, May 17, 2019. https://www.washingtonpost.com/technology/2019/05/17/tesla-model-autopilot-was-active-before-deadly-collision-federal-investigators-say/.

5. David Shepardson, "Tesla and U.S. regulators strongly criticized over role of Autopilot in crash," Reuters, February 25, 2020. https://www.reuters.com/article/us-tesla-crash/tesla-and-u-s-regulators-strongly-criticized-over-role-of-autopilot-in-crash-idUSKBN20J2B8/.

6. "Standing General Order on Crash Reporting," NHTSA, April 2023. https://www.nhtsa.gov/laws-regulations/standing-general-order-crash-reporting.

7. Farhang Heydari, "The Invisible Driver of Policing," *Stanford Law Review*, March 1, 2023. https://papers.ssrn.com/sol3/papers.cfm?abstract_id=4369747.

8. Nate Luce, "How the National Highway Traffic Safety Administration Enabled Pretextual Traffic Stops," Vanderbilt Law School, April 11, 2024. https://law.vanderbilt.edu/how-the-national-highway-traffic-safety-administration-enabled-pretextual-traffic-stops/.

9. "U.S. DOT and IIHS announce historic commitment of 20 automakers to make automatic emergency braking standard on new vehicles," NHTSA, March 17, 2016. https://www.nhtsa.gov/press-releases/us-dot-and-iihs-announce-historic-commitment-20-automakers-make-automatic-emergency.

10. Harvey Rosenfield, Clarence Ditlow, and Joan Claybrook, "Re: January 12, 2016 Petition Requesting AEB Rulemaking," Consumer Watchdog, May 23, 2016, https://www.autosafety.org/wp-content/uploads/2016/01/Ltr-NHTSA-re-AEB-Petition-5-21-16-PM-FINAL.pdf.

11. Audrey LaForest, "Steven Cliff closer to getting NHTSA back to the business of safety," *Automotive News*, February 7, 2022. https://www.autonews.com/regulation-safety/nhtsa-step-closer-naming-steven-cliff-permanent-administrator/.

12. Trisha Thadani, Rachel Lerman, Imogen Piper, Faiz Siddiqui and Irfan Uraizee, "The final 11 seconds of a fatal Tesla Autopilot crash," *Washington Post*, October 6, 2023. https://www.washingtonpost.com/technology/interactive/2023/tesla-autopilot-crash-analysis/.

13. "Limitations and Warnings," Tesla Model 3 Owner's Manual. https://www.tesla.com/ownersmanual/model3/en_us/GUID-E5FF5E84-6AAC-43E6-B7ED-EC1E9AEB17B7.html.

14. Ibid.

15. "NHTSA Orders Crash Reporting for Vehicles Equipped with Advanced Driver Assistance Systems and Automated Driving Systems," NHTSA, June 29, 2021. https://www.nhtsa.gov/press-releases/nhtsa-orders-crash-reporting-vehicles-equipped-advanced-driver-assistance-systems.

16. Second-Amended-SGO-2021–01_2023–04–05.

17. "Part 573 Safety Recall Report," NHTSA, January 27, 2022. https://static.nhtsa.gov/odi/rcl/2022/RCLRPT-22V037–4462.PDF.

18. Faiz Siddiqui, "Silicon Valley pioneered self-driving cars. But some of its tech-savvy residents don't want them tested in their neighborhoods," *Washington Post*, October 3, 2019. https://www.washingtonpost.com/technology/2019/10/03/silicon-valley-pioneered-self-driving-cars-some-its-tech-savvy-residents-dont-want-them-tested-their-neighborhoods/.

19. "Full Self-Driving (Supervised)," Tesla Model Y Owner's Manual. https://www.tesla.com/ownersmanual/modely/en_us/GUID-2CB60804-9CEA-4F4B-8B04-09B991368DC5.html.

20. Ibid.

21. Ibid.

22. Andrei Nedelea, "Tesla FSD Now Has Selectable Modes: Chill, Average and Assertive," *Inside EVs*, January 12, 2022. https://insideevs.com/news/560209/tesla-fsd-self-driving-profiles/.

23. Ibid.

24. ODI Resume: Tesla "Passenger Play," NHTSA, December 21, 2021.

25. Aaron Gregg and Faiz Siddiqui, "Tesla will recall more than 50,000 vehicles over software's 'rolling-stop' feature," *Washington Post*, February 1, 2022. https://www.washingtonpost.com/business/2022/02/01/tesla-recall-rolling-stop/.

26. Tesla NHTSA Recall No: 22V-037, https://static.nhtsa.gov/odi/rcl/2022/RCONL-22V037-8566.pdf.

27. Part 573 Safety Recall Report, NHTSA, February 15, 2023. https://static.nhtsa.gov/odi/rcl/2023/RCLRPT-23V085-3451.PDF.

28. Ibid.

29. "NHTSA letter to Tesla, Re: Vehicle May Fail to Stop at Stop Sign," January 31, 2022. https://static.nhtsa.gov/odi/rcl/2022/RCAK-22V037-9109.pdf.

30. @elonmusk, X, July 2, 2024. https://x.com/elonmusk/status/1808326181453775069.

31. "Tesla, Inc. Service Bulletin: Update Vehicle Firmware to Correct Seat Belt Chime Functionality," March 2, 2022. https://static.nhtsa.gov/odi/rcl/2022/RCRIT-22V045-4582.pdf.

32. Faiz Siddiqui, "How auto regulators played mind games with Elon Musk," *Washington Post*, March 27, 2022. https://www.washingtonpost.com/technology/2022/03/27/tesla-elon-musk-regulation/.

33. Fred Lambert, "Tesla owners are again losing heat in extreme cold as some heat pumps are failing badly," *Electrek*, January 12, 2022. https://electrek.co/2022/01/12/tesla-owners-losing-heat-extreme-cold-heat-pumps-failing-badly/.

34. Steven Loveday, "NHTSA Recall Clarifies Tesla Heat Pump Issue, Software Fix Coming," *Inside EVs*, February 9. 2022. https://insideevs.com/news/566343/tesla-heat-loss-nhtsa-solution/.

35. David Shepardson, "Tesla recalls over 500,000 U.S. vehicles to fix pedestrian warning sounds," Reuters, February 10, 2022. https://www.reuters.com/business/autos-transportation/tesla-recalls-nearly-579000-us-vehicles-over-pedestrian-warning-risk-sounds-2022-02-10/.

36. "Federal Motor Vehicle Safety Standard No. 141, Minimum Sound Requirements for Hybrid and Electric Vehicles," NHTSA, February 26, 2018. https://www.federalregister.gov/documents/2018/02/26/2018-03721/federal-motor-vehicle-safety-standard-no-141-minimum-sound-requirements-for-hybrid-and-electric.

37. Part 573 Safety Recall Report, NHTSA, February 15, 2023. https://static.nhtsa.gov/odi/rcl/2022/RCLRPT-22V063-8773.PDF.

38. Ibid.

39. @elonmusk, X, February 12, 2022. https://x.com/elonmusk/status/1492667516275105792.

40. "Automakers fulfill autobrake pledge for light-duty vehicles," Insurance Institute for Highway Safety (IIHS), December 21, 2023. https://www.iihs.org/news/detail/automakers-fulfill-autobrake-pledge-for-light-duty-vehicles.

41. "NHTSA Finalizes Key Safety Rule to Reduce Crashes and Save Lives," NIITSA, April 29, 2024. https://www.nhtsa.gov/press-releases/nhtsa-fmvss-127-automatic-emergency-braking-reduce-crashes.

42. "U.S. DOT and IIHS announce historic commitment of 20 automakers to make automatic emergency braking standard on new vehicles," NHTSA, March 17, 2016. https://www.nhtsa.gov/press-releases/us-dot-and-iihs-announce-historic-commitment-20-automakers-make-automatic-emergency'.

43. "Statement by Ralph Nader On Tesla Full Self-Driving (FSD) technology," Nader.org, August 10, 2022. https://nader.org/2022/08/10/statement-by-ralph-nader-on-tesla-full-self-driving-fsd-technology/.

10. The Cost of Buying Twitter

1. Jeremy B. Merrill, Rachel Lerman and Faiz Siddiqui, "Elon Musk sells roughly $5 billion in Tesla stock in series of whirlwind transactions," *Washington Post*, November 11, 2021. https://www.washingtonpost.com/technology/2021/11/10/elon-musk-tesla-stock/?msclkid=a76a08e2b45111ecb1fa721259515fe8.

2. @elonmusk, X, March 26, 2022. https://x.com/elonmusk/status/1507777261654605828; @elonmusk, X, March 25, 2022. https://x.com/elonmusk/status/150725970922463 2344.

3. @elonmusk, X, March 25, 2022. https://x.com/elonmusk/status/1507272763597373461.

4. @elonmusk, X, March 26, 2022. https://x.com/elonmusk/status/1507777913042571267.

5. Will Oremus, Elizabeth Dwoskin, Faiz Siddiqui and Reed Albergotti, "Elon Musk joins Twitter board, promises 'significant improvements'," *Washington Post*, April 5, 2022. https://www.washingtonpost.com/business/2022/04/05/elon-musk-twitter-board/.

6. Faiz Siddiqui, Douglas MacMillan and Aaron Gregg, "Elon Musk signals with $46.5 billion he's serious about buying Twitter," *Washington Post*, April 21, 2022.https://www.washingtonpost.com/business/2022/04/21/elon-musk-twitter-funding/.

7. Faiz Siddiqui, Elizabeth Dwoskin, Reed Albergotti and Gerrit De Vynck, "Elon Musk lines up growing list of investors to take over Twitter," *Washington Post*, June 1, 2022. https://www.washingtonpost.com/technology/2022/06/01/elon-musk-twitter-investors/.

8. Matt Rosoff, "Here are the people who texted Elon Musk to offer advice or money for the Twitter deal," *CNBC*, September 30, 2022. https://www.cnbc.com/2022/09/30/who-texted-elon-musk-to-get-involved-or-offer-advice-on-twitter-deal.html.

9. Exhibit H: Elon Musk Texts, Twitter v. Elon Musk, Case No. 2022-0613-KSJM, September 28, 2022.

10. Faiz Siddiqui, "Musk's Twitter investors have lost billions in value," *Washington Post*, September 1, 2024. https://www.washingtonpost.com/technology/2024/09/01/musk-twitter-investors-underwater/.

11. Exhibit H: Elon Musk Texts, Twitter v. Elon Musk, September 28, 2022.

12. Amanda Silberling and Taylor Hatmaker, "Here are some of the cringiest revelations in the Elon Musk text dump," *TechCrunch*, September 29, 2022. https://techcrunch.com/2022/09/29/elon-musk-texts-discovery-twitter/.

13. Exhibit H: Elon Musk Texts, Twitter v. Elon Musk, September 28, 2022.

14. Ibid.

15. Faiz Siddiqui, "Musk's Twitter investors have lost billions in value," *Washington Post*, September 1, 2024.

16. Miles Klee, "Here are the people who lost millions backing Musk's Twitter takeover," *Rolling Stone*, August 22, 2024. https://www.rollingstone.com/culture/culture-features/twitter-x-shareholders-court-order-diddy-jack-dorsey-1235085804/.

17. Faiz Siddiqui, "Elon Musk is worth $270 billion. He'd buy Twitter with an IOU," *Washington Post*, April 22, 2022. https://www.washingtonpost.com/technology/2022/04/22/musk-twitter-financing-tesla/.

18. Meghan Bobrowsky, "Elon Musks's Share-Selling Spree Tops $15 Billion," *Wall Street Journal*, December 22, 2021. https://www.wsj.com/articles/elon-musks-share-selling-spree-tops-15-billion-11640229872.

19. Tesla Form 10-K, 2021, United States Securities Exchange Commission. https://www.sec.gov/Archives/edgar/data/1318605/000095017022000796/tsla-20211231.htm.

20. Faiz Siddiqui, "Elon Musk is worth $270 billion. He'd buy Twitter with an IOU," *Washington Post*, April 22, 2022. https://www.washingtonpost.com/technology/2022/04/22/musk-twitter-financing-tesla/.

21. Exhibit H: Elon Musk Texts, Twitter v. Elon Musk, September 28, 2022.

22. "Amendment No. 2 To Schedule 13d/A Under the Securities Exchange Act of 1934," United States Securities and Exchange Commission. April 13, 2022. https://www.sec.gov/Archives/edgar/data/1418091/000110465922045641/tm2212748d1_sc13da.htm.

23. Ibid.

24. "Amendment No. 2 To Schedule 13d/A Under the Securities Exchange Act of 1934," United States Securities and Exchange Commission. April 20, 2022.

25. @elonmusk, X, October 24, 2022. https://x.com/elonmusk/status/1584539176997122048.

26. "Elon Musk Equity Financing Commitment letter," April 25, 2022. https://www.sec.gov/Archives/edgar/data/1418091/000110465922049844/tm2213189d8_ex99-j.htm.

27. Reed Albergotti, "Elon Musk delayed filing a form and made $156 million," *Washington Post*, April 6, 2022. https://www.washingtonpost.com/technology/2022/04/06/musk-twitter-sec/.

28. Dave Michaels, "Elon Musk's Belated Disclosure of Twitter Stake Triggers Regulators' Probes," *Wall Street Journal*, May 11, 2022. https://www.wsj.com/articles/elon-musks-belated-disclosure-of-twitter-stake-triggers-regulators-probes-11652303894.

29. @elonmusk, X, December 12, 2024. https://x.com/elonmusk/status/1867357433493872874.
30. Daniel Davies, "Morning Coffee: Elon Musk's exhausted bankers contemplate bonus devastation. The Japanese bank that's hiring where others fear to tread," *efinancialcareers*, October 5, 2022. https://www.efinancialcareers.com/news/2022/10/elon-musk-twitter-bankers.
31. Douglas MacMillan, Reed Albergotti and Taylor Telford, "Musk gets help from tech titans and a Saudi prince in Twitter bid," *Washington Post*, May 5, 2022. https://www.washingtonpost.com/business/2022/05/05/musk-twitter-financing-ellison/.
32. @Alwaleed_Talal, X, October 7, 2015. https://x.com/Alwaleed_Talal/status/15146159 56986757127.
33. @Alwaleed_Talal, X, April 14, 2022. https://x.com/Alwaleed_Talal/status/15146159 56986757127.
34. @elonmusk, X, April 14, 2022. https://x.com/elonmusk/status/1514683079968931841.
35. Exhibit H: Elon Musk Texts, Twitter v. Elon Musk, September 28, 2022.
36. Faiz Siddiqui, "Musk's Twitter investors have lost billions in value," *Washington Post*, September 1, 2024. https://www.washingtonpost.com/technology/2024/09/01/musk-twitter-investors-underwater/.
37. @Alwaleed_Talal, X, May 5, 2022. https://x.com/Alwaleed_Talal/status/15221716 41761046528.
38. Faiz Siddiqui, Reed Albergotti, Elizabeth Dwoskin and Rachel Lerman, "Elon Musk says Twitter deal is on hold, putting bid on shaky ground," *Washington Post*, May 13, 2022. https://www.washingtonpost.com/technology/2022/05/13/musk-twitter-bid/.
39. @elonmusk, X, April 21, 2022. https://x.com/elonmusk/status/1517215066550116354.
40. Amanda Silberling, "Here are some of the cringiest revelations in the Elon Musk text dump," *TechCrunch*, September 29, 2022. https://techcrunch.com/2022/09/29/elon-musk-texts-discovery-twitter/.
41. Twitter v. Elon Musk, Exhibit H: Elon Musk Texts, September 28, 2022.
42. Faiz Siddiqui, "How auto regulators played mind games with Elon Musk," *Washington Post*, March 27, 2022. https://www.washingtonpost.com/technology/2022/03/27/tesla-elon-musk-regulation/.
43. Sheila Dang, "Twitter estimates spam, fake accounts comprise less than 5% of users—filing," Reuters, May 2. 2022. https://www.reuters.com/technology/twitter-estimates-spam-fake-accounts-represent-less-than-5-users-filing-2022-05-02/./.
44. @elonmusk, X, May 13, 2022. https://x.com/elonmusk/status/1525049369552048129.
45. @elonmusk, X, May 13, 2022. https://x.com/elonmusk/status/1525080945274998785.
46. @AJDelgado13, X, May 13, 2022. https://x.com/AJDelgado13/status/15251441094255 98465?s=20.
47. Lora Kolodny, "Start-up investor Jason Calacanis raising millions of dollars for Musk's Twitter deal," *CNBC*, May 12, 2022. https://www.cnbc.com/2022/05/12/start-up-investor-jason-calacanis-raising-millions-for-twitter-stake.html.
48. Twitter v. Elon Musk, Exhibit H: Elon Musk Texts, September 28, 2022.
49. Ibid.
50. Faiz Siddiqui, Elizabeth Dwoskin, Reed Albergotti and Gerrit De Vynck, "Elon Musk lines up growing list of investors to take over Twitter," *Washington Post*, June 1, 2022. https://www.washingtonpost.com/technology/2022/06/01/elon-musk-twitter-investors/.
51. Ibid.
52. "Tesla Amendment No. 7 To Schedule 13d," United States Securities and Exchange Commission, May 24, 2022. https://www.sec.gov/Archives/edgar/data/1494730/0001 10465922064655/tm2216931d1_sc13da.htm.
53. Hamza Shaban and Faiz Siddiqui, "Here's who helped Elon Musk buy Twitter," *Washington Post*, December 24, 2022. https://www.washingtonpost.com/technology/2022/12/24/elon-musk-twitter-funders/.
54. Faiz Siddiqui, Jeff Stein and Joseph Menn, "U.S. exploring whether it has authority to review

Musk's Twitter deal," *Washington Post*, November 2, 2022. https://www.washingtonpost.com/us-policy/2022/11/01/musk-twitter-treasury-department-review/.

55. Faiz Siddiqui, "Musk's Twitter investors have lost billions in value," *Washington Post*, September 1, 2024. https://www.washingtonpost.com/technology/2024/09/01/musk-twitter-investors-underwater/.

11. Exit Plan

1. Will Oremus and Elizabeth Dwoskin, "Twitter's new CEO is bringing an engineering background to a politics fight," *Washington Post*, December 1, 2021. https://www.washingtonpost.com/technology/2021/12/01/twitter-ceo-parag-agrawal/.

2. Jacob Carpenter, "Was Jack Dorsey an absentee CEO by the end of his Twitter tenure? The evidence keeps pointing to 'yes'," *Fortune*, September 2, 2022. https://fortune.com/2022/09/02/twitter-jack-dorsey-whistleblower-poll-absent-leadership/.

3. Will Oremus and Elizabeth Dwoskin, "Twitter's new CEO is bringing an engineering background to a politics fight," *Washington Post*, December 1, 2021. https://www.washingtonpost.com/technology/2021/12/01/twitter-ceo-parag-agrawal/.

4. Ibid.

5. @elonmusk, X, May 13, 2022. https://x.com/elonmusk/status/1525049369552048129.

6. @paraga, X, May 16, 2022. https://x.com/paraga/status/1526237578843672576.

7. @paraga, X, May 16, 2022. https://x.com/paraga/status/1526237580638859267.

8. @paraga, X, May 16, 2022. https://x.com/paraga/status/1526237581419040768.

9. @elonmusk, X, May 16, 2022. https://x.com/elonmusk/status/1526246899606601730.

10. Rob Wile, "Musk is not supposed to disparage Twitter while trying to buy it. He's doing it anyway," *NBC News*, April 27, 2022. https://www.nbcnews.com/business/business-news/elon-musk-slams-twitter-after-acquisition-deal-announced-rcna26244.

11. @elonmusk, X, May 16, 2022. https://x.com/elonmusk/status/1526250477456965634.

12. Sheila Dang, "Exclusive: Twitter is losing its most active users, internal documents show," *Reuters*, October 26, 2022. https://www.reuters.com/technology/exclusive-where-did-tweeters-go-twitter-is-losing-its-most-active-users-internal-2022–10–25/.

13. @elonmusk, X, April 9, 2022. https://x.com/elonmusk/status/1512802419301826575.

14. @elonmusk, X, February 1, 2020. https://x.com/elonmusk/status/1223754759921897472.

15. @elonmusk, X, February 1, 2020. https://x.com/elonmusk/status/1223756247612186625.

16. Faiz Siddiqui and Jeremy B. Merrill, "Elon Musk reinvents Twitter for the benefit of a power user: Himself," *Washington Post*, February 16, 2023. https://www.washingtonpost.com/technology/2023/02/16/elon-musk-twitter/.

17. @elonmusk, X, May 13, 2022. https://x.com/elonmusk/status/1525291586669531137.

18. @teslaownersSV, X, May 13, 2022. https://x.com/teslaownersSV/status/1525292556270985223.

19. @elonmusk, X, May 13, 2022. https://x.com/elonmusk/status/1525293103585718272.

20. @elonmusk, X, May 13, 2022. https://x.com/elonmusk/status/1525295117489229824.

21. @paraga, X, May 16, 2022. https://x.com/paraga/status/1526237589534953472.

22. Elizabeth Dwoskin, "In reversal, Twitter plans to comply with Musk's demands for data," *Washington Post*, June 8, 2022. https://www.washingtonpost.com/technology/2022/06/08/elon-musk-twitter-bot-data/.

23. "Letter from Skadden, Arps, Slate, Meagher & Flom LLP to Twitter, Inc.," June 6, 2022. https://www.sec.gov/Archives/edgar/data/1418091/000110465922068347/tm2217761d1_ex99-o.htm.

24. Ibid.

25. Elizabeth Dwoskin, "In reversal, Twitter plans to comply with Musk's demands for data," *Washington Post*, June 8, 2022. https://www.washingtonpost.com/technology/2022/06/08/elon-musk-twitter-bot-data/.

26. Elizabeth Dwoskin and Faiz Siddiqui, "Twitter is probing Elon Musk's social circle in broad legal requests," *Washington Post*, August 1, 2022. https://www.washingtonpost.com /technology/2022/08/01/musk-twitter-subpoena/.

27. Faiz Siddiqui, Ellen Francis and Taylor Telford, "Elon Musk says deal can't 'move forward' until Twitter proves bot numbers," *Washington Post*, May 17, 2022. https://www .washingtonpost.com/technology/2022/05/17/elon-musk-twitter-deal-proof-bots/.

28. Rachel Lerman, "Five reasons the Elon Musk deal to buy Twitter could still fall apart," *Washington Post*, April 28, 2022. https://www.washingtonpost.com/technology/2022/04 /28/elon-musk-twitter-deal-risks/.

29. Elizabeth Dwoskin, Cat Zakrzewski, Will Oremus and Joseph Menn, "Twitter lawyer long weighed safety, free speech. Then Musk called her out," *Washington Post*, May 10, 2022. https://www.washingtonpost.com/technology/2022/05/09/twitter-lawyer-censor -musk/.

30. Gerrit De Vynck, Faiz Siddiqui and Rachel Lerman, "Elon Musk files to back out of Twitter deal," *Washington Post*, July 8, 2022. https://www.washingtonpost.com/technology/2022 /07/08/musk-deal-sec/.

31. Faiz Siddiqui and Gerrit De Vynck, "Elon Musk's deal to buy Twitter is in peril," *Washington Post*, July 7, 2022. https://www.washingtonpost.com/technology/2022/07/07/elon -musk-twitter-jeopardy/.

32. Richard Lawler, "It's looking more like Elon Musk could bail on buying Twitter," *The Verge*, July 7, 2022. https://www.theverge.com/2022/7/7/23199137/elon-musk-twitter-spam -account-bot-data-breakup.

33. Art Raymond, "Is Elon Musk's $44B Twitter deal about to implode?," *Deseret News*, July 8, 2022. https://www.deseret.com/u-s-world/2022/7/8/23200422/is-elon-musks-44-billion -twitter-chase-about-to-implode-spam-accounts-tesla-spacex-legal-battle.

34. Lauren Hirsch, "Twitter is ready for a legal battle to force Elon Musk to buy the company," *New York Times*, July 8, 2022. https://www.nytimes.com/2022/07/08/business/musk -twitter-deal.html.

35. Kerry Flynn, "Elon Musk's Twitter deal becomes debate topic on the platform," *Axios*, July 8, 2022. https://www.axios.com/pro/media-deals/2022/07/08/elon-musk-twitter-deal -debate.

36. Faiz Siddiqui and Elizabeth Dwoskin, "Musk's countersuit contains aggressive new claims. Twitter is rebutting them," *Washington Post*, August 4, 2022. https://www.washingtonpost .com/technology/2022/08/04/elon-musk-twitter/.

37. "Tesla Amendment No. 9 To Schedule 13d," United States Securities and Exchange Commission, July 8, 2022. https://www.sec.gov/Archives/edgar/data/1418091/000110465922078413 /tm2220599d1_sc13da.htm.

38. "Letter from Skadden, Arps, Slate, Meagher & Flom LLP to Twitter, Inc.," July 8, 2022. https://www.sec.gov/Archives/edgar/data/1418091/000110465922078413/tm2220599d1 _ex99-p.htm.

39. Faiz Siddiqui, "Twitter adopts 'poison pill' intended to thwart Elon Musk's takeover bid," *Washington Post*, April 16, 2022. https://www.washingtonpost.com/technology/2022/04 /15/twitter-poison-pill/.

40. @btaylor, X, July 8, 2022. https://x.com/btaylor/status/1545526087089696768.

41. Twitter v. Elon Musk, X Holdings I, Inc. and X Holdings II, Inc., Verified Final Complaint. https://www.documentcloud.org/documents/22084487-final-verified-complaint ?responsive=1&title=0.

42. Elizabeth Dwoskin and Rachel Lerman, "Twitter sues Elon Musk, setting stage for epic legal battle," *Washington Post*, July 12, 2022. https://www.washingtonpost.com/technology /2022/07/12/twitter-elon-musk-lawsuit/.

43. Twitter v. Elon Musk, X Holdings I Inc. and X Holdings II, Inc., Verified Final Complaint.

44. Faiz Siddiqui and Elizabeth Dwoskin, "Musk's countersuit contains aggressive new claims. Twitter is rebutting them," *Washington Post*, August 4, 2022. https://www.washingtonpost .com/technology/2022/08/04/elon-musk-twitter/.

45. Kevin Allen, "Chancellor Kathaleen McCormick '04 J.D. of the Delaware Court of Chancery delivers inaugural Patricia O'Hara Distinguished Lecture in Law & Business," University of Notre Dame Law School, December 8, 2022. https://law.nd.edu/news-events/news /kathaleen-mccormick-delaware-court-of-chancery-patricia-ohara-lecture-law-business/.

12. Lifeline

1. Elizabeth Dwoskin and Gerrit De Vynck, "Judge grants Elon Musk an October court date, in early win for Twitter," *Washington Post*, July 19, 2022. https://www.washingtonpost.com /technology/2022/07/19/twitter-elon-musk-trial/.

2. Joseph Menn, Elizabeth Dwoskin and Cat Zakrzewski, "Former security chief claims Twitter buried 'egregious deficiencies'," *Washington Post*, August 23, 2022. https://www .washingtonpost.com/technology/interactive/2022/twitter-whistleblower-sec-spam/.

3. Faiz Siddiqui, Elizabeth Dwoskin, Cat Zakrzewski and Rachel Lerman, "New whistleblower allegations could factor into Twitter vs. Musk trial," *Washington Post*, August 23, 2022. https://www.washingtonpost.com/technology/2022/08/23/twitter-musk-trial -whistleblower/.

4. Joseph Menn, Elizabeth Dwoskin and Cat Zakrzewski, "Former security chief claims Twitter buried 'egregious deficiencies'," *Washington Post*, August 23, 2022. https://www .washingtonpost.com/technology/interactive/2022/twitter-whistleblower-sec-spam/.

5. Ibid.

6. Matt Robinson and Zeke Faux, "When Elon Musk Tried to Destroy a Tesla Whistleblower," *Bloomberg*, March 13, 2019. https://www.bloomberg.com/news/features/2019–03–13/when -elon-musk-tried-to-destroy-tesla-whistleblower-martin-tripp?embedded-checkout=true.

7. Faiz Siddiqui, Elizabeth Dwoskin, Cat Zakrzewski and Rachel Lerman, "New whistleblower allegations could factor into Twitter vs. Musk trial," *Washington Post*, August 23, 2022. https://www.washingtonpost.com/technology/2022/08/23/twitter-musk-trial -whistleblower/.

8. Ibid.

9. @elonmusk, X, August 23, 2022. https://x.com/elonmusk/status/1562135640598528000.

10. Ibid.

11. Faiz Siddiqui, "Judge grants Musk request for additional data in Twitter trial," *Washington Post*, August 25, 2022. https://www.washingtonpost.com/technology/2022/08/25/musk -twitter-trial/.

12. Ibid.

13. Rachel Lerman and Faiz Siddiqui, "Judge will let Musk add whistleblower claims to case against Twitter," *Washington Post*, September 7, 2022. https://www.washingtonpost.com /technology/2022/09/07/musk-twitter-trial-no-delay/.

14. Twitter v. Elon Musk, et al., Verified Complaint, September 8, 2022. https://cdn.arstechnica .net/wp-content/uploads/2022/09/public-version-of-amended-musk-counterclaims -twitter-v-musk.pdf.

15. Rachel Lerman and Faiz Siddiqui, "Judge will let Musk add whistleblower claims to case against Twitter," *Washington Post*, September 7, 2022.

16. Faiz Siddiqui, "Elon Musk's texts reveal what led to Twitter bid, before deal fell apart," *Washington Post*, September 30, 2022. https://www.washingtonpost.com/technology/2022 /09/30/elon-musk-texts-twitter/.

17. Rachel Lerman and Faiz Siddiqui, "Judge will let Musk add whistleblower claims to case against Twitter," *Washington Post*, September 7, 2022. https://www.washingtonpost.com /technology/2022/09/07/musk-twitter-trial-no-delay/.

18. Jessica Karl, "The Twitter Whistleblower Doesn't Help Elon Musk's Case Much,"

Bloomberg, August 23, 2022. https://www.bloomberg.com/opinion/articles/2022-08-23 /twitter-whistleblower-doesn-t-help-elon-musk-s-case-much.

19. Matt Levine, "AMC Goes APE," *Bloomberg*, August 23, 2022. https://www.bloomberg .com/opinion/articles/2022-08-23/amc-goes-ape.

20. @AnnMLipton, X, August 23, 2022. https://x.com/AnnMLipton/status/15620185980 46121985.

21. @AnnMLipton, X, August 23, 2022. https://x.com/AnnMLipton/status/156202824 7298318336.

22. Matt Levine, "AMC Goes APE," *Bloomberg*, August 23, 2022. https://www.bloomberg .com/opinion/articles/2022-08-23/amc-goes-ape.

23. "Read the Letter Elon Musk Sent to Twitter with More Reasons to Terminate His Buy-out," *Bloomberg*, August 30, 2022. https://www.bloomberg.com/news/articles/2022-08-30 /full-text-read-elon-musk-s-aug-29-letter-to-twitter-to-terminate-deal.

24. "Letter from Skadden, Arps, Slate, Meagher & Flom LLP to Twitter, Inc.," August 29, 2022. https://www.sec.gov/Archives/edgar/data/1494730/000110465922095765/tm2224790d1 _ex99-q.htm.

25. "Letter from Skadden, Arps, Slate, Meagher & Flom LLP to Twitter, Inc.," September 9, 2022. https://www.sec.gov/Archives/edgar/data/1418091/000110465922098972/tm2225 585d1_ex99-r.htm.

26. Clare Duffy, "Elon Musk has publicly filed updated counterclaims against Twitter based on whistleblower disclosure," *CNN Business*, September 15, 2022. https://www.cnn.com/2022 /09/15/tech/elon-musk-twitter-amended-counterclaims/index.html.

27. Twitter v. Elon Musk, et al., Defendants' Verified Counterclaims, Answer, and Affirmative Defenses to Plaintiff's Verified Complaint, July 29, 2022.

28. William T. Quillen and Michael Hanrahan, "A Short History of the Court of Chan-cery," The Widener University School of Law, 1993. https://courts.delaware.gov/chancery /history.aspx.

29. Lewis Black, Jr., "Why Corporations Choose Delaware," Delaware Department of State Divi-sion of Corporations, 2007. https://corpfiles.delaware.gov/pdfs/whycorporations_english.pdf.

30. Ellen Bardash, "'The Time Has Come' for Musk Discovery Sanctions, Twitter's Lawyers Say," Law.com, September 27, 2022. https://www.law.com/delbizcourt/2022/09/27/the -time-has-come-for-musk-discovery-sanctions-twitters-lawyers-say/.

31. Ellen Bardash, "Special Master Appointed to Resolve Twitter-Musk Discovery Dis-putes" Law.com, September 30, 2022. https://www.law.com/delbizcourt/2022/09 /30/special-master-appointed-to-resolve-twitter-musk-discovery-disputes/?slreturn =20231027222848.

32. "Elon Musk deposition in Twitter fight rescheduled for first week of October," *Guardian*, September 27, 2022. https://www.theguardian.com/technology/2022/sep/27/elon-musk -deposition-twitter-takeover-deal.

33. Jef Feeley, Ed Hammond and Kurt Wagner, "Musk Revives $44 Billion Twitter Bid, Aim-ing to Avoid Trial," *Bloomberg*, October 4, 2022. https://www.bloomberg.com/news/articles /2022-10-04/musk-proposes-to-proceed-with-twitter-deal-at-54-20-a-share.

34. "Letter from Skadden, Arps, Slate, Meagher & Flom LLP to Twitter, Inc.," October 3, 2022. https://www.sec.gov/Archives/edgar/data/1418091/000110465922105787/tm2227435d1 _ex99-s.htm.

35. Jef Feeley, Ed Hammond and Kurt Wagner, "Musk Revives $44 Billion Twitter Bid, Aim-ing to Avoid Trial," *Bloomberg*, October 4, 2022. https://www.bloomberg.com/news/articles /2022-10-04/musk-proposes-to-proceed-with-twitter-deal-at-54-20-a-share.

36. Elizabeth Dwoskin, Faiz Siddiqui and Gerrit De Vynck, "Twitter-Musk trial delayed as sides argue over money and trust," *Washington Post*, October 6, 2022. https://www .washingtonpost.com/technology/2022/10/06/twitter-musk-court-postpone/.

37. Ibid.

38. Matt O'Brien and Barbara Ortutay, "Judge delays Twitter trial, gives Musk time to seal buyout," Associated Press, October 6, 2022. https://apnews.com/article/elon-musk-twitter-inc-technology-business-934a3b2429bed8cfeadfa6567a2e5256.

39. Elizabeth Dwoskin, Faiz Siddiqui and Gerrit De Vynck, "Twitter-Musk trial delayed as sides argue over money and trust," *Washington Post*, October 6, 2022. https://www.washingtonpost.com/technology/2022/10/06/twitter-musk-court-postpone/.

40. Olivia Raimonde and Paula Seligson, "Twitter Buyout Revives $12.5 Billion Headache for Wall Street Banks," *Bloomberg*, October 4, 2022. https://www.bloomberg.com/news/articles/2022-10-04/twitter-lbo-revives-12-5-billion-headache-for-wall-street-banks.

41. Elizabeth Dwoskin, Faiz Siddiqui and Gerrit De Vynck, "Twitter-Musk trial delayed as sides argue over money and trust," *Washington Post*, October 6, 2022. https://www.washingtonpost.com/technology/2022/10/06/twitter-musk-court-postpone/.

42. Giulia Morpurgo and Paula Seligson, "Banks on Twitter Deal Extend Debt Commitments to One Year," *Bloomberg*, April 26, 2022. https://www.bloomberg.com/news/articles/2022-04-26/banks-on-twitter-deal-extend-debt-commitments-to-one-year.

43. Elizabeth Dwoskin, Faiz Siddiqui, Gerrit De Vynck and Jeremy B. Merrill "Documents detail plans to gut Twitter's workforce," *Washington Post*, October 20, 2022. https://www.washingtonpost.com/technology/2022/10/20/musk-twitter-acquisition-staff-cuts/.

44. Ibid.

45. Laura Cooper and Alexander Saeedy, "Elon Musk's Twitter Takeover Debt to Be Held by Banks Amid Turbulent Markets," *Wall Street Journal*, October 21, 2022. https://www.wsj.com/articles/elon-musks-twitter-takeover-debt-to-be-held-by-banks-amid-turbulent-markets-11666377716.

46. @elonmusk, X, October 26, 2022. https://x.com/elonmusk/status/1585341984679469056.

47. Faiz Siddiqui, "Elon Musk dubs himself 'Chief Twit,' visits Twitter HQ with deal set to close," *Washington Post*, October 28, 2022. https://www.washingtonpost.com/technology/2022/10/26/musk-twitter-deal-chief-twit/.

48. @WalterIsaacson, X, October 27, 2022. https://x.com/WalterIsaacson/status/1585666128713371649.

49. Faiz Siddiqui, "Elon Musk dubs himself 'Chief Twit,' visits Twitter HQ with deal set to close," *Washington Post*, October 28, 2022. https://www.washingtonpost.com/technology/2022/10/26/musk-twitter-deal-chief-twit/.

50. Ed Hammons and Ed Ludlow, "Musk Tells Twitter Staff He Doesn't Plan to Cut 75% Of Jobs (1)," *Bloomberg,* October 27, 2022. https://news.bloomberglaw.com/mergers-and-acquisitions/musk-tells-twitter-employees-he-doesnt-plan-to-cut-75-of-jobs.

13. "I Just Want to Make Twitter Fun Again"

1. Parag Agrawal, Ned Segal, Vijaya Gadde, and Sean Edgett v. Elon Musk et al., Complaint for Severance Benefits, Equitable Relief, and Statutory Penalties (Erisa), March 4, 2024. https://s3.amazonaws.com/jnswire/jns-media/47/13/15482202/NORCALAgrawalvMusk.pdf.

2. Ibid.

3. Faiz Siddiqui and Elizabeth Dwoskin, "Elon Musk acquires Twitter and fires top executives," *Washington Post*, October 28, 2022. https://www.washingtonpost.com/technology/2022/10/27/twitter-elon-musk/.

4. Cat Zakrzewski, Faiz Siddiqui and Joseph Menn, "Musk's 'free speech' agenda dismantles safety work at Twitter, insiders say," *Washington Post*, November 22, 2022. https://www.washingtonpost.com/technology/2022/11/22/elon-musk-twitter-content-moderations/.

5. @elonmusk, X, October 27, 2022. https://x.com/elonmusk/status/1585841080431321088.

6. Faiz Siddiqui, Elizabeth Dwoskin and Gerrit De Vynck, "Elon Musk's planned Twitter layoffs are imminent," *Washington Post*, October 29, 2022. https://www.washingtonpost.com/technology/2022/10/29/elon-musk-twitter-takeover/.

7. Ibid.

8. Cat Zakrzewski, Faiz Siddiqui and Joseph Menn "Musk's 'free speech' agenda dismantles safety work at Twitter, insiders say," *Washington Post*, November 22, 2022. https://www.washingtonpost.com/technology/2022/11/22/elon-musk-twitter-content-moderations/.

9. Lora Kolodny, "Elon Musk has pulled more than 50 Tesla employees into his Twitter takeover," *CNBC*, October 31, 2022. https://www.cnbc.com/2022/10/31/elon-musk-has-pulled-more-than-50-tesla-engineers-into-twitter.html.

10. Elizabeth Dwoskin and Faiz Siddiqui, "Musk's inner circle worked through weekend to cement Twitter layoff plans," *Washington Post*, October 31, 2022. https://www.washingtonpost.com/technology/2022/10/31/elon-musk-twitter-layoffs.

11. Cat Zakrzewski, Faiz Siddiqui and Joseph Menn, "Musk's 'free speech' agenda dismantles safety work at Twitter, insiders say," *Washington Post*, November 22, 2022. https://www.washingtonpost.com/technology/2022/11/22/elon-musk-twitter-content-moderations/.

12. Chris Kirkham, Hyunjoo Jin and Abhirup Roy, "The inside story of Elon Musk's mass firings of Tesla Supercharger staff," Reuters, May 15, 2024. https://www.reuters.com/business/autos-transportation/inside-story-elon-musks-mass-firings-tesla-supercharger-staff-2024-05-15/.

13. Elizabeth Dwoskin and Faiz Siddiqui, "Musk's inner circle worked through weekend to cement Twitter layoff plans," *Washington Post*, October 31, 2022. https://www.washingtonpost.com/technology/2022/10/31/elon-musk-twitter-layoffs/.

14. "NAACP President and CEO, Derrick Johnson, Issues Statement on Facebook Oversight Board's Decision to Uphold the Ban on Donald Trump," NAACP, May 5, 2021. https://naacp.org/articles/naacp-president-and-ceo-derrick-johnson-issues-statement-facebook-oversight-boards.

15. Rebecca Hersher, "What Happened When Dylann Roof Asked Google For Information About Race?," *NPR*, January 10, 2017. https://www.npr.org/sections/thetwo-way/2017/01/10/508363607/what-happened-when-dylann-roof-asked-google-for-information-about-race.

16. Naomi Nix, Drew Harwell and Cat Zakrzewski, "Musk meeting with civil rights groups upsets his fans," *Washington Post*, November 2, 2022. https://www.washingtonpost.com/technology/2022/11/02/musk-twitter-bans-trump/.

17. Drew Harwell, Taylor Lorenz and Cat Zakrzewski, "Racist tweets quickly surface after Musk closes Twitter deal," *Washington Post*, October 28, 2022. https://www.washingtonpost.com/technology/2022/10/28/musk-twitter-racist-posts/.

18. Reis Thebault, Danielle Paquette and Justine McDaniel, "Paul Pelosi attack video shows break-in, assault with hammer," *Washington Post*, January 27, 2023. https://www.washingtonpost.com/nation/2023/01/27/paul-pelosi-attack-video/.

19. Elizabeth Dwoskin and Faiz Siddiqui, "Elon Musk deleted a tweet about Paul Pelosi. Here's why that matters," *Washington Post*, October 31, 2022. https://www.washingtonpost.com/technology/2022/10/30/musk-deleted-tweet-pelosi/.

20. Stan Greene, "The Awful Truth: Paul Pelosi Was Drunk Again, And In a Dispute With a Male Prostitute Early Friday Morning," *Santa Monica Observer*, October 29, 2022. https://www.smobserved.com/story/2022/10/29/opinion/the-awful-truth-paul-pelosi-was-drunk-again-and-in-a-dispute-with-a-male-prostitute-early-friday-morning/7191.html.

21. Drew Harwell, Taylor Lorenz and Cat Zakrzewski, "Racist tweets quickly surface after Musk closes Twitter deal," *Washington Post*, October 28, 2022.

22. Kurt Wagner, Edward Ludlow, Jackie Davalos, and Davey Alba, "Twitter Limits Content-Enforcement Work as US Election Looms," *Bloomberg*, October 31, 2022. https://www.bloomberg.com/news/articles/2022-11-01/twitter-limits-content-enforcement-tools-as-us-election-looms.

23. Grace Kay, "The Twitter manager who went viral for sleeping on the floor of company HQ survived Elon Musk's layoffs," *Business Insider*, November 7, 2022. https://www.businessinsider.com/manager-viral-sleeping-twitter-elon-musk-takeover-survived-layoffs-2022-11.

24. @esthercrawford, X, November 2, 2022. https://x.com/esthercrawford/status/1587709 705488830464.

25. @esthercrawford, X, November 2, 2022. https://x.com/esthercrawford/status/1587819 812301918209.

26. Naomi Nix, Nitasha Tiku, Will Oremus and Faiz Siddiqui, "Elon Musk's Twitter bid frustrates employees. That's a risk for him," *Washington Post*, April 15, 2022. https://www .washingtonpost.com/technology/2022/04/14/twitter-employees-elon-musk/.

27. @elonmusk, X, October 30, 2022. https://x.com/elonmusk/status/1586831721386766337.

28. Elizabeth Dwoskin, Faiz Siddiqui, Gerrit De Vynck and Jeremy B. Merrill "Documents detail plans to gut Twitter's workforce," *Washington Post*, October 20, 2022. https://www .washingtonpost.com/technology/2022/10/20/musk-twitter-acquisition-staff-cuts/.

29. Elizabeth Dwoskin and Faiz Siddiqui, "Musk's inner circle worked through weekend to ce- ment Twitter layoff plans," *Washington Post*, October 31, 2022. https://www.washingtonpost .com/technology/2022/10/31/elon-musk-twitter-layoffs/.

30. Faiz Siddiqui, "Elon Musk begins mass layoffs at Twitter," *Washington Post*, November 4, 2022. https://www.washingtonpost.com/technology/2022/11/03/elon-musk-twitter-layoffs/.

31. @elonmusk, X, November 2, 2022. https://x.com/elonmusk/status/1587670513819729920.

32. Naomi Nix, Drew Harwell and Cat Zakrzewski, "Musk meeting with civil rights groups upsets his fans," *Washington Post*, November 2, 2022. https://www.washingtonpost.com /technology/2022/11/02/musk-twitter-bans-trump.

33. @elonmusk, X, November 2, 2022. https://x.com/elonmusk/status/1587668703834955778.

34. Faiz Siddiqui, "Elon Musk begins mass layoffs at Twitter," *Washington Post*, November 4, 2022. https://www.washingtonpost.com/technology/2022/11/03/elon-musk-twitter-layoffs/.

35. Faiz Siddiqui, Naomi Nix and Will Oremus, "Advertisers fleeing, workers in fear: Welcome to Elon Musk's Twitter," *Washington Post*, November 4, 2022. https://www.washingtonpost .com/technology/2022/11/04/twitter-layoffs-musk/.

36. @elonmusk, X, November 4, 2022. https://x.com/elonmusk/status/1588538640401018880.

37. @stillgray, X, November 4, 2022. https://x.com/stillgray/status/1588560500023267328.

38. @elonmusk, X, November 4, 2022. https://x.com/elonmusk/status/1588613591275827200.

39. Faiz Siddiqui, "Elon Musk begins mass layoffs at Twitter," *Washington Post*, November 4, 2022. https://www.washingtonpost.com/technology/2022/11/03/elon-musk-twitter-layoffs/.

40. Ibid.

41. Barbara Ortutay and Matt O'Brien, "Twitter slashes its staff as Musk era takes hold on platform," *Associated Press*, November 5, 2022. https://apnews.com/article/elon-musk-twitter -inc-business-layoffs-c0334da78b3af9faf2f43cf3f6e52ffa.

42. Teddy Amenabar, "'Not a tweep anymore.' Twitter layoffs likely to exact an emotional toll," *Washington Post*, November 4, 2022. https://www.washingtonpost.com/wellness/2022/11 /04/layoffs-stress-anxiety-twitter/.

43. Ibid.

44. Elon Musk, *CNBC*, May 16, 2023.

45. Alex Heath and Mia Sato, "Elon Musk's Twitter layoffs leave whole teams gutted," *The Verge*, November 4, 2022. https://www.theverge.com/2022/11/4/23439790/elon-musk-twitter -layoffs-trust-and-safety-teams-severance.

46. Faiz Siddiqui, Naomi Nix and Will Oremus, "Advertisers fleeing, workers in fear: Welcome to Elon Musk's Twitter," *Washington Post*, November 4, 2022. https://www.washingtonpost .com/technology/2022/11/04/twitter-layoffs-musk/.

47. Lora Kolodny and Laren Feiner, "Read Elon Musk's first email to all Twitter employees: Remote work over, company needs subscriptions to survive downturn," *CNBC*, November 10, 2022. https://www.cnbc.com/2022/11/10/read-elon-musks-first-email-to-all-twitter -employees.html.

48. @elonmusk, X, November 1, 2022. https://x.com/elonmusk/status/1587498907336118274.

49. Ibid.

50. @elonmusk, X, November 1, 2022. https://x.com/elonmusk/status/1587500060853424129.
51. Rachel Lerman and Cat Zakrzewski, "Elon Musk's first big Twitter product paused after fake accounts spread," *Washington Post*, November 11, 2022. https://www.washingtonpost.com/technology/2022/11/11/twitter-fake-verified-accounts/.
52. Drew Harwell, "A fake tweet sparked panic at Eli Lilly and may have cost Twitter millions," *Washington Post*, November 14, 2022. https://www.washingtonpost.com/technology/2022/11/14/twitter-fake-eli-lilly/.
53. Rachel Lerman and Cat Zakrzewski, "Elon Musk's first big Twitter product paused after fake accounts spread," *Washington Post*, November 11, 2022. https://www.washingtonpost.com/technology/2022/11/11/twitter-fake-verified-accounts/.
54. Victor Ordonez and Stephanie Wash, "Meeting audio reveals Musk told Twitter staff either return to office or 'resignation accepted'," *ABC 7 News*, November 11, 2022. https://abc7news.com/elon-musk-audio-recording-ends-remote-work-twitter-return-to-office-email-employees/12440688/.
55. Joseph Menn, Cat Zakrzewski, Faiz Siddiqui, Nitasha Tiku and Drew Harwell, "Twitter's content moderation head quits as departures alarm the FTC," *Washington Post*, November 10, 2022. https://www.washingtonpost.com/technology/2022/11/10/twitter-security-resignations.
56. @elonmusk, X, October 4, 2022.

14. "Welcome to Level 2 of Hell"

1. Faiz Siddiqui and Jeremy B. Merrill, "Musk issues ultimatum to staff: Commit to 'hardcore' Twitter or take severance," *Washington Post*, November 16, 2022. https://www.washingtonpost.com/technology/2022/11/16/musk-twitter-email-ultimatum-termination/.
2. Ibid.
3. Lora Kolodny, "Elon Musk demands Twitter staff commit to 'long hours' or leave: Read the email," *CNBC*, November 16, 2022. https://www.cnbc.com/2022/11/16/elon-musk-demands-twitter-staff-commit-to-long-hours-or-leave.html.
4. Joseph Menn, Nitasha Tiku, Faiz Siddiqui and Cat Zakrzewski, "Hundreds said to have opted to leave Twitter over Musk ultimatum," *Washington Post*, November 18, 2022. https://www.washingtonpost.com/technology/2022/11/17/twitter-musk-easing-rto-order/.
5. Clare Duffy and Oliver Darcy, "Twitter employees head for the exits after Elon Musk's 'extremely hardcore' work ultimatum," *CNN Business*, November 18, 2022. https://www.cnn.com/2022/11/17/tech/twitter-employees-ultimatum-deadline/index.html.
6. Joseph Menn, Nitasha Tiku, Faiz Siddiqui and Cat Zakrzewski, "Hundreds said to have opted to leave Twitter over Musk ultimatum," *Washington Post*, November 18, 2022.
7. Ibid.
8. Joseph Menn and Cat Zakrzewski, "Musk summons engineers to Twitter HQ as millions await platform's collapse," *Washington Post*, November 18, 2022. https://www.washingtonpost.com/technology/2022/11/18/twitter-death-watch-chaos-resignations/.
9. Ibid.
10. Will Oremus, "Musk, defending his Tesla pay, says he'll shift focus from Twitter," *Washington Post*, November 16, 2022. https://www.washingtonpost.com/technology/2022/11/16/elon-musk-tesla-trial-pay/.
11. Ibid.
12. Ibid.
13. Hunjoo Jin and Tom Hals, "Elon Musk says he will find a new leader for Twitter," *Reuters*, November 16, 2022. https://www.reuters.com/technology/elon-musk-says-he-expects-reduce-his-time-twitter-court-testimony-2022-11-16//.
14. Will Oremus, "Musk, defending his Tesla pay, says he'll shift focus from Twitter," *Washington Post*, November 13, 2022. https://www.washingtonpost.com/technology/2022/11/16/elon-musk-tesla-trial-pay/.

15. David Shepardson and Hyunjoo Jin, "Senator Warren, Tesla investor turn up heat over Musk's Twitter role," Reuters, December 19, 2022. https://www.reuters.com/world/us/us-senator-questions-tesla-board-chair-over-musk-purchase-twitter-2022-12-19//.

16. Faiz Siddiqui and Rachel Lerman "Elon Musk's role at Tesla questioned as Twitter occupies his attention," *Washington Post*, December 16, 2022. https://www.washingtonpost.com/technology/2022/12/15/elon-musk-tesla-twitter/.

17. "Letter from Senator Elizabeth Warren to Tesla Board," December 18, 2022. https://www.warren.senate.gov/imo/media/doc/2022.12.18 Letter to Tesla Board on Musk Concerns.pdf.

18. Lora Kolodny, "SpaceX, Tesla, and Boring Company execs are helping Elon Musk at Twitter, records reveal," *CNBC*, December 8, 2022. https://www.cnbc.com/2022/12/08/spacex-tesla-and-boring-company-execs-helping-musk-at-twitter.html.

19. @elonmusk, X, December 19, 2021. https://x.com/elonmusk/status/1472754632325795843.

20. @elonmusk, X, March 18, 2023. https://twitter.com/elonmusk/status/1637193767697408001.

21. @elonmusk, X, December 14, 2021. https://x.com/elonmusk/status/1470858546153762819.

22. Cat Zakrzewski, Faiz Siddiqui and Joseph Menn, "Musk's 'free speech' agenda dismantles safety work at Twitter, insiders say," *Washington Post*, November 22, 2022. https://www.washingtonpost.com/technology/2022/11/22/elon-musk-twitter-content-moderations/.

23. Seth Dillon, "Twitter Suspends The Babylon Bee," *The Babylon Bee*, March 22, 2022. https://babylonbee.com/news/twitter-has-shut-down-the-bee.

24. Cat Zakrzewski, Faiz Siddiqui and Joseph Menn, "Musk's 'free speech' agenda dismantles safety work at Twitter, insiders say," *Washington Post*, November 22, 2022. https://www.washingtonpost.com/technology/2022/11/22/elon-musk-twitter-content-moderations/.

25. @elonmusk, X, November 18, 2022. https://x.com/elonmusk/status/1593673339826212864.

26. @pwnsdx, X, December 21, 2022. https://x.com/pwnsdx/status/1605442608603463680.

27. Faiz Siddiqui, "Twitter brings Elon Musk's genius reputation crashing down to earth," *Washington Post*, December 24, 2022. https://www.washingtonpost.com/technology/2022/12/24/elon-musk-twitter-meltdown-tesla/.

28. @elonmusk, X, April 9, 2022. https://x.com/elonmusk/status/1512785529712123906.

29. Joseph Menn, "Elon Musk uses QAnon tactic in criticizing former Twitter safety chief," *Washington Post*, December 12, 2022. https://www.washingtonpost.com/technology/2022/12/12/musk-child-porn-qanon/.

30. Cat Zakrzewski and Faiz Siddiqui, "Elon Musk's 'Twitter Files' ignite divisions, but haven't changed minds," *Washington Post*, December 3, 2022. https://www.washingtonpost.com/technology/2022/12/03/elon-musk-twitter-files/.

31. @elonmusk, X, November 28, 2022. https://x.com/elonmusk/status/1597336812732575744.

32. Express, "Irritable Bar Syndrome," *Washington Post*, August 22, 2013. https://www.washingtonpost.com/express/wp/2013/08/22/irritable-bar-syndrome/.

33. Mike Isaac and Ryan Mac, "As Elon Musk Cuts Costs at Twitter, Some Bills Are Going Unpaid," *New York Times*, November 22, 2022. https://www.nytimes.com/2022/11/22/technology/elon-musk-twitter-cost-cutting.html.

34. "Musk orders Twitter to cut infrastructure costs by $1 billion—sources," Reuters, November 3, 2022. https://www.reuters.com/technology/musk-orders-twitter-cut-infrastructure-costs-by-1-bln-sources-2022-11-03/.

35. Ryan Mac, Mike Isaac and Kate Conger, "Musk Shakes Up Twitter's Legal Team as He

Looks to Cut More Costs," *New York Times*, December 13, 2022. https://www.nytimes.com /2022/12/13/technology/elon-musk-twitter-shakeup.html.

36. Ina Fried, "Exclusive: Apple to pause advertising on X after Musk back antisemitic post," *Axios*, November 17, 2023. https://www.axios.com/2023/11/17/apple-twitter-x-advertising -elon-musk-antisemitism-ads.

37. Gerrit De Vynck and Adela Suliman, "Elon Musk courts Twitter advertisers as he seeks new streams of revenue," *Washington Post*, November 1, 2022. https://www.washingtonpost .com/technology/2022/11/01/elon-musk-twitter-verification-stephen-king/.

38. Faiz Siddiqui, "Twitter brings Elon Musk's genius reputation crashing down to earth," *Washington Post*, December 24, 2022. https://www.washingtonpost.com/technology/2022 /12/24/elon-musk-twitter-meltdown-tesla/.

39. @elonmusk, X, November 28, 2022. https://x.com/elonmusk/status/15973368127325 75744.

40. Cat Zakrzewski and Faiz Siddiqui, "Elon Musk's 'Twitter Files' ignite divisions, but haven't changed minds," *Washington Post*, December 3, 2022. https://www.washingtonpost.com /technology/2022/12/03/elon-musk-twitter-files/.

41. @mtaibbi, X, December 2, 2022. https://x.com/mtaibbi/status/1598828932395978752.

42. @mtaibbi, X, December 2, 2022. https://x.com/mtaibbi/status/1598829996264390656.

43. Faiz Siddiqui, "Twitter brings Elon Musk's genius reputation crashing down to earth," *Washington Post*, December 24, 2022. https://www.washingtonpost.com/technology/2022 /12/24/elon-musk-twitter-meltdown-tesla/.

44. Ibid.

45. Cat Zakrzewski, "Employees prevented Musk from breaking federal Twitter order, FTC finds," *Washington Post*, February 21, 2024. https://www.washingtonpost.com/technology /2024/02/21/x-twitter-jordan-ftc-musk/.

46. Ryan Mac, Mike Isaac and Kate Conger, "Musk Shakes Up Twitter's Legal Team as He Looks to Cut More Costs," *New York Times*, December 13, 2022. https://www.nytimes.com /2022/12/13/technology/elon-musk-twitter-shakeup.html.

47. @DonLemon, X, March 13, 2024. https://x.com/donlemon/status/17679756784845 58306.

48. @elonmusk, X, November 6, 2022. https://twitter.com/elonmusk/status/15894149585086 91456.

49. Drew Harwell and Faiz Siddiqui, "Musk bans Twitter account tracking his jet, threatens to sue creator," *Washington Post*, December 14, 2022. https://www.washingtonpost.com /technology/2022/12/14/elonjet-twitter-suspension-jack-sweeney-talks/.

50. Ibid.

51. @elonmusk, X, December 14, 2022. https://x.com/elonmusk/status/16031901551077 94944.

52. Drew Harwell and Taylor Lorenz, "Musk blamed a Twitter account for an alleged stalker. Police see no link," *Washington Post*, December 18, 2022. https://www.washingtonpost.com /technology/2022/12/18/details-of-musk-stalking-incident/.

53. @drewharwell, X, December 14, 2022. https://x.com/drewharwell/status/16031335490 32669185.

54. Paul Farhi, "Musk suspends journalists from Twitter, claims 'assassination' danger," *Washington Post*, December 16, 2022. https://www.washingtonpost.com/media/2022/12/15/twitter -journalists-suspended-musk/.

55. @elonmusk, X, December 15, 2022. https://twitter.com/elonmusk/status/160357372597 8275841.

56. Paul Farhi, "Musk suspends journalists from Twitter, claims 'assassination' danger," *Washington Post*, December 16, 2022. https://www.washingtonpost.com/media/2022/12/15 /twitter-journalists-suspended-musk/.

57. @elonmusk, X, December 15, 2022. https://twitter.com/elonmusk/status/16035879708
32793600.

58. Drew Harwell and Taylor Lorenz, "Musk blamed a Twitter account for an alleged stalker. Police see no link," *Washington Post*, December 18, 2022. https://www.washingtonpost.com
/technology/2022/12/18/details-of-musk-stalking-incident/.

59. Jeremy Barr and Sarah Ellison, "Musk unsuspends some reporters on Twitter. But their companies never left," *Washington Post*, December 17, 2022. https://www.washingtonpost
.com/media/2022/12/17/musk-twitter-journalist-suspension-media-react/.

60. @bariweiss, X, December 12, 2022. https://x.com/bariweiss/status/16023641971944
32515.

61. @bariweiss, X, December 12, 2022. https://x.com/bariweiss/status/1603788344470556674.

62. @elonmusk, X, December 16, 2022. https://x.com/elonmusk/status/16037971715721
17505.

63. @bariweiss, X, December 16, 2022. https://x.com/bariweiss/status/1603908561741889536.

64. Filip Timotija, "'Twitter Files' journalist Matt Taibbi: Musk proved to be 'very disappoint-ing' on free speech issue," *The Hill*, March 16, 2024. https://thehill.com/homenews/media
/4536394-twitter-files-journalist-matt-taibbi-musk-disappointing-free-speech/.

65. Dalton Bennett, Samuel Oakford, Gerrit De Vynck and Monique Woo, "From Jared Kush-ner to Salt Bae: Here's who Elon Musk was seen with at the World Cup," *Washington Post*, December 20, 2022. https://www.washingtonpost.com/investigations/2022/12/20/elon
-musk-spotted-world-cup-final/.

66. Emma Roth, "Twitter abruptly bans all link to Instagram, Mastodon, and other compet-itors," *The Verge*, December 18, 2022. https://www.theverge.com/2022/12/18/23515221
/twitter-bans-links-instagram-mastodon-competitors.

67. @paulg, X, December 18, 2022. https://x.com/paulg/status/1604556563338887168.

68. Faiz Siddiqui, Cat Zakrzewski and Marisa Iati, "After backlash, Elon Musk is stak-ing his leadership on a Twitter poll," *Washington Post*, December 19, 2022. https://www
.washingtonpost.com/technology/2022/12/18/twitter-policy-links-to-social-sites/.

69. @Snowden, X, December 18, 2022. https://x.com/Snowden/status/16046069143729
84832.

70. @elonmusk, X, December 18, 2022. https://x.com/elonmusk/status/16045889048286
00320.

71. @elonmusk, X, December 18, 2022. https://x.com/elonmusk/status/16045930576763
00288.

72. @elonmusk, X, December 18, 2022. https://twitter.com/elonmusk/status/1604616426
114932737.

73. @elonmusk, X, December 18, 2022. https://twitter.com/elonmusk/status/160461686367
3208832.

74. @elonmusk, X, November 18, 2022. https://twitter.com/elonmusk/status/16046176439
73124097.

75. @elonmusk, X, November 18, 2022. https://x.com/elonmusk/status/15937679537069
21985.

76. @elonmusk, X, November 23, 2022. https://twitter.com/elonmusk/status/15954738758
47942146.

77. @elonmusk, X, November 6, 2021. https://x.com/elonmusk/status/14570646977824
89088.

78. Robert Frank, "Elon Musk faces a $15 billion tax bill, which is likely the real reason he's selling stock," *CNBC*, November 7, 2021.https://www.cnbc.com/2021/11/07/elon-musk
-faces-a-15-billion-tax-bill-which-is-likely-the-real-reason-hes-selling-stock.html.

79. @elonmusk, X, November 6, 2021. https://x.com/elonmusk/status/1457064697782489088.

80. @elonmusk, X, November 6, 2021. https://x.com/elonmusk/status/1457066048944066565.

81. Jeremy B. Merrill, Rachel Lerman and Faiz Siddiqui, "Elon Musk sells roughly $5 billion in

Tesla stock in series of whirlwind transactions," *Washington Post*, November 11, 2021. https: //www.washingtonpost.com/technology/2021/11/10/elon-musk-tesla-stock/.

82. @elonmusk, X, December 15, 2022. https://x.com/elonmusk/status/1603609466301059073.

83. @elonmusk, X, December 17, 2022. https://x.com/elonmusk/status/1603982891179839488.

84. @elonmusk, X, December 18, 2022. https://x.com/elonmusk/status/1604650028999405568.

85. Faiz Siddiqui, Cat Zakrzewski and Rachel Lerman, "No word from Musk on whether he will resign. He lost a poll he said he's abide," *Washington Post*, December 19, 2022 https://www.washingtonpost.com/technology/2022/12/19/musk-twitter-ceo-poll/.

86. @elonmusk, X, February 12, 2023. https://x.com/elonmusk/status/1624876021433368578.

87. Faiz Siddiqui, Cat Zakrzewski and Rachel Lerman, "No word from Musk on whether he will resign. He lost a poll he said he's abide," *Washington Post*, December 19, 2022. https://www.washingtonpost.com/technology/2022/12/19/musk-twitter-ceo-poll/.

88. @elonmusk, X, December 19, 2022. https://twitter.com/elonmusk/status/1604981780548767744.

89. @elonmusk, X, December 19, 2022. https://x.com/elonmusk/status/1604985324505030658.

90. @elonmusk, X, December 20, 2022. https://x.com/elonmusk/status/1605372724800393216.

91. Faiz Siddiqui, "At Elon Musk's 'brittle' Twitter, tweaks trigger massive outages," *Washington Post*, March 6, 2023. https://www.washingtonpost.com/technology/2023/03/06/elon-musk-twitter-outages.

92. Walter Isaacson, *Elon Musk* (New York: Simon & Schuster, 2023), 445.

93. Ibid., 513.

94. @elonmusk, X, March 6, 2023. https://x.com/elonmusk/status/1632794008060567552.

95. Elizabeth Dwoskin, "Twitter experiences a widespread global outage," *Washington Post*, December 28, 2022. https://www.washingtonpost.com/technology/2022/12/28/twitter-global-outage/.

96. Walter Issacson, *Elon Musk* (New York: Simon & Schuster, 2023), 517.

97. Faiz Siddiqui, "Twitter repeatedly crashes as DeSantis tries to make presidential announcement," *Washington Post*, May 24, 2023. https://www.washingtonpost.com/technology/2023/05/24/elon-musk-ron-desantis-2024-twitter/.

98. Walter Issacson, *Elon Musk* (New York: Simon & Schuster, 2023), 517.

99. Marianna LeVine, Faiz Siddiqui, Hannah Knowles, Tirsh Thadani and Drew Harwell, "Trump returns to X with technical glitches, softball questions from Musk," *Washington Post*, August 12, 2024. https://www.washingtonpost.com/technology/2024/08/12/trump-returns-x-elon-musk-interview/.

15. "Can Elon Musk Do Whatever He Wants and Not Face the Consequences?"

1. Will Oremus, "Musk, defending his Tesla pay, says he'll shift focus from Twitter," *Washington Post*, November 16, 2022. https://www.washingtonpost.com/technology/2022/11/16/elon-musk-tesla-trial-pay/.

2. Samantha Delouya, "Elon Musk changed his name to 'Mr. Tweet' on Twitter after a lawyer accidentally called him that during a Tesla shareholder trial," *Business Insider*, January 23, 2023. https://www.businessinsider.com/lawyer-calls-elon-musk-mr-tweet-during-tesla-trial-twitter-2023-1.

3. Faiz Siddiqui, "Elon Musk stands by 'Funding secured' tweet in trial testimony," *Washington Post*, January 23, 2023. https://www.washingtonpost.com/technology/2023/01/23/elon-musk-tesla-trial/.

4. Renae Merle, "Tesla's Elon Musk settles with SEC, paying $20 million fine and resigning as board chairman," *Washington Post*, September 29, 2018. https://www.washingtonpost.com /business/2018/09/29/teslas-elon-musk-settles-with-sec-paying-million-fine-resigning -board-chairman/.

5. Faiz Siddiqui, "Elon Musk found not liable in federal trial over 'Funding secured' tweet," *Washington Post*, February 3, 2023. https://www.washingtonpost.com/technology/2023/02 /03/elon-musk-tesla-verdict/.

6. Faiz Siddiqui, "Musk, defending 'Funding secured' statement, downplays impact of Tweets" *Washington Post*, January 30, 2023. https://www.washingtonpost.com/technology/2023/01 /20/elon-musk-tesla-trial/.

7. Rebecca Elliott, "Elon Musk Flags Tweets' Limitations in Tesla Trial," *Wall Street Journal*, January 20, 2023. https://www.wsj.com/articles/elon-musk-among-next-set-of-witnesses -in-tesla-tweets-trial-11674192908.

8. Faiz Siddiqui, "Musk, defending 'Funding secured' statement, downplays impact of Tweets" *Washington Post*, January 30, 2023. https://www.washingtonpost.com/technology/2023/01 /20/elon-musk-tesla-trial/.

9. Transcript of Trial Proceedings, Re Tesla, Inc. Securities Litigation, February 3, 2023.

10. Michael Liedtke and the Associated Press, "In trial, Elon Musk is cast as a liar who cost regular Tesla shareholders millions of dollars," *Fortune,* January 18, 2023. https://fortune .com/2023/01/18/elon-musk-trial-tesla-funding-secured-tweet-shareholders/.

11. Faiz Siddiqui, "Elon Musk found not liable in federal trial over 'Funding secured' tweet," *Washington Post*, February 3, 2023. https://www.washingtonpost.com/technology/2023/01 /20/elon-musk-tesla-trial.

12. Transcript of Trial Proceedings, Re Tesla, Inc. Securities Litigation, February 3, 2023.

13. @elonmusk, X, February 3, 2023. https://x.com/elonmusk/status/1621653950947799042.

14. Faiz Siddiqui, "Elon Musk found not liable in federal trial over 'Funding secured' tweet," *Washington Post*, February 3, 2023. https://www.washingtonpost.com/technology/2023/02 /03/elon-musk-tesla-verdict/.

15. Gerrit De Vynck and Cat Zakrzewski, "Musk's celebrity lawyer now plays key role in Twitter overhaul," *Washington Post*, November 6, 2022. https://www.washingtonpost.com /technology/2022/11/06/alex-spiro-musk-twitter-lawyer/.

16. Faiz Siddiqui, "Elon Musk found not liable in federal trial over 'Funding secured' tweet," *Washington Post*, February 3, 2023. https://www.washingtonpost.com/technology/2023/02 /03/elon-musk-tesla-verdict/.

17. Erick McCormick, "Tesla Trial: did Musk's tweet affect the firm's stock price," *Guardian*, January 23, 2023. https://www.theguardian.com/technology/2023/jan/28/tesla-trial-elon -musk-what-you-need-to-know-explainer.

18. Faiz Siddiqui, "Elon Musk found not liable in federal trial over 'Funding secured' tweet," *Washington Post*, February 3, 2023. https://www.washingtonpost.com/technology/2023/02 /03/elon-musk-tesla-verdict/.

19. @elonmusk, X, February 1, 2023. https://x.com/elonmusk/status/1620664851663319042.

20. Faiz Siddiqui, "Musk's securities fraud trial begins over Tesla 'Funding secured' tweet," *Washington Post*, January 17, 2023. https://www.washingtonpost.com/technology/2023/01 /17/elon-musk-tesla-trial/.

21. Zoë Schiffer and Casey Newton, "Yes, Elon Musk created a special system for showing you all his tweets first," *Platformer*, February 14, 2023.https://www.platformer.news/yes-elon- musk-created-a-special-system/.

22. Faiz Siddiqui and Jeremy B. Merrill, "Elon Musk reinvents Twitter for the benefit of a power user: Himself," *Washington Post*, February 16, 2023. https://www.washingtonpost .com/technology/2023/02/16/elon-musk-twitter/.

23. @elonmusk, X, February 17, 2023. https://x.com/elonmusk/status/1626556852816470024.

24. @elonmusk, X, February 14, 2023. https://x.com/elonmusk/status/1626520156469092353.

25. Faiz Siddiqui and Jeremy B. Merrill, "Elon Musk reinvents Twitter for the benefit of a power user: Himself," *Washington Post*, February 16, 2023. https://www.washingtonpost .com/technology/2023/02/16/elon-musk-twitter/.

26. Ibid.

27. Ibid.

28. Elon Musk, *Don Lemon Show*, March 18, 2024.

29. @elonmusk, X, February 14, 2023. https://x.com/elonmusk/status/1625695877326340102.

30. Arjun Kharpal, "Elon Musk aiming to appoint his successor as Twitter CEO by the end of 2023," CNBC, February 15, 2023. https://www.cnbc.com/2023/02/15/elon-musk-aiming -to-appoint-new-twitter-ceo-by-end-of-2023.html.

31. Rachel Lerman, Taylor Telford and Faiz Siddiqui, "Elon Musk is unfathomably rich. Her's where his money is stashed," *Washington Post*, June 15, 2024. https://www.washingtonpost .com/technology/2024/02/01/elon-musk-wealth-net-worth-companies/.

32. Sanj Atwal, "Elon Musk suffers worst loss of fortune in history amid 'market madness'," *Guinness World Records*, January 6, 2023. https://www.guinnessworldrecords.com/news/2023 /1/elon-musk-suffers-worst-loss-of-fortune-in-history-amid-market-madness-731988.

33. Aditya Soni and Eva Mathews, "Tesla shares suffer New Year's hangover on demand worries, delivery issues," Reuters, January 3, 2023. https://www.reuters.com/business/autos -transportation/tesla-shares-start-2023-lower-worries-over-weak-demand-logistical -issues-2023-01-03/.

34. Faiz Siddiqui, "Elon Musk says he's sleeping on a couch at Twitter and his dog is in charge," *Washington Post*, April 12, 2023. https://www.washingtonpost.com/technology/2023/04 /12/elon-musk-twitter/.

35. Katharine Schwab, "San Francisco Is Investigating the Bedrooms Elon Musk Installed At Twitter For Possible Code Violations," *Forbes*, December 7, 2023. https://www.forbes .com/sites/katharineschwab/2022/12/06/elon-musk-twitter-bedrooms-san-francisco -investigation/?sh=50f3f7c1af15.

36. Faiz Siddiqui, "Elon Musk says he's sleeping on a couch at Twitter and his dog is in charge," *Washington Post*, April 12, 2023. https://www.washingtonpost.com/technology/2023/04 /12/elon-musk-twitter/.

37. @elonmusk, X, May 11, 2023. https://x.com/elonmusk/status/1656748197308674048.

38. @elonmusk, X, May 12, 2023. https://x.com/elonmusk/status/1657108798480470018.

39. @elonmusk, X, May 12, 2023. https://x.com/elonmusk/status/1657050349608501249.

40. @elonmusk, X, July 23, 2023. https://x.com/elonmusk/status/1682964919325724673.

41. @elonmusk, X, July 25, 2023. https://x.com/elonmusk/status/1683946564115394561.

42. "Brightly flashing 'X' sign removed from the San Francisco building that was Twitter's headquarters," *Associated Press*, August 1, 2023. https://apnews.com/article/twitter-x-sign -lightup-san-francisco-elon-musk-fa81d70c13c98a2cc7f03c2561a01258.

16. Autopilot Grounded

1. @elonmusk, X, July 2, 2020. https://x.com/elonmusk/status/1278764736876773383.

2. Faiz Siddiqui and Jeremy B. Merrill, "17 fatalities, 736 crashes: the shocking toll of Tesla's Autopilot," *Washington Post*, June 10, 2022. https://www.washingtonpost.com/technology /2023/06/10/tesla-autopilot-crashes-elon-musk/.

3. Sean O'Kane, "Tesla ignored safety board's Autopilot recommendations, chairman says," *The Verge*, February 25, 2020. https://www.theverge.com/2020/2/25/21152984/tesla-autopilot -safety-recommendations-ignored-ntsb-crash-hearing.

4. @elonmusk, X, February 12, 2023. https://x.com/elonmusk/status/1624873453949014017.

5. Faiz Siddiqui and Jeremy B. Merrill, "17 fatalities, 736 crashes: the shocking toll of Tesla's Autopilot," *Washington Post*, June 10, 2022. https://www.washingtonpost.com/technology /2023/06/10/tesla-autopilot-crashes-elon-musk/.

6. Ibid.

7. Trisha Thadani, Faiz Siddiqui, Rachel Lerman and Jeremy B. Merrill, "Tesla drivers run Autopilot where it's not intended—with deadly consequences," *Washington Post*, December 10, 2023. https://www.washingtonpost.com/technology/2023/12/10/tesla-autopilot-crash/.

8. Ashley Halsey, "NTSB says driver in fatal Tesla crash was overreliant on the car's 'Autopilot' system," *Washington Post*, September 12, 2017. https://www.washingtonpost.com/local/trafficandcommuting/ntsb-says-driver-in-fatal-tesla-crash-was-overreliant-on-the-cars-autopilot-system/2017/09/12/38e5f130–9730–11e7–82e4–f1076f6d6152_story.html.

9. Trisha Thadani, Faiz Siddiqui, Rachel Lerman and Jeremy B. Merrill, "Tesla drivers run Autopilot where it's not intended—with deadly consequences," *Washington Post*, December 10, 2023. https://www.washingtonpost.com/technology/2023/12/10/tesla-autopilot-crash/.

10. Faiz Siddiqui, Leo Sands, Aaron Gregg, Trisha Thadani and Rachel Lerman, "Tesla conducts largest-ever recall for 'insufficient' safety controls after exclusive Post report on Autopilot," *Washington Post*, December 13, 2023. https://www.washingtonpost.com/technology/2023/12/13/tesla-autopilot-recall/.

11. Ibid.

12. @rohanspatel, X, December 13, 2023. https://x.com/rohanspatel/status/1735154510484431333.

13. "Update Vehicle Firmware to Prevent Driver Misuse of Autosteer," Tesla.com. https://www.tesla.com/support/vehicle-firmware-prevent-autosteer-misuse.

14. Geoffrey A. Fowler, "Testing Tesla's Autopilot recall, I don't feel much safer—and neither should you," *Washington Post*, December 31, 2023. https://www.washingtonpost.com/technology/2023/12/31/tesla-autopilot-recall-test/.

15. Nora Eckert and Ben Foldy, "Tesla's Recall Fix for Autopilot Irritates Drivers, Disappoints Safety Advocates," *Wall Street Journal*, January 29, 2024. https://www.wsj.com/business/autos/teslas-recall-fix-for-autopilot-irritates-drivers-disappoints-safety-advocates-f9ca0eb4.

17. The Technoking Has No Clothes

1. Tornetta et al. v. Musk et al., Post-Trial Opinion, January 30, 2024. https://corpgov.law.harvard.edu/2024/02/01/tesla-musk-case-post-trial-opinion/.

2. Ibid.

3. @elonmusk, X, January 30, 2024. https://x.com/elonmusk/status/1752455348106166598.

4. @elonmusk, X, February 1, 2024. https://x.com/elonmusk/status/1753271394408829106.

5. @elonmusk, X, February 7, 2024https://x.com/elonmusk/status/1755260480514293867.

6. @elonmusk, X, January 30, 2024. https://x.com/elonmusk/status/1752491924848820595.

7. @elonmusk, X, February 1, 2024. https://x.com/elonmusk/status/1752922071229722990.

8. @elonmusk, X, February 14, 2024. https://x.com/elonmusk/status/1757924482885583112.

9. Tom Krisher, "Elon Musk's Neuralink moves legal home to Nevada after Delaware judge invalidates his Tesla pay deal," *Associated Press*, February 10, 2024. https://apnews.com/article/elon-musk-neuralink-brain-implant-corporate-move-nevada-delaware-09c2eee269beebccf9a701f21ea2b9f7.

10. @TeslaBoomerMama, X, December 5, 2024. https://x.com/TeslaBoomerMama/status/1864847823902236884.

11. @elonmusk, X, June 13, 2024. https://x.com/elonmusk/status/1801278941698703399.

12. Tesla: Form 8-K, United States Securities and Exchange Commission, June 13, 2024. https://www.sec.gov/Archives/edgar/data/1318605/000110465924071439/tm2413800d31_8k.htm.

13. Tornetta v. Musk et al., Opinion Awarding Attorneys Fees and Denying Motion to Revise the Post-Trial Opinion, December 2, 2024.

14. Trisha Thadani and Faiz Siddiqui, "Judge rejects Elon Musk's $56 billion pay package, despite shareholder vote," *Washington Post*, December 2, 2024. https://www.washingtonpost.com/technology/2024/12/02/elon-musk-pay-package-rejected-tesla-delaware/.

15. @elonmusk, X, December 2, 2024. https://x.com/elonmusk/status/1863740336331170304.

16. @breakingbaht, X, November 15, 2023. https://x.com/breakingbaht/status/1724892505 647296620.
17. @elonmusk, X, November 15, 2023. https://x.com/elonmusk/status/17249082874712 72299.
18. @elonmusk, X, November 15, 2023. https://x.com/elonmusk/status/17249326192034 20203.
19. @elonmusk, X, November 15, 2023. https://x.com/elonmusk/status/17249339802760 84909.
20. Eric Hananoki, "As Musk endorses antisemitic conspiracy theory, X has been placing ads for Apple, Bravo, IBM, Oracle and Xfinity next to pro-Nazi content," *Media Matters*, November 11, 2023. https://www.mediamatters.org/twitter/musk-endorses-antisemitic -conspiracy-theory-x-has-been-placing-ads-apple-bravo-ibm-oracle.
21. Eli Tan, "This is the growing list of companies pulling ads from X," *Washington Post*, November 20, 2023. https://www.washingtonpost.com/technology/2023/11/17/elon-musk-x -companies-pulling-ads-anti-semitism/.
22. @elonmusk, X, November 21, 2023. https://x.com/elonmusk/status/17257144149079 28696.
23. Frances Vinall and Timothy Bella, "Musk's X sues Media Matters after report shows ads next to pro-Nazi posts," *Washington Post*, November 21, 2023. https://www.washingtonpost .com/business/2023/11/21/musk-media-matters-x-lawsuit-ken-paxton/.
24. @GerberKawasaki, X, November 16, 2023, https://x.com/GerberKawasaki/status/17252 19518186995834.
25. @GerberKawasaki, X, November 16, 2023. https://x.com/GerberKawasaki/status/172522 4994983022602.
26. @elonmusk, X, November 15, 2023. https://x.com/elonmusk/status/1724932619203 420203.
27. @elonmusk, X, November 15, 2023. https://x.com/elonmusk/status/17248967364126 60188.
28. @elonmusk, X, January 13, 2024. https://x.com/elonmusk/status/1746999488252703098.
29. Gerrit De Vynck, "Elon Musk targets advertisers who boycott X with expletive-filled rant," *Washington Post*, November 29, 2023. https://www.washingtonpost.com/technology/2023 /11/29/elon-musk-advertiser-dealbook/.
30. Lora Kolodny, "Elon Musk claims advertisers are trying to 'blackmail' him, says 'Go f——— yourself'," *CNBC*, November 29, 2023.https://www.cnbc.com/2023/11/29 /elon-musk-to-advertisers-who-are-trying-to-blackmail-him-go-f----yourself.html .
31. Ibid.
32. Ibid.
33. Dan Primack, "Elon Musk's X gets another valuation cut from Fidelity," *Axios*, December 20, 2023. https://www.axios.com/2023/12/31/elon-musks-x-fidelity-valuation-cut.
34. Faiz Siddiqui, "Elon Musk's uphill battle to win greater control of Tesla," *Washington Post*, January 28, 2024. https://www.washingtonpost.com/technology/2024/01/28/elon-musk -tesla-control/.
35. Al Root, "Tesla Cybertrucks Are Rusting. There Are Fixes for That," *Barron's*, February 18, 2024. https://www.barrons.com/articles/tesla-cybertrucks-rusting-fixes-f10209fb.
36. @elonmusk, X, December 12, 2022. https://x.com/elonmusk/status/16022784772347 28960.
37. @chazman, X, February7, 2020. https://x.com/chazman/status/1755366988870725901.
38. @elonmusk, X, February 7, 2024. https://x.com/elonmusk/status/1755411084939501860.

Afterword

1. Maria Sacchetti, Faiz Siddiqui and Nick Miroff, "Elon Musk, enemy of 'open borders,' launched his career working illegally," *Washington Post*, October 27, 2024. https://www .washingtonpost.com/business/2024/10/26/elon-musk-immigration-status/.

2. @elonmusk, X, November 7, 2024. https://x.com/elonmusk/status/18545763106993
48325.

3. @elonmusk, X, October 19, 2024. https://x.com/elonmusk/status/1847731937168826582.

4. @elonmusk, X, October 19, 2024. https://x.com/elonmusk/status/1847775059823218967.

5. @elonmusk, X, November 11, 20224. https://x.com/elonmusk/status/18560735301375
26564.

6. Julia Ingram, "Elon Musk spends $277 million to back Trump and Republican candidates,"
CBS News, December 6, 2024. https://www.cbsnews.com/news/elon-musk-277-million
-trump-republican-candidates-donations/.

7. @elonmusk, X, November 10, 2024. https://x.com/elonmusk/status/1855810991709475099.

8. @realDonaldTrump, X, November 13, 2024. https://x.com/realDonaldTrump/status
/1856658569124262092.

9. Rob Wile and Lora Kolodny, "Elon Musk asks voters to brace for economic 'hardship,'
deep spending cuts in potential Trump Cabinet role," *CNBC*, October 30, 2024. https://
www.nbcnews.com/business/economy/economy-if-trump-wins-second-term-could-mean
-hardship-for-americans-rcna177807

10. @jason, X, November 22, 2024. https://x.com/Jason/status/1860016850240680355.

11. Elon Musk, *TCN*, October 7, 2024. https://www.youtube.com/watch?v=k89aYdZOC_I.

12. Faiz Siddiqui and Rachel Lerman, "Musk has long history of squabbles, investigations with
federal agencies," *Washington Post*, November 15, 2024. https://www.washingtonpost.com
/business/2024/11/15/elon-musk-trump-government-efficiency-agencies-investigations/

13. "Ayn Rand," *Stanford Encyclopedia of Philosophy*, June 8, 2010. https://plato.stanford.edu
/entries/ayn-rand/#WhatEthiWhyDoWeNeedIt.

INDEX

Jada Chin

FAIZ SIDDIQUI is a technology journalist with *The Washington Post*, covering companies such as Tesla, Uber, and Twitter (now X) for the Business Desk. His reporting has focused on transportation, social media, and government transformation, among other issues. His work has earned multiple Society of Professional Journalists Mark of Excellence and Hearst Journalism awards, and his writing has also appeared in *The Boston Globe* and on NPR.